IN TENSION BETWEEN
ORGANIZATION AND PROFESSION

In Tension between Organization and Profession

Professionals in Nordic Public Service

Carola Aili, Lars-Erik Nilsson,
Lennart G. Svensson & Pamela Denicolo (eds)

NORDIC ACADEMIC PRESS

Nordic Academic Press
P.O. Box 1206
221 05 Lund, Sweden
info@nordicacademicpress.com
www.nordicacademicpress.com

Typesetting: Stilbildarna i Mölle, Frederic Täckström
Cover: Jacob Wiberg
Cover illustration: *Man Freed from Puppet String*, Images.com/Scanpix/Corbis
Print: ScandBook, Falun 2007
Print run: 1 2 3 4 5 6 7 8 9 10
ISBN 978-91-85509-02-7

Contents

Carola Aili & Lars-Erik Nilsson

Tensions – let the doctor give an example

This book is about what it is like to be a professional in today's public sector organizations where higher sick leave, burnout, decreasing resources, increasing demands for professional development, rapid changes in organizations, new forms of leadership, and client-oriented practices are part of the professional's working life. Our prime focus is the individual professional and the challenges these tensions personally represent. We aim to contribute to the understanding of tensions professionals need to handle, thereby promoting a dialogue on issues such as 'What conditions do new professional tasks require?' 'Which new competences are needed?' What impact does the implementation of new technology have on professionals?

Professions in Nordic countries

The chapters of this book focus on professions that have developed parallel to the expansion of the welfare state (Bertilsson, 1990). This expansion has placed new demands on public services, leading to the restructuring of public sector organizations, the development of new professions expected to carry out political reforms, the division of labour through jurisdiction, and to the forming of more specific professional identities (Macdonald, 1995). Professionals in a welfare state have a problematic relation to the ideal definition of a profession, as Freidson puts it, 'a set of institutions which permit the members of an occupation to make a living while controlling their own work' (Freidson, 2001, p. 17). Since the welfare state is governed politically, the work and the education of the professionals is a political question or, as Svensson puts it, 'Within state organizations compromised decisions

7

are formed with respect to the relative strength of interest groups' (the authors' translation, Svensson, 2002:30). Professional corporations form an important group in the society, and the state has legitimized them through delegating control and self-regulation to the professional bodies. Professionals need to be aware of their responsibilities and duties in order to be able to perform their work; they must know about political governance and political goals as well as professional knowledge and mission.

The symbiosis of the professional groups and the state (Government) works its way down to street level, to the local workplace. Changes at the governmental level are mediated to the local organizations not only via the government, but also via the professional groups themselves through government-regulated education and research (cf. Macdonald, 1995). Sometimes government and the professions are not in step, thereby producing tensions and challenges for the individual professional. This kind of situation can be illustrated by the implications of the idea of citizenship conceptualized in liberal gloss about the individual's fundamental right to express a personal opinion (Moghaddam, Slocum, Finkel, Norman, Mor, & Harré, 2000) leading to clients claiming 'their rights'. Professionals have to consider these claims, even at times when they are unable to fulfil them for lack of resources, or at times when they conflict with professional judgement. Thus, professionals have to work in tension between professional and organizational demands, while at the same time considering issues of client empowerment.

The changes we describe are typical of a system of ideas, influenced by Anglo-Saxon new liberalism, called New Public Management (NPM), which has spread through the western world during recent decades (Hood, 1995). Efficacy and effectiveness are central notions of NPM. Public sector organizations should be managed by budget and quality control. A guiding principle is that social progress can be achieved by enhanced productivity (see Agevall, 2005). Productivity should increase as a result of creating independent production units. The quality of the services produced, such as education, health and social care, are to a high extent left to the professionals, clients and/or parents regarded as critical consumers. As an outcome, local political decisions to a large extent move from the level of politicians to the civil servant level (Montin, 2002). According to Agevall (2005), a founding postulate of NPM is the 'notion that people cannot be trusted' (p. 97). Consequently the client cannot trust the professional, who might act out of self-interest, while the professional cannot trust the client, who might take advantage of the situation. This state of affairs can also be applied to the relation between politicians and professionals.

The concept of tension

When we set out to write this book, we were initially concerned by the alarming reports we have mentioned. We regarded *tensions* primarily as a result of the pressure that public sector organizations put on professionals, who try to protect professional interests and autonomy while carrying out discretionary work. This way of conceptualising the relation between the state and professionals as a source of conflict has been a typical approach in research (Freidson, 1970; Sarfatti-Larson, 1977; Abbott, 1988; Brint, 1994; Svensson, 2002).

As our work on the book progressed, other conceptions of tension emerged. It seemed likely that tensions, mediated by both professional *and* organizational interests, constitute a dynamic framework within which individual professionals renegotiate their individual rights, duties and obligations. In these processes they have to take into account demands from colleagues, clients, families and significant others, by trying to assess whether these new demands can be encompassed by their profession and by themselves personally, and then by deciding which demands to prioritise. A desire to control work in the name of effectiveness and quality is typical both for professionals and the institutions of the state, but often in different ways. At the same time, both parties advocate autonomy for professionals in the name of responsibility and individualisation.

The theory of professions also brings focus to the *tensions* between what is considered to be optional for the profession, the public and/or the client (Freidson, 2001). A conceptualisation of tensions as conflicting interests, inter- and intra-professional disputes, and general dissonance has proved to be helpful, enabling some of the authors to illuminate important issues in a productive way. Other authors conceptualise tensions more as a field of uncertainty exacting consideration or as new strategies where tensions even create opportunities for the individual to act in new and better ways, even providing new career paths.

The word 'tension' encompasses the ideas of dissonance or competing requirements as well as boundary work and border crossings. Lipsky (1980) claims that politics comes into being through the professionals' meetings with their clients, e.g., in the hospital ward or in the classroom. This process is not trouble-free, however, since the professionals frequently are faced with dilemmas that are difficult to make sense of and to handle, thereby leading to a different kinds of 'politics' than intended.

Professionals in tension fields – a historical perspective

Are these the worst of times for professionals or just other times? At least tensions are not new phenomena. This can be demonstrated with a glimpse at the history of the medical profession as a doctor describes what it meant to be working in the rural areas of Sweden during the first part of the nineteenth century:

> 'It will not hold up in the long run that, as it is now, provincial doctors at the same time need to manage health care and the new and increasingly more demanding social care. It is, as we know, totally new principles presently being worked out and applied in health care. Until now one has focused on how to cure deceases, now one begins to understand that this is not enough, there is a need for earnest attempts to work to prevent them. And it is this part of the problem that increasingly falls on the provincial doctor. But as his work is now laid out he does not have the time for this new activity in a real efficient manner.'
> 'Can you give an example, Doctor?'
> 'Yes, many. I'll satisfy myself with one. There was a question about the housing of an agricultural labourer receiving allowance in kind under the vicarage in my district. The house was being renovated, and I had made a specific request that it should be furnished with a heating system. Fine! So I am away on a journey on official business, and the Dean calls a meeting and makes the meeting decide not to install the heating system.'
> 'Why?'
> 'Why? He regarded it as not suitable that his labourers should have a heating system when he did not.'
> (Nordström, 1938 [Lortsverige (1938)/§ 1. Prosten och stataren])[1]

Nordström's dialogue illustrates that the welfare state, despite its often positive connotations, may well be a locus of tension and gives nourishment to professionals reasoning about moral values, redistribution of goods, rationales for action, professional responsibilities, division of labour, forms of control and so forth. These are issues that trouble the individual professional. What it means to be a doctor is in some respects still the same. Doctors are concerned with the health of their patients, with diagnosis, what medicines to prescribe and similar issues. In other respects, what it means to be a doctor has radically changed. The scenario illustrates an emerging political will to make better living conditions. The doctor presents it as a result of advances in medical science, saying that there is a connection between health and housing. He pinpoints changes in technology that he considers to be important to public health. He demonstrates that a social factor such as distribution of wealth and social status influences how he can perform his work.

Finally, he forewarns of a particular division of labour between doctors and social workers. Change produces professional difficulties that need to be dealt with; he cannot easily work out how he can manage with the resources at his disposal. The Nordström scenario also illustrates issues of occupational identity. Whether the provincial physician should be a health worker or more of a social worker is a dilemma that he needs to handle. Identity is often regarded as a product of social structures. Abbott (1988) suggests that for professions whose jurisdiction is a product of laws, rules and acceptances formed in different arenas, these laws, rules and acceptances may be sources of identity. Changes in jurisdiction thus challenge that identity.

Continuous change in public sector organizations

Change is a ubiquitous phenomenon (Braudel, 1972; Freeman & Perez, 1988) and metaphors such as post-industrial, information society, postmodern, risk society or knowledge society are used to describe the changes. The implementation of New Public Management has brought about continual reforms and changes in Scandinavian public sector organizations, processes often implemented to increase efficiency *and* to promote service quality. Street-level bureaucrats often connect these changes with increased workload and demands for efficacy and efficiency (Sarfatti-Larson, 1977). Individuals and groups are often required to take the initiative and engage in the development of quality and work processes. Their initial creative and responsible efforts

to enhance quality are often squandered by impediments and limitations that put job satisfaction in jeopardy. Job satisfaction, defined as
attitudes based on judgement of relevant aspects of work and work
situation is strongly related to well-being and health (Karsten, Koning & Van Schooten 2007).

We propose that the conflicting aspects we have described relate to
ideas of what it means to perform professional work and to be a professional. Vermeulen (1997) shows that tensions between these ideas
and actual work conditions affect motivation. Furthermore, the professionals in non-profit sector organizations often experience deficient
working conditions (Light, 2002) such as poor technological equipment and support and few opportunities for professional development.
Additional complications are indistinct forms of recognition, since
unclear standards of performance make it difficult both to encourage
those who do a good job and to reprove those who perform inade-
quately. The latter can be dealt with internally, by professions with a
strong jurisdiction (Abbott, 1988). However in countries where the
expansion of professional organizations has been fundamental to the
development of the public sector, this is seldom carried out to its full
extent.

In organizational settings, changes are often expected to take place
at organizational level, team level and at individual level. The authors
of this book discuss the likely effects of these changes by (1) adding
the professional level and the professional body and (2) exploring which
tensions these processes bring about among the different organizational levels.

In the following chapters we use various perspectives to exemplify
the kind of tensions that these change processes bring about for the
professionals of our time. We propose that there are change processes that are harmful to the professional, even at times when professionals themselves come to grips with them and sometimes act as driving
forces in the process. There are reasons to investigate these tensions
and what makes them injurious. Under which circumstances can the
will to do a good job be harmful? When does new knowledge, other
ways to think or new technology become a burden instead of a
resource in professional work? Under what circumstances will professional life turn into dystopia? What does the future have in store for
the heirs of 'the good doctor'?

This book reports and discusses research projects in Norway, Denmark and Sweden. All chapters have been discussed in workshops, and all authors have taken active part as referees and discussants for several chapters. Carola Aili and Lars-Erik Nilsson have been first referees for all chapters and have operated as general editors. The final referees have been Lennart Svensson and Pamela Denicolo. We are thankful to Kristianstad University for financial support.

Notes

1 These paragraphs have been extracted from Lubbe Nordström's book *Lort-Sverige*. The publication of Nordström's book coincided with the growth of the welfare state in the Nordic countries. Through his writings, overcrowded living conditions, sanitary inconveniences and health problems were vividly depicted as conditions shared by large parts of the population. These descriptions informed contemporary society about the life of 'ordinary' people and contributed to a critical debate about common responsibilities for the welfare of all citizens. Nordström's texts and radio broadcasts became part of the debate on what has metaphorically been called the 'people's home'. In hindsight they can be seen as foretelling the building of what is more commonly referred to as the welfare state in most countries.

Preamble

Initially developed as tools by and for the medical profession in order to better the quality of medical interventions, the National Quality Registries in Sweden have recently attracted the attention of the authorities as potential tools for resource allocation. In this scenario there is a possible tension between the interests of the medical profession and those of the authorities. In this chapter Lars H. Hansen analyses and discusses the emergence and current development of the registries, focussing on possible dilemmas or tensions between the actors who have an interest in the registries.

Lars H. Hansen

Discretion, quality and control

The medical profession and National Quality Registries

Introduction

The object of study in this chapter is the Swedish National Quality Registries. It is a case study that primarily describes these registries, but it also analyses some possible dilemmas or tensions among or between the actors who have an interest in the registries. The quality registries have been developed by the medical profession as a means for improving the quality of medical interventions. In short, a National Quality Registry is a systemised way of collecting individual-based data on diagnoses, treatments and outcomes regarding a specific kind of disease or medical intervention (for instance diabetes or hip replacement). Physicians fill in a form (on paper or on-line) after having treated a patient. Data from the whole country are then being compiled and analysed at the registry centre responsible for running the registry. The magnitude of this data collection makes it possible to rather quickly compare the outcome of different treatments, and thereby promote the use of 'best practice'. However, it also makes it possible to compare the performance of hospital departments and even individual physicians.

Awareness of the existence and scope of the registries is now spreading to other groups than physicians, and there is a growing demand – especially among the authorities – for registry results. The reason for this interest is that data from the registries can be used as a means for monitoring the outcome of the healthcare system. There is also a rising interest from both the media and ordinary citizens for recent registry data, something which can be explained by the media's devoted interest in the Swedish public healthcare and the rather recent option for citizens to choose relatively freely between caregivers around the country. Up till very recently registry data have, however, not been accessible for anyone outside the medical speciality that is controlling the registry.

National quality registries represent different kinds of phenomena for different actors. For the medical profession the registries are primarily a means to improve medical quality, which is achieved by collecting and analysing data on a specific type of medical intervention. From this perspective, a quality registry is nothing but an organization for the collection and management of data. From the point of view of politicians, civil servants and ordinary citizens (i.e. the everyday users of healthcare services) quality registries have a more wideranging purpose than 'only' to develop medical quality. For these groups the registries can function as a system for the comparison and/or control of different care units. This is a notion that comprises the outspoken vision from the National Board of Health and Welfare that information from the registries shall be accessible for politicians, civil servants, patients and their relatives (National Board of Health and Welfare [NBHW], 2002).

The purpose of this study is to describe, analyse and discuss the National Quality Registries and their role within the Swedish healthcare system. It is the registries' emergence, development, and application, together with a number of actors' opinions about the registries that have been studied. The empirical data that the analyses are based upon consist of interviews with people that have been involved in the development of the registries, documents from the registries and different national and local authorities, and articles in professional journals.

In order to understand and explain the development of the quality registries and how they affect and are affected by the context in which they appear, theories about professions and standardisation have been utilised. The approach is qualitative and can be described as a constant movement between theorising and analysing the empirical material.

The development and context
of the National Quality Registries

Traditionally, the progress of medical interventions has more or less ubiquitously been considered as the result of the medical professions' development of already existing and new methods of treatment. During a couple of decades there has, however, been an increasing awareness that a more systemised approach towards the advancement of medical interventions can be used for quality improvement. The National Quality Registries exemplify this. They have been established by specialities within the medical profession, with the purpose of improving medical treatment by what can be learnt from large scale data collection:

> The National Quality Registries have been developed to fill the gap left by the lack of primary monitoring systems. The quality registries collect information on individual patient's problems, interventions, and outcomes of interventions in a way that allows data to be compiled for all patients and analyzed at the unit level. Since the registries are national, the entire country is in agreement on what indicates good care. This also makes it possible to compare different units. (Swedish Association of Local Authorities and Regions [SALAR], 2005 p. 6)

The first registries were started in the mid seventies as research data bases with financial support by research funds. The first registry was the Swedish Knee Arthroplasty Register which was started in 1975. The aim of this registry was 'to give early warning of inferior designs and present average results based on the experience of a whole nation instead of that of highly specialized units' (Robertsson, Lewold, Knutson & Lidgren, 2000, p. 8). Since its inception this registry has registered more than 65,000 knee surgeries, and all units in Sweden that routinely perform knee arthroplasty surgery participate in the registry work (Swedish Knee Arthroplasty Register [SKAR], 2006).

In 1979 the Swedish National Hip Arthroplasty Register became the second Swedish registry, and during the eighties only a few new registries were started. In the beginning of the nineties there was a great increase in the number of new registries, and since then several registries have been started each year. Today, the majority of registries are financed directly by the state. At present (2006) Sweden has 58 registries that receive economic support from the Swedish Association of

Local Authorities and Regions (SALAR)[1] and the National Board of Health and Welfare (NBHW). Not all registries receive support however; in 2005 more than 100 registries requested funding for 2006 (SALAR, 2005).

Thus, even though the first registry was started as early as 1975 it was not until the early 1990s that the expansion of registries really took off. The reason for this rather slow beginning was that no one actually considered the registries to be anything else than tools for improving the purely medical quality. However, during the late eighties the so called quality movement swept over organizations around the world (Røvik, 2000). This movement can be summarised by the concept Total Quality Management (TQM), and a predominant feature of this management ideal is to continuously measure critical variables in order to control and, thus, improve the 'production' process (Bergman & Klefsjö, 1995).

It was at that point in time when TQM was the vogue that SALAR became aware that the registries could be used as devices for measuring and comparing the outcome of medical interventions on a national level. Thus, it was their inherent potential as information systems that strongly contributed to SALAR's decision to support the registries. This is not surprising since quality management practices are heavily dependent upon means to make 'objective' comparisons, i.e. they need numbers (statistics) to operate properly. The data provided by the registries can be instrumental in this since they make it possible to compare the results of individual hospital departments with the national average.

Notwithstanding their potential as management tools, all the quality registries have been established as professional tools by and for the medical profession. And even though the registries have become established and in some sense institutionalised as a part of the health-care sector's total quality work, they are still to be found within the medical research or scientific paradigm. Both regarding the choice of what to measure (i.e. the variables that make up each registry's questionnaire) and the way in which data are collected, compiled and presented research practice serves as guidance. However, the variables that are used need not be carved in stone, and pressure from groups outside the medical profession might change the picture.

The organization of the registries is rather decentralised since each registry is managed and administered from a department at a hospital somewhere in the country. At this so called 'registry centre' each registry has a responsible 'registry manager' who is a highly competent specialist in the registry field. The other partaking departments around the country report their data to the registry centre where all data are being compiled and analysed. The registry centres are to be found all over the country, but almost all are located at the large university hospitals.

The registries are not totally independent however. In order to receive economic support from the authorities they have to apply for funding from the Executive Committee for National Quality Registries, which is made up of representatives from the National Board of Health and Welfare, the Swedish Association of Local Authorities and Regions, the Swedish Society of Medicine, and the Swedish Society of Nursing. The Executive Committee decides on the allocation of financial resources to the registries (SALAR, 2005), and it also discusses and prepares 'matters of strategic importance for the development and use of the registries, and takes different practical initiatives to support the development' (National Board of Health and Welfare [NBHW], 2001, p. 12). In order to be entitled for economic support a registry must satisfy a number of conditions, for instance be supported by the relevant professional speciality association, organize conferences and deliver reports on registry results (NBHW, 2000).

So, even though the registries are national, they do not have a common national centre. The one thing that is common to all of them is the conditional funding from the authorities granted by the Executive Committee. However, in addition to the registries, since 2002 the authorities also support three competence centres that 'aim to promote the development of new registries, create synergy effects by collaboration among registries (e.g., in technical operations, analytical work, and use of registry data to support clinical quality improvement), and helping to make registry data beneficial for different users' (SALAR, 2005, p. 8). The competence centres are supposed to develop a broad know-how of registry work, i.e. knowledge about how registries should be organized, and how registry data can be analysed and interpreted. Consequently they are manned not only by physicians, but also by statisticians, programmers, epidemiologists, and social scientists. The three competence centres are also located at hospitals around the country, and each has focussed on a connected number of specialities: diseases of the eyes, musculoskeletal diseases, and cardiovascular diseases and cancer.

The concrete results of some decades of registry work can be summarised as follows. In many cases it has been possible to establish a harmonisation of medical interventions for a certain medical problem. For instance, the findings by the Swedish National Hip Arthroplasty Register have led to recommendations regarding certain operation methods, which have had the result that Sweden has a comparatively low percentage of revisions (Swedish National Hip Arthroplasty Register [SNHAR], 2003). In some cases the findings have disclosed deviations which cannot be explained by differences in patient characteristics. These differences regarding interventions can only be explained by differing practices or knowledge among doctors at the units in question. Data from the registries have also been used for research to a rather great extent, which means that results from the registries via research in the long run can have an effect on medical practice.

All in all, the registries seemingly work as intended regarding medical aspects. Also, the number of registries is constantly increasing, and by means of the competence centres the central support for the registries is improving. The National Board of Health and Welfare has, however, expressed hopes that the registries eventually can be used for even more purposes than today.

The vision of the National Board of Health and Welfare is that aggregated data from the national quality registries shall be easily accessible to the medical profession in the whole country, and to politicians and civil servants in the management and development of healthcare. The information from the registries shall also be accessible to patients and relatives in order to meet their information needs when it comes to knowledge of different clinics' or departments' treatment results and waiting time for the choice of care giver. For this to be possible a continued dissemination of knowledge of the registries is necessary. The healthcare system is facing the challenge of – to a far greater extent than hitherto – finding ways of distributing this information in a manner which will give citizens a meaningful and comprehensible basis for their own decisions. In the future registry data are expected to function as a basis for decisions by hospital management and local authorities regarding the management, development and follow-up of healthcare on both regional and local levels (NBHW, 2002, pp. 9–10).

Now, before getting on with the analysis, the primary problems or questions of this study must be addressed. But first, the actors affecting the registries must be specified. In the above description of the registries and how they are organized it should have become evident that there are a number of actors involved in the registry field as a whole. The primary actor is of course the medical profession represented by the speciality associations that control the registries. We also have the authorities (both national and local) represented by the National Board of Health and Welfare (NBHW) and the Swedish Association of Local Authorities and Regions (SALAR) who are providing the financial resources needed to run the registries. These groups are all represented in the Executive Committee for National Quality Registries, which means that they have a direct influence on the development of the registries. Two other groups must also be mentioned. First, the citizens that come in contact with the healthcare system (both patients and their relatives), and, second, the media that continuously is monitoring everything that is going on within the public sector. Neither the media nor the public at large have a direct influence on the registries, but they can – by highlighting results or choosing between different care units – give impetus to certain changes.

The following analyses will centre around three themes. The first theme concerns what is being measured (i.e. the set of variables that make up each registry), and who is deciding what to measure. From an ideal typical professional perspective the registries should primarily be used to audit and – consequently – develop medical interventions. There is a research paradigm within the medical profession which makes this perspective more or less natural, and since it is physicians who take the initiative to and start registries the result is that what gets measured in a registry (i.e. the variables of the registry) emanates from a medical development and scientific research interest. The authorities are, on the other hand, arguing that the registries should be used both for management decisions and citizens' choices of caregivers, which eventually can affect the priorities regarding what to measure. In short, this theme deals with possible consequences of categorisation.

The second theme concerns standardisation, i.e. the question whether the registries should be made more similar regarding both organization and content. The competence centres, the use of a common protocol to describe the registries, and an amount of pressure from the authorities that certain variables (for example on gender) all contribute to a possible standardisation. This is a process that can affect both the already existing registries, and also the way that new registries are being set up.

The third and final theme has to do with the results of the registries. Who are the results intended for and how is registry data presented? This is in essence a question of transparency and ownership over the data being produced by the registries. If results from the registries were to be presented in a manner that made it possible for politicians to use them for decisions on resource allocation and for citizens to use them to choose between care givers, it could possibly alter the current relationships between the actors involved in the field. There is an inherent paradox concerning registry work and its possible effects on the medical profession. On the one hand, it can strengthen the medical profession as a whole due to the apparent improvements in medical interventions. On the other hand, registry results can be used to force units to comply to an identified best practice, regardless of whether individual physicians agree with the recommended practice or not. There is also the possible scenario that national and local authorities use registry results in order to justify for instance the concentration of certain interventions to highly specialised units. Thus, it is possible to discern a potential tension between the actors involved in the field.

The power of categories

In professional work both diagnosis and treatment have specific classification systems, which Abbott (1988) denotes 'a profession's own mapping of its jurisdiction, an internal dictionary embodying the professional dimensions of classification' (p. 41). Within the jurisdiction of the profession lies the right to classify a problem or – with other words – make a diagnosis. In order to classify/diagnose there must be a classification at hand, even if it only consists of two categories. The classification system of diagnosis defines what problems or symptoms fall under the jurisdiction of the profession, while the classification system of treatment brings together the problems or symptoms that requires the same treatment. The right to develop, use and change classification systems is to some extent what professional jurisdiction on the work place is all about.

The classifications that are being used by professions are primarily developed for scientific purposes and based upon scientific theories of how the world is organized (for instance the periodic system). Classifications that from the outset have been developed within a science can, however, become incorporated into a bureaucratic organizations set of classifications and – in connection to this – be transformed to a standard, which means that the future development of the classification can be guided by aspects other than purely scientific ones (Hansen, 2001; Starr, 1992). If a scientific classification develops into a standard, and that standard is being used by the government to audit and monitor for example processes within the healthcare sector, it will be hard for the profession that has the scientific 'ownership' of the original classification to argue full control over the use and future development of the classification.

When the knowledge of individual professionals is being codified and fit into classification systems, the individual professional becomes a part of a large scale information system where most of the professional work – at least in theory – becomes measurable. The classification of everything that is being done and performed within the professional work is however something of a double-edged sword for the profession. On the one hand, it makes it easier for the profession to make claims on jurisdiction by making their work clearly visible to everyone: – This is what we do, it is based on this specific knowledge and therefore we want to have an exclusive right to perform all work in the field. On the other hand, a far reaching standardisation of the classifications within the jurisdiction can have negative consequences for the autonomy of the profession. A classification standard is – by virtue of its comparatively fixed categories – relatively easy to understand for groups outside the profession. Abbott (1988) writes that 'results that are too easily measurable lead to easy evaluation from outside the profession and consequent loss of control' (p. 46). Also Bowker and Star (1990) have noted a similar possible consequence and imply that all classification systems that make work visible also make surveillance of the work easier.

The variables of a registry constitute a more or less conscious mapping of what belongs to the professions jurisdiction. What variables ought to be included in a registry and how they should be weighted is an indication of the perspective on quality from the view of the registry managers. If a registry only consists of medical variables it is a strong indication that those responsible for the registry view quality as the result of medical interventions. There have, however, been several debates on whether the variables used by a registry are really those that can best measure the quality in that specific field. In a debate regarding the measurement of quality within the field of surgery Per-Olof Nyström (chief physician at the department of surgery at Linköping University Hospital) suggested that the most reliable quality indicator/variable is post-operative time of care since it 'is an objective and quantitative result which is easy to measure and that describes the total effect of medical, organizational and social processes in healthcare. Therefore, post-operative time of care is an excellent variable for meaningful quality measurement' (2004, p. 184).

Lately, variables based on the patients' own experiences have been introduced in the registries. One such variable is work ability, which is being used by the Swedish Rheumatoid Arthritis Registry. Patients can – prior to the visit to the hospital – via access to a webpage report their data on the subjective variables included in the registry (for example work ability). When they meet their doctor they can talk about the results together and also discuss possible treatments. In this way, the patient has become a much more active actor in the whole care process.

The use of more subjective variables based on patients' experiences makes it possible to use the registries for more purposes than to improve the medical interventions, in particular in combination with reports that are accessible and comprehensible to the wider public. Such reports can be the base for patients' choice of hospitals, for demands on care units regarding patient reception, and as base information when deciding on what treatments are most motivated regarding the economy of the society. Using variables which are based on the patients' experiences is undoubtedly a kind of adaptation to the ideal of the quality movement, which states that it is the demands and expectations of the customers that define the quality of the service (Bergman & Klefsjö, 1995). Therefore, the inclusion and exclusion of variables in the registries (and who decides what variables to be used) is of utmost importance concerning the development of the registries and how they are going to be used in the future.

For those responsible for the healthcare of society quality registries can be a contribution to their goal to fulfil the demand that they should carry out systematic and continuous quality work. It must, however, still be with the active cooperation from the profession. In the annual report from the Swedish National Hip Arthroplasty Register (SNHAR, 2003) it is argued that the 'key to our success is that the register is owned by the profession, and that it is thus perceived to be meaningful for everyday development' (p. 2). Ultimately, this concerns the autonomy and jurisdiction of the profession. If the set of variables in the registries begins to stray away from the traditional medical paradigm, there is an apparent risk that physicians in their everyday practice choose (if the have that option) not to partake in the registry work.

Standardisation

Even though it is not clearly spelled out, there is a growing pressure suggesting that the registries should become more similar, both regarding form and content. Concerning the formal aspects it is a question of a standardisation of the application for funding, a standard for the presentation of the registries (protocol), and an ambition to harmonise the design of the annual reports. The standardisation process regarding content is propelled by demands that certain variables should be included in the registries (for example subjective health measures), by starting national competence centres which – by providing support for registry building – create models for the design of registries, and by requests that new registries must include specific variables that shall function as quality indicators for Swedish healthcare as a whole. This means that a process of standardisation can be underway without one individual actor pressing in that direction. It is more a question of a number of initiatives that – taken together – make up what appears as a single process.

The increased public funding means that pressure is building from the financiers to get their requests fulfilled. It becomes harder and harder to argue that the voluntary part of the registry work is an excuse concerning what the principals wish to get from the registries. Competence centres can be looked upon as the solution to a problematic that has been a topic for discussion in the Executive Committee for quite a while, i.e. how the development and quality of the registries can be improved. From the point of view of the committee registries do not function equally well depending for instance on varying competence regarding statistics and epidemiology. Each speciality has seemingly developed their own registry without learning from the experiences of others.

A far reaching standardisation may lead to a decrease in the autonomy of the individual practitioner. According to Jacobsson (2000) the professional practice with its subjective and continuously trying approach to the sequence diagnosis, inference, and treatment can even be threatened.

> If standardization is carried too far, as with systems of medical expertise, it may even be viewed as a threat to professional expert knowledge. The claims to special knowledge by professional groups have a kind of 'sacred quality' that is hard to reconcile with requiring that everything be put in writing. (p. 44)

A standardisation of the professional practice can therefore be conceived of as a threat against the expert knowledge that is the essence of the profession.

Do we want the world to know?

There is an ongoing debate on how data should be presented. Actors outside the profession (politicians and civil servants in particular) have requested that the results from the registries should be presented in a way that is comprehensible also to the layman. During a meeting with the Executive Committee for National Quality Registries in 2001 it was discussed whether there was a need for two types of annual reports: one for the profession and another for politicians and civil servants. The committee did recognise the need for 'layman reports', but concluded that it was not possible to demand that type of reports from the registries yet.

There is an apparent scepticism among many physicians regarding other groups' access to results from the registries. However, we also find proponents of greater transparency within the profession. For instance, in an article in *Läkartidningen* (the official journal of the Swedish Medical Association) Andreen Sachs (chief physician medical advisor for SALAR) and Theodorsson (professor of clinical chemistry and chairman of the Medical Quality Council) (2002) argue that the quality of medical interventions must be displayed publicly if society's confidence for healthcare is to be maintained:

> In essence, this concerns society's trust in the healthcare system. As a consumer you are used to continuously assess the content and quality of goods and services. For the most part, as a consumer of health-

care you unfortunately lack the corresponding information. In order to strengthen the patient's standing access to an open account of the quality of healthcare is a self-evident ingredient. (p. 800)

In this quotation the individual (the patient) is presented as an active consumer who is both willing and able to choose between healthcare services from different producers. To be able to make informed choices patients must, however, have access to relevant information.

Many within the medical profession obviously do not trust the media and the public at large regarding their ability to interpret and understand data from the registries, and there has been cases where single hospitals has been pointed out by the media as below the national average for certain interventions (Örn, 2004). On the other hand, many civil servants think that results from the registries should be presented openly for each and every hospital (NBHW, 2002). Behind this ambition for increased transparency we find an image of the registries both as something which can serve as some kind of consumer information to the public, both also function as pressure on the individual hospitals to develop their treatment in accordance with best practice. There is a notion that greater transparency leads to changes, and that it is only units that have genuinely bad results that will be criticised in the media. In opposition to this, we have the opinion that the public and the media are not capable of understanding the results because of their complexity. Johan Calltorp (professor of health and care administration) (1999) argues that the medical profession has to retain the trust of their principals and defend their professionalism.

> It is difficult to see any other way to achieve this than by carrying out an active quality assessment by the best means possible within the profession. This includes a scientific discussion about methods, source of errors, and limitations. After this professional self evaluation results are presented to the principals in an intelligible manner. If the medical profession does not actively take these steps we can surely anticipate legislation. This would surely result in both inferior quality comparisons and a loss of autonomy for physicians, something which is closely connected to the concept profession itself. (p. 2567)

Here we can see how the question of transparency is connected to the question of the autonomy of the medical profession. And maybe the profession must allow some degree of insight into the registries as a trade-off in order to maintain the ultimate control over them. To stubbornly refuse insight may lead to an increased pressure from other actors, which in the end can lead to coercive measures. The increased pressure towards transparency is partly a result of increasing economic support where those who are financing the registries want to get more out of them. It is also a result of an increasing awareness of the existence of the registries, which means that some actors (for example the media) now are demanding to have access to registry data. A couple of examples can elucidate the ongoing process towards greater transparency and the debates surrounding it.

For several years the Swedish National Hip Arthroplasty Register has openly published results for individual hospitals. However, there is a limit to what data are accessible to the public (SNHAR, 2005).

> The confidential information to the individual units includes detailed information about the causes of their own failures during the last five years and a case-mix profile, thereby providing a basis for local efforts to achieve improvement. Each unit's own results are compared with the national average. (p. 2)

In May 2003 Swedvasc (Vascular Registry in Sweden) decided to publish hospital specific results to the public. This was not an uncontroversial decision however, and there were critics who argued that as long as the quality of the reporting to the register is not fully acceptable the results will also be indefinite, and therefore not suitable for publication. In an interview the chairman of Swedvasc, Martin Björck, voices another view (Ohlin, 2003).

> Nobody denies that there are a great number of sources of error. We have been very hesitant. But we have been criticised for not publishing our results, so now – after much pondering – we have decided to make the results available to the public, says Martin Björck.
>
> In order to avoid misunderstandings the presentation is going to be intelligible to non-surgeons. Hospitals that have results below the average shall be allowed to enclose a commentary. If a hospital cannot explain a bad result maybe it is better if they stop operating, argues Björck. Not all data in the registry are being published. It is limited to twelve quality indicators and the result after four typical interventions that concerns large groups of patients (p. 2668)

Both Swedvasc and the hip registry are examples of how it is possible for the profession to combine transparency in a registry with continued control over the registry work itself and what results are being published.

Even though everyone seems to be in agreement that there is an ongoing process towards increasing transparency, it is not possible to identify one single actor or group of actors who can be argued to be the prime mover behind the process. Rather, it is a question of a combined effect of many actors' world views, and there is obviously an ongoing discussion between the authorities and those responsible for the registries on how to achieve more transparency without loss of control for the profession.

The entire discussion about transparency can be interpreted as an ongoing struggle for the power over the registries between the parties involved. However, there are no open fights between groups with fundamentally differing views. As time has passed, the principals have become more and more interested in the potential of the registries, which has resulted in both increased financing and rising expectations. The transparency struggle is not so much a question of whether outsiders should have access to registry data at all, but rather a question of the form and detail of public data. The medical profession does not want to let go of the control over when, where, and how data are being published since that would mean letting go of the professional self control. This is hardly surprising because it is a part of the profession's monopoly of its own basic scientific knowledge.

Summary and conclusion

National quality registries have developed from a purely medical quality tool into a potential instrument for resource allocation (either via citizens' choices of care giver or by way of decisions by local and central authorities). For the clinically active physicians quality registries are tools for the development of medical quality. For the authorities the registries constitute a possible future system for comprehensive quality audit and resource allocation. For the patients, finally, results from the registries can function as guidance when choosing between different hospitals. Of course, these actor groups all have a common interest in the development of medical quality. However, there is an apparent possible tension between them since the agenda of both the authorities and the public at large can have consequences for the future discretion of the medical profession.

As a consequence of the quality movement's advent in Swedish healthcare new possibilities emerged for the research registries. In particular the requirement that the quality work of all units should be audited meant that there was a need for tools that made possible comparisons both over time and between units and regions. The understanding that the quality registries might become this tool marked the beginning of the rapid development during the nineties. Further, SALAR and the NBHW could count on the profession to have a predominantly positive view of the registries since they had been developed by the profession with the purpose of developing the medical quality.

Both the pressure for increased transparency and the pressure for increased similarity can have consequences for the medical profession's jurisdiction. According to Abbott (1988) it is primarily in the professional work that the jurisdiction of the profession is created. Every registry consists of a number of variables that are considered as vital for the understanding and treatment of a particular disease, and aggregated data are supposed to answer the question of how to become more efficient in the treatment. To be able to control which variables ought to be included in a registry and what status they ought to be given is undoubtedly a question of being able to control the work process. It is partly a question of the individual professional's self control (i.e. the Doctor who examines, diagnoses, and treats patients in accordance with his or hers acquired competence). However, it is also a question of the autonomy of the whole profession; in this case the right for a group of doctors who are specialised on a particular disease to define what is essential in the treatment (i.e. what variables are to be included when measuring the quality), and also to interpret the results of the treatment.

Results from the registry work might eventually mean that the diagnosis and treatment of certain diseases can become a considerably easier process than up till now. To be able to define, classify, and – as a consequence of this – be able to clearly measure the result of a treatment makes it also possible to control and direct. This does not imply a direct threat against the discretion of the medical profession however. Instead, it might trigger a change in parts of the work process, for instance that nurses take over some parts of the treatment. All in all, the development of the registries might eventually turn into somewhat of a dilemma for the medical profession. While improving the quality of medical interventions registry results can also lead to a demystification of the work of the profession, which might lead to a loss of control over the work process.

Further, this study has also shown that elements in the new forms of quality management that has developed within the public sector since the mid eighties have also had an impact on the quality registries. The new doctrine emphasises customer focus and measurability, and for the quality registries both the process towards increased transparency and a growing standardisation implies an advance towards these central aspects of quality management. Also, the use of variables that take account of the patients' experience of the care process means undoubtedly an adjustment to the ideal of the quality movement, i.e. that the demands and expectation of the customers defines the quality of the service.

Notes

1 Most of the material was collected during 2002–2004 when the author was working in a research project that concerned professional autonomy and quality management (Bejerot & Hasselbladh, 2001), that resulted in a report on the registries (Hansen & Adam, 2004). The study was supported by a grant from The Swedish Council for Working Life and Social Research (1999–0239).
2 The Swedish Association of Local Authorities and Regions (SALAR) is the federation for the county and regional councils that administrate matters that are too costly to handle at the municipal level, in particular public health and medical care.

Preamble

If we have to document our professional actions, will we then only perform the actions that we are supposed to document? This question reflects the content of this chapter.

Lena Agevall & Karin Jonnergård

Management by documents – a risk of de-professionalizing?

Introduction

We have witnessed an upsurge of documents that are to be used as new devices for steering and standardization of professional work in both public and private sectors (Ivarsson Westerberg, 2004; Svedberg Nilsson, Henning & Fernler, 2005). Examples of such documents are handbooks for public servants, local instruction catalogues, service guarantees, standards of quality, action plans for different activities, and action plans as contracts with clients. The rationale behind these types of documents is often to increase the transparency of work processes and to specify the demands that may be made on different groups of employees. The documents thus directly and indirectly influence the performance of different vocational groups.

However, the type of influence or the extent to which performance is influenced is still unclear. This issue may be particularly relevant for professionals, that is, individuals who 'have been trained to perform complex tasks independently and to solve problems which arise in the performance of these tasks using their experience and expertise' (Derber & Schwartz, 1991, as cited in Abernethy & Stoelwinder, 1995, p. 2). Expert knowledge and its situation-based applications imply that the standardization and measurement of professional conduct have been seen as difficult. Professionals' work has therefore been based on self-control, including the creation of common knowledge and professional norms and standards, rather than administrative control. Introducing the management of professions by documents challenges traditional autonomy as well as the traditional control of groups of professionals, and may increase the tension between professions and organizations. More specifically, one may ask if management by documents has any impact on professionals' knowledge, core values, and ethical responsibilities, and if so, how? How are professionals' autonomy influenced and what kind of control does management by documents entail?

In this chapter we develop a theoretical framework for investigating management by documents. We begin by discussing the concepts of control and traditional professional control. Additionally, the concept of professionalism is presented as an ideal type, and the meaning and application of professional knowledge is discussed. The effects of management by documents on professions and professional knowledge are then investigated. The chapter concludes with some propositions regarding the effect of documents as a control device for professions.

Different types of control

Control has been defined in multiple ways. In research on organizational control, control usually has the connotation of either domination, that is, the execution of power, or regulation, that is, the direction of action towards a desirable state or goal (Scheytt, Soin & Metz, 2003). Both of these connotations are present in situations where control is executed; they may be seen as different dimensions of control. In this chapter we delimit the content of control to situations where it is used to coordinate or accomplish work tasks. In addition, we will highlight the regulative aspect of the concept of control. This perspective highlights issues such as which types of control are appropriate in different situations, and how different types of control influence action. One point of departure for our discussion is Ouchi's (1979, 1980) ideal types for forms of control and different control situations.

According to Ouchi (1979), the type of control applied to a work process depends on when it is possible to control a work task. In principle, the work task may be controlled (1) before performance; (2) through control of the action during the performance, manuals, or other forms of action control; or (3) after the performance, through measurement and reward of the results of the performance. The choice of control type is dependent on the controlling party's knowledge of the transformation process or work process at hand, and the possibility to measure the output of the work task. If the transformation process is predictable, control may be carried out during the action; if the results are measurable, control may be carried out through output controls. However, if the transformation process is ambiguous, varied, or situation-dependent, and the results are not easily measurable, neither output controls nor action controls are possible. In this case, control may be executed through control of the premises of the action. This may be done through socialization into common norms and/or knowledge frameworks that guide actors when performing their work tasks (cf. Collin, 1990).

Ouchi (1980) also differentiates between different contexts in which various types of control may be applied. He defines three ideal types: market, bureaucracy, and clan. Markets may be used for control when transactions are easily specified (i.e., the result is measurable) and when variations in the transformation processes are low. Bureaucracy may be used when the process variations imply that coordination is necessary. However, when the results of the work tasks are difficult to measure and the transformation processes are varied, strong goal congruence between the involved actors is needed in order to achieve the desired state or goals. In this case, what Ouchi (1979, 1980) labels clan is the most appropriate control context. The clan is characterized by a clear division of authority (seniority), common norms and values (communion, cf. Barnard, 1938). Control takes the form of premises control, and traditions that are transferred between the generations of clan members serve to evaluate the results of actions. Ouchi classifies the traditional way of controlling professions as premises control, and considers professions to be a type of clan. Ouchi's framework is summarized in figure 1.

In conclusion, normative control theories assume a relation between the specific character of the object of control and the form and context of control. For professions this implies that the control form has to be adjusted to the specific character of the type of work at hand. We will therefore continue by investigating the specific characteristics of professions, their relationship to professional control, and the implications that arise when professional control is exchanged for behavioural or output control, as in the case of management by documents.

Figure 1: Ouchi's framework for control (cf. Ouchi, 1979, 1980; Collin, 1990).

Conditions determining the control type			
		Knowledge of the transformation process	
		Perfect	Imperfect
Ability to measure output	High	Behaviour or output control Price information Market or bureaucracy	Output control Price information Market or bureaucracy
	Low	Behaviour control Rule information Bureaucracy	Premises control Tradition information Clans

Professional knowledge, norms, and control
Professionalism as an ideal type

Freidson (2001) has systematically spelled out a third logic, an ideal type of professionalism, by contrasting professional work with the ideal-typical descriptions of the free labor market and the ideal-typical, rational-legal bureaucracy. In this view, professionalism contrasts both with Max Weber's ideal type of rational-legal bureaucracy and with the ideal-typical description of the free market. According to Freidson, what constitutes professionalism in its pure form is the co-presence of the following five interdependent elements:

- specialized work in the officially recognized economy that is believed to be grounded in a body of theoretically based, discretionary knowledge and skill and that is accordingly given special status in the labor force;
- exclusive jurisdiction in a particular division of labour created and controlled by occupational negotiation;
- a sheltered position in both external and internal labour markets that is based on qualifying credentials created by the occupation;

- a formal training programme lying outside the labor market that produces the qualifying credentials, which is controlled by the occupation and associated with higher education; and
- an ideology that asserts greater commitment to doing good work than to economic gain and to the quality rather than the economic efficiency of work (p.127).

The elements are mutually dependent, forming an internal logic – an ideal-type. While no ideal-type can reflect the real world, the concept of an ideal-type is a useful heuristic device. The fixed nature of the abstract ideal-type serves as an unchanging point for comparisons with the changing empirical world. The internal logic of the ideal-type means that deviance in one element has an indirect effect on the others, and when deviances increase, we are able to understand de-professionalization processes. Additionally, the ideal-type concept dissolves the debates about how to define contested concepts such as profession and semi-profession, because it offers a combinatorial approach that can be applied to all forms of work, not only those organized as professions.

In the following, we will elaborate on the meaning of professional knowledge and the norm system, including the commitment to doing a good job, and ethics. The reason for the analytical separation between knowledge systems and norm systems is that it is important to investigate how disturbances in the norm system will propagate into the knowledge system and vice versa (cf. Abbott, 1988).

Development of professionalism

According to Freidson (2001), professions are built on a body of knowledge and skills. Abstract theory and autonomous judgment is accordingly the core of professional knowledge. In addition to this, professional work also requires trained skills, and the steering mechanism of professionals' problem solving is 'double sided':

> When the diagnostic strategies of physicians are studied, two kinds of processes are prominent in their thinking-aloud protocols: processes of direct *recognition*, where presence of a symptom leads almost immediately to hypothesizing a disease that might be its cause, and processes of *search* ...Thus the search is conducted alternately in each of two environments: the physician's mental library of medical knowl-

edge and the patient's body. Information gleaned from one environment is used to guide the next step of search in the other (Simon, 1985, p. 105).

Recognition is an essential aspect within the professionals' knowledge system. Recognition has to be learned through trained skill- and experience-based application of the theoretical knowledge. The need for the trained skill- and experience-based application of theoretical knowledge implies that becoming a professional is a process that involves learning the intrinsic values of the profession as well as learning to adjust to the clients' needs. To understand this learning process, we employ the learning model put forth by Dreyfus and Dreyfus (1986, 2005).[1] The model is used as an analogy to increasing professionalism. A brief overview of some of the essential elements of the model's different stages – *novice, advanced beginner, competent performer, proficient performer*, and *expert* – is presented below.

Novice

Individuals at this first learning level recognize facts, characteristics, and rules without any reference to the particular situation in which they occur. The rules can be generalized to all similar situations, and are not dependent on context: they are context-independent. Individuals judge their skill by evaluating how well they have followed the rules they have learned (Dreyfus & Dreyfus, 1986, p. 21; Flyvbjerg, 2001, p.13). Consequently, individuals do not feel so much responsibility for their actions, provided they have not made a grave mistake (Dreyfus & Dreyfus, 2005, p.782; Flyvbjerg, 2001, p. 11).

Advanced beginner

At this stage individuals have gained further experience and are now learning to recognize relevant elements in different situations. They see similarities between other experiences in similar situations. In other words, advanced beginners possess a base for action, which contains both context-independent and context-dependent elements. Even advanced beginners experience a limited sense of responsibility for the consequences of their actions. For both novices and advanced beginners, an undesirable result – if not involving a grave error – will, for example, be explained by inadequate rules (Dreyfus & Dreyfus, 2005, p. 783; Flyvbjerg 2001, p. 12).

Competent performer

With increased experience, the number of recognizable elements becomes overwhelming, and individuals have to learn to prioritize. Competent performers learn to prioritize through a hierarchical form of decision-making. The competent performer chooses a plan. This plan prescribes which aspects in the situation are important and which are not. The individual 'feels responsible for the consequences of the choice, precisely because selecting a plan cannot be done objectively, but must nevertheless be carried out in order to be able to act competently' (Flyvbjerg, 2001, p.13). At this stage there is *a qualitative leap concerning the evaluation* of the task.

> At this stage, the result depends on the learner's choice of perspective, the learner feels responsible for his or her choice. Often, the choice leads to confusion and failure. But sometimes things work out well, and the competent student then experiences a kind of elation unknown to the beginner ... If we were disembodied beings, pure minds free of our messy emotions, our responses to our successes and failures would lack this seriousness and excitement (Dreyfus & Dreyfus, 2005, p. 784).

Dreyfus and Dreyfus argue that the more competent performers become emotionally involved in their tasks, the more difficult is becomes for them to move back to the detached rule or maxim-following stage of the advanced beginner. They cite an example from Patrica Benner's research on nurses:

> Unless the trainee stays emotionally involved and accepts the joy of a job well done, as well as the remorse of mistakes, he or she will not develop further... In general, resistance to involvement and risk leads to stagnation and ultimately to boredom and regression (Dreyfus & Dreyfus, 2005, p. 785).

We argue that emotional involvement is not only important for the general development of vocational knowledge, it is also required if the norm system is to be used in day-to-day practice at work. Emotional involvement is essential within the knowledge system, and can also be interpreted as a steering mechanism connected with the norm system. Polanyi (1978) also argues for the importance of intellectual passions for guiding scientific work:

> The overwhelming elation felt by scientists at the moment of discovery, an elation of a kind which only a scientist can feel and which science alone can evoke in him…The outbreak of such emotions in the course of discovery is well known, but they are not thought to affect the outcome of discovery. Science is regarded as objectively established in spite of its passionate origins…I want to show that scientific passions are no mere psychological by-product, but have a logical function, which contributes an indispensable element to science.…Only a tiny fraction of all knowledge facts are of interest to scientists, and scientific passion serves also as a guide in the assessment of what is higher and what of lesser interest; what is great in science, and what relatively slight .…Any process of enquiry unguided by intellectual passions would inevitably spread out into a desert of trivialities (pp. 134–135).

As we interpret it, 'elation' is another essential element of professional knowledge, an indispensable steering mechanism within the system of knowledge. In other words, without *emotional involvement* no further learning of professionalism is possible. We can compare Polanyi's words above with the idea that resistance to involvement leads to stagnation, boredom, and regression. Our interpretation is that the terms elation, passion, and emotion can be seen as synonyms for the same phenomenon: the concept of emotional involvement.

Proficient performer

Professional performers are immersed in their jobs. At this stage, individuals intuitively recognize a specific perspective, and then analyse what to do. That is, they 'must still *decide* what to do' (Dreyfus & Dreyfus, 2005, p. 787). One important aspect here is to recognize that there is a problem or an opportunity:

> The proficient marketing manager will keep his finger on the pulse of the product market through reading and listening to everything from formal reports to gossip. One day he may decide, intuitively, that a problem or opportunity exists and that product repositioning should be considered. He will then initiate a study of the situation, quite possibly taking great pride in the sophistication of his scientif-

ic analysis while overlooking his much more impressive talent – that of recognizing, without conscious thought, the simple existence of the problem (Dreyfus & Dreyfus, 1986, p. 30).

Thus, recognition becomes vital at this stage of learning. Recognition, we argue, is an important part of the knowledge system, because in order to develop professionalism, it is necessary to be able to discover any practical problems within the situational context. 'The *proficient performer*, immersed in the world of skilful activity, *sees* what needs to be done, but she/he *decides* how to do it' (Dreyfus & Dreyfus, 2005, p. 787).

Expert performer

'The *expert* not only sees what needs to be achieved; thanks to vast repertoire of situational discriminations, he or she also sees immediately how to achieve the goal' (Dreyfus & Dreyfus, 2005, p. 787). Dreyfus and Dreyfus argue that it is the ability to make more subtle and redefined discriminations that is the difference between the expert and the proficient performer:

> Among many situations, all seen as similar with respect to plan or perspective, the expert has learned to distinguish those situations requiring one reaction from those demanding another. That is, with enough experience in a variety of situations, all seen from the same perspective but requiring different tactical decisions, the brain of the expert gradually decomposes this class of situations into subclasses, each of which requires a specific response. This allows the immediate intuitive situational response that is characteristic of expertise (Dreyfus & Dreyfus, 2005, p. 787).

The expert's behaviour is intuitive. According to Simon (1985), 'most intuitive leaps are acts of recognition' (p. 105). Additionally, qualified practical knowledge has to be modified in new situations (e.g., Rolf, 1991, p.112; cf. Polanyi, 1973). The ability to do this is a precondition for being able to adapt to the clients' needs. Dreyfus and Dreyfus argue that if one asks 'an expert for the rules he or she is using, one will, in effect, force the expert to regress to the level of a beginner and state the rules learned in school' (2005, p. 788).

In relation to Freidson's ideal type, the two last stages in the Dreyfus and Dreyfus learning model – the proficient performer and the expert performer – would be judged as being 'professional.' Freidson's ideal-type includes the aspects of expert knowledge and experience, as well as judgment of the best practice to apply in a given situation. To these, the Dreyfus and Dreyfus learning model adds the importance of *emotional involvement,* recognition *of the situation at hand,* the possibility to *evaluate* the task and to *act in accordance with one's evaluation* as basis for professional performance. These aspects are critical for the application of professional knowledge, but are also relevant for the application of professional norm systems. Perhaps these stages are necessary for the development of professionals' norm systems and sense of commitment.

Perceiving professional situations

Henriksen and Vetlesen (1998) argue that the Dreyfus and Dreyfus model may be used in order to facilitate an understanding of ethics in a broader perspective. Of course, no one can be an expert on ethics, but people are able to learn to recognize situations that demand moral evaluation and judgment (cf. Brytting, 2001). The professional individual has to observe that there is a moral dimension within the situation; the situation should invite the individual to engage in reflection on the moral and ethical aspects of various actions (Brytting, 2001; cf. Henriksen & Vetlesen, 1998). If the individual fails to observe this dimension within the situation, no ethical reflection will take place and the action will not be based on ethical deliberation.

One may define two levels of ethics.[2] One is *universal principles,* the other is the *practical ethic* within a situational context.[3] Only when the concrete, specialized context is taken into account can the ethical norms be translated into the ethics of practice (cf. Freidson, 2001, p. 215). Concerning ethics, *recognition* can be considered an interconnected mechanism between professional norm systems and knowledge systems.

If we refer to the work of Aristotle, we are reminded of *phronesis* as a type of knowledge. Aristotle distinguished between *episteme, techne,* and *phronesis.* Episteme concerns knowledge and universals that are invariable in time and space. Such knowledge is built on analytical rationality. Techne is related to art and craftsmanship. It is context-dependent and concerns the application of technical knowledge and skills; it is built on a pragmatic, instrumental rationality. Phronesis (or prudence) involves practical knowledge and practical ethics.

> We may grasp the nature of prudence [*phronesis*] if we consider what sort of people we call prudent. Well, it is thought to be the mark of a prudent man to be able to deliberate rightly about what is good and advantageous ... But nobody deliberates about things that are invariable ... So ... prudence cannot be science or art; not science [*episteme*] because what can be done is a variable (it may be done in different ways, or not done at all), and not art [*techne*] because action and production are generically different. For production aims at an end other than itself; but this is impossible in the case of action, because the end is merely doing *well*. What remains, then, is that it is a true state, reasoned, and capable of action with regard to things that are good or bad for man ... We consider that this quality belongs to those who understand the management of households or states. (Aristotle's *Den Nikomachiska etiken*, 1988, pp. 163–164, cited in Flyvbjerg 2001, p. 56–57.)

To sum up, phronesis concerns ethics. It is context-dependent, variable, and pragmatic and it concerns deliberation of values connected to praxis. What we can learn from phronesis is the connection between knowledge and ethics. These two aspects are required for trust of the professionals (cf. Koehn, 1994). The 'good or bad for man' is present 'in' expert knowledge. Expert knowledge in this sense is ability to perform 'good' actions (cf. Rolf, 1991, p. 112).

Professional work thereby includes the performance of 'complex task[s] independently and to solve problems which arise in the performance of these tasks using their experience and expertise' (Derber & Schwartz, 1991), where not only the knowledge, but also ethical judgments in the form of phronesis are vital ingredients. To sum up, essential elements for professional practice are the ability to *recognize* the situation at hand, to *evaluate* the work needed, and to *feel emotionally involved* in solving the problems at hand. A precondition for professional practice is therefore to exercise discretion in one's choice of action in the specific situation and to exercise self-control in the work situation. The concepts of recognition, evaluation, and emotional involvement are thus important analytical devices for understanding the effects of changing control mechanisms within professions.

43

Traditional professional control

The specification of professional work above implies that neither the work processes themselves nor their performance outcomes are possible to predict beforehand. Accordingly, Ouchi categorizes professions as a group that applies clan control, based on premises control. This idea has been further developed into the notion of professional control, or professionalism as a control form (Abernethy & Stoelwinder, 1995; Fournier, 1999). Building on Orlikowski (1991), Abernethy and Stoelwinder maintain that professional control occurs when organizations hire personnel who not only 'have the necessary knowledge and experience to perform complex tasks, but ... have also been socialized to act independently without formal administrative control and can search for and implement desired solutions' (1995, p. 3) Professional control thus stems from social control within the social group and has it roots outside the organization (Orlikowski, 1991). This control may be carried out by colleagues, or by the association that organize the profession (cf. Erlingdóttir & Jonnergård, 2006).

Fournier (1999, p. 289) further develops the specification of professional control; it is a form of disciplinary logic that is built upon the professionals' ability to establish control over professional knowledge, the personal conduct of practitioners, and their practices as such. As a form of disciplinary logic, professionalism emphasizes the importance of being considered legitimate by society (clients) and to consider oneself as 'appropriate'. In other words, the way society interprets what it means to be a professional defines the limits and the possibilities of professional control. According to Fournier, this implies that

> individuals are governed not through a monolithic and all-powerful State, but through systems of 'truth' [...], through the proliferation of expert practical knowledge (e.g. psychology, medicine, law and accounting) that serves to constitute human beings as autonomous subjects with a responsibility (or even an interest) to conduct their life in appropriate way. (1999, p. 284)

The social construction of an 'appropriate' professional or professional group occurs on both the collective and the individual levels. On the collective level, professionals as a social group have to legitimize themselves by referring to certain values outside of the profession itself, for example, the public good. On the individual level, this legitimacy must be put into action. According to Fournier, this is done through the notion of *competence*. She claims that

> through the notion of competence, truth and knowledge are translated into a code of appropriate conduct which serves to construct the subjectivity of the professional practitioner. Truth governs not by controlling directly the acts (or event) of the knowledge of the professional practitioner but by making sure that the practitioner is the sort of person who can be trusted with truth. Thus an important characteristic of professional competence is the reliance on technologies of the self (i.e. through careful selection and strong doses of socialisation) rather than merely on technologies of domination. (1999, p. 287)

In summary, traditional professional control rests upon the socialization of behaviour patterns that have been transferred from generation to generation through education, bodies of knowledge, and ethical rules. As such, it is to be viewed as premises control rather than behaviour control or output control, where the premises are formed by the mechanism of legitimacy of the professions in the eyes of the society and the social construction of 'appropriate' professionals. This form of control is a condition for performing complex tasks and the situation-specific application of knowledge. At the same time, these kinds of situations and tasks are required if traditional professional control is to be effective.

Documents as a new type of control

In the public sector, different types of documents have always been used to regulate the relationships between the political, administrative, and professional parts of public organizations. The design of documents such as budgets and transcripts of political decisions are actually the way in which the public sector has traditionally organized its activities. Political decisions have provided the outline and budget processes have set the boundaries for these activities (e.g., Wildavsky, 1977; van Gustern, 1976). Using Ouchi's (1979) concepts, one may say that this is a type of premises control in which the politicians set the premises, but there is still substantial freedom in how the work is executed and the people performing the activities are permitted to decide which methodology or technology to use. From the perspective of the professions, one may say that these organizational conditions correspond to the conditions for professional control. This type of situation provides a basis for the integration of professional control in organizational settings and lowers the tension between organizations and professions (Abernethy & Stoelwinder, 1995).

Today, management by documents[4] has started to play a substantial role in the management of both public and private organizations. Two aspects of management by documents are important to discuss: The first aspect is the content of the documents; the second is the demands for documentation that most often come along with the managerial documents. During the past two decades, documents that go beyond specifying the frames for different activities to include specific rules for actions have become more frequent. Examples of this type of document include instruction manuals, service guaranties, quality standards, action plans for different activities, and action plans as contracts with clients, which to a high degree specify the performance of professionals or semi-professionals. Seen from the perspective of formal standards, professionals become performers who simply carry out pre-established tasks. This is one aspect of what we call managerial documents and management by documents.

A second aspect of management by documents is an increased demand for documentation. Professionals are required to spend an increasing amount of time on documenting their work, filling in forms, writing up reports and evaluations, etc. As a result, the actual work – providing health care – may suffer. One example of this is quality assurance programmes in the health care sector (e.g., Erlingsdóttir, 1999; Erlingsdóttir & Lindberg, 2005). These new programmes mean that health-care providers suddenly have been exposed to extensive demands for documentation. Similarly, the school system is exposed to increased demands for the documentation of education and the development of the pupils (see Persson, this volume). The increased demands for documentation can be seen as part of the increased transparency that is a salient trend in today's society (see Sahlin-Andersson, 2000).

The new control devices lead to what we call *management by documents*. As such, they differ from the professional control that was discussed above, and have led to a new form of control for professionals. Comparing management by documents with Ouchi's (1979, 1980) control types, management by documents entails action or behavioural control, that is, a control form more suitable for bureaucracy than for professions. In addition, it entails output control, which is achieved through documentation.

Our research questions are: Does management by documents have any impact on professionals' knowledge, value base and ethical responsibilities, and if so, how? Given the preceding discussion regarding professions and professional control, the question may be more precisely stated as: How do managerial documents influence professionals' freedom to act, and how does management by documents influence the recognition, evaluation and emotional involvement of professionals?[5] In the next section, we will identify, discuss, and analyse some examples.

The implications of managerial documents

We will base our discussion on three main examples. These will be presented briefly below, after which we will discuss the possible effects on the recognition, evaluation and emotional involvement of the profession in relation to these examples.

According to Prottas (1979), there is a risk that the ability to use knowledge can decrease because of the simplistic use of rules: 'First, it tends to specify behaviour and not the rationale for behaviour... Second, this approach to rule-making makes illicit an unavoidable part of street-level bureaucrat's work, that is, the exercise of discretion' (p. 95). In similarity to Ouchi (1979), Prottas asserts that prescriptive rules are a poor way to control professionals' behaviour. Freidson (2001) cautions against standardization because of the risk that unanticipated knowledge will be lost or because clients may be hurt: 'Where service is being provided to individual humans in need, standardization runs the risk of degrading the service to some and failing to serve appropriately those who fall outside the norm' (p. 218).

To understand if management by documents has any impact on professionals' knowledge, value base, and ethical responsibilities – and if so, how – we must focus on three phenomena: recognition, emotional involvement, and evaluation, all of which are embedded within the professionals' knowledge system and connected to the professionals' norm system. We argue that this focus is important for understanding how prescriptive rules cause disturbances and how these disturbances will propagate into professionals' norm systems and systems of knowledge. Disturbance in the knowledge system will have an impact on the norm system, and vice versa. Some empirical examples are presented below and a secondary analysis is provided to test the analytical tools we have chosen.

Examples of management by documents
Quality systems [6]

Because professionals have traditionally been responsible for quality control, quality systems can be seen as a against input premise control, but also as a break against the professionals' traditional evaluations of their own work. And as Freidson argues, it is this monopolistic control that is the essential characteristic of ideal-typical professionalism (2001, p. 32).

For example, Reed (1995) argues that quality management practices may be understood as a form of organizational control and surveillance and as an ideological narrative and organizational strategy of the 'enterprise culture' that became prominent in the 1980s.

Other evidence (Erlingsdóttir & Jonnergård, 2006) has shown that different professions use different ways to handle the requirement for quality systems. Erlingsdóttir and Jonnergård's study included the auditing field and health care sector. They found that the auditor's professional associations were proactive and edited the implementation processes. Within the auditing field, the idea of quality was connected to work processes and involved the standardization of the quality system as such. Because of these organizing devices, auditing businesses are protected from public control as long as they maintain at least a certain degree of quality.

Within the health care sector, the idea of quality assurance was embedded within the philosophy of New Public Management, strengthening the effects New Public Management has had within this field. Physicians reacted as a professional group; they were not interested in the idea of quality assurance. For the health care sector, the idea of quality assurance has reinforced centralization because of the increased claims of transparency on the operational level. The differences between the two professions are related to their different types of knowledge base and how they legitimize their specialized work.

> Comparing these results with another research project concerning nurses' strategies for handling quality-assurance programs (Blomgren, 1999), the importance of a knowledge base and the ways to legitimize specialized work are once again illustrated. The quality assurance was in this case used as a way to make 'make nurses' practical work more abstract by making it more distinct and visible [and] was also a way of enhancing their professional aspirations' (Blomgren, 1999, p. xvi)

The nurses became proactive and they developed a common way to document their work and at the same time consider how the quality of all tasks could be improved. The quality assurance programme was a method for assuring an acceptable level of care despite increasing requirements for economic efficiency. However, for the nurses the quality system had two other purposes besides the quality of patient care: (1) the documents protected the nurses in case of incidents, because the documents showed that the nurses had done what was required for safe and proper care; and (2) the creation of the quality-assurance programmes had the potential to improve the status of the nurses' work as a profession (Blomgren, 1999, pp. 152–153).

There are, for our purposes, some interesting elements in Blomgren's research results. First, in terms of context-dependent knowledge, describing all dimensions within the nurses' work is problematic because of the tacit dimensions of context-dependence. As Polanyi (1973, p. 88) argues, experts can 'indicate their clues and formulate maxims, but they know many more things than they can tell, knowing them only in practice, as instrumental particulars, and not explicitly, as objects.' This point of view compels us to ask the question: Which practical knowledge will be lost in the quality document developed by the nurses?

The phenomenon of 'quality' as such is also problematic. Quality has many dimensions and must be context-dependent. Even though people can recognize quality, when they encounter it in a specific situation, they cannot describe all of the elements embedded in the actual quality they recognize (cf. Agevall, 2002). We will employ Wittgenstein's (1992. p. 43) concept of 'family similarities' to understand the complexities of quality: 'various similarities between the members of a family intervene with and cross each other: height, facial features, eye color, way of walking, temperament etc.' (our translation). We argue that the perception of quality is essential for professional knowledge and norm systems.

Another problem with quality assurance programmes is that they do not improve quality in the long term: '[Quality assurance] may even suppress the development of better quality by promoting complacency, or suppress improvement by stifling innovation ("the book says we must do it this way")' (Morgan & Potter, 1995, p. 181).

Will context-independent rules interfere with the recognition of what is important and what is not within the situational context? This question covers two types of recognition: the ability to recognize practical problems and possibilities, and the ability to recognize situations that require moral or ethical sensitivity. If quality assurance suppresses the possibility for people to modify their knowledge in new situations or to improve quality, it may lead to propagation of the norm systems of the profession, that is, the commitment to do a good job.

Additionally, how should we interpret the result that shows that quality assurance documents tend to protect nurses in case of incidents because they had done what is required for safe and proper care? Is it an example of regression from the proficient or expert performer stages to a lower level of novice or advanced beginner with limited responsibility and greater reliance on rule following? As mentioned above, at the competent, proficient, and expert stages in Dreyfus and Dreyfus's learning model, individuals feel personally responsible for their own choices and actions, and a sense of individual responsibility is essential to ethics. Furthermore, if our interpretation is correct, the documents may undermine the emotional involvement that is essential for the commitment to do a good job and that is one of the core elements of professional work, embedded within the knowledge system and explicit in the norm system.

Services catalogues and local guidelines

In his research on care manager reform for organizing the care of the elderly, Blomberg (2004) found that

> documentation, specialization, standardization and formalization are all associated with the reform and also theoretically viewed as neces-

> sary elements for increasing the bureaucratic (formal) control of activities. But it is seen also to consist of discrete informal control. When the managers talk about their job they stress the importance of discarding cost elements and concentrating on needs. At the same time … the formalization of needs-assessment was accompanied by increased restrictiveness in allowing for assistance. The reform paves the way for and is followed by tighter cost control. (p. 211)

Standardization means that the different kinds of service benefits are determined beforehand, for example, in catalogues. Each part of a given service contribution is prescribed: its content, scope, methods, and quality are grounds for the prices in contracts between purchasers and providers. Even if there are some possibilities for discretion in the decision making process, there is a risk that the elements within the services catalogue will be the norm and thus the standards. Blomberg (2004, p. 212) argues that there is some evidence that the work of care managers is transforming into a gatekeeper role. This raises the same concerns that we voiced earlier about the risk of professionals regressing to the advanced beginner and novice stages.

Another example of these 'new documents' is the local municipal guidelines concerning the provision of personal assistance to the disabled. In some municipalities, the guidelines are not always in accordance with the law, and they often amount to restrictions of services for disabled individuals (Socialstyrelsen, 2005, p. 23). A relevant question here is: How will a professional individual react to this type of description in the local municipal guidelines? Will she or he react against the prescriptions or will she or he follow the rules even though they break the law? That is an empirical question and the answer concerns the ethics of the professions – the norm system. If there is a break down of the norm system, it will propagate into the knowledge system.

International Standard on Auditing

In 2006 all auditors in the European Union (and in several other places in the world) began to follow one common standard for auditing: the International Standard on Auditing (ISA). The standard includes detailed recommendations for the way the audit should be planned and carried out. According to the ISA standard, each step of the audit process must be documented. Additionally, the larger auditing firms have developed substantial computer-based work programmes and lists of issues for the different parts of the audit process. In general, smaller auditing firms most often use standardized computer programmes developed for these functions by specialized computer companies. This standardization has developed during a number of years; it is far more comprehensive than it was previously, and it is obligatory that all auditing forms adhere to it. The impact of this standardization of the auditing profession has been questioned. While some dread a de-professionalization (cf. Öhman, 2004), other welcome the opportunity to concentrate on the other side – the evaluative side – of auditing (cf. Mason *et al.*, 2000).

Learning recognition is a part of the process of learning to become a professional. In the case of auditing, this entails being able to detect a problem in a company's control system, risk management, or accounting. The ISA standard may be both a support and an obstacle in this respect. On the one hand, it should be a support because it covers the basic situations that an audit is supposed to cover. On the other hand, if recognition is primarily given to documentation, an auditing problem whose occurrence has *not* been taken into account in the documentation may be overlooked or ignored. However, another development may be just as relevant. It is possible that the standards for being a professional will diminish. As the focus is increasingly put on following the standards, the experience and knowledge needed to be able to recognize problems not mentioned in the standards could diminish. This may lead to differentiation and de-professionalization within the profession. This might not influence professionals' autonomy as such, but it could influence their ability to recognize and evaluate different situations, an ability which is a vital aspect of professional expertise.

The evaluation aspect has to do with the ability to judge the situation and make a choice between different alternative actions. The main choices in the audit process concern what issues and control processes to examine more closely and how to evaluate the various accounting choices made by the company.

Concluding propositions

Management by documents entails both behavioural control and output control. First, the content of the documents implies behavioural control, whereas the demands of documentation entail output control and make it possible to assess professionals' compliance to the documents. There is a high degree of probability that the behaviour control and the output control will reinforce each other when professionals' autonomy and their ability to control and evaluate their own work is decreased.

The examples above illustrate deviations from Freidson's ideal type of professionalism. In these examples professionals' autonomy and their ability to control their own work have been restricted. Furthermore, they have partly lost their ability to decide what is quality in the professional field. Concerning the control of the professions, we have identified a shift from professional control to other forms of control.

With the basis on the theoretical discussion and the empirical examples, we derive the following propositions. These are intended to be the basis for further empirical investigations.

Prescriptive documents lead to behaviour control and will:

• cause decreased emotional involvement – a detached and technical view of work, and
• reduce professionals' recognition of practical problems and possibilities, diminishing their ability to recognize situations that require moral and ethical sensitivity, and
• lead to a new way of evaluating professional work, that is, a decreased sense of individual responsibility for one's own work.

Interference with the essential elements within the knowledge system causes a professional to regress from being a proficient or expert performer to the stages of advanced beginner and novice, and the decline within the knowledge system will propagate into the norm system.

Documentation as a means of measurement and cost efficiency leads to output control and may cause:

- a re-orientation of emotional involvement from the situation at hand to the possible outcome, and
- the possible direction of recognition towards dimensions included in 'the measuring-rods', and
- the evaluation to include new criteria for decision connected to the output measures.

Output control may lead to changes within the ethical norm system and professionals' commitment to doing a good job. In other words, the control system evolves from being based on value-rationality (phroneses) to being based on a form of instrumental rationality (cf. techne), and changes within the norm system may propagate into the system of knowledge and vice versa. If these tentative propositions come true, de-professionalizing processes will occur.

Notes

1 We use the concept of *profession* in a very broad sense. The purpose is to include recognized professions as well as occupational groups that are struggling for jurisdictions and professional status.
2 These elements are, as we interpret it, mutually dependent on each other. Doing a good job includes elaborating, refining, and extending a body of knowledge and skill. In other words, professionals are not able to do these things without the possibility to control their own work. Doing a good job also includes the ethical aspect of serving others' needs apart from any self-interest (cf. Freidson, 2001, p. 108). We agree with Freidson: the essential element of what we call the *norm system* is the commitment to do a good job, which is in turn built on the 'devotion to use the disciplined knowledge and skill for the public good' (pp. 217–218) rather than striving for economic gains, quality, and efficiency.
3 Dreyfus and Dreyfus's learning model has received most criticism because they do not explicitly define what they mean by *rules*. But there is consensus that a person with qualified knowledge does not consciously refer to rules (Rolf, 1991, p. 112). We deem this consensus satisfactory for our purposes.
4 In this article, we use *ethic* and *moral* as synonymous concepts.
5 Gilligan (1982) puts forth a similar argument: 'While an ethic of justice proceeds from the premise of equality – that everyone should be treated the same – an ethic of care rests on the premise of non-violence – that no one should be hurt' (p. 174).
6 These documents differ from 'traditional steering documents' in the public sector (such as decrees or statutes), as they have their origin in management control rather than in traditional public administration (Cooper, 1990).
7 There is currently a discussion whether New Public Management (NPM) entails de-professionalization or re-professionalization (cf. Abernethy & Stoelwinder, 1995; Selander, 2001). Most of this discussion belongs to the 'cynical approach' to

professions (cf. Brante, 1988) and concerns the division of power and tasks between different occupations. Because we are interested in the effects on professional's systems of knowledge and norms systems, we do not enter this discussion.

8 There are different kinds of quality systems. Some examples are Total Quality Management (TQM), Quality Assurance, and Quality Accreditation.

Preamble

There is a general understanding that teachers must become users of information and communication technology; in this regard, positioning theory has been used to analyse the social and historical shifts in teachers' rights, duties, and obligations associated with using such technology. Analysis of policy documents demonstrates that these rights and duties have historically been reserved for future teachers. Data for his chapters have been drawn from material collected by the research projects *ICT and Learning in Teacher Training* funded by the Knowledge Foundation through its research programme LearnIt.

Lars-Erik Nilsson

Talking 'tools for learning'

Positioning teachers in discourses
on information and communication technology

Introduction

'Tools for Learning – A National Programme for ICT in Schools' is
the English title of a Swedish Government Communication
(1997/98:176). Its text introduced the largest effort to that date to
implement information and communication technology (ICT) in the
Swedish school system. It is the contention of this study that the translation does not do full justice to either the Swedish title or the contents of the Communication. The Swedish title, *Lärandets verktyg:
nationellt program för IT i skolan*, implies that IT tools *are* the contemporary tools needed for learning. Without them, there *cannot* be
learning worthy of a knowledge society; without their use, schools will
lose their institutional legitimacy and teachers their legitimacy as professionals. We analyse political discourse on teachers' professional identity from a long-term perspective, arguing that Swedish policies concerning ICT implementation have always invoked the name of 'teachers in the future'. Teachers as a group have never been positioned as
users. Thus policies have introduced a tension between public expectations and the possibilities open to the profession, i.e., collective professional interests.

In 1995, the Swedish government claimed that it was a matter of
national urgency that Sweden should endeavour to become an information society (SOU, 1994, p. 118). Implementing a new infrastructure based on computerized digital technology was considered pivotal
to such a transition and education one of three strategic areas for related political action. Through this drive, pressure was put on teachers

to become ICT users. In 1998, the Swedish government initiated its largest effort to that point to implement ICT in the Swedish school system, in Government Communication 1997/98:176, 'Tools for Learning' (ITiS, 1998). The contents of the Communication indicated that it was the aim of the Swedish government to ensure that modern technology was used by the teaching profession. Taken as a whole, the policy suggestions make available a professional identity for teachers as users of digital and networked ICT and also specify the type of user a teacher must become. This chapter contributes to our understanding of the construction of contemporary teachers' professional identity against the backdrop of the implementation of this technical infrastructure.

Professional tools and professional identity

It is often said that schooling is such a stable activity that someone from an earlier century could walk into a classroom of today, instantly know what kind of place s/he was in, and accurately assess what was going on. S/he would immediately recognize the teacher, the board, the marker, and the seating arrangement with students in their desks and know what is going on. Be that as it may, policies on ICT in education in most countries clearly suggest that governments want a shift away from whiteboards, books, and pens. In Swedish ICT policies, teachers' prior professional identity is challenged by the use of the metaphor 'tools of learning'. Through this metaphor, the government establishes premises not only for new tools that teachers are duty-bound to use in their daily work, but also for what their learning environments should be like and how the teaching and learning done in them should be organized.

Thus, political visions appear to be constraining the kind of professional identity teachers can forge. Teachers, should they yield to central policies, would need to change how they work. In ICT policies, although perhaps not in everyday school activities, a new teacher emerges, one who works with a computer, smart board, video projector, and global connection. To the extent that a teacher subscribes to the identity of a lecturer with a marker and a whiteboard, this identity can be said to be threatened by government policies and parliamentary decisions.

Politics, organizations, tools,
and the construction of professional identity

The introduction to this chapter stressed political initiatives. Ahrne (1996) asserts that research into the effects of politics on administration has been scarce; in research into ICT implementation in education, however, this concern has been paramount. There are a number of studies that suggest that external influences have been important in shaping the implementation of technology in education (Jedeskog, 2000). According to the perspective guiding the present study, the envisioned change in the use of teaching tools exerts pressure on the individual teacher concerning how to make sense of professional identity. Of course, there is much more to the relationship between teachers and their tools than simply *what* tools they use; ultimately, the relationship also concerns *what kind* of professional identity teachers can seek, given the legislation passed by governments, and perhaps even more so given how this is being implemented. Can they become expert users and control the use of these new tools? In short, what kinds of tool users can they become?

Svensson (in press) asserts that most of our social landscape is dominated by formal organizations. Ideally, organizations, whether public or professional, provide scaffolds for individual professionals, and ideally, these scaffolds are a source of strength. Being part of an organization, however, also means giving up some of one's independence (Ahrne, 1990; Svensson, in press). In discourse on professional work and professionals, it is generally assumed that decisions concerning how to perform work are (a) based on scientific (i.e., professional) knowledge that is (b) gained in formal training; moreover, the assumption is that (c) the professional will draw on personal experience and (d) ideological commitment in applying such knowledge to various cases (e) in the interest of doing good work within the jurisdiction of her/his profession (cf. Friedson, 1994). While individual professionals seem to have the final say in all these respects, it is also clear that they need to concede to organizational demands from both public and professional organizations. They must, as it were, comply with political dictates while following evidence-based research into best practice. To add further complexity, they must do this while taking into account 'the particular demands of the organization to perform services for us as citizens, clients, customers, or users according to more or less well-defined societal contracts' (Svensson, in press, my translation). Professional autonomy, if not an illusion, is at least a right circumscribed by concessions to the political arena, organizations, and other interests; this also ought to be true when it comes to the use of professional tools.

The controversies that swirl about the issue of teacher autonomy and control latch on to this general debate, concerned not so much about whether there *is* autonomy and control but rather whether teachers are *gaining or losing* control. The political pressure put on teachers under the aegis of reform and 'new managerialism' can in itself be taken to indicate that teachers are losing control. Much research into the implementation of technology supports such a conclusion. Cuban (1986) claims teachers were provided with tools that were not designed for them and that they could not see the point in using; computers were thus regarded as unable to contribute much to student learning (Cuban, 1986, 2002). Metaphors such as 'top-down' (Riis, 1991) and 'push' (Riis, 2000) paint a picture of reform from above or at least from outside the organization. Söderlund (2000), on the contrary, argues that control is shifting and that decisions about technology have moved down the organizational hierarchy, thus aligning himself with statements about teachers gaining more control over their work (see Carlgren & Marton, 2000). Warschauer (2000) illustrates this tendency towards growing professional control in a study that demonstrates how two different groups of teachers use technology for completely different ends, one group using technology to facilitate higher-order thinking skills to prepare students for academic studies and the other to facilitate the production of web and multimedia material to prepare students for the marketplace.

Positions in policies and reports

The data in this chapter comprise texts about teachers and technology in the form of Government Bills, Communications, and reports. The preferred perspective from which to analyse the texts assumes that an individual's access to professional tools is determined in a field of tension in which the individual's rights and duties/obligations are continuously negotiated. Positions relative to ICT are made available for teachers in discourse at different organizational levels. These positions are considered dynamic in the sense that they depend on several constantly shifting factors: conditions in local moral orders, the unfolding of conversations, story lines in documents, and discourse in the course of history. It is implied that tensions between professions and organizations about the rights and duties to use professional tools are constitutive of the individual professional and of the kind of professional identity that can be made available but is also contestable. That is, professional identity is foremost a discursive construction.

This reasoning aligns with positioning theory (Harré and van Langenhove, 1999b; Harré and Moghaddam, 2003), according to which positions are considered to be built up of clusters of rights (demands that can be placed on others), duties (demands that others can place on you), and obligations (demands that you place on yourself). These clusters make up ensembles of positions associated with sometimes contradictory expectations as to what people can, should, and may do. They allow us to see the individual within the profession, rather than just the professional stepping into a role that has been pre-cast for the profession.

To demonstrate these points, the data in this article have been chosen to illustrate how ensembles of positions are made available for teachers in talk about ICT and how these positions suggest different rights and duties to use technology. Precisely because positioning theory asserts that positions are highly contingent on context, the data consist of a heterogeneous set of texts chosen from various historical and social contexts from the 1980s through the first five years of the new millennium. The first text is taken from the Project for Research on INteractive Computer-based Education SystemS – PRINCESS (Kollerbauer, Jansson, Köhler, & Yngström, 1983). The second text is a policy document from the Swedish National Board of Education calling for the first efforts to introduce computers into the school system (National Board of Education, 1986). The third text is the English version of the Swedish Government Communication, 1997/98:176, 'Tools of Learning', representing the most substantial political effort to that point to implement ICT in the Swedish school system. This English version was published by the project organization, 'ICT in Schools' (ITiS), that was an outgrowth of the Communication; it is this version to which I refer in the present study, and quotations from the Communication will accordingly be cited as

61

'ITiS, 1998'. The fourth text is an excerpt from the latest Government Bill (2004/2005:175) on ICT. The texts have been grouped to form a historical sequence covering Swedish policy making from the nineteen seventies to the year 2005.

The subject, the object, and the excluded

In 1971, the Swedish government gave the National Board of Education a directive to examine the possibility of introducing education *about* computer technology into Swedish secondary and upper-secondary schools. 'About' suggests a right and duty to know about computer technology rather than a right and duty actually to *use* them. A series of projects were set up, one of them being the PRINCESS project. The primary issues were what kinds of computer support could benefit education and what kind of hardware and software would be required (Kollerbauer *et al.*, 1983, p. 40); regarding teachers and technology, it is asserted that 'the teacher too, must be regarded as a subject' (p. 17).

Positioning teachers as *subjects* implies agency, as is clearly illustrated where the relationship between teaching and technology was described. Teaching should still be the realm of the teachers (Kollerbauer *et al.*, 1983, p. 17, 38). Here the project takes a different view from that common at the beginning of the century, when technology was expected to replace teachers and make teaching more effective (cf. Cuban, 1986). This view also stands in marked contrast to Swedish attempts to introduce technology for programmed instruction approximately two decades earlier, when technology was supposed to take over instruction (SOU, 1963:, Malmquist, 1961). There are other implications. Subjects cannot be replaced. If teachers were to be subjects they needed to become competent users, and it was suggested that their use of technology could aid their professional development (Kollerbauer *et al.*, 1983, p. 17).

The normative stance that teachers should be subjects had design implications; computer support should be designed in such a way that it could supplement but not replace teachers (Kollerbauer *et al.*, 1983, p. 17). To become genuine subjects, teachers should have the right to decide how computers should be used, the particular needs they should meet, and the disciplinary content for which they should be programmed. They should be tutors or invigilators rather than lecturers, and also have a duty to provide human assistance for students' individual use of computers (pp. 35, 38) based on professional disciplinary knowledge.

Contemporary teachers were, however, restricted by views of pedagogy; in relation to pedagogy, they were positioned as *objects*. Basic principles of computer support were adopted from contemporary Swedish curricula by the PRINCESS project. These normative ideas changed gradually as policies introduced a shift in pedagogical focus from individualization towards collaboration, and an interest in Piaget and problem-based computer support during the project years (Kollerbauer *et al.*, 1983, p. 44). This shift influenced design. According to Lindh (1997), one important influence of the project on subsequent policies was the idea that training programmes had to be designed so as to allow users to pose the questions.

From the outset, the project was dominated by the ideal that all relevant experts should be allowed to contribute to the design process; in fact, one recommendation was that teachers should participate in design. A variety of professional groups became involved. Researchers were involved in programming and conducting scientific studies (Kollerbauer *et al.*, 1983, p. 216). Engineers worked on hardware. Disciplinary specialists were allowed to advise regarding content that ought to be targeted for computer support. Teachers and students were allowed to provide input on usability issues. These 'designer teachers' were required to be knowledgeable and able 'to define relevant problem areas and really take part in and influence work on the development of computer support' (p. 70). A central belief was that teachers were experts on content rather than pedagogy, and that it was in the former domain they should have both the right and the duty to supply specialist knowledge. In this, the project aligned itself with ideas that emphasized participant design and assessment, consistent with the Scandinavian model of design (cf. Ehn, 1993) and constructionist technology assessment (Zuiderent, 2000). Practical design work, however, led to the conclusion that this model of user participation had failed. To be subjects with the right to take part in the design process, disciplinary specialists were also obliged to know about design and technology. Expectations concerning teacher involvement in design based solely on knowledge of disciplinary content were considered unrealistic (Kollerbauer *et al.*, 1983, p. 70). This was a kind of 'catch 22'. In short, while the project paid lip service to a participatory model in which disciplinary specialists had the right to influence computer support, only those disciplinary specialists who developed expertise in design could acquire active and influential positions in the design process, that is, be positioned as subjects in relation to their future work tools.

Particularly interesting in connection with the issue of teachers' professional identity were the differences in treatment accorded the subjects and the *excluded*. Two different trajectories appear to have been used. The project team argued that competence development should vary according to the role in the design process. Only one teacher in every disciplinary field in every school was to have the right to competence that would allow her/him to adapt computer support and influence how the support was set up. Developing such competence on the part of all teachers was considered a waste of resources (Kollerbauer *et al.*, 1983, p. 226–228). Only these 'competent' experts could be subjects included in the process of designing and assessing computer support. The rights and duties of these teachers are particularized through their participation in a design experiment and different roles in education. The excluded only needed to know about computers, and it was obvious that when it came to teachers in general, only *future* teachers could become subjects with the right to use computers – and use them according to official policies.

Given the ideology guiding the project, one explanation seems plausible. There was an immediate need of disciplinary expertise to carry out the project. For that purpose, the project produced an ensemble of particular positions logically possible for project teachers, including disciplinary specialists, co-designers, and users who were active and competent driving forces - in short, subjects. As has been shown, these positions were highly occasioned and contextual. They particularized what it meant to be a subject or an object, not only relative to technology, but to pedagogy, disciplinary knowledge, and design. They said more about individual teachers' rights and duties in the context of the project than about their rights and duties relative to ICT for teachers as a group at the time.

The 'super user', the disciplinary specialists, the trainees, and the excluded

At the same time, one of the first administrative-level policies concerning computers in education was formulated by the Swedish

National Board of Education. Several problems were dealt with in the policy, including what kind of teacher competence would be required for implementing computers in education and how to develop such competence. This policy lets us see how the rights and duties of teachers in general and of special groups of teachers in particular were viewed at the time. The text *Utbildningen inför datasamhället* [Education in preparation for a digital society] (National Board of Education, 1986) contains an often-quoted passage that states that students should have the right to such knowledge of computers and their use, that they can take on the societal responsibility to influence the development of the technology (pp. 10–11). It is crucial that education about computers and their use become part of compulsory education – although not implemented in all subjects. Students are to be treated as subjects relative to technology, but what about teachers? Who should be responsible for achieving these objectives? In view of what was said about students and the importance of computer technology in society, one might suspect that teachers would be treated as a group in which rights and duties were shared by all individuals in the profession. Instead, the text displayed similarities to the PRINCESS project text, and the teaching profession was not treated as a homogeneous group. Rather, positions associated with various rights and duties emerged from within the profession.

One way to scrutinize how rights and duties are distributed is to look at the rhetoric of urgency. Urgency is not an issue in this case, since what we need to prepare for, although certain, is not impending. However, this requires that we distinguish between present and future needs. It was recognized that teachers in different stages of education and different disciplines needed different knowledge and skills (National Board of Education, 1986, p. 17). The chief difference in terms of teachers' rights concerned the right actually to learn to use computers, a right reserved for teachers in vocational education who were obliged to prepare students for an industry that already used computers and thus had to master computers themselves; in other words, in their field, computer use was an *urgent* problem. Disciplinary needs positioned *disciplinary specialists* in a similar manner, though the need appeared less urgent and, most importantly, served to distinguish between specialists rather than present them as a group with homogeneous rights and duties. Some disciplines – most notably science and maths – were considered environments in which computer use would play a prominent role; thus, knowledge of and ability to use computer support were considered important in these disciplines, unlike in the humanities.

Rights and duties were also differently allocated to individuals according to their placement in the educational system. It was considered essential to start preparing the next generation of teachers, *the trainees*. All student teachers in teacher training, even those in areas that still lacked a curriculum including computer studies, should have a right to fundamental training. Discourse about student teachers' rights and duties extended beyond mere knowledge and use of computer technology. Following the line of reasoning used in the PRINCESS project, trainees should be subjects, not objects, relative to technology and should gain knowledge of technology, be able to use technology, and cultivate a creative and critical approach to technology. The theory and methods of computer support introduced to the trainees must be of high quality and prepare them for expertise in pedagogy rather than in technology. While policies introduced a range of rights for student teachers, these were not matched by corresponding duties to learn through requirements in the examination syllabus.

Most teachers in service were almost completely excluded. In upper-secondary school and adult education programmes it was recommended that at least one teacher, a 'super user', in every disciplinary area should have deeper knowledge of computers, through either competence development or teacher training. In the nine-year compulsory education system, it was considered sufficient to have one or two teachers with in-depth ITC knowledge in every municipal school management area under one headmaster. Knowledge of how to use a computer was only to be a prerequisite for those teaching subjects that required computer use. For the moment, efforts to educate teachers in service 'due to a scarcity of resources had to be limited to those immediately affected by changes in curriculum' (National Board of Education, 1986, p. 18). Teachers were thus positioned as objects of resources grounded in discourse on money, hardware, software, and resources for training – to mention just a few of the issues cited – though individual teachers could be individually positioned in various ways. Resources needed to be allocated to those most immediately in need of them. The excluded were not considered as needing much computer training at all, at least not right away. Some teachers did not need more than a single training programme. 'Super users' needed deeper knowledge and, after they completed basic training, it was thus deemed important to provide them with ongoing competence development involving computer specialists. Thus teachers were treated as a heterogeneous group. The rights and duties of teachers *in general* did not extend to learning more than their students did, and it was asserted that 'as a benchmark for minimum standards, teachers should receive education in the same proportions as students receive it' (p. 18).

Different trajectories were constructed for different teachers. What applied to student teachers, vocational teachers, disciplinary specialists, and even students does not apply to teachers *in general*. It was only considered *preferable* that all teachers be educated about computers. No matter how important knowledge of computers was regarded, most teachers had fewer rights than students and other personnel did, and the line of reasoning adopted was that society and educational organizations would change as older generations were replaced by younger ones. Once again, it was obvious that a coherent professional identity was not being established or fostered.

While ideology and competence were the main positioning devices evident in the text from the PRINCESS project, access to technology, economic resources, and immediate needs surfaced as positioning devices in the text from the National Board of Education. These positioning devices were used rhetorically to particularize the teaching profession. Age, diploma, disciplinary affiliation, type of employment, and personal interest became important factors, not just affecting the duties of individual teachers, but also determining whether individuals in the profession were positioned as entitled to computer education and hence to use, advise on the design of, and make actual changes to computer support. A result of this process is commented on by Jedeskog (1996), who claims that in this period computer users were recruited from the disciplinary fields of science and technology, but seldom from the humanities or social sciences, turning the computer into an instrument for men in white lab coats. It was not urgent that non-science and non-technology teachers be involved as users, nor to ensure that teachers as a group were knowledgeable about computers.

The afraid, the incompetent, and the competent

A decade later, 'urgency' became an important rhetorical catch phrase, as awareness of the Internet entered political consciousness. Sweden's political aim was to become a world-leading user of ICT by 2010. Government Bill 1995/96:125 proclaimed that education was one of three strategic areas in which political efforts were needed if the transformation into an information society were to succeed. Pedagogical use of ICT should be implemented in education within three years, and it became important for *all* teachers to master ICT. It was asserted that 'all true change in schools must take place through the teachers, who are and will remain key figures in learning'; this could only happen if teachers were given 'ample scope to utilise the new technology' (ITiS, 1998, p. 18). Pedagogy, not technology, should lead the way. It appeared as though there was a firm resolution at the national government level that the teaching profession must be equipped professionally to take the lead, with some help from private initiatives, parents, and students.

Story lines about urgency made several positions available in 'Tools for Learning' (ITiS, 1998). Teachers in educational organizations in an information society need to be active and competent users of ICT to remain key figures. Teachers need overall knowledge of computer technology: they must understand how to set up learning environments, develop multimedia, and communicate in networked environments; they must have basic knowledge of operating systems and applications, and have developed work ethics and knowledge of legal rules and their effects on the learning environment. All these were listed as the demands that should be placed on *all* teachers hoping to position themselves as digitally *competent* professionals. Furthermore, teachers were supposed to be able to use ICT tools in their own professional work and professional development, including communication outside the classroom, lesson planning, quality management, and personal competence development. In addition, they were also expected to understand the implications of political decisions and curriculum requirements regarding how ICT should be used.

Teachers were collectively positioned both as competent subjects with the right to influence the development and use of technology and define its proper use in education, and as the objects of ideologies that prescribe certain ways to use technology. According to Government Communication 1997/98:176, 'Tools for Learning', technology must be used to support problem-based, student-active, teamwork-focused, and multidisciplinary forms of learning, and teachers must use technology outside the classroom and for school development. These normative statements positioned teachers as a homogeneous group of professionals obliged to possess the knowledge and skills required for the multi-purpose use of ICT in education.

The project 'ICT in Schools' (ITiS) was an outgrowth of Government Communication 1997/98:176. Other subject positions, sometimes offering striking contrasts to those made available in the Communication, were made available to teachers, thus introducing a tension. The foreword to a special edition of the Communication, produced by the Delegation for ICT in Schools and signed by Ylva Johansson, then the Minister of Education, states that

> We must therefore ask the right questions when we address the relationship between education and ICT. We must dare to ask whether we have an education system capable of giving every child access to the opportunities afforded by the new technology. Do teachers and other adults know enough to dare to use ICT as an educational tool in school teaching? (ITiS, 1998, Foreword)

This story line about competence is only present in the ITiS version of the Communication. It conveyed the impression that there was a gap between an education system with multi-competent teachers capable of giving students access to new technology and an education system with *incompetent* and *afraid* teachers who cannot guarantee students access to new opportunities. In this foreword, the Minister stressed the need for an assessment. The question is posed whether teachers and other adults 'know enough to dare to use ICT as an educational tool' (ITiS, 1998, Foreword). The phrase 'teachers and other adults' suggests that teachers are not the only ones who can support the use of ICT in education. What other groups could the minister have been thinking of and what were their qualifications? Was she only referring to parents and their ability to help students, or perhaps to employees of private companies, as mentioned in Government Bill 1975/76:125? Was she perhaps referring to the 'global learner' or to the learner's personal network, as they were referred to in the Communication? The Minister gave examples of the kind of professional challenges teachers and 'others' may face and lack sufficient knowledge to handle. They will have to: manage education that is 'affected by the constant availability of unstructured information'; 'venture to use information and communication technology (ICT) to bring about development of school work'; and to use technology to 'contribute to a new focus on pupils learning' (ITiS, 1998, Foreword). The professional position offered is one implying that some teachers are unable to perform tasks for which they have also been positioned as key figures. They are positioned as wanting. At the same time, they appear to have the duty, as teachers, to take on a range of challenges posed by new technology. The Bill and the Communication offered a new position for teachers, describing them as competent users, while implying that part of the profession should be positioned as incompetent.

How can this gap be closed, given that even 'incompetent' teachers apparently have rights? These new demands cannot be placed on the teaching profession until its members are competent. A collective 'we' – perhaps the government, state, or society at large – was held accountable for teachers' fear and incompetence, and it was considered important that these institutions dared ask the right questions. Therefore it must be 'a question of equality of opportunity for schools to provide universal access to this technology, and to the capacity to use it, for their pupils' (ITiS, 1998, Foreword).

Miller (1994) talks about how the rhetorical presence of *kairos* creates a sense of urgency regarding technology forecasting. Here, the Minister's forecast depicts knowledge of technology as something that will create an advantage. The opportunity, there for the taking, is presented as one 'we' cannot effort to miss. 'We' must turn our society into an information society; to do this, 'we' need to change our infrastructure and provide for the competence of school professionals. This situation is not presented as primarily the duty of teaching professionals, but rather as a demand placed on the collective 'we'; placing such demands implies that it is the right of all teachers to be found wanting.

The ITiS project was launched approximately two years after the Communication. ITiS aimed to provide all teachers and students with access to e-mail, all schools with acceptably fast broadband connections, and 40 per cent of the teachers with a personal computer and competence development. Interestingly, when it comes to rights to personal tools and competence development, 'all teachers' seems to be defined as roughly 40 per cent of them, leaving it open to interpretation exactly what demands incompetent professionals were in a position to place on their organizations. In this respect, the Communication was reminiscent of the text from 1986, and it must be asked whether the rest of the teachers – i.e., the other 60 per cent – were to be responsible for their own professional development, had the right to other training, or simply had the right to remain incompetent and afraid of working with computers.

What appears as an urgent call for all teachers to support the transformation to an information society has now been particularized as an effort that gives rights to and demands duties of a narrower group of teachers. Ensembles of positions have been made available in the text. The main text of the Communication presents an ideal professional position in which the individual teachers are obliged to make full use of the tools available to them as communicators, facilitators, learners, team workers, planners – indeed, as almost anything a competent teacher may need and see fit to be. The foreword also makes available the position of incompetent, which entails the right to be uninformed, afraid, wanting, and reluctant.

The digitally competent and the wanting

The currently in force Government Bill dealing with ICT (Government Bill, 2004/05:175) shares the primary objectives of earlier government legislation and policies. Now, however, people are considered as *already* living in and needing to improve on an information and communication society; accordingly, the three main objectives of this Bill are

- 'to enhance trust in ICT' [att öka tilliten till IT],
- 'to increase competence in using ICT' [att öka kompetensen att använda IT], and
- 'to increase access to information society services' [att öka tillgängligheten till informationssamhällets tjänster]. (p. 33)

Issues concerning teacher and student access to hard infrastructure and communication were treated as aims that had already been dealt with through the ITiS project. The remaining problems concerned provision of content and services (Government Bill, 2004/05:175, p. 106) and could be dealt with through: public-private partnerships (p. 109), the Swedish Schoolnet (pp. 110–111), a soft infrastructure with open standards for rational information management (p. 111), and access to research (pp. 106, 114). In the Bill, the government committed itself to creating an infrastructure to support teachers in working with content and learning about research. Such support was presented as the right of teachers at all levels and in all specialities, whether *digitally competent* or *wanting*.

Among priorities were 'efforts to increase IT (ICT) competence among those working in the field of education, and to take into account the demands on competence in an information society in directives about future revisions of course plans and curriculum' (Government Bill, 2004/05:175, p. 106). These were presented, in the language of new public management, as efforts to 'contribute to reaching the intermediate goal set for quality in this Bill'. The need for greater digital competence is discussed from the vantage point of needs – in an information society, and at different levels in the educational system – and signals that a number of teachers are still found wanting. The idea of a more or less direct relationship between the demands of an information society and demands placed on education is signalled by demands for curricular revisions. Professional competence and such revisions are considered to contribute to achieving the partial aim of increased quality, placing far greater demands on teacher competence. This is tied to the idea that each individual will require knowledge of ICT, because economic growth depends on digital and media competence on the part of both teachers and students. Such knowledge must 'encompass the students' interest, attitudes, awareness of security issues, and ability to use information and communication tools in a secure manner to search for, store, compile and critically value information, and to present results, create new knowledge and communicate with others as active citizens' (p. 108).

Teacher competence is derived from the needs of both society and students, and general categories, such as 'pedagogues' or 'teachers', are used rather than specialized categories that distinguish between different kinds of teachers, categories such as 'disciplinary specialists' or 'vocational teachers'. Demands to 'be knowledgeable and to keep informed about new possibilities introduced by information technology' (Government Bill, 2004/05:175, p. 108) are set forth as general demands placed on the profession as a whole with few distinctions. Higher education is treated separately from lower education, with a particular section dealing with demands for teacher training and a small subsection covering preschool and preschool personnel. Today's teachers were found wanting when viewed through the eyes of the future; the demands placed on them are far reaching, and it is suggested that they lack sufficient knowledge to be able to educate, such that they can meet the competence needs of an information society. Once again, governance in the name of the future is invoked, as was also the case in the earlier policies. Does this imply that all teachers are currently found wanting, or only that teachers are found wanting only with respect to future demands? What is striking about the story line on competence is that it problematizes the point made in the naming of the Government Bill. The notion of a change 'From an IT policy for society to a policy for the information society' (Government Bill, 2004/05:175) is lost in the notion of governance in the name of the future. The IT society or information society is not here yet, and the demands placed on teachers are for tomorrow. This line of reasoning about continuously increased demands for knowledge typifies discourse on the information society.

In education, the demands are specified as high digital and media literacy for both teachers and students, no distinctions being made between the two. All teachers have a duty to know, form attitudes, use, create, and be active in relation to technology. Still, these demands have the power to differentiate between teachers who are digitally competent and those found wanting in this respect. In the section devoted particularly to competence, precise demands are placed on teachers but also limitations. The requirement 'continuously to take advantage in the possibilities afforded by information technology' is coupled with the statement 'at the same time as resources are limited' and a requirement to use 'digital resources developed for flexible learning, for example self-study material'; this is qualified by the proviso that all this can be accomplished 'in a cost-efficient manner so as to provide teachers with ICT competence' (Government Bill, 2004/05:175, p. 108).

Thus, readiness to prepare for future demands became the focus when it came to competence. Though teachers have a *collective* duty to be knowledgeable and hence able to meet new competence demands, the competence development enterprise is itself constructed as an *individual* project. Competence development according to the new Bill does not follow the ITiS concept of having tutored teacher-teams learning by working together (for a description of the ITiS concept, see Karlsson, 2003). Neither is it the kind of individual project described in Becker and Riel (2000), in which 'teacher leaders' engaged in projects, wrote presentations and summaries, and attended conferences to learn more about the advances in their profession. Resource limitations still serve as devices positioning teachers as responsible for their own competence and development of it. The same devices also set limits on the demands that can be placed on organizations. The Bill opens up the possibility of all teachers demanding that the State provide cost-effective digital resources, in a self-study format, for teachers' individual competence development; reciprocally, teachers have a duty to use these resources to develop their competence in a cost-effective way.

Four cost-effective resources are singled out: public-private partnerships, research databases provided by libraries and the research community, courses and content modules provided by peers, and courses and content modules provided by the National Agency of Education and other related authorities. The importance of access to research is stressed, and it is claimed that 'a prerequisite for teacher competence development is that schools are easily able to access information about and gain access to pedagogical texts and to the results of research into the use of ICT in school, among other matters' (Government Bill, 2004/05:175, p. 108). Only in the PRINCESS project was the connection between ICT use and access to a professional knowledgebase previously made relevant. Now, open access is presented as a goal, and the Swedish National Library and the universities can collaborate to achieve it, at least providing open access to everything produced in Swedish Universities. Mastery of technology also includes the obligation to base one's knowledge and skills on evidence. The position of being considered literate in an information society is defined in terms of clusters of rights and duties; among these is the *right* of teachers, for example, to have access to academic research, and hence their *duty* to exercise this right, and base their working knowledge on up-to-date academic work in their field.

It had earlier been established that student teachers also have a right to know about ICT and its uses in education and to develop the skill to use it (SFS 1993:100, appendix 2), but now, with the latest Bill on ICT, this *right* has been written into the examination syllabus as a *requirement*. In a story line about student teachers, the government states that teacher training institutes must set a good example when it comes to using ICT for administration and pedagogical development. As well, developments in the entertainment industry are seen as giving rise to new demands regarding how to present educational material, so teacher education must 'take a broad perspective on, for example, information management, source criticism, law, ethics and creative activity' (Government Bill, 2004/05:175, p. 111).

Few groups of teachers were singled out in this new Government Bill, but references were added to teachers at teacher training institutes who are able to use advances in the entertainment industry in presenting educational content, to student teachers who are obliged to know about the pedagogical use of ICT and to master its use, and to preschool teachers. These three groups were all encouraged to harness the advantages of ICT. Approaching ICT in a *'critical and reflective manner'* will let them put ICT to its best use. Preschool teachers have a right to state-funded competence development if they venture to use ICT. Otherwise, teachers are treated as a group that is obliged to master the technology of the society of the future and this technology's pedagogical uses, but that possesses few rights when it comes to developing this competence.

Implementation of technology and teachers' positions

This chapter has contributed to an understanding of the construction of teachers' contemporary professional identity against the backdrop of a new technical infrastructure. The positions uncovered in this analysis clearly illustrate the ambiguities in normative texts about teachers' professional identity with respect to ICT. There is a tension between the general positions available to future teachers and the positions available to individual contemporary teachers, a tension posing a threat to their legitimate standing as professionals.

Two pairs of relational positions

In discourse about implementing technology in the educational system, the activities of the profession have been ascribed explanatory power. Teachers have been regarded as resisting such technology implementation. The analysis carried out in this chapter points in another direction. Two pairs of relational positions found in the analysed policy documents provide a good description of the rights and duties teachers in general may have as tool users: the user versus the non-user, and the subject versus the object. As illustrated in the tables below, these pairings reveal that teachers in general have been excluded from rights and duties such as taking part in design, influ-

	Subject	Object
Rights	Influence purchase of hardware and software, instructional design, and use of technology	Leave decisions about design and use to other actors
Duties	Inform regarding experiences and contribute to knowledge of pedagogical and disciplinary applications	Leave control to engineers and systems people; follow norms established in curricula

	User	Non-user
Rights	Have access to hardware, software, and competence development	Stay uninformed about the use of computers; learn as much as students do about computers and society from a disciplinary perspective
Duties	Learn how to use computers; use computers to prepare students for working life and future society, and teach them about and with computers	Develop competence about computers and society from a disciplinary perspecitve; teach students about computers

encing pedagogy, using computers and networked technology, and being trained to use technology – to mention a few examples.

It is uncontroversial to claim that the implementation of ICT in education has been unsuccessful, that education has lagged behind while implementation in the rest of society has succeeded, that until recently few teachers have been ICT users, that teacher ICT competence has been low and training scarce, that educational use has been second to administrative, and that the technical infrastructure has been scarce, user unfriendly, and unreliable (for examples of such reasoning, see O'Neill & Baker, 1994; Cuban, 1986, 1993, 2002; Jedeskog, 1996; Riis, 1991; Robertson, 2002). What is more controversial is to claim that teachers follow the trajectories set up for them in policy; they are the 'pig in the middle' with respect to local opportunities, contemporary possibilities, and visions of the future.

In much debate, teachers are blamed for failures to implement technology and 'teacher bashing' has been a result (Cuban, 1986). Teacher bashing threatens the roles awarded them and their claims to professionalism. They have, for example, been positioned as technophobes afraid of using technology, thus more or less involuntarily resisting its implementation. Teachers have also been positioned as gatekeepers who, for various reasons, intentionally resist ill-founded attempts to implement technology and object on the grounds that little support for implementation can be derived from their professional knowledge-base. Most of these explanations derive from a view of teachers as comprising a more or less homogeneous professional group with rights and duties drawn from a relatively stable moral order that required them to be competent ICT users. This chapter concludes that such a position has only been open to a few of them.

What has been illustrated in this analysis is that there are different types of teachers in both existing local and historical moral orders. At no point in contemporary history have teachers been collectively positioned as ICT users or, perhaps more importantly, as *competent* users. The most important results indicate that policies only made the position of competent user available to future users, such as student teachers, disciplinary specialists, and those involved in educational development projects. As subjects, these users should have a right to influence their use of technology and a duty to use technology to prepare students for a future society in which this technology is an important part of the infrastructure. Individual members of the profession are part of an ever-changing moral order in which individual professionals have different rights and duties.

From the viewpoint of positioning theory, classifications tend to be dynamic and contingent on culture and history (Harré & van Langenhove, 1999a). According to such a perspective, teachers can hardly be expected, either as individuals or a group, to display only historically consistent traits. Individuals may be both teachers in discourse about tools and various kinds of teachers with different rights and duties. They may first of all be consumers, hackers, 'tech gods', addicts, or even men in white lab coats, as suggested by Cuban (1986, 1996), Postman (1996), Becker and Riel (2000), Nilsson (2005a, b), and Jedeskog (1996, 2000). They may also, as in our analysis of policy documents, be subjects, objects, users and non-users, future users, designers, disciplinary specialists, and competent or incompetent.

Positions and control of professional tools

There is one remaining concern. Interest in tensions between organizations and occupations/professions regarding the issue of tools has a long history. This relationship has been widely discussed over the centuries, and the discourse has encompassed a broad spectrum of concepts, including alienation (Marx, 1974), technology and power (Marx, 1974; Ure, 1835), division of labour (Babbage, 1835; Taylor, 1942/1972), industrial organization (Woodward, 1965), labour and skills (Braverman, 1977), and technology and design (Checkland, 1981; Ehn, 1993). Today the discourse takes in discussions of science and technological systems (Hughes, Pinch, & Bijker, 1987; Bijker, 1995), technology assessment (van Langenhove & Bertolink, 1999), and, for that matter, technology and learning (Säljö, 2005). Such discourse, also represented in this volume (cf. Agevall & Jonnergård, chapter 2; Hansen, chapter 1; Ljung-Djärf, chapter 14; Nilsson, chapter 13 – this volume), has been intrinsic to attempts to account for the results of the diffusion of technology in education.

The implementation of technology is regarded as having been carried out in a top–down fashion (Riis, 2000), leaving little room for teachers to exercise initiative and, as Cuban (2002) would have it, without taking teacher competence into account. From Cuban's perspective, teachers can, or at least should, refuse to use the technology, because they cannot see any professional gain from using it. Given that history, the context and culture of education would tend to support the use of ICT, but not the profession (Cuban, 2002). Teachers might, on the other hand, become victims of technological push (Riis, 2000) and be forced to use technology. The analysis of policy documents and reports drawing on the ontology of positioning theory sets teachers' professional use of tools in a slightly different perspective. There has never been a case in which central political and administrative bodies ordered teachers to implement and become users of ICT in the first place. Not only did policy makers leave room for professional teachers to remain non-users, they even positioned them as non-users by arguing that resources were scarce. There was nothing for teachers to refuse to use and no technology to push on them. Access to computers and resources for competence development did not allow for any but particular teachers to become users; most in the profession were positioned as non-users. As such, they had neither the right nor the duty to work with the new technology. Instead, there was a wish that they would learn at least as much as all their students were learning about the technology. They also had the right to become users in a distant future, and successively more and more teachers were positioned as users. They were included in government efforts and were given rights to use new services. A minority of them earned the right to have computers as personal tools, and by the end of the millennium it was still possible to position teachers and student teachers as lacking competence and to accept that they did not work with computers because they were afraid.

External control

Still, it must be said that ICT was pushed into the education system without education professionals expressing a need for it. This must be considered to have been a top-down initiative, potentially influencing how teachers go about their work. However, what remains to be seen is precisely where control over these tools will end up. By the mid 1980s, the idea of school computers emerged, and funds were made available to encourage schools to buy them, suggesting organizational-level control. Gradually, hardware became a closed box, incorporating standardized solutions. What kind of technology should be used was a question that disappeared from the political agenda as technology became simply 'off-the-shelf' products equipped with software designed by industry. Today, ICT can be construed as an outpost of new managerialism. Software for reporting on student absences and development and for economic reporting has entered the scene. This would seem to indicate that teachers have gradually become objects of technology they are obliged to use but lack the right to influence. According to this perspective, teachers have become victims of a technology that is advocated by the education system but has not been specifically designed to solve their professional problems (cf. Cuban, 1986; Säljö, 2002).

A slow revolution

At the same time, open access initiatives give teachers access to professional databases, collegial networks, and an endless array of software. Movery and Rosenberg (1998) argue that new technologies seem to have a fifty-year development cycle, starting out with a narrow range of uses and ideas for use and gradually maturing into multi-purpose technologies. According to that line of reasoning, we are facing a slow revolution (Gilbert, 1996), and therein lies the rub. As the technological perspective was replaced by a focus on services, a range of new possibilities that could be framed as pedagogical discourse, and also in terms of new managerialism, were presented in policies. In the ongoing political rhetoric, *services* such as word processing, e-mail, and the Internet – not computers *per se* – were presented as necessary for teachers to use in pedagogical and other professional activities. The competent teacher must thus be able to use these services. It would appear as though teachers in general were pressured by their organization to use these new services, and access to them was forced on the system through the ITiS project. There can also be considered to have been a pull as well. Teachers had the right to choose their own projects, but were obliged to base their decisions about how to use, design, and conduct these projects with reference to the governments' normative stance on pedagogy. Policies make certain positions available. With few exceptions, the idea that teachers must be subjects who can make decisions concerning their use of technology remains. Teachers are the true agents of change in education, as was said in the later texts; on the other hand, they are also the objects of policy decisions (Lind, 1997). This tension leaves ample space for future research into teacher positions and technology.

Concluding remarks

At the outset of this chapter, a less-than-subtle indication was made that, at least in political discourse, the teaching profession indeed may be positioned as one that is out of touch with the tools considered their professional tools. A question was raised about the possible consequences of such a situation for legitimate claims from the profession to be professional educators. To conclude, talk about technology makes certain positions available. Some of these effectively position teachers as incompetent and afraid, giving them the right to refuse to use ICT. A provisional answer to the question of whether the teaching profession can refuse to use tools designated as 'tools for learning' at the legislative and administrative levels must at least provisionally be met with an emphatic 'Yes'. Not only could they do so, but they were seemingly expected to. In the short run, such a position does not harm the professional standing of teachers. However, what it means in the long term to the individual professional who is afraid of these tools, who is incompetent and refuses to use them, is another matter and one worth looking into.

Preamble

What can studies of occupational trajectories provide when interested in development and change over time in an organizational field? In this article on development and change of Swedish municipal adult and the welfare state professionals there, traditional ideas on reform and restructuring are challenged.

Ingrid Henning Loeb

Municipal adult education
Teacher trajectories and clashes of incentives

Introduction

Sweden has a tradition of adult education dating back to the popular movements at the end of the 19th century. Municipal adult education (MAE) has been a part of the public sector, offering elementary and secondary education for adults since 1968. It was launched by the 1967 Adult Education Reform Act after adult education had become a crucial and central issue in Swedish educational policy and labour market policy in the 1960s, when the parallel school system was abandoned and a nine-year compulsory school was introduced, as well as modernized secondary education.

Initially, MAE was, to a great extent, the means of providing 'a second chance' for the 'educational reserve' that had previously been denied the opportunity of secondary education. Four goals for MAE were gradually formulated and reinforced between 1967 and 1975 in a series of government bills: 1) equality, 2) democracy, 3) economic growth and 4) the satisfaction of individual preferences. These goals have applied as general goals over time, but the emphasis has differed (cf. Fransson & Larsson, 1989; Lundahl, 1997; Lumsden Wass 2004).

Although the goals of MAE on the one hand have been the same over the years, on the other hand disparate ideas, concepts and techniques concerning how the MAE–state relationship should be structured, administered and organized have been brought up. From the early 1980s, as in all other organizational fields in the public sector, different forms of decentralization models and restructuring concepts have dominated. MAE can be said to have been a landing site for 'travelling' New Public Management ideas and models (cf. Hood, 1991; Czarniawska & Joerges, 1996). However, MAE is not only a site of reform and restructuring – it is also a field of adult educational practice, of learning, of teaching, and of developmental work by teachers.

This article is based on a dissertation thesis (Henning Loeb, 2006) which was part of a research project – 'Transforming Incentives in Swedish Adult Education' (2002–2005) – funded by the Educational Sciences Section of the Swedish Research Council. The purpose of the study was to describe and analyse development of and changes in MAE, from the mid-1970s until the 21st century, based on life history studies with teachers who have worked in MAE – teaching different subjects, and in different municipalities – since the early 1970s. Studying and analysing MAE through life history studies provided the opportunity to understand development and change in this specific field in the public sector from a point of departure that had not previously been investigated – i.e. that of lived context.

In this article, the trajectories of the teachers are initially presented, contextualized by help of the analytical tools that have been worked with: concepts from time-geography. How can development and change in MAE over three decades be analysed? How can the transformations for the welfare state professionals working there be analysed? With help of concepts from institutional theory (DiMaggio & Powell, 1991) an elaboration is made on how the different MAE organizations, in which the four teachers work, develop in similar or homogenous ways, and a presentation of a periodization is brought forth. What significance to development and change over time can be ascribed to, for example, reforms? What is the significance of these reforms when thinking of the trajectories and their turns – and of the organizations they are coupled to? What other incentives for development and change are discernable? What is the role of these? Those are questions dealt with.

Of specific interest are the veers of three of the four trajectories, the dramatic turns which occur in the late 1990s, as two consecutive restructuring shifts operate simultaneously. On the one hand, there are strong incentives for what can be labelled as 'extended [teacher] professionalism' (cf. Lortie, 1976). On the other hand 'quasi-marketisation' (cf. Whitty, Power & Halpin, 1998; Beach, 2004) constructions are introduced in full force. This, what is conceptualized as 'a clash of incentives', is put forth and analysed. The concluding part of the article is a discussion on the effects of the changing conditions for the welfare state professionals and their organizations in this part of the public sector. Are others defining professionalism? What is the impact? Or can 'extended professionalism' be discerned? How, in that case, is it manifested? These questions are dealt with in the closing parts of the article.[1]

Part 1: The trajectories of the teachers

I have configured my research data and worked with 'narrative analyses' as described by Polkinghorne and the result is four 'storied narratives' (Polkinghorne, 1995), four 'genealogies of context' (Goodson, 1992). Concepts from time-geography, an approach originally suggested by Torsten Hägerstrand (1970), have been brought in as tools for understanding the teacher trajectories – to conceptualize how the trajectories have been formed – and to organize plots of trajectories in space-time.

Central to the time-geography perspective is the fact that space and time is an inseparable unit: *space-time*. Everything individuals (or other entities) do takes time and occurs somewhere – space-time provides the resources and the constraints. Hägerstrand defines three types of *constraints*: capacity constraints, coupling constraints and institutional constraints. An individual's movements/activities in space-time makes a *path*, a space-time path (also called a *trajectory*), which can be studied, related to e.g. constraints, and analysed. A path (or trajectory) also makes it possible to study 'the continuity of succession of situations' (Hägerstrand, 1982, p. 323) – *situation* is another core concept of the perspective. Finally, two concepts from time-geography are *project* and *diorama*. The concept of project consists of the individual's intentions, of space-time possibilities and the 'storehouse of culture', as put by Hägerstrand (p. 325). The concept of diorama is used to relate the individual to other entities – the 'thereness aspect' of the concepts is what is essential.

The teachers have worked with MAE since the mid-1970s with the exception of Maria, who began in 1981. They have taught different subjects: Gustav has worked with maths and physics, Anna with English and history, Britta with Swedish, history, social studies and (mainly) Swedish as a second language. Maria began teaching subjects equiv-

85

alent to grades 4/5–9, but has been involved solely with literacy projects since 1994.

All the stories include certain reforms and incentives for change: the curriculum for adult education established in 1982, the restructuring of the Swedish school system in 1990/1991 in which professional freedom and local responsibility was to substitute steering by regulations, and the five-year national adult education project the Adult Education Initiative (AEI, in Swedish Kunskapslyftet) 1997–2002. One of the central aims of this project was to transform MAE in order to match ideas about lifelong and flexible learning, and through this project quasi-marketization of municipal adult education was established, and multiple 'providers' emerged.

Gustav's trajectory

Gustav's first MAE diorama is in a centrally located building in one of Sweden's larger cities, in the mid 1970s. He gets introduced to the job and the field by his colleagues and head teachers. He attaches great importance to the school and 'climate' there. MAE was important in the city, and the school had, as he puts it, a strong identity. Gustav describes the early years as intensive. He talks about the spirit of the time: 'I happened to begin when there was this spirit of the time, when [MAE] was being built up and expanding'. Connected to this spirit of the time was Olof Palme, the minister of education at the time. Gustav talks about the high level of ambition of the teachers at the school where he taught, and he remembers how challenged he was and how he sat at home in the kitchen during late evenings, preparing his math examples and different explanations.

In Gustav's trajectory, projects are closely connected to his subjects. Over the years, he works with developing educational packages, is involved in discussions on course content, test construction and forms of assessment. In the 1980s, commissioned education for companies and public organizations becomes a large part of his job. In the 1990s, he gets involved in other types of projects: with a national group working with standardized course tests, with an ICT project, and with designing and distributing distance education on the Internet. His story of the early 1990s is also about study trips he made to other countries.

With the AEI (the Adult Education Initiative) the situation

86

changes in the municipality: in 1999 an adult education board – a meso arena of structuring and ordering adult education – is established and Gustav's MAE unit becomes one of many 'providers'. The MAE units in his city are first downsized and in 2001/2002 turned into a freestanding company owned by the city council. Flexible learning and flexible courses become a norm and Gustav reflects critically on these kinds of study forms. According to Gustav, to advocate that is putting the form in the centre, not the pedagogical content or the subject matter, nor the individuals. He is convinced that best results are achieved when people study together in groups, and the teacher can use the group as a means for discussion and perspectives.

Gustav's trajectory is the most dramatic of the four in the study. In 2002, the time coinciding with the very end of our interview-series, the municipal company lost its mandate in the tendering processes. Gustav and some 300 staff were transferred to a 'holding project' where the purpose was to find new jobs in the municipality. Today Gustav is a teacher at a comprehensive school.

Anna's trajectory

The storied narrative of Anna's early years at MAE – also the mid 1970s – is about how stimulating she thought it was teaching adults English and History and about her work methods, but it is also a story about MAE being housed in the building of an upper secondary school, with no special space for the students and no workroom for the teachers. These coupling and institutional constraints are prominent.

In the second part of the 1980s, her working methods gradually change towards more individualisation and project work. The explanation she gives for this development is the 1982 curriculum for adult education and the influx of different groups of students with different needs. A new headmaster becomes an important person for the development of MAE in the municipality – he has political connections and visions, manages to create space for MAE and builds up an identity for it. In Anna's narrative, the development in the 1980s becomes 'an explosion' in the 1990s when MAE gets a structure of its own. The staff can arrange better schedules for the students and the teachers get a workroom where they can place their materials and can plan and produce things together.

At the end of the 1980s, Anna and her colleagues begin working with more elaborated forms of individualization methods and some years later they move to a special building, which also houses an EU project on Open Learning. The teachers work collaboratively and, in Anna's words, they were 'ahead of the new curriculum' (introduced in 1994). Staff from other municipalities pay educational visits. Anna also works on changing working methods in her history classes during these years, but this is more problematic. Her way of doing things differently emanates from studying the history of ideas at university – i.e. primarily via content and not via form.

Also in Anna's municipality, MAE becomes one of several providers during the AEI, with 30% of the 'market'. Similar to Gustav's case, a pedagogical concept based on flexibility is prescribed; here without a time schedule for different subjects and without fixed terms, and also strongly favoured by the school leaders. The plot developed into an organizational drama in 2001, and the representatives for the teacher union called for the Labour Inspectorate to come to the school to make an inspection. The school leadership was ordered to take four measures, the most important of which, Anna emphasizes, was that the school leaders must investigate organizational factors concerning burden of work, in order to prevent ill-health, and to take measures to rectify the situation. After the inspection, the municipality came up with an action plan, and for a year all the staff met in groups with a professional counsellor in order to establish a new organization. Slowly, things turned around and by the time of the study in 2003, there are once again work schedules and organized courses at the MAE.

Maria's trajectory

Maria began working in MAE in 1981, teaching basic adult education, i.e. subjects equivalent to grades 4/5–9. The initial part of her story is – as in Anna's story – a diorama with constraints: adult education in a remote corner of the compulsory school building. However, it is expanding: when she begins working in 1982, there are two teachers in basic adult education, at the beginning of the 1990s there are eight. The development of Maria's organization is, like Anna's, connected to a school leader with political knowledge. In the early 1990s, MAE has premises of its own, located in a central building and with 'an identity' and 'high status'.

Maria's trajectory is explorative. She attends in-service training from the outset and after having worked a year or two she and one of her colleagues become involved in a project initiated by the county education department intended to implement the MAE Curriculum 1982. A recurrent theme in the plot of Maria's trajectory is trying out different methods and pedagogical concepts. She began to work more and more with students in need of literacy training and since 1994 she has only worked in this field. Maria's trajectory becomes both a reflective and a pragmatic path towards a practice that works well for this target group. She tries out and rejects different ideas and finally finds a theory that she agrees with. In time, a matching methodology and model is developed, with strict routines and tools for adults with reading and writing difficulties.

The trajectory of the literacy activity that Maria is responsible for is dynamic and stable, but the rest of the organization goes through major changes. In the early 1990s up until the AEI a development takes place that, in Maria's words, 'is revolutionary'. But with the AEI, a major restructuring takes place. This results in multiple providers, prescribed flexi study forms by the municipal order agency, and repeated cuts in Maria's organization. Her story of the recent years is one of economic imbalances and MAE administrators being replaced. Rather than the aimed for and commonly spoken ideas on flexibility, there is turbulence and uncertainty.

Britta's trajectory

Britta's trajectory is special because it extends from being an adult education student at Hermod's correspondence institute in the 1950s and 1960s to being an adult education teacher at a folk high school and to being a teacher at MAE from 1976. A recurrent theme in her story is about daily practice and the importance of connecting to adults' experience and cultural and historical background. Her appreciation of MAE structure is also frequently emphasized, and through the years she is involved in various projects organizing adult learning activities and environments – e.g. a library at the school. From the mid-1980s, Britta becomes increasingly involved in working with students who study Swedish as a second language. In the 1990s, she and her colleagues develop interdisciplinary models, in order to provide a coherent structure for these students. Like Maria, Britta works with the implementation of the 1982 MAE Curriculum on behalf of the county education department. Britta attaches great importance to this curriculum and the work that the school was doing at that time. When she explains developmental projects carried out much later on, she refers to the tradition they have had at the school since the days of working with the curriculum of 1982. She also attaches importance to the building, which they moved to in 1984, where they still work today. With a centre for MAE, a community for students and teachers is established.

In contrast to the others, there is a continuity 'in the successions of situations' in Britta's trajectory, over the decades and through reforms. In her municipality other providers were only given 20% 'of the market' after the introduction of the AEI. In Britta's words, the municipal politicians from several parties have guarded MAE – they have had occasional contact with different teachers at MAE, have paid visits to the organization and she thinks they have been of the opinion that it works well. This implies that the teachers have been able to complete projects, e.g. EU projects that Britta has been involved in.

The collaboration with Britta takes place a year before she retires. When asked what her reflections are on the development of adult education, Britta points out that 'the wheels turn'. Individualism, flexibility, distance learning and student responsibility were what characterised Hermod's correspondence institute where she once studied as a young adult. A point she wants to make is that MAE and its structure with teachers, classes and groups was originally established because many adults did not complete their studies at Hermod's or via other flexible arrangements.

Part 2: Comprehensive analysis of the development of MAE

A periodization of three eras is the starting point for comprehensive analysis of the four trajectories in MAE – a periodization grounded in the disparate ideas and techniques on how the education-state relationship is to be structured, administered and organized. The governing principles of each era have comprised expressed implications for the teacher trajectories in this study. Briefly, the classification looks as presented in the table below.

Swedish municipal adult education		
Era 1	Era 2	Era 3
1968–1990	1991–1997	1998–
Centralism with decentralization efforts	Decentralization, goal-steering and 'extended professionalism'	Reforming adult education: Quasi-markets and 'flexibility'

Two restructuring shifts make up the basis for the division of 'eras'. Up until 1991, MAE, as well as the other parts of the Swedish educational system, was funded by earmarked state money, time-tables for courses were fixed. Curriculum and syllabi were rather detailed – although in the 1982 curriculum for MAE, local planning and organization was emphasized.

In the comprehensive analysis of the development of the field, concepts from DiMaggio's and Powell's discussion on institutional isomorphism (1991) are used, to capture and argue how the teacher trajectories – and the different MAE organizations which the four teachers work in – develop in similar or homogenous ways. DiMaggio and Powell identify three mechanisms through which isomorphic change occurs: '(1) *coercive isomorphism* that stems from political influence and the problem of legitimacy; (2) *mimetic isomorphism* resulting from standard responses to uncertainty; and (3) *normative isomorphism*, associated with professionalization.' (ibid., p. 67).

The data show that the central government model – and the mechanisms of coercive institutionalism – are strong up until the implementation of the MAE curriculum reform in 1982. With that curriculum, local planning and shaping of adult educational practice enter the stories and increasingly play a greater role in the narratives. Consequently, although Era 1 properly is labelled as an era of centralization and of government control, the trend in MAE is towards 'looser coupling' (cf. Weick, 1976) to central state bureaucracy. These studies show that in the 1980s the field of MAE stabilizes not through coercive pressures, but through mimetic and normative mechanisms. Educational visits are made, best practices are introduced, directors of studies work hard to find ways of establishing structure and an 'identity'. When the Swedish school system is restructured in 1990/1991 and coercive isomorphism is defused by the government, mimetic and normative isomorphic mechanisms are already operating strongly in MAE.

There are a number of parallel local processes and projects going on in the early 1990s. There is the story of the path to a MAE structure, and stories of how projects started when the teachers, students and staff were gathered in the same building. Packages of various kinds for various target groups, multiple efforts to arrange and rearrange and integrate groups, courses, collaboration with e.g. the library, with 'Open learning', etc. 'Travelling' (cf. Czarniawska & Joerges, 1996) pedagogical ideas circulate, are adopted for a while in one way or another, or set their mark in practice more permanently in one way or another. The dominating gestalt of Era 2 is new or concerns ongoing projects.

During the years of 'the withdrawal of the coercive central state' the development towards normative isomorphism is strong. In the 1994 curriculum and in the so-called school development agreement in 1995, the idea of professionalism was heavily emphasized. The rhetoric pointed towards 'extended' responsibilities, 'extended' professionalism and greater autonomy for the local schools, and the professional teacher is described as the key to 'school improvement', working in teacher teams, in collaboration with others (cf. Carlgren, 2000; Sundkvist, 2000). Dioramas of the four trajectories show how involved they all were during these years, collaborating with others, developing and improving projects and education models. When they describe their work at that time, they talk about it in terms of school development.

The second restructuring shift in the 1990s – the five-year Adult Education Initiative (1997–2002) – is the point for a veer in three of the four trajectories. The restructuring of MAE resulted in the establishment of quasi-marketization, municipal order boards, purchasing processes and the entry of a variety of AE providers brings about a radically different 'institutional environment' (cf. Scott & Meyer, 1994) for the organizations that the trajectories are connected to. In all the organizations except Britta's, the teaching staff is reduced through the years and MAE is repeatedly re-structured. From the order boards and other actors in the institutional environment there is pressure to deliver flexible and individualized MAE of a different kind than previously. With the concepts of institutional isomorphism, this restructuring shift with the pressure to deliver a certain kind of MAE can be termed as a shift towards neo-coercive isomorphism. In the era of 'flexibility' this is paradoxically about providing and delivering a certain kind of model, and this attachment to one kind of form can be termed 'neo-formalism'.

The neo-coercive mechanisms of Era 3 and this way of restructuring clash with the predominant mimetic and normative mechanisms embedded in the restructuring shift that took place in the early 1990s with the withdrawal of the central state and the idea of defusing coercive pressures. This clash is evident in several situations in the trajectories and can be conceptualized as a 'clash of incentives'. The two restructuring shifts operate simultaneously from the late 1990s onwards, and the material shows how quasi-market models are strong instruments of change and how goal-steering, local curriculum development, teacher collaboration and local development projects quickly can be de-stabilized by market technologies.

Part 3: The teaching profession in MAE

A shift of focus from the above, focusing on the development of the field of MAE, towards an investigation of the teaching profession in MAE and its development, provides further possibilities of in-depth analysis. Issues here are on how the teaching profession in MAE can be conceptualised, and how the transformations of the teaching profession in this specific field can be discussed.

The MAE teaching profession and its standing

In accordance with sociological researchers like Whitty (1997), Brante (1999), Castro (1999) and others, I regard teachers in MAE as welfare state professionals. In comparison with teachers in the Swedish compulsory school system, there are some differences of significance. Firstly, although the Swedish policy was one of building MAE, there was never a designated teacher education for adult education. None of the teachers in the study had come across any adult education issues during their teacher education. Teacher education was oriented towards subjects, method, levels, and aimed at teaching children and youth – there were no courses focusing on adult education or adult learning. Thus, when the teachers (and most of their colleagues) begin working with adult education, all of them except Britta (who has been a student at a correspondence institute and has also worked there and in a folk-school) have no professional knowledge or experience from working with adults. In that way, teaching adults, working with adults etc. is something solely learnt 'in situ' – in and through adult-educational practice. Secondly, compared to other teacher groups in the Swedish public sector, teachers in MAE have also been – and are – dependent on occasional directed state education projects, on temporary policy priorities and on educational labour market measures in a way that teachers in the compulsory school system are not. Both the way in which this specific group of teachers continuously are in the situation of adjustment to state priorities and the fact that there is no teacher education for adult education provides a basis for judging the status of the group as of a less stable standing than that of teachers in the compulsory school system.

However, teachers in MAE often have high academic degrees in the subjects they teach. This, together with their grading authority, provides a standing described as 'socially sanctioned expertise' (cf. Beckman 1989). Moreover, features in MAE such as commissioned education for local companies, public administrations and organizations also give room for a different, more loosely coupled, connection to the state than teachers in the compulsory school system. The trajectories of the teachers include periods in the late 1980s and early 1990s when the MAE organizations made good profit and teachers could attend courses, participate in further education and travel to other countries on study visits.

The development of the MAE teaching profession

The development of the profession up until 1997 follows one trend of decentralization incentives or rationality: welfare state professionals, their practice (and their organizations) develop best when given more autonomy. This is introduced in the curriculum of 1982, is reinforced in the late 1980s, and is the underlying principles of the restructuring of the Swedish school system in 1990/1991 and the subsequent reforms with the 1994 curriculum and in the so-called school development agreement in 1995 – a five-year regulation of the teachers' employment conditions. As mentioned above, the idea of extended professionalism is formulated in policy documents adherent to the reforms. This development of greater autonomy for professionals is not contradictory to – but rather in line with – the 'normative value systems' (cf. Evetts, 2003) of educational researchers such as e.g. Goodson and Hargreaves (1996) who have outlined components for what they call 'principled professionalism'. The components of the principled professionalism they have put forth are strongly connected to continuous developmental and critical collaborative work, driven by a belief in social practice and moral purpose. The teacher trajectories in these studies provide many examples of developmental projects, committed work to solve ongoing problems of daily practice, collaborative learning, in-service training, filed visits, etc. Borrowing a concept from Knorr Cetina (2001), this all together shows dioramas of 'epistemic cultures'.

The introduction of the AEI implies clashing incentives for welfare state development and change – this constitutes a contradictory decentralization trend with new expert groups or cultures. In accordance with the national goals of the project, each municipality was responsible for its own local organization and development, but a special national delegation with representatives of several ministries and an operative secretariat managed the five-year project. Lumsden Wass (2004) analyses the role of these agencies as 'governing techniques' to spread the message of restructuring and new forms of MAE. On a local level, a municipal project leader was appointed in each and every municipality to manage and administrate the arrangements of the AEI and these project leaders had close communications with the national secretariat. Lumsden Wass formulates the shift in terms of that 'power was transformed from the board of education to the municipal executive board of the municipal council'.

Although the key ideas of the first wave of restructuring operate simultaneously,[2] the basis of the new expert cultures – of the national operative secretariat, the local project leaders and new meso-arenas of municipal order boards – is a of a different normative value system and with a 'new language of learning' (cf. Biesta 2004). The normative value system of these new expert groups with the new ideas of flexible learning, of delivery, of quasi-market structures and accountability are part of an international new public management trend, articulated in policy documents like OECD's 'Lifelong learning for all' (1996) and the 'EU memorandum on lifelong learning' (2000).

What is the impact of 'the new expert groups' on the professionals and the organizations? As shown in the study, these 'expert groups' have great impact on the trajectories and the situation can be said to disempower teachers as others begin to define the profession and professionalism for them. On the other hand, examples in my material suggest teacher resistance and struggle for other solutions. The neo-coercive mechanisms for institutional change are strong but are also contested by teachers who can be said to have appropriated ideas of decentralization, ideas such as that of 'extended professionalism'. As Anna's trajectory showed, the teachers managed to fight for and accomplish a structure they could agree on. Neither can Maria's trajectory be classified as one towards disempowerment: rather, it is the story of an earnest and importunate struggle for adult literacy students in her municipality. The teachers in Britta's organization are the one's least exposed to new expert groups: local politicians there have very much kept to the classic arrangement to provide municipal adult education by the municipal provider. However, as Britta's story tells, teachers in MAE are involved in continuous discussions with local political representatives from different parties. Gustav's trajectory is the most dramatic: MAE is transformed to a free-standing municipal company which quite soon lost its mandate in the tendering processes and that puts an end to his almost 30 years in MAE. But due to intense debate, critique etc. initiated by the staff, and the outcome of subsequent political processes, his organization was re-erected in 2004, and now provides 20% of MAE without being part of tendering processes.

Conclusion

The investigations made here of development and change in Swedish municipal adult education with life history studies as point of departure give the possibility to challenge traditional ideas on reform and restructuring. On the one hand, reforms and restructuring are reflected in practice and have import on the trajectories and their turns, but the material also strongly show how the field develops through 'travelling ideas', mimetic processes, the setting up of new (local) projects and so on. Actually, some strong themes have showed how the field has developed and changed by conditions not directly coupled to a reform or a restructuring programme – the consequences of organizing all MAE in the same school building is one example. The role of stabilizing processes and activities for and in development and change is emphasized in this material– the plots of the teacher trajectories are much about ways in which projects take shape gradually. On the contrary, there are also some striking examples of how projects destabilize through restructuring.

The clash of incentives with the AEI and quasi-market models that I have outlined shows how powerful this model has been in this organizational field of the Swedish welfare system. However, the plots of the trajectories of the teachers also indicate why there have been strong local clashes and not just undivided adaptations to this new public management reform. Previous incentives for decentralization seem to have promoted a group of welfare state professionals who in the neo-coercive situation fight for what they consider to be professional.

Notes

1 In an article in *Policy Futures in Education* (Henning Loeb, 2007), my analysis is focused on the development and change of the field of MAE. In this contribution, the focus is rather on the welfare state professionals and the issue of professionalism in this field.

2 The school development agreement of 1995 was a five-year agreement which later was prolonged, the curriculum of 1994 is still present.

Preamble

One important organizational factor that influences psychosocial work climate and generates job-related stress is role conflict. From an empirical perspective, this article places the emphasis on the experience of role conflicts in an organization that is characterised by client work, indistinct and multifaceted goals, and conflicting expectations. This article describes how role conflicts are formed and experienced by treatment assistants at a drug abuse treatment centre.

Sandra Jönsson

Role conflicts among treatment assistants

A basic condition in social work is that social workers stands in the 'front line' and are forced to handle at least two kinds of realities: the *organization* and the *client* (Leppänen, Jönsson, Petersson, & Tranquist, 2006). On the one hand, the work is conducted within the scope of certain organizational conditions: The organization sets up the goals, drafts job descriptions, distributes financial resources, recruits staff members and supplies employees with special competence development and work methods. On the other hand, the bulk of the work is conducted in relation to clients with disparate needs, demands, problems and expectations (Leppänen *et al.*, 2006). Consequently, social workers often experience different role expectations from diverse agents inside and outside the organization. These expectations are not static or stable over time but are formed and developed in the societal context.

With the influence of new public management, the organization and the actual work in many human service organizations (e.g. social services) have gone through major changes. One tendency is the increased focus on economic values and norms. Another is the trend to look at the clients as customers with 'the right' to choose and select special services within the public sector. From the perspective of new public management there is an ambition to develop methods in order to measure achievements and goal fulfilment. There is also a desire to find measurable goals in the organizations (Agevall, 2005).

All these organizational aspects can result in a stressful work situation as the workers have insufficient opportunities to act in accordance with the needs of client orientation, i.e. to provide good care and service. Bennet, Ross and Sunderland (1996) support this stance in studies illustrating that the incapability to provide adequate care was experienced as a major stressor by the workers. Their conclusion was that burnout might be the consequence of organizationally imposed criteria for what constitutes success and a good job, criteria that are in opposition to the worker's professional and personal values and ethics. Therefore, conflicts can arise between idealistic role models and a harsh reality, resulting in emotional strain (Söderfeldt & Söderfeldt, 1997).

The aim of this article is to illustrate from an empirical perspective how treatment assistants at a drug abuse treatment centre experience situations where they have to manage expectations and demands from different actors such as the management, colleagues and clients.

In order to obtain an understanding of the characteristics of social work, the article commences with a general description of relevant organizational aspects. This involves a brief description of the research process, the treatment centre and the participants. Subsequent to this, there is an account of the empirical material. The article concludes with a discussion.

A client-oriented work setting

When individuals come into contact with human service organizations, they are defined as clients and become the 'raw material' for the transformation process (Hasenfeld, 1983). The bulk of the social worker's day involves interacting with clients. Hence, in social work, the relationship between clients and social workers is considered an important factor with regard to how the work situation is perceived by the social worker.

When the work concerns drug abuse treatment, the very core of the work process lies in the relationship with the clients (Acker, 1999; Billquist, 1999; Lloyd, King, & Chenoweth, 2002). These workers tend to become personally involved in the client's life situation and the relationship can sometimes become very close and intimate. Within the social services and in particular drug abuse treatment, client work can accentuate a number of important existential and moral questions regarding clients' integrity, private life and financial situation (Hallsten, 1983; Stjernö, 1983). Typically, the interactions with the clients call for personal involvement of a kind that is not evident in many other professions (Hallsten, 1983). The work is often characterised as emotionally demanding, and sometimes decisions must be made in open conflict with the client. For instance, in client work with drug abusers there is often open or hidden hostility that could complicate the client interactions. This will naturally affect the caregiver in numerous ways. Research has established emotional exhaustion to have an especially high correlation with job demands, high workload and role conflicts (Le Blanc, de Jonge, & Schaufeli, 2000).

Vague and complex goals

Another characteristic of the human service organizations is that the political goals are generally comprehensive, vague and complex (Häggroth, 1991; Lundquist, 1992; Rombach, 1991). There are a number of general descriptions of aims that contain vague formulations regarding the client's rights. This means that these descriptions allow free scope for the organization to organize the work in order to attain its specific goals.

In the area of social work, social workers are often forced to handle special conflicts as a result of the Swedish Social Services Act. Many of the sections in this act only mention the overall goals for the organization, and do not specify how these goals should be implemented in the more practical aspects of their work. Furthermore, in some cases the law prescribes contradictory goals. One such example in the Swedish context is the disagreement between the law's intentions to respect the client's integrity and the intention to make the client take measures in order to become self-supporting (Kullberg, 1994).

Multiple expectations

Since the Swedish human service organizations are financed with public funds, there are many parties interested in how the work is organized. In the area of social work, this means that the needs of the clients are defined by a number of players, including the clients themselves, social workers, professional organizations, managers and politicians representing citizens in general as well as the clients. This indicates that the social worker must assimilate different views of what client needs are according to what can be morally or legally justified (Eriksson & Karlsson, 1990).

Hasenfeld (1983) describes the assimilation of different views as a 'boundary role' between clients on the one hand, and organizations and politicians on the other. A boundary role of this type could be expected to engage a significant amount of role conflict and role ambiguity (Pousette, 2001).

Role conflicts

From this general description of the organizational features it is evident that social workers and treatment assistants working conditions are complex, characterised, among other things, by different kinds of role conflicts. The role stress theory focuses on the interaction between the characteristics of the organization, the characteristics of the person and the characteristics of the interpersonal relations within the organization (Kahn, 1964). Role conflicts can be described as a situation when a specific individual (in this case the treatment assistants) is faced with conflicting expectations. In a work setting the management, clients, and colleagues have dissimilar expectations. In order to manage these demands, the individual makes a personal interpretation of the situation (Thylefors, 1991).

Kaufmann and Kaufmann (1998) suggests four kinds of role conflicts. (1) Intra-projector role conflict: when one person gives two contradictory messages to the role taker. (2) Inter-projector role conflict: when two or more persons communicate the role taker contradictory expectations. (3) Inter-role conflict: when one person has several roles to fulfil. (4) Person-role conflict: when the personal values and attitudes are incompatible with the expectations that are placed on the job role by the organization.

Studies have shown that lack of congruent expectations and demands from people in the workplace are psychologically uncomfortable and may induce negative emotional reactions, diminish effectiveness and job satisfaction, and decrease the employee's intent to remain a member of the organization (Allen & Mellor, 2002; Burke, 2002).

Diary-in-group as a research procedure

This article is based on a study of treatment assistants working at a drug abuse treatment centre. The centre is administered by the social services, and comprises both treatment wards and non-institutional care. At the centre, the treatment is based on a milieu-therapeutic perspective, where the overall organizational goal is to create a platform from which the client can continue the changing process towards a drug-free life. At the centre, the clients participate in activities such as discussion groups, male/female groups, social groups, cleaning, physical exercise and other activities of a more creative quality. The time spent in treatment varies and is generally tailored individually; however, the treatment typically lasts from six to nine months.

The participants in this study work as treatment assistants at the centre (assumed names). Patricia, 30 years old, has worked in the area of drug-abuse treatment for five years. Annie is 54 years old and has worked in the field for 11 years. Tom, 48 years old, has worked with drug-abuse treatment during the last 20 years. Sheila 24 years old, has recently graduated from school of social work and has worked in the field for 1 year.

In this study the diary-in-group method was used (Lindén, 1996; Lindén & Torkelsson, 1991; Symon, 2004). The diary-in-group method can be described as a technique that combines different kinds of diaries with group discussions. This method is based on the notion that it can be fruitful to combine the individual subjective perspective reflected in the diaries with the social construction process during group-interactions. In the study, the participants were requested to keep a diary during five working days that was to contain notes about situations, feelings and thoughts related to their work experience.

- Each diary entry was discussed in a group session and the time devoted to each diary varied from 1 to 1,5 hours. Each session opened with one of the authors reading aloud from his/her own diary and the other participants listened and tried to start their own associative process. As soon as anyone in the group was making associations with something specific, something recognisable, or had questions about something, the reading was interrupted and a group discussion followed. Four sessions were held at intervals of approximately two months.

- The analysis was based on the transcribed group discussions and can be described as inductive, aiming at illustrating situations where the treatment assistants experienced role conflict.
- One advantage of the diary-in-group method is that the diary study allows access to ongoing everyday behaviour in a relatively unobtrusive manner. This allows the immediacy of the experience to be captured (Symon, 1998). However, it is difficult for the researcher to have power over the participants writing. If the diaries are written long time afterwards, this might affect the diary notes as well as the content of the following group discussions.

The experience of role conflicts among the treatment assistants

The analysis of the group discussions revealed that the treatment assistants experience a work situation that is characterised by multiple expectations and demands. These expectations originate from clients, managers, relatives, social services and colleagues. These are closely correlated with the different roles that the treatment assistants experience.

Within the group, the roles are described as being linked to each other and the assistants experiences that these often alternate from one situation to another. In the analysis, the following role conflicts appeared: practical father vs. good mother, caregiver vs. being a fellow human being, caregiver vs. friend, and private vs. working life. These conflicts are related to each other and originate from a complex work situation. In the following text, quotations from the group discussions are shown in asindented text.

Practical father vs. good mother

As described earlier, client-related work often means that the workers alternate between 'personal' and 'professional' behaviour. In the group, discussions were depicted where the assistants felt that they did not act in a professional manner. When the treatment assistants used the term 'professional' they were referring to the role that is connected to the actual treatment work. According to the treatment assistants, these roles cannot completely be separated and the tension between the personal and the professional roles can vary depending on the situation. During the daytime, when the majority of the work can be described as 'treatment work', they seldom experience any role conflict. However, during evenings and weekends this conflict becomes more apparent.

When it comes to the managers' expectations and to a certain extent those of the colleagues, the participants described these as wide-ranging and at times laden with conflict. On one hand they feel that they are expected to act as home helpers, ensuring that the clients tidy their rooms, ordering furniture, purchasing supplies etc. On the other hand there are expectations and demands to embrace the role of a caregiver. The latter is described by one of the participants as a role that is on a 'different level'.

The expectations that colleagues and management have of the caregivers have implications for the clients. For instance, if the staff's working hours for the most part involve cleaning and coordinating purchases, less time will be spent with the clients. This can cause conflicts or tensions for the caregivers as they have to decide whether they should prioritise practical aspects of the job or spend quality time with the clients. One of the participants clarified this dilemma when saying: 'should I be the good mother or the hands-on father?' What stands out in this situation is the fact that they describe a work situation where time is allocated for working in a caring capacity but not for the more practical aspects of the job. Furthermore, the treatment assistants also feel that there is no scope for sitting down to have conversations with the clients. A quote from one of the participants (translated from Swedish):

> ... for the actual caretaker role there is time allocated in a way, then you have to juggle with the rest of the time to squeeze in the 'practically oriented father', the 'dear mother', or more care in one way or another. (Sheila)

Caregiver vs. being a fellow human being

The treatment centre has affiliations with the social service and clients concerning various issues such as vacancies at the treatment centre. These contacts are at times perceived as taxing, as the workers often find themselves in a conflicting situation where on the one hand they have to be a 'fellow human being' and on the other they have to restrict themselves to the framework of the job. Examples of such situations included when a former client stood outside the treatment centre and wanted to be enrolled on the treatment programme again, or when a person called and wanted to be admitted to the treatment centre. Another participant described a situation where they had to decline a woman who wanted to be admitted. The caregiver found it hard to decline admission to a person who was in such obvious need of help:

> the woman who called us here, that I have declined once and who basically is begging us 'please accept me, where am I supposed to go?', you see, you have their life in your hands or that is what it feels like at least, and it is not easy, it is not easy and it tears you apart. (Patricia)

In these discussions the participants expressed the conflict between the role as a caregiver and that of being a fellow human being, 'where the heart is saying one thing and the mind/brain says another'. This conflict becomes very obvious when it concerns former clients. The treatment assistants find it more difficult to decline somebody that they have a relation to and whose circumstances they are familiar with.

> it was really hard ... it was a guy in my group ... he was denied a place in the middle of the night ... it was hard to close the door. (Annie)

This type of role conflict accentuates the question concerning what work with other people really entails and how it affects the worker. One of the participants said, 'we're here to help them in some sort of way. If I had followed my heart, I would have given in allowed many many more another chance but as you have to listen to your mind the end result is that they will be refused a place.'

Caregiver vs. friend

Many of the clients will remain at the treatment centre for long periods of time and the therapeutic work is carried out in close collaboration with the clients. This often results in situations where they have to dictate where the boundaries are. For instance, it could involve clarifying right from wrong. Consequently, the caretakers often feel that they are perceived as an 'angry and nagging mum'. Furthermore, some caregivers find it difficult to have this approach to adults who in some cases are older than they are themselves. Another employee uses expressions such as 'crook and police' and 'cat and rat' to describe situations occurring at the centre, i.e., being the one who is always chasing something or somebody, which is experienced as taxing and tiresome.

Another conflicting situation that is exemplified in the discussions concerns when a caregiver says yes and is perceived as a friend, and when they say no, conflicts arise. One of the caregivers described it as follows:

> ... in many situations it is easier to say yes rather than no. If you say no you have to back up your no ... it can be really difficult to validate your no sometimes ... it is much easier to say yes ... because then you are just a mate, and it won't be as difficult. (Sheila)

Within the group they describe it as failure when they do not have proper backup for their arguments for rejection and when they feel that the clients have too much control. One of the participants described a situation with a client where the person in question was nagging and fawning. This caregiver meant to say that in a stressful situation it is easier to say yes rather than no. After situations like these the caregiver might feel as if the client was given the upper hand, which can have negative consequences.

A situation that is described as out of the ordinary is when they are on call duty. During call duty the assistants work alone for one evening and night. One of the participants felt a significant discrepancy between working in the daytime and the evening, because the role changes. One participant describes it as follows:

> In the evening ... you go back to being an employee ... it is their free time, it is really up to them what is going to happen or not, I mean you don't push them to do stuff in the same way as you do during the daytime. (Sheila)

Another issue that is characteristic of the experience of role conflict is when the caregivers and clients are doing some sort of activity that is extracurricular. This can involve bowling, swimming or the like. These activities differ from the ordinary activities in that the staff have lowered their guard and will be less of a professional and display more of a personal side. The difference between acting out the private person as opposed to the professional is that the former displays emotions more openly. Some members of the group mentioned that they felt vulnerable and more exposed in these situations. One of the participants described it as follows:

> ... well, when working here your personality will be displayed, but in various ways it will be shaded by the fact you have to act professionally ... but when we do various things such as bowling ... then you become a private person in a different way ...(Tom)

In discussions about the professional and the private role it becomes apparent that there is ambivalence embedded in this concept. On the one hand the discussions take the stance that it is important for the clients to encounter the staff's more private and personal emotions and viewpoints. On the other hand the discussions concern how the staff's behaviour can leave an impression on the clients, i.e., the clients' perception of the staff. One treatment assistant expressed it as follows:

> what will the consequence be that I show that I can be angry? At the same time, I must express it somewhere and I can't go around smiling all day and be positive and happy as things affect me as well, and they must face that elsewhere too ... one is only human. (Patricia)

Private vs. working life

In many human service organizations the staff is often described as a tool. In other words, it is the personnel's knowledge, personality and experience that will decide what the outcome will be like.

In the discussions with the treatment assistants it became apparent that in many circumstances they try to separate their working life from their private life. They indicate that these are two separate arenas that should not be merged. One of the caretakers described how she has a specific point on her way to work where she alters from being a private person to being a professional. She means that it is important that you let go of work when you are at home, because 'you can't be here 24–7'. The ability to let go of work is something that takes time to get habituated to. In the discussions it became clear that the group's private life is sacred. One of the participants said that she wants to keep her private life to herself and does not want any of the clients to know what she gets up to, which means that she reveals very little about what she does in her spare time. Some find it unsettling that the clients know where they live or that they can run into them outside work. One of the participants explained that running into clients or former clients outside work is taxing, as they will be reminded about their situations. The group feels a certain degree of responsibility for the clients, and find it strenuous to have to deal with these situations outside the work context.

As was mentioned earlier, it is clear that the clients have an idealised view of the staff. One of the participants described a situation when he and his colleague were sitting at a restaurant drinking wine when a client had approached him and been very taken aback. As a result of this the client will probably have a different view of the staff at the treatment centre that can have consequences for the treatment outcome.

Discussion

The work that is carried out at the treatment centre is performed in a complex reality that primarily is characterised by staff working in close proximity to clients (Acker, 1999; Billquist, 1999; Lloyd et al., 2002). Other than the closeness to clients, the work is also characterised by vague and unspecific goals that will have consequences and affect the expectations that the caregivers feel that various actors have of them. The purpose of this study was to place the focus on an important aspect of the work, namely the experience of role conflict at work. Whether or not the staff experience role conflict at work has implications as this will have consequences for the individual and the organization (Kahn, 1964). Research studies have indicated that the way in which role conflict is experienced is connected with other aspects of the job such as work satisfaction and job performance (Kahn, 1964; Le Blanc et al., 2000). There is also a strong correlation between the experience of role conflict and how the work demands are experienced. By means of the results of this study it can be established that the work situation at the treatment centre is governed by various kids of role conflicts. As we have seen, these conflicts occur when one and the same person is faced with a pool of expectations from diverse actors. The aspect that stands out most in the empirical material is the central position the clients have in the treatment assistants' workday. In many situations the clients are important actors, and this fact is naturally linked to the fact that the majority of the work that the caretakers carry out is in close interaction with clients.

In the present study the participants have described numerous situations where they experience some kind of role conflict for various reasons. One kind of conflict that was brought to the surface was the 'inter-projector role conflict', i.e., the kind of role conflict that takes place because two or more people have different expectations of a person. This kind of conflict was exemplified under the heading 'practical father vs. good mother'. The caregivers felt that the management expected them to tidy the clients' rooms, purchase materials for various creative activities, or order furniture for the public areas. At the same time, the clients wanted time for conversations, social interactions or walks.

Typically the treatment assistants are stuck in a situation where they have to prioritise the more practical aspects of the job, which at times leads to job dissatisfaction as many of the treatment assistants feel that it is the client relationship that is the core of their job. Hence, the expectations stem from two sources, the management and the clients.

Another type of conflict that was described concerned inter-role conflicts, i.e., the extent to which individuals perceive that the roles they are engaged in serve to facilitate versus conflict with one another. This type of conflict was obvious in many situations that were described by the caregivers. One such example is when the treatment assistants cannot assist/provide help for all the clients that want to be admitted to the treatment centre. Their inner voice or their more altruistic side might say that one should help the clients although they discontinued their treatment programme earlier in the week. The professional role might say that the clients must follow the rules that are set and that there is little point in trying to help the clients unless they are 100 percent motivated. The inter-role conflict also becomes clear when it concerns the role of a 'caretaker' and that of a 'friend'. The caretaker takes on a more professional stance, where it is expected that he or she maintains the boundaries and distinguishes right from wrong. Through the role as a friend the caregivers get closer to the clients by letting go of all the demands and the relationship is relaxed. The third type of role conflicts that were described illustrates what is known as person-role conflict. This type of conflict is characterised by when a person's values and attitudes are incompatible with the expectations that are placed on the job role by the organization. Among the treatment staff this kind of conflict occurred in situations where the heart says one thing whilst the brain says another. In other words, it concerns situations where you as a fellow human being want to take care of the clients but at the same time the professional perspective accentuates that one has to act in a different way.

During the discussions it became apparent that the treatment assistants are well aware of their complex work situation. During the conversations they could stress and illustrate the disparate role conflicts that occurred and often had unique labels for these conflicts. On the basis of these descriptions it can be established that many of the conflicts encompass dilemmas that can be related in one way or another to how the professional role is perceived. In the discussions the participants spoke implicitly about what it really entails to be professional or why it is perceived as problematic to uphold this role. It is evident that the staff experience difficulties in describing and relating to the professional role. In the discussions situations are exemplified where they have acted more or less professionally. The discussions incorporated the fact that during the daytime, when there are scheduled activities, role conflicts do not surface in the same way as during the evenings or weekends. For instance, on those occasions when the caregiver is alone with the clients (for instance during on-call duty or evening hours) it is difficult to maintain the professional role. This can be due to a feeling of insecurity that occurs in those situations or instances when the worker is alone with the clients. Perhaps the worker is acting out the private role in an attempt to establish a relationship as a friend. However, as the workers abandon the professional role they feel uncertain about how the more private role affects the clients and the treatment process. The conflicts that have been described here have to some extent their foundation in the organizational conditions.

A problem that is recurrent in many human services and also at the treatment centre is the fact that the goals of the organization and its practices are vague and unclear (Hasenfeld, 1983; Lipsky, 1980). Consequently the personnel in the organization, and in particular those who work directly with the clients, will have to interpret the organizational goals, on their own or together with the team, in such a way that they will fit the everyday practical operations (Lipsky, 1980). This will have the end result that one organization can contain several interpretations of what the purpose of the work is or what the organizational goals are. With regard to the work at the treatment centre, this can have consequences for what they should interpret 'treatment work' and 'professional practice' as encompassing. Another difficulty in organizations with vague goals is that staff can find it difficult to know what they should prioritise in their workload. Among the treatment assistants this became apparent when they had non-scheduled activities: they find it difficult to know whether they should prioritise the more practical/administrative assignments or the client contacts.

Other studies with the focus on client work have found that staff often find it difficult to judge when the job has been completed (Pousette, 2001; Söderfeldt & Söderfeldt, 1997; Söderfeldt et al., 1996). Another organizational aspect that in many ways affects how the work situation and role conflicts are experienced has to do with the organization's resources. According to Lipsky (1980), staff working in human service organizations often experience that limited resources restrict them from carrying out their job properly. Lipsky argues that there will be consequences when there are restricted possibilities for the workers to carry out their job satisfactorily or when the staff in question has to abandon their professional norms in order to handle the current situation. For the treatment assistants this type of scenario became very obvious when it for instance concerned the more practical aspects of the job. As an example, when there is no person employed specifically to handle tasks such as purchasing furniture and materials, this will have implications for how much time the treatment staff can allocate to the clients. According to Lipsky (1980), many employees in human service organizations feel that too much of their working day is devoted to administrative duties and too little time is spent with clients. This can result in a demanding work situation where the employees do not experience that they can perform the work in a satisfy-

ing way. For example, studies have shown that the inability to perform a satisfying job is regarded as a fundamental and important
stressor in work (Bennet *et al.*, 1996).

Preamble

Teaching as a profession can be described as 'personalised professionalism', while nursing in comparison appears as more collective. This applies both at the level of the individual professional, the work-place, as well as the level of the profession as a collective. An argument that new forms of control are undermining professionalism thus seems too simple; threats to professionalism may just as well come from within the profession as from the outside.

Joakim Caspersen

Aspects of professionalism

Collective nursing – personalised teaching?[1]

Introduction

Do new forms of control in public sector undermine professionalism? Major changes in the welfare states of the western world have occurred in recent decades. The introduction of New Public Management (NPM) models in most, if not all, parts of the public sector have brought about changes in public employees' everyday life. Although the term NPM often takes on different meanings for different people in different settings, and has no agreed upon definition of what it actually complies (Christensen & Laegreid, 1999), it can be said to be characterized by 'a large category of institutional changes [...] affecting expenditure planning and financial management, civil service and labour relations, procurement, organizing and methods, and audit and evaluation on a government wide-basis' (p. 170). Professionals working in the public sector have experienced this development hands on, with the 'adoption of performance indicators, quality system management, contract systems, and deregulations' (ibid).

The development towards a more controlled and specified professional work is often referred to as 'deprofessionalization' (Hyland, 1996; Parkin, 1995) or as 'proletarianization' (Turner, 1993). The thesis of deprofessionalization was first articulated by Haug (1973) as a 'revulsion to [...] syrupy ideas about the future' (Haug, 1988, p. 49) presented by forecasters of the professionalised society (for instance, Halmos (1970) and Freidson (1971)), despite Wilensky's (1964) and Becker's (1962) earlier call for caution. Modernisation and new forms of control are assumed to pressure the highly valued freedom and autonomy of the professionals, undermining their professionalism. As Evetts (2003) puts it: '(professions) [...] have been perceived as under threat from organizational, economic and political changes, [and] are portrayed as experiencing a reduction in autonomy and dominance, [and] a decline in their abilities to exercise the occupational control of work' (p. 396).

Whether reorganizations in the public sector are undermining professionalism or not, is not a straightforward question. It involves both the nature of the work the professionals perform, the development of the professions as professions, and there are wide variations between organizations in the same profession. If an empirical investigation of this question is to be undertaken, one possible approach would be to look at it from the point of view of the individual professionals.

This paper examines how Norwegian teachers and nurses report on what can be considered three different aspects of professionalism. This will be interpreted in the light of recent reorganizations in Norwegian public sector, the background of the respective professions as well as the nature of the work they perform. The discussion focuses on what has been said to be the three core issues of professionalism; autonomy, service-orientation and expertise (Bottery, 1996; Eraut, 1994; Wilensky, 1994).

Teaching and nursing are very interesting professions for comparison. They are both what is often referred to as 'weak professions', (see for instance Wise, 2005), which means that their legitimacy as professions, with all the advantages this might imply, is more difficult to achieve than for the so called strong professions (medicine, law.) Teaching and nursing have taken on this battle with somewhat different means, and with somewhat different results. As will be elaborated below, nurses can be said to have increased their status while teachers have decreased theirs; the respective professional associations have adopted rather different strategies in their struggle; and they are situated differently in the organizations of which they are part, and these organizations also differ significantly.

There are (at least) three important and associated aspects of professionalism: expertise (or a specialist knowledge-base), altruism (or a service-orientation), and autonomy (Bottery, 1996; Eraut, 1994). Expertise refers to the possession of an exclusive knowledge and practice. Autonomy refers to the professionals' need and right to exercise, control entry into and practice within the professions, legitimated by their expertise. Altruism refers to the ethical concern by the professional group for its clients (Bottery, 1996), or a moral commitment to serve the interests of clients (Eraut, 1994). As Freidson (1988) has argued, expertise and serv-ice-orientation serves as legitimization for autonomy, both at the indi-vidual and collective levels. This will be expanded in the following and linked to the case of teaching and nursing in Norway.

New forms of control in Norwegian teaching and nursing

Dahle and Thorsen (2004) address the general modernisation of the public sector in Norway. They argue that the control and privatisa-tion of public services often associated with the NPM ideology has become an important way of organizing the Norwegian welfare state, but perhaps not to the same extent as in many other European coun-tries. However, recent reforms in both the education and health sec-tors in Norway have accentuated the turn towards more control and greater demands on efficiency and accountability.

The Norwegian Hospital Reform, implemented in 2002, transferred the ownership of hospitals from the counties to the central govern-ment and organized the hospitals as state owned health enterprises. In addition, the system of financing of the hospitals was altered and patients were given the right to choose where to receive treatment. This was widely acknowledged as a transition towards more market-oriented solutions in the health sector and, along with this, a bureau-cratisation and the implementation of an audit culture (Dahle & Thorsen, 2004; Kjekshus, 2003). This reform also brought with it changes in the organization of the daily work in the health sector. Kjek-shus (2003) argues that along with the bureaucratisation of the hos-pitals came new demands of loyalty to the institution instead of the profession, and more emphasis on financial performance and goal achievement. It entailed a reduction in the professional autonomy and increased control over the distribution of time and money. Kjekshus's argument would suggest that nursing has experienced a drift towards less individual autonomy and more organizational control.

The educational sector in Norway has undergone several reforms in recent decades. Changes have been made in primary and second-ary school as well as in higher education. The strongest changes have probably been the curricula reforms made in primary and secondary education in 1997 ('Reform 97'). The implementation of detailed cur-ricula in all subjects has been described as a Norwegian neo-conservative New-Right ideology with the adaptation to an economic view on education, and education as a means for future economic growth (Hovdenakk, 2004). It has been argued that the 1990s was the decade of educational reforms (Karlsen, 2002), and that while the pedagogic of the 1970s put the development of the student in centre, the educational politics of the 1990s was oriented towards political concerns (Hovdenakk, 2004). However, it is an empirical question whether curriculum changes actually changed the everyday work of the teacher.

Attempts have been made to analyse to what extent the curricula actually were directing the work of the individual teacher, and one of the findings was that the curriculum was the most important planning tool for the teachers (Imsen, 2003), and had a clear influence on teachers' work at the individual level. But the implementation did not mean a clear cut development towards more direct control of teachers' work. On the one hand 'school and municipal reforms in the 1990s decreased the influence of the professional, [and] new principles of management and administration, service quality and user quality have come to the fore' (Helgøy, 2003, p. 55). On the other hand many teachers 'managed to transform the reforms into pedagogical tools and the teachers are still in daily control in the classroom' (ibid, p. 55). The positive aspects of standardised goals and quantitative performance measures are also emphasized in international research on teachers and nurses (Stronach, Corbin, McNamara, Stark, & Warne, 2002).

As will be discussed later, there are some inherent features in the nature of teachers' work that still makes it an individual task, and whereby it is evasive of many forms of direct control. But so far, it seems reasonable to suggest that both teaching and nursing in Norway have implemented new forms of control in a way that affects the practice of the individual professional.

Autonomy

One of the key features of the ideal type of professional is that their assumed knowledge allows them, both at an individual level and at a collective level, to have some kind of freedom or autonomy. Autonomy refers first of all to the whole profession, and 'the argument is that only the profession itself can define and judge the competence and good conduct of its members' (Eraut, 1994, p. 224). This would be autonomy at a collective level, and self-regulation is the manifestation of this collective autonomy. Autonomy also refers to individual autonomy, the opportunity to control and plan one's own work. Freidson (1988) makes a distinction between a collective level and an individual level. He refers to the collective level as socio-economic autonomy, and the individual level as technical autonomy. The former refers to the opportunity to select the economic terms of work and the location and social organization of work; the latter refers to deciding the technical content of work. Freidson stresses that it is the technical autonomy that is the key feature of the status of the professions.

In practice, there are differences in the autonomy granted at the level of the profession as a whole, as well as differences between professions in their members' opportunity to be autonomous in their professional practice (Eraut, 1994). Different professions are situated in different positions in different organizational hierarchies. This is very much the case when comparing teaching and nursing. In hospitals, the hierarchy is differentiated, with doctors at the top and with nurses, auxiliary nurses and technicians placed lower in the hierarchy. In schools, the staffs consist mainly of teachers and the organizational structure is fairly horizontal.

Abbott (1988 pp. 125–129) argues that there is a distinction between autonomous and heteronomous professions. Autonomous professionals work mainly for themselves or for professional peers, while heteronomous professionals are employed by organizations not headed by others from their profession. At almost all places of employment, nurses are part of an organization run by others than nurses. Hospitals are large bureaucratic organizations: they are organized as hierarchies, and have a complex division of labour. In the local health services the organizations are smaller, but are still differentiated and frequently led by others than nurses. As Abbott also exemplifies, nursing is a heteronomous profession. Schools, on the other hand, are more uniform organizations, with a less expanded hierarchy. Teachers comprise most of the workforce, and the leader of the organization, the principal, is frequently a teacher.

As mentioned, the introduction of new managerial methods is often linked to discussions on deprofessionalization or proletarianisation of the professions, claiming that the new forms of control and management are undermining autonomy. The independent professional is becoming the bureaucrat (Freidson, 1986, pp. 158–159). In Figure 1,

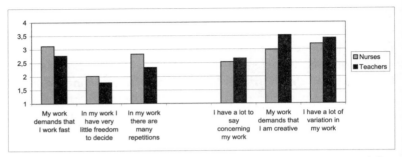

Figure 1. Description of work situation, mean values. Mean values on different statements about work situation, three years after graduation. Scale is from 1 (not at all) to 4 (very much so). N varies from 201–205 (teachers) and 223–229 (nurses). All differences are significant at the 0,05 level (t-test.) Source: Stud-Data.

newly qualified teachers' and nurses' experience of their own work situation is presented. All questions can be considered describing aspects of individual autonomy.[2]

It would make no sense to comment on the absolute level of the mean values in the diagram; it is the comparison between the groups that is interesting. The differences between the groups are not very great, but the pattern is clear. Teachers report fewer demands from their work, more freedom to decide and fewer repetitions in their daily work. They also report slightly, but significantly, more influence on their work and the work demands more creativity by teachers than nurses. Teachers report more variation in their work than nurses. The differences all point in the same direction: teachers, more than nurses, experience autonomy at the individual level.

On the one hand, this can be considered as a reflection of the nature of the work teachers and nurses perform. From the beginning teaching was a more independent and autonomous profession than nursing. Historically, the teacher was the leading figure in the local community, and was the learnéd man who had the freedom to organize the daily work by himself (Karlsen & Kvalbein, 2003). Nursing, on the other hand, did not have the same independent position, but was subordinate and nurses were an assistant to the medical doctors.

The liberal role of teachers and more restricted role of nurses was also related to the gender stereotypes associated with the profession.

It has been argued that the early formation of professions was strongly influenced by the gender organization and gender stereotypes in society at large (Greiff, 2006), and that this gendered organization still affects the way professions are understood. This would imply that nursing, as a traditional female profession, was associated with values such as maternal care, consideration, religious calling and serving other peoples' interests. Teaching, at least in its early days, was an exclusively male profession, and had values such as conscientiousness, strength, vigour and also values of responsibility such as providing for the family, and economic responsibility. The greater autonomy of the teachers was perhaps influenced by rather stereotypical understandings of gender.

As shown, teaching and nursing have had rather different developments from their occupational starting points. Nursing has been more of a subordinate profession, while teaching from the start was a rather independent and autonomous profession. Teaching was more or less exclusively a male profession, while nursing is and always have been a female-dominated profession. The gender composition in teaching has now changed (about 70 per cent of teachers today are women (Caspersen, 2006)), but the nature of teachers' and nurses' work is still different with regards to the autonomy they have at the individual level.

The differences between the groups could also imply that the pressure on professional autonomy, or the deprofessionalization or proletarianisation of the professionals, has been greater in the health sector, and that this is the reason for the differences between the groups. If it is assumed that the NPM ideology has gained a foothold in the educational sector as well as the health sector, our findings suggest that teachers have managed to maintain a rather autonomous role and the possibility to control their own work situation in a way that is not found in nursing. However, such an interpretation is difficult. There are differences concerning work situation, differences in professional strength, differences in the development of the professions, differences at work-place level in terms of resistance to change; a whole multitude of factors are interacting and affecting the outcome.

Freidson (1986) argues that there are differences at the individual level between teachers and nurses and the work they perform. Although much has changed during the more than twenty years that have passed since Freidson made his analysis, his general point still seems valid. Nurses are part of a 'very elaborate, highly technical division of labor among a number of occupations ordered both by specialisation and authority.' (p. 165). This elaborated division of labour and the technical elements in many parts of the sector 'creates constraints on individual discretion that are greater than appears to be the case for most other professions' (ibid.). Teachers, on the other hand, are somewhat opposite to nurses. Although the school system can be organized as a bureaucratic organization, and the educational sector may be implementing strict regimes of control and monitoring, teachers have a 'distinct autonomy stemming from the way the teacher's position in the classroom is insulated from systematic observation and control even by peers' (p. 161). Nurses' work can be characterised as collective, and this makes it easier to control. Teachers' work is individualised and evades direct supervision.

Service orientation

Professions are connected to and legitimised by an intrinsic motivation for choice of career (Freidson, 2001). At both at the individual and collective level, professional autonomy is not only claimed by the nature of expertise, but also by service orientation or ethicality (Freidson, 1988, p. 360). 'After all, unless the profession's expertise is guided by a concern with the good of humanity, it may not put it to good use' (ibid.). Freidson's discussion concerns the regulation of the professions, or more specifically, how the professions regulate themselves and their members. The argument is that ethicality is not shown in the attitudes that the professionals claim, but in the action they perform. These actions are under the regulation of the profession. Attitudes may be a prerequisite to good behaviour, but do not assure that good behaviour follows. In the analyses presented later, teachers' and nurses' perception of the degree to which they are able to perform tasks in line with their ethical orientation is addressed.

In nursing and teaching, both historically and today, the intrinsic motivation is closely connected to an orientation towards other people, often referred to as altruism. In everyday language, altruism and altruistic actions are often used about 'unselfish regard for or devotion to the welfare of others'.[3] The term is often used about actions that do not give any form of reward for the subject performing the action, but in Bottery's definition the subject might very well achieve

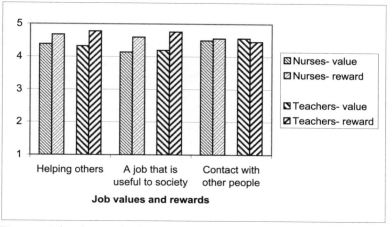

Figure 2. Job values and job rewards at graduation and two and a half year later, mean values. Mean values on statements about what students want from work (job values), and to what degree they feel they get to realise the same job values in their work situation two and a half years later (job rewards). Scale is from 1 (not important/not at all) to 5 (very important/very much). N varies from 154–159 (teachers) and 150–156 (nurses). Source: Stud-Data.

personal gain from such actions. The important component is the ethical concern for others.

It has been argued that today's youth find new meaning in helping others (Jensen & Tveit, 2005). It is not the altruistic, unselfish and self-sacrificing orientation that characterises modern care-workers; increasingly, people choose to help others for personal gain, directly or indirectly through the gratitude and appreciation they receive from the patient. With reference to Ziehe (Ziehe, 2000; Ziehe, Fornäs, & Retzlaff, 1993; Ziehe, Nielsen, & Fornäs, 1989), Jensen and Tveit claim that the energy and motivation one finds in helping others comes from the reward it gives one's self. Other-orientation is combined with self-interest if one is to become a skilled professional, and the difference between self-interest and other-orientation becomes blurred.

In Figure 2 the job values and rewards of teachers and nurses are presented. The students in their final year of education are asked to rank on a five-point scale from 1 (not important) to 5 (very important) the importance of different job characteristics when considering a job offer. These are referred to as 'job values'. Two and a half years after graduation the students are asked to rank on a five point scale the degree to which their work provides them with opportunity to realise different job values. These are referred to as 'job rewards'. Only job values and rewards that correspond with a traditional other-orientation is presented.[4] The main finding is that both teachers and nurses are very much 'other-oriented', and that they find the opportunity to realise these other-oriented values in their work.

One part of the argument concerning reorganization of public sector and the implementation of NPM is that moral responsibility for the work is taken away from the individual professional, thus minimising the role of the professional. As Jehnsen and Lahn (2005) aptly put it: 'Reducing morality to a question of legislation, systems and rule following may over time reduce the capacity of professional groups to set standards, produce meaning and instil a sense of moral responsibility among their members: in short, the very notion of professionalism may be undermined' (p. 306). The hypotheses one could infer from this is that in our case teachers and nurses will feel incapable of realising the more altruistic values connected to their professions. However, figure 2 indicates that the intrinsic motivation of both teachers and nurses is very much alive, and that the work situations for both teachers and nurses provide them with good opportunity to realise these job values.

One of the arguments for introducing new forms of control could be interpreted in terms of distrust in the professionals' service-orientation, or their desire to work for the public interest (Evetts, 2006). Professionals are restricted by introducing strict rules and procedures, and the expectation would then be that the inclination to work for the public good would be low in the profession. The findings in Figure 2 can be interpreted otherwise, where both teachers and nurses rate the other-oriented values high. However, the control forms can also be interpreted in terms of quality assurance. It is important that the services professionals provide are of a high standard, and control mechanisms are one way of providing this. Another way is making sure that they have sufficient founding in the knowledge-base of their profession, an issue that will be addressed in the next section.

Expertise

As shown, there are differences in teachers' and nurses' experiences of their work situation, and this could be due both to differences in implementation of new forms of control, as well as differences in the work they perform and differences in the history of the professions. It also seems clear that the service-orientation is vibrant at the individual level, and that both teachers and nurses feel that they their work provides them with good opportunities for realising these job values.

A third element in professionalism is expertise, or esoteric knowledge. Autonomy is supported by knowledge of such a nature that only the professionals themselves are able to determine what is wrong in specific situations, and only the professionals themselves are able to decide the actions to taken.

The period of professional training lays the foundation for the professional knowledge which legitimises autonomy. It is also the means the profession as a collective has to control entry into the profession. The General Teacher Education in Norway is four years, while nursing education is three years. A bachelor's degree in nursing qualifies for work in all parts of the health sector where nurses are present; the generalist teacher education qualifies for work in primary and secondary school.

One approach when addressing the question of knowledge in professions is to assess the quality and amount of substantial knowledge the professionals have. Another approach is to examine how they regard and evaluate knowledge and what kinds of knowledge they find important for their professional practice. Heggen (2005) has analysed how students of teaching, nursing, social work and pre-school teaching value the importance of formal knowledge, personal abilities, values/attitudes and practical skills at the start of their study and at the end of their study. In the first semester of study almost 75 per cent of nursing students rated formal knowledge as very important. In teaching the share rating formal knowledge as very important was a little less than 60 per cent. In the sixth semester[5] the same students were asked to rate the same questions again. Now a little more than 80 per cent of the nursing students rated formal knowledge as very important. The share had increased. Amongst the teacher students the opposite had happened: Less than 50 per cent now rated formal knowledge as very important. Heggen also found that students of social work

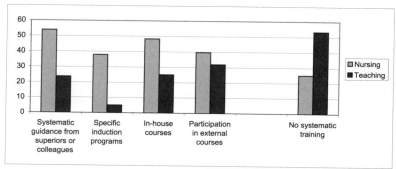

Figure 3. Reported training of newly educated teachers and nurses. Percentage of teachers and nurses reporting having participated in different induction programmes, N= 232 (nursing) and 219 (teaching). Source: StudData.

and teaching rated formal knowledge as less important than the other three types of knowledge.

While nurses became more confident that formal knowledge was important in their professional practice during their education, teachers became less convinced of the same. What can cause this difference? Heggen suggests that this reflects a general difference between the teaching and the nursing profession in the understanding of professional competence.

Another important aspect of professional competence is the continuing development of competence, and the induction of newly qualified professionals. There are interesting differences between teachers and nurses also at this level and which could be referred to as the system level.

Teaching and nursing in Norway are somewhat opposites when it comes to organized training of newly qualified, and also regarding continuing professional development. While both health organizations and personnel in Norway are obliged by law to participate in professional development programs to secure safe quality practice (Bjørk, Hansen, Samdal, Tørstad, & Hamilton, 2007), there is no such obligation for Norwegian teachers (OECD, 2005). So-called 'clinical ladder' programs were introduced in Norwegian hospitals during the 1990s (Bjørk et al., in press). This period was characterised by nursing shortage, and in-house career programs were considered an effective means by which to attract and retain nurses. This coincided with a political emphasis on quality assurance in health care settings. These systems started out as a method for recognition and have developed towards formal systems for development of competence. The Norwegian Nurses Organisation (NNO), a strong and powerful union in Norway, has pushed for the implementation of these kinds of competence programs. By law, all health organizations and personnel are obliged to secure safe quality practice through continuing development of competence.

In Norwegian teaching, there is no statutory provision for continuing professional development. In a comparison between all OECD countries, a little more than 40 per cent of Norwegian teachers had attended a professional development program in the previous three months according to principals (OECD, 2005). This places Norway near the median of the 30 participating countries, more than 20 percentage points behind countries such as the U.K. and Sweden. As accounted for by the OECD, teacher induction programmes in Norway are based upon mentoring. School principals assign an experienced member as a mentor and these mentors are then provided with training funded by the Ministry of Education and Research. This leaves the schools and the newly qualified teacher with plenty of leeway to organize the induction activities themselves.

In Figure 3 more than fifty per cent of the newly educated nurses report that they have received systematic guidance from superiors or colleagues, while less than twenty-five per cent of the teachers report the same. More than fifty per cent of the newly educated teachers report that they have had no systematic training at all compared to twenty-five per cent of the nurses. It is evident that nurses meet a completely different induction system than teachers. This is also supported by the fact that nurses, more so than teachers, think that their training has been sufficient for performing their work[6].

The findings suggest that newly qualified teachers are largely left on their own, at least compared to the newly qualified nurses. Can the autonomy of the professional teacher lead to non-intended consequences in that the newly qualified professional teachers are left on their own? Eraut argues that for teachers professional autonomy is juxtaposed with isolation from colleagues (Eraut, 1994). Professional autonomy is perhaps at the cost of an organized entry intro working life.

Personalised professionalism and professional accountability

Professionalism consists of three elements where expertise and service orientation lays the foundation for the autonomy which the professionals are granted both at the individual and collective levels. New forms of management in the public sector have been said by some to undermine professionalism. In the material presented students of both teaching and nursing report a strong service orientation. They also report that they have the opportunity to realise these values in their work three years later. Another finding was that teachers reported having more freedom to make decisions at an individual level than nurses. On the other hand, more than half the teachers reported not to have participated in any systematic training, while only about a quarter of the nurses reported the same. Heggens' (2005) findings suggest that this personalisation of teaching also has consequences for their professional knowledge base.

Karseth and Nerland (2007) have examined discourses of knowledge in four professional associations in Norway, among them Norwegian Nurses' Organization (NNO) and the Union of Education Norway (UEN) (the teachers' union). Both associations are engaged in issues concerning knowledge development and pursue this by various means. First of all, Karseth and Nerland find a difference in the importance given to different kinds of knowledge. They portray the NNO as an association which has emphasised scientific knowledge, while UEN is the opposite, advocating practice-based and personal knowledge.

Karseth and Nerland also find differences in how the associations safeguard professional practice, and the UEN and the NNO have to some extent chosen opposite strategies. Direct intervention in professional practice can be contrasted with emphasizing individual autonomy and discretionary decision-making, and UEN has emphasised the individual practitioners' right to decide, while the NNO has been a proponent of a more directly controlled work situation.

Thirdly, Karseth and Nerland distinguish between a restorative and a progressive strategy where the NNO and UEN again can be said to have chosen opposite strategies: the NNO as a progressive agent, UEN as a restorative. While the NNO has emphasised expansion and a constant need for new knowledge and techniques, the UEN appears to have been more occupied with restoring past glory.

Teaching as a profession can thus be characterised as personal or individual and restorative rather than progressive: nursing can be considered scientifically oriented, collective and progressive. The differences are clear, and reflect the earlier findings well. From the material presented here, an appropriate characteristic of teaching as a profession could be 'personalised professionalism', while nursing has a more collective character.

Personalised professionalism sounds almost like a contradiction. One of the characteristics of a profession is a collective knowledge-base instead of a personal experience or ability. If the personal or individual was the foundation for the profession, there would be no need for expensive or time-consuming education of professionals. If the individual professional was to perform acts of discretion based solely on personal judgement, it would not invoke any trust in the public whatsoever.

To say that anti-professionalism is the case in Norwegian teaching is, of course, far too drastic, but it does seem obvious that teaching and nursing have taken rather different paths and approaches and that this manifests itself at many levels today. If knowledge is considered as the foundation for professionalism, then teachers' approach to knowledge, both at the level of the individual professional (the valuation of knowledge), at the system-level (the low reported levels of participation in induction programs and continuing professional development), and at the level of the professional association (in terms of the UEN's strategies), seems rather fragile. Further research investigating these differences between the professions more thoroughly, at all the levels mentioned, would be of considerable interest.

The first question asked in this paper was whether new forms of control in the public sector are undermining professionalism. The answer seems no less difficult now than in the introduction. There are many aspects that need to be taken into account such as the nature of the work, the resistance towards new forms of control at different levels, and the actual implementation of new forms of control at the micro-level. It seems as threats to professionalism may come from many directions. If one of professionalisms distinctive features is specialised knowledge, then it seems as the threat can come just as much from within the profession as from outside. Furthermore, the question itself, whether new forms of *control undermine professionalism,* can be argued *a priori* to accept the traditional dichotomy 'between "economy" (bad; audit culture; deprofessionalizing; impositional, etc.) and "ecology" (good; professional; solidary; voluntarist, etc.)' (Stronach et al., 2002, p. 124).

An alternative way of understanding the implementation of new forms of control in public sector is to see them as *responses* to threats to professionalism. The introduction of new forms of control in the public sector is not only explained by a desire for increased efficiency, but also as a counterweight to claims of decreased trust in the professions (Evetts, 2006), due to both an increased level of education in the population (and thus a general inflation of professional knowledge), malpractice scandals and a widespread 'value-for-money' thinking.

Mintzberg (1983) argues that there are inherent dysfunctions in professional bureaucracies, and a lack of opportunity to 'correct deficiencies that professionals themselves choose to overlook' (p. 206). Professionals can be incompetent or unconscientious, and no two professionals are equally skilled. From the outside this is understood as a lack of external control, and the cure is to 'use direct supervision, standardisation of work processes, or standardisation of outputs' (ibid, p. 210). The introduction of methods for making professionals accountable for their actions is then a way of reinstating the trustworthy professional. But this effort of reinforcing the accountable professional may have unintended consequences. 'Trust is to be replaced by accountability, but accountability seems to result in the standardization of work practices' (Evetts, 2006, p. 525).

Evetts (2002) has argued that the traditional concepts of autonomy and self-regulation no longer, if it ever did, fits as a description of professional work; the important characteristic is the opportunity to perform acts of discretion. In the same manner as autonomy is legitimised by the professional knowledge, so is the opportunity to perform acts of discretion. A standardisation of work could imply a reduction of professional autonomy or a reduced opportunity to perform acts of discretion, not with the specific intent of reducing it, but with the intent of reinstating the professional as trustworthy.

This would nevertheless coincide badly with the ideological pursuit for autonomy in the professions, and is thus perceived as undermining professionalism. Mintzberg (1983, p. 211) argues that this kind of standardisation is contrary to the nature of the professional work, and professional work cannot be effectively performed if the operator, i.e. the professional, does not have it under control. Even if professional work could be effectively performed under different forms of direct control, the professionals themselves are likely to resist it. As Eraut puts it: 'Accountability has been presented to the professional workers more as an external control mechanism than as a strengthening of their moral and professional obligations: and hence as threat to autonomy rather than a consequence of it' (1994, p. 225).

A final caution should be made in interpreting the results. Although questions concerning work in sectors that have implemented NPM models in various forms have been addressed in this paper, this should not be read as an analysis of the implementation of NPM models. This would demand longitudinal data and more elaborate alternation between the micro and the macro levels. Another potential source of error is the recruitment of individuals into different professions. Could the higher participation in induction programmes and continuing professional development in nursing than teaching be explained by individual variations? Both these questions would make interesting topics for further research.

Notes

1 I would like to thank all those that have contributed valuable comments and suggestions on different versions of this paper, especially professors Jens-Christian Smeby and Arne Mastekaasa at the Centre for the Study of Professions, Oslo University College.

2 All findings presented in this paper without references to other publications are from the Norwegian StudData-survey, a panel survey following students from 20 different professions and 11 different institutions from the first year of professional training, the final year, three years after graduation and six years after graduation. The findings presented here are from a panel that graduated spring 2001, and was followed up spring 2004. For more information see http://www.hio.no/content/view/full/1059. However, all interpretations are solely the author's own responsibility.

3 Merriam Webster online: http://www.m-w.com/dictionary/altruism.

4 For more expanded analyses of job values and job rewards among Norwegian teachers and nurses, see for instance Caspersen (2006) or Dæhlen (2005).

5 One year is divided in two academic semesters in Norway.

6 Nurses average significantly higher on a scale from 1 to 4 compared to teachers, on the statement 'The training has been sufficient for performing my job in a good way'.

Preamble

The average Swedish head teacher has a teaching background. She is the superior of 50–80 teachers. In her job she has to handle clashing interests and ideals in relation to diminishing financial resources, and while doing so she is often the target of criticism. Her work situation has changed considerably over the years. Nowadays she spends more time on administration and managerial issues then on pedagogic leadership. She often gets caught in the middle while trying to balance the diverging expectations from above, to be a 'pedagogic principal' and an 'efficient manager' with those from below, to be an 'administrator and human resource manager' and a 'surety' for good study results .

Marie-Louise Österlind,
Pamela Denicolo & Curt R. Johansson

Head teachers caught in the middle or on top of things?

Introduction

Sweden's approximately 6,000 municipal schools play a central role as child educators and nurturers. Since few private alternatives exist and the actual options to choose a school are limited, children and parents are often reduced to accepting the prevailing conditions of the local school. In national evaluations, and in the public debate, head teachers are often identified as key figures whose achievements are vital to the quality of the work performed in these schools, the pupils' study results and wellbeing and the teachers' and other staff members' work situation.

The demands made on local schools and their head teachers have become increasingly heavy over the last decades. The head teachers' responsibilities have increased while their authority has diminished. Financial cutbacks and organizational restructurings have been widespread and, although everyday activities have become more turbulent, psychologists, counsellors and assistant head teachers have decreased in numbers, adding to the head teachers' heavy workload (The Swedish Association of School Principals and Directors of Education, 2007). Concurrently the strong symbolic value of authority and edification associated with the title head teacher has depreciated. Today the head teacher position is not so much sought after, status and income have decreased in value (Söderberg Forslund, 2000) and many head teachers leave their positions prematurely[1] (The Swedish Association of School Principals and Directors of Education, 2007). Those who stay on the job have to balance contrasting expectations from national and local authorities, teachers, pupils, parents and the public. While doing so they risk being 'caught in the middle' between the local school administration and the teaching profession.

Many of the expectations from national and local authorities can be derived from the two contrasting leadership ideologies (ideals) *new public management* and *pedagogic leadership*. Below these concepts and their implications for the head teachers' professional role are discussed in the light of major changes that have affected the Swedish school organizations and their head teachers during the last decades.

In the second part of this chapter results from a study in which Swedish head teachers reflected over their leadership and their schools are presented. Two diverging personal approaches to the head teacher role are elaborated through the portraits of the two head teachers Richard and Maria (pseudonyms).

New Public Management goes to school

In the 1980s a new set of ideals regarding public sector organizations spread through the western world. This 'ideology', frequently called *New Public Management*, alternatively known as *entrepreneurial government* (Thomson, 2004), is rooted in Anglo-Saxon new-liberalism and is strongly influenced by leadership and management theories generated to fit the conditions in private sector organizations. In Sweden this meant that the prevailing ideals of 1970s, such as participation and co-determination (Eriksen, 1997), were replaced by a counter-ideology primarily focused on economy, efficiency and effectiveness. Other major characteristics of this movement are: decentralization of responsibility and authority from national to municipal level; a shift from management by rules and regulations to management by objectives; and a tendency to give preference to general leadership skills before expert knowledge. In the present day *New Public Management* is still the prevailing ideal in many Swedish municipalities (Montin, 2002).

Focusing on economy, efficiency and effectiveness

To promote efficiency is a principal aim within New Public Management. One effect of the strong emphasis on the efficiency objective, partly forced by necessity as lower growth rate in the national economy and a capping of the municipal tax led to decreasing incomes for the municipalities (Svedberg, 2000),[2] being that local municipal organizations have to balance decreasing financial resources and demands for retained or increased quality (Wallenberg, 1997; Montin, 2002).

Consequently head teachers have had to balance national politicians' requirements for educational results with local decision makers' imperative demands to keep within the budget (irrespective of the pupils' needs and research results), while bearing in mind that a head teacher considered disloyal to local resolutions can be forced to leave her/his position (The Swedish Association of School Principals and Directors of Education, 2007).

Decentralising responsibility and authority

The Swedish decentralization and deregulation process, initiated by the Government's education policy from 1976, cumulated in the early 1990s, when the municipalities (in 1991) assumed the responsibility for the compulsory comprehensive school (grundskolan) and the upper secondary school (gymnasiet), their right to determine matters concerning the local school organization being further extended by the new local government law of 1992 (Svedberg, 2000)[3]

The underpinning ideals and expected outcomes from the decentralization process diverge over time. The decentralization of school management in the late 1970s influenced by well-fare state ideals, was intended to endorse participation and co-determination (Ekholm, 1992). Whereas in new public management, the prevailing ideal in the 1990s, decentralization of responsibility and authority from national to local level is regarded a means to *delimit professional autonomy at the local level* (Thomson, 2004, p.49).

Reviewing the outcome of the decentralization of political decision-making processes, from Governmental to community level, Svensson (1998) found that an increased focusing on leadership issues strengthened the head teachers' positions through their increased priority to interpret laws, policies and objectives. The hierarchical order was sharpened and the gap between the head teachers and their members of staff was increased.

Shifting from management by rules
and regulations to management by objectives

How to control the work processes is a major concern in any organization. Whereas public sector organizations traditionally have been controlled by the use of bureaucratic techniques such as rules and regulations, the new 'regime' was reinforced by management by objectives, where goal fulfilment was assessed via measurements of efficacy and productivity, result analysis and other types of evaluations (Montin, 2002).

The implementation of management by objectives (MBO) has not been trouble-free. Frequent and continuous problems being: vague and at times contradicting objectives; unclear distribution of liability and authority; strongly restricted freedom of action for solving tasks (especially financial matters); intervening politicians and superiors who give inadequate support; and head teachers struggling with role ambiguity and difficulties to find their place in the picture while frequently performing unqualified administrative work (National Agency for Education, 1998; 2004). To make things work out head teachers have to improvise in the spirit of the objectives while being governed by other circumstances (Hultman, 2001), expecting little or no support from teachers often sceptic to the prevailing MBO discourse (Svedberg, 2003), although the shift from direct to indirect governance forms (rules vs. objectives) has smoothed the progress of professional groups wanting to gain ascendancy over the implementation of political decisions (Berg, 2003).

Changing recruitment policies
– Favouring general leadership skills over expert knowledge

By tradition, head teachers have been recruited amongst teachers considered to be exemplar pedagogues, often from the school in question (Ekholm, 1992). Whilst 'old' leadership ideals were oriented towards expertise knowledge, the 'new' ideal type of public sector leadership is management oriented, the managers' primary task being to motivate their staff members to attain the organization objectives (Montin, 2002). The favouring of management skills has broadened the recruitment basis for head teachers to non-traditional groupings such as pre-school teachers, recreational pedagogues, military officers, economists and others. The effects of the two differing *recruitment strategies* (specialist vs. generalist) have been the subject of debate. The *traditional recruitment policy* is considered to promote teachers' professional autonomy, since these head teachers have been found disinclined to implement political decisions which might dispute the prevailing norms and school staff routines (Ekholm, 1992). However Svensson (1998) found that the *recruitment of non-traditional groupings* has lead to an increased freedom of action for the professional groups working in municipal organizations, since the lack of expert knowledge and/or professionalism (such as head teachers with no teacher training or other pedagogic experience) often 'turns' head teachers into administrative managers, rather than leaders developing the core activities. Thus this suggests that the head teachers' professional background is not what foremost determines their prospects of exerting an influence on the teaching profession.

Summing up

Above we have explored the concept New Public Management and its effects on Swedish municipal head teachers' professional roles. We have found that the de-regularisation and de-centralization of the school and the strong local focus on administrative leadership and cost efficiency has lead to an increasingly complex work situation for the head teachers, who spend more time on administrative work at the expense of educational matters (Svensson, 1998), thereby involuntarily being turned into managers and administrators rather than pedagogic leaders (Svedberg, 2003). Research shows that the situation described above is not a unique Swedish phenomenon.[4] The effects on the head teachers' role and work situation, in Sweden as in most western countries, being so extensive that it is justified to ask: *What is educational about educational administration?* (Evans, 1999, p. 20). A drastic remedy is prescribed:

> If educational administration, in both practical and academic aspects, is to become a strong practice, with the capacity to contribute seriously to the work of educators, it needs to be reconstituted from the ground up as a pedagogic practice. (Evans, 1999, p. 129)

The elusive nature of pedagogic leadership

Among national decision makers and in the academic and professional discourses the educational aspects of school management, conceptualised as *pedagogic leadership*, are and have been at the centre of attention. However if one tries to pin down the nature of this concept one finds that its connotations diverge as follows: being an educational role model, being a good adult educator, being the leader of a learning organization, being a leader of an organization where learning (education) is the end rather than the means to leading the school in accordance with the national curriculum and the local education policies (Svedberg, 2003).

Even though the *dream of the good pedagogic leadership runs like a line of thought* (Svedberg, 2003, p. 93) through the specialist press, the elusive nature of *pedagogic leadership* has proved problematic to the Swedish head teachers. This has been acknowledged by the National Agency of Education who has found that Swedish head teachers perceive their role as pedagogic leaders both problematic and indistinct and consequently that the conception of *pedagogic leadership* needs to be further elaborated (National Agency of Education, 2004).

In the national educational discourse the ideal head teacher is portrayed as an educational leader who: *takes an active part in the heart of school operations, i.e. the teaching process* (Nytell, 1991, p. 20); ardently implements the national objectives found in the curriculum in such a manner that teachers and other staff members comprise these objectives; and identifies and supports local development projects (Ministry of Education and Research, 1992; 1994). These notions are also to be found in the national professional training programme for head teachers in which the participants are expected to acquire and put into practice a *democratic, learning and communicative leadership founded on the national curriculum,* (National Agency of Education, 2001, p. 2).

The National Agency for Education emphasizes the head teachers' role as mediators and correspondents of politically formulated objectives and intentions. The head teacher is expected to *correspond the political message to the extent that it is not only accepted but internalized by the school staff* (National Agency for Education, 1998, p. 58). Whether the local school development proves to be a success or not is to a high extent ascribed to the individual head teacher's leadership qualities. Either the head teachers are able to exercise a purposeful leadership over the pedagogic work or they are unable to disrupt a school culture that hinders progress.

The notion of an impending conflict of interest between national and local interests can be recognized in the quotation from the national head teachers training program goal document below, which states that after finishing their education, the participating heads should be:

> better equipped to shoulder the responsibility that the curriculum and other decrees enjoin on the head teachers as well as to specify the prevailing conditions of their schools and to claim their school's requirements towards the local policy-making authorities (National Agency of Education, 2001, p. 3).

The underlying expectation from national decision makers is that the ability to balance the diverging requirements and obligations is a mandatory qualification for any head teacher:

> If the head teacher is unable to successfully balance [finances and administration vs. pedagogic leadership] his/her suitability for the job can be questioned (SOU 2004:116, p. 102).

Caught in the middle or on top of things

Above we have deliberated the concepts of *new public management* and *pedagogic leadership*, two contrasting 'ideologies' embedded in the, at times, conflicting expectations which head teachers of Swedish municipal schools have to balance. Whilst they are expected to be a 'pedagogic principal' by *national policy makers, scholars* and *fellow members of the head teacher profession* (Ministry of Education and Science, 2004; National Agency of Education, 2004; Svedberg, 2003), the expectations raised from *local policy makers* are those of the head teacher being an 'efficient manager' (Montin, 2002; Ministry of Education and Science, 2004). These conflicting *ideals* bring about *goal conflicts* [quality vs. effectiveness] leading to *conflicting loyalties* [politicians vs. organization vs. profession] (Wallenberg, 1997; Eriksen, 1997; Montin, 2002), which need to be handled by the individual head teacher.

The situation is further complicated by the expectations of *pupils, parents and the public* who, ascribe good study results foremost to strong head teacher-ship expecting the head teacher to be the 'surety' of quality (Ekholm, Blossing, Kåräng, Lindvall, Scherp, 2000), and by those of the *teaching profession* who tend to favour head teachers who foremost act as 'administrators and human resource managers' leaving the pedagogic development to the teachers (Nytell, 1991; Blossing, 2002).

Head teachers have to balance the diverging expectations described above with personal incentives and conceptions of how to 'do a good job' in order to be a professional head teacher (Svedberg, 2003). The head teachers' prospects of role fulfilment are dependent on the legitimacy that their can obtain. The *manager* needs legitimacy from above [local politicians and superiors] and the *pedagogue* needs legitimacy from below [teachers and other staff members, pupils and parents] (National Agency for Education, 1998). While financial measures makes it relatively easy to assess managerial capacity, the elusive nature of the concept *pedagogic leadership* is an aggravating circumstance for head teachers trying to live up to expectations.

In circumstances like these strong professional values can serve as guidance for the individual. The Swedish head teachers, however, are likely to find signposts pointing in opposite directions. While Lärarförbundet (The Swedish Teachers' Union), the largest union for teachers and head teachers, recently renamed their periodical from 'School Leadership News'[5] to 'Management & Leadership: the magazine for professional school leaders'[6] implying that the head teacher profession has embraced the management oriented values of new public management. Yet, an ombudsman interviewed in the very same magazine stated that: 'We in Lärarförbundet regard teachers and head teachers as members of *one* profession' (Samma yrkesetik för alla, 2007.)

The above leads us to assume that the Head Teacher profession in today's Sweden is a profession in transition. Being heterogeneous and indefinite, it is unlikely to endorse the individual head teachers, sandwiched between the local school administration and the teaching profession, endeavouring to balance the demands made by the Government (through the national school laws and statutes and the national curriculum), local school politicians and municipal superiors, teachers, parents, pupils and the public. These demands can be found embedded in the contrasting ideologies *pedagogic leadership* and *new public management*. Consequently the individual head teacher is in danger of being caught in the middle between conflicting ideals and interests groups as Figure 1 illustrates.

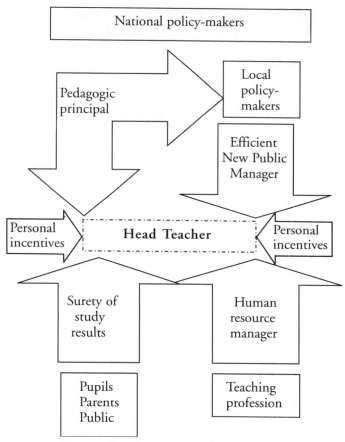

Figure 1. Caught in the middle.

A dead dangerous job

Head teachers work in *complex and interdependent cognitive, emotional and practical worlds* (Day, 2004, p. 22). Head-teacher-ship is an extensive emotional sensemaking process, which involves the individual head teacher's entire personality. Their ability to define, redefine and fill their professional role and to put leadership into practice is determined by individual factors related to personality, competence and professional background and loyalties, but also by local school cultures and traditions such as the diverging expectations of the main figures on the school arena, some of whom demanding a priority pupil-oriented, high quality education whereas others prioritise efficiency and financial rigour. These are strong constricting forces, acting in opposing directions (Svedberg, 2000).

We put forward that being a head teacher is no longer a matter of choosing between being a leaders of pedagogues or a pedagogic leader, but rather a matter of being able to successfully combine both roles, while balancing the expectations about efficient public management with those about pedagogic leadership. An added stumbling block for head teachers with a strong sense of responsibility is that their authority is not always increased to cope with this scenario.

> Everything is my responsibility. If you start thinking about what a head teacher should do you might just as well go home and pull the covers over you It is a dead dangerous job. What ever happens it's my responsibility. (Hultman, 2001, p. 67)

Is it possible to manage the unmanageable?

If the individual head teacher endeavours to take on all tasks and responsibilities single handed, like a *Jack of all trades*, while trying to come up to diverging expectations while handling conflicting objectives, interests and loyalties, there is a considerable risk that the head teacher might feel caught in the middle. This is the result of trying to manage an unmanageable situation. The only way out is to leave their position or, if things come to the worst, to leave the head teacher profession.

Nevertheless, if the head teacher succeeds in combining the best from the two prevailing ideals, *new public management* and *pedagogic leadership,* and while doing so manages to balance diverging expectations and handle conflicting objectives and clashing interests, the head teacher might stand a good chance of coming out on top.

The study – Swedish heads reflect on their leadership and schools

In what follows, the issues raised above are discussed in relation to the results from an interview study in which ten Swedish head teachers reflected on their leadership and their schools. The study was conducted at the beginning of the reorganization process within the Department of Education and Childcare in a Swedish municipality concerned with the definition of new managerial roles and the redefinition of traditional managerial roles, among others the head teacher role. Thus, the participating head teachers were still enmeshed in the traditional roles redolent of the former organizational structure.

A constructivist approach

The foundational precept of this study is that the individual's constructions of his or her social reality are of high importance since they orientate and mediate individual action. This construction process is assumed to take place on two levels: the internalisation of meanings established by others (Berger & Luckmann, 1966) and the construction of a unique understanding of the surrounding world (Kelly, 1955).

It has been claimed that the two perspectives are antagonistic but, according to Gergen (1999), the two theories can be combined into a constructivist approach in which individuals are considered to construe the world mentally but that this construction process also involves categories supplied by social relationships. Warren (2004) provides an argument that extends this line of thought:

> Personal construct psychology and social constructionism, taken together as complementary, make a formidable assault on the problem of understanding our psychological and social life – our psychosocial life. Separately they are limited in the depth of the insights they can offer (p. 41).

Participants and procedure

The participants, who contributed to the design of the research project as well as sharing their views within it, were ten head teachers whose schools were situated within the municipality. These schools covered the range of school types and sizes present in that municipality while the participants, approximately half of the population of head teachers, reflected the balance of male and female in that population. Each had had training as teachers and had several years of experience both as teachers and as head teachers.

The interviews were performed by a repertory grid[7] procedure, an interview technique developed by Kelly (1955) in order to facilitate the exploration and elaboration of parts of our construct system that are unarticulated or implicit. The interviews were used within an interpretivist setting, involving the participants' individual reflection on, and discussion of the results (Denicolo & Pope, 2001).

The repertory grid procedure involves participants in identifying elements (people or objects) that are representative of the theme in focus for the interview and then considering them in pairs, triads or as a whole group to identify similarities and differences between them on a range of dimensions. These bi-polar dimensions, termed constructs, provide an indication of the most salient attributes of the focal topic for that participant (Smith, 1995).

Two interviews were performed with each participant: one on the theme 'leadership' and the other on the theme 'schools'.

For the interview on 'leadership', each head teacher individually was asked to identify 'persons important to your implementation of leadership' (elements). Thereafter they were asked to consider these persons in triads to identify similarities and differences (constructs) between them on a range of dimensions. This procedure was concluded by including 'I as leader' as an element, thereby engaging the participants in reflecting on their own leadership in relation to the earlier identified ranges of dimensions.

In the second interview the head teachers were asked to compare and contrast a range of 'schools' (elements): own school now; own school ten years ago; a school like own school but better; a school like own but not as good; own school as I would like it to be; own school as I think the Government would like it; own school as I think the municipal administrators would like it. Thus the element set was negotiated, with the heads choosing particular schools from their own experience that fitted each general descriptor, but the constructs, or salient attributes, were elicited from the participants.

Österlind interviewed the participating head teachers. Each interview took place in the head teacher's own school while the grids were compiled using the Rep Grid II computer program (Gaines & Shaw, 1990). Each interview was concluded with a feedback session in which the graphic representations of the grid results were presented, elaborated and discussed. The individual interviews took between one

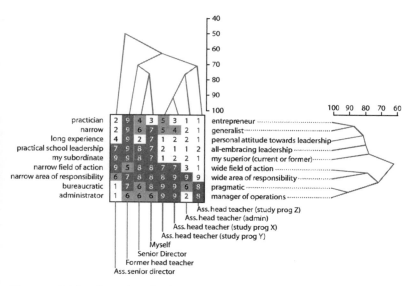

Figure 2. Richard's grid on leadership.

and two hours, the majority taking almost two hours. All interviews were recorded on audio tape which allowed the discussion around the choice of construct labels and ratings to inform the interpretation of the graphic representations of the grids.

The Rep Grid II program provides an analysis of the links between the elements and also those between the constructs, performing the least sum of differences calculation on the rating scales that were used to differentiate the position of each element along the construct dimension. The results are presented in the form of a dendogram or a tree diagram, providing clusters of similarly construed elements or similarly rated constructs, an example of which is given in Figure 2. These formed the basis of the feedback to participants and the foundation of the main results presented here. However, the main results also draw on the elaborations and explanations provided by the participants during the course of the grid interviews, as described above, in addition to the basic grids used as illustrations.

Results – balancing contrasting ideologies and expectations

Below we present aggregated results from the interviews related to the two interview themes *school leadership* and schools. Thereafter we proffer an in-depth illustration of the results through the portraits of the two head teachers, Richard and Maria (pseudonyms).

Traces of pedagogic leadership and new public management

All the head teachers mention assistant head teachers and municipal senior managers as 'persons important to their own execution of leadership'. Some also mention former superiors, personal friends, own children and/or spouse. Neither teachers, pupils nor parents are mentioned as persons important to the head teachers' own execution of leadership. These people appear, at group level, embedded in important aspects of schools (constructs) in the subsequent interviews on the theme 'schools'.

The head teachers' explorations of the differences and similarities between their important persons reflect the duality in all of their leadership ideals. However, each has a different proportion of constructs related to either new public management ideals or pedagogic ideals.

The ideas of new public management is depicted, using phrases drawn from the grids, as a head teacher who is a *goal-oriented organizer* and *decision-maker* with *wide area of responsibility* and *sphere of activity*; a head teacher who is a *pragmatic entrepreneur* and *generalist* with a *personal attitude to leadership*. The ideals representing a pedagogical leader show the picture of a head teacher who is not only a *competent pedagogue* but is one *who inspires confidence*, is a *good judge of character* and a *good listener*.

The head teachers could be distributed across a dimension that had at one end a high proportion of new public management ideals and a low proportion of pedagogic ideals while the other end the reverse description applies. The majority of head teachers had an even balance or a high proportion of pedagogic ideals.

Less money but better schools

According to the head teachers, *ten years ago* the economic situation was much better and the pupils and their parents were 'easier', but the school was not a generally better school.

The head teachers' constructions of their own schools *today* show that, even though the financial resources have diminished, and the pupils and their parents are 'worse'; in all they still consider their school today the better school. This apparent anomaly is mainly due, according to the participants, to the fact that both the staff (teachers and assistant head teachers) and the head teachers themselves have higher pedagogic competence. In the school of today the pedagogic role is changing from the lonely teacher who is 'king' or 'queen' in the classroom to teachers that co-operate and work in teams, while the pupils are treated as individuals with personal skills and needs rather than as whole groups or classes.

The head teachers' constructs about what constitutes an *ideal school* from the perspective of the municipality or the Government are barely differentiated but both could differ from the head teachers' own ideal school. Often the head teachers considered themselves as more 'realistic' in their views of what is the 'possible' ideal school than the administrators in the municipality who were perceived as immersed in more bureaucratic issues.

Meet the two head teachers Richard and Maria

Below follows an in-depth illustration of two head teachers' constructions of school leadership and schools. The two case studies were chosen to represent the extreme poles of the dimension described above which combines proportions of new public management and pedagogic viewpoints. Head teacher 1 ('Richard') is the head of a '*gymnasieskola*', the equivalent of a Sixth Form College in England, serving students aged between 16 and 19 years. Head teacher 2 ('Maria') is the head of two '*grundskolor*', linked Primary / Secondary Schools in England, serving pupils aged between 6 and 16 years. Both of these participants, like the rest, are in their middle years, have had considerable teaching experience and have been in their present position for at least three years. Any further details would identify them, which would breach confidentiality. Thus these examples serve to illustrate two contrasting approaches that emerged from the combined data of the study.

Richard – a confident new public manager

Richard's constructions of '*good*' school leadership indicate the strong influence of New Public Management ideals. He sees himself as a *prac-

147

titioner and a *generalist* with a *personal attitude towards leadership* who demonstrates an *all embracing leadership*. He regards himself as a head teacher with *a wide field of action* and a *wide area of responsibilities* who is both an *administrator* and *responsible for operations*.

The persons that Richard mentions as important for the execution of his leadership fall into two groups: A) his assistant head teachers and B) the municipal school administration's senior manager and the school's former head teacher. He places the administration's assistant senior manager outside of the other groups. Richard construes his assistant head teachers, along with the assistant senior manager, as conventional practitioners with long experience but, whilst his subordinates deal with practical school leadership, the assistant senior manager represents an all embracing leadership.

Richard places himself in a group with two other men who have a wide area of responsibility. One of them, the first person who came to Richard's mind as important to his leadership, was the former head teacher, whom he seems to regard somewhat as a role model. The third man, the senior manager, and himself score slightly less highly than the former head teacher on the construct poles that he viewed as positive. This former head teacher was certainly more entrepreneurial than Richard himself, but Richard considers himself to have a wider field of action. His senior manager received similar scores to Richard except that Richard sees himself as having a more personal attitude towards leadership whilst the senior manager draws on his tacit knowledge derived from long experience. Richard does not mention teachers, pupils or parents (as elements or constructs) in the interview on leadership. Teachers and pupils appear within constructs in the second interview (on schools).

In the school interview, Richard describes *his school ten years ago* as close to *a school like yours but worse*. He describes these schools, which form a separate group from the other schools, as *centralised* schools with *poor quality technical equipment* where the *teachers work alone* with their *focus on classes* rather than on the individual pupils. He characterises teachers' work as pedagogic *conformity* (the original Swedish word is 'enfald', which has a double meaning: *simplicity*) which *neglects the individual pupil's* needs in favour of a concentration on performance indicators such as *marks/grades*.

The scores for elements 3 and 5 (*your school as you want it to be* and *a school like yours but better*) provide an indication of the construct poles that Richard favours. His school now scores quite well on the construct *focus on individuals* and on having *schools within the school*. It is also doing much better than it did ten years ago in terms of *technical facilities, teachers working in teams, pedagogic diversity* and *care for pupils* although it is doing less well than the Government and the local authority wants it to do in terms of the last three constructs. When Richard talks about his school today he states 'I have embraced the development during the 90s'... 'The decentralization is not carried out to the extent I'd like it to'... 'The teachers might not always want to.'

Richard's constructions of his school as he would like it to be are a *decentralised school* with *several schools in the school* where the *teachers work in teams*. The work in this ideal school is characterised by *pedagogic diversity* and *caring for pupils who are treated as individuals*. Marking should be restricted to allocating a general grade (e.g. Pass with distinction, Pass, Fail) rather than being concerned with relatively trivial detail. Richard's ideal school is close to his constructions of the governmental and municipal school ideals (which are regarded as very similar), but in the interview he pointed out that what he puts in the grid concerning *his idea* of how the local education authority would like his school is just that. 'To be honest I don't think anyone knows how BUN [the municipal school administration] would like it [my school].'

Combining the results of the two grids from Richard, a picture emerges of a head teacher who knows his own value as a municipal middle manager but also one who balances two sets of ideals. He leans towards new public management leadership ideals in the leadership interview but in the school interview he also espouses the ideals of pedagogic leadership. He seems to find little difficulty in marrying the two ideals, using aspects of each as appropriate to circumstance.

Maria – a self-doubting pedagogic principal

Maria, who is the head of two schools, describes herself as *goal-oriented*, a relatively good *organizer* and *decision-maker*, a *good judge of character* but who has *less confidence in how much she can inspire others*. She considers herself as a *good judge of character* with *good pedagogic competence* and *sufficient financial knowledge*. Whilst Richard describes himself closest to the municipal senior manager and the former head teacher, Maria feels closest to her assistant head teachers. To her, the senior municipal manager, along with other representatives of the municipal administration, form a separate group. Maria also mentions a politician (who was used to represent all politicians serving on the Education and Childcare board). The politician(s) Maria describes as responsible at central level, with good financial knowledge but less pedagogic competence, not offering such a good service to her as head teacher. She sees the politician(s) as goal oriented, good decision-makers and organizers, but less confidence inspiring and not such good judges of character. They have different values to hers.

Maria's constructs about her senior municipal manager show us a picture a senior manager with good (sufficient) pedagogic knowledge, but with less good financial knowledge who gives good service to his head teacher. He is a senior manager who, to a higher extent than the other representatives of the administration and the politician(s), shares her values and is confidence inspiring and a good judge of character. However, he is also someone who is less goal-oriented and is a less good decision-maker and organizer than herself.

Maria does not mention teachers, pupils or parents (as elements or constructs) in the interview on leadership but they appear within constructs in the second interview (on schools).

When Maria explores the school theme, including both of her present schools as elements, her constructs, to a large degree, are focused on person centred issues in contrast to Richard's constructs, which are more operation centred.

Maria's two *schools of today* have several similarities. They both have teachers working in teams and have got 'half way' towards the municipal and governmental ideals. In both schools, moves have been made towards increasing pupils influence, but they still do not meet her expectations. In both schools, the level of competency in the Swedish language of pupils has 'degenerated' during the last eight years (which is partly due to the increasing influx of pupils from foreign countries) as has the parents' engagement.

Today both schools suffer from lack of financial resources whereas eight years ago financial resources were affluent. According to Maria the schools differ in that the assistant head teachers and teachers are less 'competent' in school B. The competence of the assistant head of *school A* Maria considers being equivalent to her own and the work in this school is described as being flexible with staff taking responsibility. In *school B* the assistant head is considered less competent, the staff think conservatively and the work is prosaic.

She describes her two schools eight years ago as being very conventional with a less competent head teacher and assistant head teacher; with little influence from the pupils although they had a better knowledge of the Swedish language and their parents were more engaged. *School A* was more conservative than today and the staff were co-operating poorly, whereas *school B* was as conservative then as it is considered to be today, yet the staff were co-operating more than the staff of school A.

When Maria talks about *ideal schools* she can recognise that one of her schools (A) is moving near to meeting her ideals and the other school is not far behind. However, when ideal schools are compared with what Government and municipal school administration want, a much larger disparity can be observed. Maria, in her interview, commented that these official bodies expected her to perform miracles with little financial support. She felt she had a more down to earth view of what was practicable.

Combining the results of both grids provided by Maria, a picture emerges of a head teacher who is struggling to manage two large, under-financed schools with a large immigrant population, yet she is achieving some of her goals. However her values are somewhat at odds with those she perceives as demanded by officialdom and this tension results in her lack of confidence in her own competence.

Maria clings steadfastly to her pedagogic values, which she sees as different to most administrators senior to her. To her, goals related to finance and administrative issues are less relevant than those related to person management and teaching competence. In her first grid she is clearly positioned with her assistant head teachers who maintain a teaching background and she separates her group from her superiors and those with a clear administrative role.

A review of the study

The approach and the methods allowed the head teachers to express their constructs about their professional situation at a particular time in their careers and in the historical development of educational practice in the municipality. They also reflected on their previous constructs about leadership and schools and it may well be that changes in circumstances will further effect their construing. However, in reviewing their grids (see Figure 2), all ten head teachers averred that the grids portrayed authentically a picture of their views at the time. They declared that the interviews, with immediate feedback, enabled them to consider their roles as head teacher in a more reflective way than they were able to do when caught up in the rushing streams of activities that form their professional lives.

The Head and the Teacher

The word head teacher has no equivalent in today's Swedish school system. The title of Richard's and Maria's job is 'rektor'. In this study the word head teacher makes a very good metaphor, depicting the different approaches to their work with Richard representing the 'Head' and Maria the 'Teacher'. Because he feels on top of things and is mainly concerned with administrative matters, Richard is able to set himself higher goals than those he thinks are expected of him. On the other hand Maria perceives the expected goals to be beyond reach and sets herself more personally realistic goals related to pedagogic improvement. It is interesting to note than Richard explicitly said, and Maria implied, that what was expected from them by the local Education Authority was unclear. To Richard this ambiguity is not a problem, on the contrary it widens his 'freedom'. To Maria it means that she does not get the support that would likely help to reduce some of her self doubts.

We have used the case studies of Richard and Maria to illustrate the range of reactions of the whole group of ten head teachers to co-existing ideologies in the system. This range is bounded by, at one end, head teachers who internalise new public management ideals and use them to develop the organization of the schools. At the other end of the range are head teachers who maintain allegiance to pedagogic leadership skills, perhaps resisting, ignoring or not engaging with new public management, but find them criticised for less administratively organized schools. Richard and Maria hereby demonstrate the extremes of the range of views presented by the ten head teachers, although Maria's story portrays the more common balance between new public management and pedagogy.

Achieving individual equilibrium

The results from our interviews with acting head teachers indicate that this ambiguity can be more or less challenging to the individual head teachers. We propose that head teachers can handle this tension between organization and profession by developing a personal approach to the head teacher role, hereby accomplishing a personal equilibrium.

The ten head teachers in this study reflect the dilemmas outlined in the introduction to this paper. They are striving to balance the principles of the *pedagogic leadership* with those derived from *new public management*, some with more apparent success than others. All of them are struggling to produce increased quality, in spite of decreasing financial resources, and to secure also the benefits of research and development while working in an unstable and insecure climate. The head teachers are in a sense having to mediate the demands (perceived) coming down from the local education administration and those from the national Government with those coming from teaching staff, parents, and pupils.

They need to develop psychological mechanisms to cope with the disparity between what their budgets can afford and public expectations raised by previous welfare ideals combined with developments in research and technology. This can be achieved by adopting different strategies related either to management ideals or to pedagogical ideals derived from their previous teaching profession. Each has to reconstrue their view of their leadership role and of their school becoming both leaders of pedagogues and pedagogic leaders in order to balance the contrasting demands of the role.

Notes

1 During the years 2000 to 2006 43% of the 2261 members in the Swedish Association of School Principals and Directors of Education [Skolledarförbundet] left the profession for reasons other than retirement.

2 The schools' financial situation was further complicated by the expiration of the national sector grants directly intended for school activities in 1993.

3 The fulfilment of the intentions in the National school legislation, curriculum and other national policies is overseen by the National Agency of Education.

4 For an international comparison see Evans (1999), Day (2003) and Thomson (2004).

5 Skolledningsnytt.

6 *Chef & Ledarskap Tidningen för professionella skolledare.*

7 The repertory grid interview is 'a well-used technique within psychological research' (Cassel & Walsh, 2004, p. 61). For additional examples on how the repertory grid interview has been used within educational and organizational research see e.g. Denicolo & Pope, 2001; Linander, 2002; Österlind, 2002-b; Österlind & Denicolo, 2006.

Preamble

At the end of the last century, the role of the nurse handling the hospital ward administration changed from a mainly clinical job to a purely administrative one – implying that the patient was left behind. However this shift has not always been accompanied by shifting expectations on the incumbent of the role which could be examplified with the fact that the ward managers feel that their co-workers expect them to participate in the clinical work on the ward. This questioning of the legitimacy of ward managers is described in terms of different time horizons between professional identity and organizational role.

Calle Rosengren & Mikael Ottosson

From white dress to white collar

A historical perspective
on the hospital ward administrator

Introduction

Contemporary studies on working life indicate that the ways in
which we live and make our income are undergoing revolutionary
changes. Among other things being put forward are the development
of information and communication technology (ICT), an increased
globalization of markets and a general shift towards customer-orien-
tated production systems. However, the rapid transition of work
organization could be contrasted with more stable cultural structures.
In connection with this, Beck (1992) and Hydén (2002) argue that
dramatic changes within social systems are not automatically followed
by corresponding changes in norms and values. They argue that
expectations are based on historical experience rather than on the present situation – a circumstance that could create a gap between reality and ideology. The tension between different time horizons, which
Beck and Hydén discuss, is made explicit in the following quotation
from one ward manager.

> Yes, the staff members don't think I live up to their expectations. They
> feel disappointed with me. And I can understand them because they
> can't see the new role of the leader. The longstanding tradition is that,
> on a ward like this, you've had someone who was called a ward sis-
> ter. And that meant that you had administrative chores but were also
> involved in the clinical work. [...] and our role isn't designed like that.
> We are employed on totally different premises. We're employed to
> develop the operation. [...] But we're not employed to work clini-
> cally. And that's a bit hard to understand.

In the quotation, the ward manager expresses how expectations of her as a leader are based on tradition rather than present organizational setting. In order to understand the varying expectations posed on the ward managers a historical perspective is needed. According to Henriksen (2002), Nilsson (2005) and Petersson (1993), ward administration was traditionally handled by the most skilled nurse on the ward. Besides her clinical chores, she was responsible for manning the ward, educating its staff and mending supplies and equipment. Basically, the position consisted of ensuring that the present needs of the ward were matched with the proper personnel and equipment. Despite her administrative chores, she was foremost a nurse and as such was naturally part of the operative clinical work.

During the second half of the twentieth century, the administrative structure of Swedish public health care evolved dramatically and became an extensive bureaucratic apparatus. This development can be illustrated by the fact that the administrative staff increased 27 times in number during this period in relation to that of physicians, whose number only increased 6 times. Nurses came to play a significant role in this bureaucratization process. In his thesis *Gender, Salary and Careers – The transformation of the nursing profession during the twentieth century*, historian Sune Dufwa (2004) points out that the number of nurses with an administrative function increased during this period to comprise 8 percent of the total medical staff at the end of the past century. Studies indicate that increased bureaucratization has led to a purification of everyday work on the wards (Dufwa, 2004). At the end of the past century, administrative functions became clearly separated from clinical functions. The nurse handling ward administration filled her working day with paper work rather than with traditional clinical work. Hence, the role of ward administrator became increasingly 'managerial' in orientation.

Aim and purpose of the article

One way to study the increased health care bureaucracy is to analyse in what way changed organizational roles are related to more stable cultural structures such as professional identities. The present article examines a series of interviews with a group of nurses who work with administration and on separate wards in one county council, Region Skåne, in Sweden. The interviews were conducted during 2005 by Calle

Rosengren as a part of his doctoral studies. The main question, which structured the interviews, was how they perceived the increase in administrative chores in their role as ward managers. A total of nine interviews were conducted. At the time of the interviews, six of the respondents were working as ward managers. Two of the interviewed nurses were working as the above six respondents' immediate superiors, and both had previous experience as ward managers. The final interviewee came from central administration. Eight of the respondents were female and one was male. As the material is rather small, any generalizations being made are not primarily based on a representative sample. In this article, the interviews are rather used to serve as illustrations and exemplifications in a discussion on organizational roles, historical change and professional identity.

The aim of the article is to identify any conflicting expectations placed on the ward managers and to try to discover how individual ward managers deal with the tensions inherent in the role. How do the ward managers perceive the different expectations placed on their role and in what way are these expectations handled? An additional aim of the article is that it should constitute a foundation for further studies in which historical changes and professional identity are analysed in terms of psychosocial work environment. In a time when most public organizations are experiencing constant reorganization, it is interesting to pose questions regarding how identities are constructed and maintained in turbulent and shifting contexts (see Sennet 1998).

Health care bureaucracy and the nursing profession

Seen in an international perspective, the Swedish health care administration is not unique. In most Western countries, ward manager posts are occupied by nurses (Salvage & Heijnen, 1997). In a study of British ward administration it is shown that nurses with administrative functions are the foundation of the British health care hierarchy (Savage & Scott, 2004). It is also shown that different hospitals have designed the positions in different ways. The health care administrations in Britain and Sweden are shown to have major similarities. In both countries, the foundation of ward administration is constituted by a balance between nurses' administrative and clinical tasks. This construction could be expected to contribute to a situation in which different, and conflicting, expectations are placed on this occupational role.

The dramatic expansion of the health care system in both Britain and Sweden during the twentieth century must be seen in light of the build-up of the post-war welfare state. In Western countries, an expansive health business has been built up, the aim of which is to produce good care for citizens as well as a healthy and strong nation. In both countries, this public and tax-financed expansion has been transformed into a period marked by heavy-handed economic and reorganization measures. Hospitals, nursing homes and clinics have been closed at the same time as societal demands for efficiency and financial control have increased. Concurrently with this transformation of the medical services, the character of nursing has also changed. Traditional nursing has become capital intensive and medically and technically more advanced. This process has brought about increased demands on the skills and knowledge of personnel.

One way of meeting these challenges has been to rationalize the operation through personnel specialization. In the medical services, doctors and nurses have faced increased demands on their special training. At the same time as demands on advanced knowledge have increased dramatically, the breadth and extent of medical personnel's knowledge has been reduced. As the work has been split up the administrative tasks have been given to specialized administrators – the ward managers. From a management perspective, the changes in the role of the ward manager could be described as moving from hands-on leadership – with authority derived from extensive knowledge of the clinical operation – to a leadership focussed on resource planning. In terms of the competence needed to carry out the assignment, the transition has implied less emphasis on clinical skills and more on administrative skills. However, even given these new demands, ward administrators are still recruited from the regular nurses on the ward. Regarding the title of the person who is given this role, the two most common are 'ward sister' (avdelningsföreståndare) and 'ward manager' (avdelningschef). The former implies a focus on clinical chores and patients and the latter on administration and staff. In moving towards an increased focus on administration, ward manager has become the most common title. This conceptual change is clearly indicative of the above-mentioned ideological shift in the public sector. However, it could be questioned whether this conceptual shift has been accompanied by changed staff expectations.

'The ward staff want you to be'

Henriksen's (2002), Nilsson's (2005) and Petersson's (1993) picture of
the early ward manager as being the most skilled nurse on the ward
is also corroborated in the interviews. One of the ward managers states:

> You usually took the person who had been working the longest time
> on the ward, for example the old lady who knew everything about
> surgery. It was she who became boss… because that was pretty nat-
> ural. Of course she knew how to do everything.

Concerning the character of this 'old lady', a clear image of a very
authoritative character emerges. This is a general perception among
the respondents and can be illustrated by a small anecdote told by one
of the ward managers.

> When I was a nurse I worked under an old traditional ward sister
> who practically owned the whole ward. […] She had a bell so every
> time she'd gone the round with the chief physician. She did it by her-
> self. We weren't allowed to follow. […] So she had a bell she rang. In
> the hallway. Then we'd all come running.

As the quotation indicates, the traditional ward sister's authority was
mainly based on her profession as a nurse and less on her managerial skills. She was a very salient person on the ward, and the leadership she performed was of a hands-on character. The ringing of the
bell can be seen as a clear expression of the hierarchical relations on
the ward. One of the interviewed ward managers' immediate superiors describes the change in the role as moving towards an increased
focus on personnel and a decreased focus on the patient.

> Today's ward managers are so much more. They don't work like that.
> The ward managers of today don't even have a relationship to the
> patient. They are pure administrators. Their focus is primarily on staff
> members.

Here, the bureaucratization process is seen as leading to a purification of daily chores on the ward and, thus, you become either an
administrator or a carer. The supervisor gives several reasons as to why
this change in focus has occurred.

> Today, labour laws and working life are designed in such a way that
> personnel administration demands an awful lot. In some ways, I guess
> it was simpler before. The ward sister of the past she could both

> work... have a patient perspective and still busy herself with paper-work in some way... it was easier back then. Things didn't move as fast as today. Back then you probably had more time so that you could have both perspectives. It's completely impossible today.

The informant perceives that the health care organization of today is more complex in nature than previously, which in turn makes it diffi-cult, or sometimes even impossible, to combine clinical and adminis-trative work. If we look in detail at the ward manager's work, it still con-sists – much like it did before – to a great extent of manning the ward and solving daily problems there. One ward manager puts it as follows:

> Yes, big as well as small problems appear all the time. From someone who wants to change work shifts to big problems [...] like someone who is sick-listed for serious things and the like. It can happen in the blink of an eye. And cooperation problems within the work group. That a patient has a complaint. So a lot of things occur during the day that I didn't know about in the morning when I came in.

As the ward manager describes it, much of the work is reactive, in the sense that it is unplanned. But at the same time, it is also expected of the ward manager that he/she be proactive and visionary in develop-ing the quality of the ward. As one ward manager expresses it: 'It's a lot about visions. I have many ideas. About how we should work more customer oriented here for example.'

A general perception among the interviewed ward managers is that people's prior experiences of ward managers still linger on – such as the expectations placed on them. They feel this especially among the older generation or those who have worked in the medical services for a long time. They consider that personnel of this kind have very clear expectations with regard to the ward manager. While the elder-ly personnel expect the ward manager to perform clinical tasks, the younger ones see the ward manager as a pure administrator. One of the ward managers says:

> The ward staff want you to be... to know the patients... to be able to answer any question. At the same time, you are expected to do work on the ward, help the others in the morning rush. Perform everyday work. After that you are expected to take care of rehabilitation and human resource development. The problem is that there are old expec-tations too. Particularly from those who have been around for a while, those who have worked for many years and have old views. I think

that many of the new nurses and assistants have a different view of the ward manager, but the ones who have worked in the old days… sometimes you can hear: 'The ward sisters could do it before – why can't you do it now?'

According to this ward manager, the conflict between the present situation and expectations is most obvious in those who have worked as nurses and assistants for some years. They have expectations with regard to the ward managers that are based on previous experiences and the historical development of the medical services.

'Is she on the Internet or what?'

It is not self-evident that every aspect of the ward manager's work is viewed upon as work at all. In the interviews, a clear distinction appears between clinical and administrative work, such that paper work does not count. 'The ward manager of the past she could both work… have a patient perspective and still busy herself with paperwork in some way…' The perception of what constitutes work is a cultural construction and therefore varies from time to time and from organization to organization (Silvén, 2004). Irrespective of institutional care, the culture on the ward is based on the nursing profession. As was made clear above, nursing training is distinguished by its clinical elements, explaining why only caring has come to be considered work. In addition to this indistinctness regarding the ward manager's work, the increase in administrative tasks has resulted in a situation in which the ward manager's work is not as visible as the clinical work. Thus, the ward managers themselves as well as their staff can experience that they are not doing anything.

> I mean my worst fear as a new ward manager was that someone should ask: 'What have you done today?' 'Well, what have I done today? Talked to a lot of people.' Still I've been busy with work all day. When somebody asked me as a nurse 'What have you done today?' 'Oh, I've transported this many patients to the operating room, I've taken this many blood samples, I've done this many intravenous drips, I've tended to this many wounds.' 'Cause that was concrete in some way. That was real work. And I'll tell you that this attitude is sometimes held towards directors' work. Recently I met a doctor. So I asked 'Where is our boss?' And then he said: 'He's working today.' 'Oh really, I responded. I thought he did that everyday.' 'But he's performing an operation.' That says a lot!

A conclusion that can be made from the quotation above is that administrative work is sometimes not regarded as 'real work' – a circumstance that the ward mangers perceive is a cause for suspicion among their co-workers. This is explicated by one of the ward managers' immediate superiors, who says 'I know that many ward managers sometimes feel frustration when people look into their office and say "All right, there she is sitting at her computer again. Wonder what she's doing? Is she on the Internet or what?"'

The fact that work has become more administrative in character means that it is no longer as bound to the ward facilities as it used to be, which, for example, opens up for telecommuting. The question to be asked then is: Is work conducted outside the ward facilities perceived as 'real work'? And the answer is: No. Similar to the different perceptions of concrete clinical work versus more abstract administrative work, the respondents experience that this kind of work is looked upon with suspicion by other staff members. In this connection, the ward managers claim that they are expected to be present during office hours – an expectation that can be deduced from the ward manager's historical role as a very visible person on the ward. If the ward manager were to telecommute, it is presumed that the staff would view such work as not working at all. 'No, personally I don't think that would work for me. I would probably feel guilty if I left earlier one day. And think that "Now they think I'm not doing anything at all"'.

As mentioned earlier, much of the change in the design of the ward manager's role is that clinical chores have been reduced or ceased all together. However, the interviews show that several of the respondents still spend a great deal of their time on clinical chores and that they are committed to such chores. The fact that they were conducting nursing tasks was something they felt was perceived very positively by the staff. 'What a great boss who is out there!' Moreover, the informants feel that decisions made on the basis of personal experience receive more attention.

> In some way I think that I'll get more trust if I say 'This looks very bad. You really have to do this better.' Then they'll have an easier time accepting it if I've been out there and seen it in person. […] It's not just a desk product so to speak.

In other words, administrative experience does not count – it is, as we saw, not even considered work. In order to gain increased respect

– and at the same time make their work more visible – the ward manager performs clinical work with no pay – outside his/her line of duty. In certain contexts, the ward manager is not free to make this decision at all, but, due to an acute need, must throw him-/herself into the clinical work.

> Last year it happened that I sat on this chair and in came a colleague, a midwife, and screamed at me that I had to come. Then I had to take care of a couple. And help out with that delivery. There was simply no one else.

Here, the ward manager takes on the traditional female role as the caretaker. Nursing is not merely salaried work, but, as shown in previous research (Dufwa, 2004), can also be considered a calling. This calling underlies the role as a nurse as well as the role of being a human being – you cannot let a fellow human being come to harm because you are 'sorting your paper'. The ward managers who did not perform clinical chores explain this in terms of their lack of clinical competence. They argue that because they have not been working clinically for a long time, they feel they do not have sufficient knowledge of new routines and equipment. The argument that it is simply not their job is not enough. By referring to their lack of competence in conducting nursing tasks, they are downgrading their professional competence as nurses, and at the same time showing that the administrative chores of the ward manager are not enough to dispel the demands of the calling.

'Then I'm dressed in white'

As mentioned in the beginning of the article, professional identities must, in relation to organizational roles, be seen as rather stable over time. Central to the understanding of professional identities is that they are based on conceptions of masculinity and femininity. Studies on working life history show that different professions have a clear gender encoding depending on the specific historical context from which they have evolved (Wikander, 2006). By tradition, the nursing profession is associated with what are traditionally regarded as feminine qualities such as thoughtfulness, empathy and sensitivity (Björklöf, 2006; Greiff, 2006; Ekstrand, 2005). The connection between the nursing profession and gender is made explicit in our language, in that a nurse is also called 'sister' – a fact that has led to certain problems of designation. What do we call a male nurse (Dufwa, 2004)? It is reasonable to assume that changes in the medical services have made traditional gender encoding problematic.

In the medical services, it is not only the professions that have a specific gender encoding but, according to Alvesson and Due Billing (1999), also the organizational hierarchy. Like many other businesses, the health care hierarchy is marked by a pattern in which women are found near the bottom and men near the top. What will happen when a female nurse makes a career and perhaps even becomes the superior of male doctors? Is a career in the medical services encoded as masculine, in that it moves from caring (feminine) to management (masculine)? Macdonald (1995) argues that the role of the ward manager must be seen in relation to the professional project of nurses. The ward manager was to ensure greater autonomy for the nurses working within the hospital organization. Is the ward manager then to be seen as a protector of her fellow sisters, which, according to Macdonald, was the original purpose of the role, or is she to be seen as a traitor to her sex – a traitor who wants to get closer to the men at the top of the hierarchy? From this point of view, the conflict could be analysed as disloyalty on the part of the ward manager towards her fellow sisters.

One former sister, who became a ward manager, supports this interpretation when she describes her career move as a break with the female collective on the ward.

> It's a large group. It's a strong group of women. Only women. It's a tradition. We don't have many men [...] Most staff members have worked here for many years and they're a strong group, welded together, with different wills. First I just said no... definitely no!

The above picture of women's relations to their gender role and career is confirmed by Lindgren (1992). In her study of career patterns in the medical service, she found that a woman who strives upwards in the hierarchy is looked upon with suspicion. Their female colleagues said that such women just wanted to get closer to the doctors, that they were more interested in their superiors than in their fellow sisters (Lindgren, 1992). It is reasonable to assume that making a career within an organization with explicit gender encoding is problematic. It is also reasonable to assume that a woman who moves upwards in this kind of organization is defying traditional gender patterns. This interpretation is supported by the fact that the interviewed male ward manager said that he did not experience any role conflict in his work. Although our empirical foundation is small, it seems fairly clear that the relationship between nurses and the ward managers has gender implications and that the female ward manager runs the risk of being excluded from the female fellowship.

However this interpretation, that nurses who pursue a career as ward manager are looked upon as traitors to their sex, could be complemented and nuanced from several different perspectives. One obvious fact is that organizational hierarchies not only express a gender encoding, but also reflect class. In line with Sverre Lysgaard's (2001) analysis of the relation between 'the workers' collective' (Arbeiderkollektivet) and management, it could be assumed that the nurse who pursues a career is also considered to be disloyal towards and to lack solidarity with colleagues on the ward. By moving closer to the doctor – who not only symbolizes male dominance, but also the upper class – the ward manager betrays the other nurses both as fellow sisters and as colleagues. Another consequence of the nursing profession's clear female gender encoding is that patient care constitutes the core of the profession (Greiff, 2006). Thus, by moving away from the patient – leaving the white dress and becoming a white-collar worker – the ward manager leaves the core of the nursing profession – the patient – behind.

In this article, two different expectations have been discussed, that of the administrator and that of the nurse. Ward managers are supposed to be colleagues, women, nurses and supervisors simultaneously. Similarly to other professionals, the ward manager uses different symbols to indicate identity, and in cases of conflict to indicate which identity applies at the moment. In order to indicate our position in relation to others, we use language in different ways; we assume different postures in relation to superiors and subordinates; we use titles and nametags to show who we are (Barth, 1994; Ottosson, 1999; Peterson-Royce, 1982). Within the health care service, as in other uniformed professions, clothing is perhaps the most important symbol in different situations. One way of handling tensions between being an administrator and being a nurse is in the selection of clothing. One of the ward managers mentions white clothing as a symbol of her clinical role. 'Then I'm dressed in white. Yes. 'Cause they know that when

I'm wearing white I'm working clinically. Then I'm available.' This quotation illustrates that this ward manager marks a difference between the person performing clinical work and the one performing administrative work through her choice of clothing. When she leaves her administrative role, the white dress replaces 'the white collar' – an indicator of the fact that there actually exist two roles that the ward manager must handle within his/her working day.

Conclusion

The present article has focused on the establishment of ward managers as a sub-profession of the nursing profession. During its initial phase, this establishment could be seen as reflecting the nursing profession's ambition to gain a higher degree of self-determination inside the medical service organization. When the administrative apparatus enlarged during the twentieth century, the participation of nurses with administrative functions became more common. At the end of the century, the role of the ward manager changed from a mainly clinical job to a purely administrative one. At the same time, the ward managers feel that their co-workers expect them to participate in the clinical work on the ward. The descriptions provided by the informants also show that the predominant view of what characterizes 'the real work of a nurse' focuses on its clinical elements. Our present interpretation, based on the interviews, is that this view of the nature of the work involves a questioning of the legitimacy of ward managers. Moreover, we can see the origins of the tension in the ward manager's role in the nursing profession's gender encoding. The nurse (the woman) who makes an administrative career (ascribed to men) runs the risk of being seen as a traitor to her sex. Taken together, the interview material shows that ward managers often see themselves as partially renounced by the nurse collective and that they, therefore, even see themselves as suspicious characters.

They leave the professional fellowship of the nursing group; they receive new duties that have little if any connection with their professional training as nurses. A majority of the interviewed ward managers say that their posts have become purely administrative and that they do not have time enough to participate in clinical work on the ward. Despite this experienced alienation, most of them occasionally perform clinical work. When they, like their predecessors, are performing the role as the 'most skilled nurse', they secure their authority on the ward. Sometimes they perform clinical chores with the explicit ambition to maintain their competence as nurses; sometimes because they must do it – they are trained nurses surrounded by ailing and sometimes even dying patients; sometimes they do the work simply because they find it stimulating and enjoyable. In other words, the clinical work performed by the ward manager does not necessarily have to be seen as a symbolic action in relation to certain expectations deduced from the nursing profession, but could rather be seen, from the individual's point of view, as a valuable and necessary action.

Preamble

This chapter is based on a survey of Swedish and international police research. A fundamental task in police work is discussed: dealing with dilemmas. These have to be handled in a judiciously way by the police officers, as there are no absolute answers to the question of how to act in various situations. The reasoning is linked to questions about multifunctional organizations and competence.

Lena Agevall & Håkan Jenner

Dealing with dilemmas
A fundamental task in police work

Introduction

The police should 'be both helpers and overturners ... should act with a wave of the right hand but clench the left one ... be both soft and firm and preferably at the same time' – this statement can be found in a 1983 document from the Swedish Police Association (as cited in Lundquist, 1988, p. 106, our trans.). This quote reflects the topic of this chapter, namely, understanding police work as a way of managing contradictory and complex demands.[1] We will try to describe some of the demands put on the police force, and from this description identify various dilemmas that individual police officers must learn how to deal with. This article is based on a survey of Swedish and international police research focusing on this aspect. In line with Lundquist (1991) we differentiate between conflicts, when in quandary there are oppositions between two considerations and it is obvious which one the officer should choose professionally and ethically (e.g. if an officer is offered a bribe), and dilemmas, when two quandaries are in opposition and the officer cannot be quite sure which choice is the best to make. As a frame of reference for this reasoning we employ theories on multi-functional organizations and competence assessment.

Police work – just like pedagogical and social work – is defined by a constant lack of absolute answers about how to act in various situations. Instead, these types of work are characterized by questions about how to deal with dilemmas in a moral manner. Dilemmas that are typical for pedagogical work are discussed by, for example, Fritzén (1998), who shows that the teacher must balance between aspects such as given – created (content of knowledge), passive – active (student participation), and control – openness. Analyses of social workers' role from this perspective have been conducted by Jenner (1995). Typical dilemmas for social workers include being both a fellow human being and a person of authority, taking into consideration the social rights of the client without taking on all of the responsibility, and respecting the client's integrity while at the same time having an obligation to report and investigate.

From a pedagogical viewpoint, this may be understood in terms of the competence that comes with the profession (cf. Ellström, 1998). This *competence in action* is influenced by the qualities inherent in the individual or the situation. In turn, the individual aspect affects two sides of competence: formal and actual. The two do not always coincide. For example, one may have undergone training that provides formal qualification for a profession, but in practice one may have difficulty dealing with the tasks that one is faced with. Individual competence must also be seen in relation to the demands and terms of the task. Competent handling of tasks is, thus, a function of the knowledge acquired by the person involved, the characteristics of the tasks, and the prerequisites under which to deal with the tasks (Fritzén & Gerrevall, 2001).

We begin our account by pointing out some characteristics that police officers share with other professions. This introduction situates police work in its professional context.

Being in-between contradictory demands

There are mutual demands on those who are public employees. They work in organizations with elected management, which means that they are part of the parliamentary chain of control and the citizens are the foundation of this. Those working in public organizations have a social commission and are governed by laws and regulations. Public employees are also expected to continuously and simultaneously consider the values found within the framework of our joint value system, or *our public ethos* (Lundquist, 1998).

Public organizations are multi-functional; there is a multi-criteria problem in that there are several, and often contradictory, objectives and values that need to be addressed simultaneously. Being able to handle conflicts of objectives and values thus becomes an important part of one's competence (Christensen *et al.*, 2005, p. 16; SOU, 1997:57, p. 150). We may identify what is usually called *public operations' dialec-*

tics, which means the search for the correct balance between compassion and flexibility, and between impartiality and the strict application of regulations (Lipsky, 1980, p. 15; Lundquist, 1998, p. 123). One needs to maintain law and order and handle cases in an impartial, matter-of-fact way without being overly formal (Christensen *et al.*, 2005, p. 216). One needs to show compassion and be flexible while still operating within the realms of the law.

The work categories that fulfil a societal mission in direct contact with citizens are called *street-level bureaucrats* (Lipsky, 1980). They are at the borders of organizations and meet citizens face-to-face in their daily work. They cannot predict their workdays, what situations they will encounter, or how many problems they will be faced with; nor can their work be monitored. This means that police officers, as well as other street-level bureaucrats, have a certain amount of freedom to act. The meeting between street-level bureaucrats and citizens is particularly delicate because the meeting occurs face-to-face. The *style* of the meeting is important. It is one thing to be treated abruptly in a written letter, but it is most likely far worse to be confronted with arrogant, unsympathetic, or inconsiderate treatment in person (Lundquist, 1998, p. 124). The style of the meeting, that is, making sure to treat citizens with respect and consideration, must therefore be seen as part of the competence required by public employees.

The administrative ethical aspect may be generally approached starting with the considerations that an official in a western democracy needs to adhere to (Figure 1).

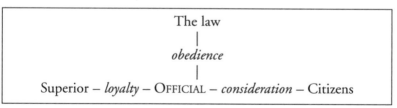

The law
|
obedience
|
Superior – *loyalty* – OFFICIAL – *consideration* – Citizens

Figure 1. Basic considerations for officials in public organizations (based on Lundquist 1991, p. 45).

Lundquist points out the following:

> One of the foundations in public ethics is that the official should obey the law and act loyally towards his superiors. None of these relations

can be isolated. At the same time as the official needs to obey the law and act loyally towards his superior he must also show consideration towards citizens. *Of course there is nothing here to suggest that these three demands cannot contradict one another* [italics added]. (Lundquist, 1991, p. 59, our trans.)

On a different level, there is also consideration shown towards colleagues. Consideration towards colleagues may also give rise to ethical conflicts and dilemmas.[2] *Competence in action* is about responsible actions when it comes to handling both practical and ethical dilemmas. The phenomenon we are trying to capture is comparable to what Aristotle called *wisdom – phronesis*. It includes considering the things that may vary, good judgment, and 'a disposition to act in accordance with actual thought to what is good or bad for people' (Aristotle, Swedish trans. 1988, p. 164, our trans.).

The ideal here is *the reflective practitioner*. This term, which was coined by Schön (1983), applies to people who are *researchers in practice*, people who reflect on the phenomena that they encounter, and on the previous interpretations that are implicit in their actions. Similarly, Molander (1996) stresses that fact only becomes knowledge when you use it in practice. He speaks of *knowledge in action*. Simply put, it is not important to be able to answer correctly, but rather to be able to *act* correctly and in a good manner.

This requires context-based judgments and skills, that is, a know-how understanding. Know-how understanding[3] is based on *quality regulations in social communities – in practice*. We cannot speak of individual practices, since they are a collective phenomenon. Quality regulations mean, if we look at the police force as an example, collective regulations for what good police work entails and the standards that serve as tacit knowledge in one's actions (cf. Rolf, 1991).[4] We may illustrate this by taking a closer look at the quotation below regarding how some police officers feel that they, quoted by Bittner (1967), should act in their interactions with skid row inhabitants:

> Patrolmen view a measure of rough informality as good practice vis-à-vis skid-row inhabitants. By this standard, patrolmen who are 'not rough enough,' or who are 'too rough,' or whose roughness is determined by personal feelings rather than by situational exigencies, are judged to be poor craftsmen. (p. 701)

If we analyse the above quotation, we may infer that there are not only quality regulations in practice but also that which Molander (1992, p. 77) would call *reasons* for actions: 'To ask for reasons and to give reasons means that a certain terminology and a certain type of answer is accepted, or rejected. Question and answer entails "a normative control station."' We realize that a situation-based necessity may be a reason, but that personal feelings may not. We realize that the degree of force officers find appropriate for managing a given situation depends on the situational context. We also realize that 'not rough enough' – 'too rough' functions as a basic rule, that is, open-ended rules require one to make a personal assessment in a situational context. The rules are, in other words, context based. That which is accepted is found within the framework of *learned application*. This means that others thus accept the application of the rule within the same line of work (Agevall, 1994, p. 43).[5]

Despite the similarities that exist between working as teachers, social workers, and police officers, there are also specific differences, determined by the specific societal mission, the tasks, and the governing demands. The question one needs to ask is thus: What characterizes police work? The answer to this question, according to Skolnick (as cited in Knutsson & Granér, 2001, p. 80), is that the characteristics of police work involve:

- exposure to dangers and threats
- being viewed as an authority
- needing to work quickly and efficiently

Individual factors can also be found in other lines of work; however, it is the combination of these three that is seen as typical for police work. Additionally, the police force is the occupational group that has been given authority to use restraint (Police Act § 8) and force against citizens. The directives in the Penal Code regarding self-defense (Penal Code §1 chapter 24) and legal authorization (Penal Code §2 chapter 24) in addition to the Police Act §10 provide the police with the authority to use force under certain circumstances (Knutsson & Granér 2001).

The various components that constitute the specific work of the police force are used as starting-points for the analysis of the situation-based demands that police officers face and have to deal with on the job:

- Emphasis is put on danger and threats and the authority aspect. The question of quickness and efficiency primarily regards the issue of whether this may 'influence' the aspects just mentioned.
- The different characteristics of police work may be described separately, but should at the same time be seen as being interlinked with one another.
- We disregard the fact that there are different defined tasks and/or units within the police force, that is, that the importance or frequency of the different factors may vary, which ought to influence the police officers' views of what is considered to be 'proper police work' (Knutsson & Granér, 2001, p. 82). Here we look for the general features.

Being exposed to danger and threats

When a patrolling officer is called to a scene, he or she must be prepared to meet potentially frightened, intoxicated, confused, angry, hostile, wounded, or violent people. Police officers are faced with situations that may be of the utmost life-or-death importance. To manage these situations, officers must make use of their authority – they have to 'take charge' (Wilson, 1989, p. 37). In these situations, there is an imperative to *act*, and this is the essence of police work. At the same time, this imperative involves being able to deal personally with dangers and threats. Furthermore, decisions in these situations must often be made quickly. To shed some light on the complexity of the situation as regards dangers and threats to one's person, three aspects will be addressed: attention and caution as part of knowledge, relationships between police officers, and strategies used when meeting different citizens.

Attention and caution

Police officers are trained to deal with potential danger. They are trained to recognize what is normal and to sense the danger of that which is abnormal (Ekman, 1999, p. 13). Perception–attention becomes an important part of their know-how understanding regarding the situational and the particular. It may involve the ability to realize that there is a problem or to read a situation, and police officers develop a 'police eye' that they use to see and interpret their surroundings. The police eye concept, which in some sense may be compared to a 'clinical eye' in the field of healthcare, was introduced by Finstad (2001). In an ethnographic study, Finstad observed Norwegian police officers in charge of law and order and noticed that police officers in a patrol car see more than the average person on the street does. Andersson (2003), who studied local police officers, says that this 'sweeping eye of the local policeman' seemed more and more apparent. She writes of 'an interpretation scheme in which they [the police officers] distinguish between crime and law-abiding behaviour, between order and disorder' (p. 75).

An important ingredient in police officers' know-how understanding seems to be the development of an approach characterized by attention and caution (cf. Shearing & Ericson, 1991, p. 492). To understand the importance of attention and also the predictability of cooperation between police officers, we may look at what Weick and Roberts (1993) call the *collective mind*: 'a pattern of heedful interrelations of actions in a social system' (p. 514). This means a close social connection[6] between behaviours. This is particularly important for work in which one wrong step may result in great danger or harm.

Weick and Roberts begin with the concept of *know-how* and extend their analysis to the collective level. It is important to make a contribution to the current situation while simultaneously predicting the other person's actions (representation) so that your actions are adjusted to the other person's actions (subordination). Through the development of attentive actions in social systems, risks and accidents are avoided. Weick and Roberts maintain that this includes dependability and reliability. They caution that collective mind should not be confused with mature or developed groups, and exemplify this with the phenomenon *groupthink* as a combination of a developed group and an undeveloped collective mind.

When interrelated behaviours are broken down, this leads to carelessness. People can, as we know, work both for and against each other:

> Individuals represent others in the system in less detail, contributions are shaped less by anticipated responses, and the boundaries of the envisaged system are drawn more narrowly, with the result that subordination becomes meaningless. Attention is focused on the local situation rather than the mutual situation. People still may act heedfully, but not with respect to others. Interrelation becomes careless. (Weick & Roberts, 1993, p. 371)

Transferred to police work, in which one wrong step may have drastic consequences, this means that the interrelated behaviour and coordinated actions determine how well police officers succeed in managing potentially dangerous and problematic situations. Being able to predict how their partners will act is also something that police officers emphasize: 'He [the colleague] must be predictable and not subject you to any dangers; you must know what he will do' (police officer interviewed in Ekman, 1999, p. 97, our trans.).

Relationships between police officers

Apart from the predictability aspect, the officer also stresses the importance of being able to trust one's colleague:

> From a security perspective, it is important to be able to trust your colleague; if there is tumult you want to know that your back is covered and that the colleague will not withdraw. (police officer interviewed in Ekman, 1999, p. 97, our trans.)

Trust between colleagues is highly valued and has two sides: It involves knowing that the person you work with will not fail you, that he or she will do everything to help you in a dangerous or threatening situation. However, it also involves being able to assist the other person in the same situation. Granér and Knutsson (2000, p. 113) observe that the scenarios that police officers fear involve finding themselves in situations in which they cannot help their colleague – having to leave a colleague behind. This fear may even be greater than the fear of being injured. This is one positive side to relationships between police colleagues that is often mentioned.

Trust as a phenomenon is multi-dimensional and may be defined in various ways. However, we may stipulate that trust is about expectations and convictions. Lawton (1998, p. 71) observes that people believe and expect that others will act in a particular way and that these expectations are related to their previous experiences. Thus, trust reduces the complexity of the future: 'we take things on trust.' It is vital in order for people to trust others. How people decide to act depends on how much they trust in and are able to predict the behaviour of others. Trust is an integrative mechanism that creates and upholds solidarity, social relationships and systems (cf. Weick & Roberts, 1993, p. 378). It is visible in relationships and in the maintenance of relationships. A *high-trust relationship* is characterized by the following:

> Participants share goals/values
> They have diffuse long-term obligations towards each other
> There is open-ended support
> They communicate openly and honestly
> They rely upon each other
> They give each other the benefit of the doubt
> (Fox, 1974, as cited in Lawton, 1998, p. 74)

Sharing for example objectives and values and being able to engage in open and honest communication are two ingredients in a trusting relationship. If a police officer does something unethical or illegal, his or her colleague must be able to openly object and discuss it. In other words, police officers must be able to tell their colleagues if they are doing something that they think is wrong. The following extract from an interview with a police officer illustrates this:

> Well, for the most part I think that I would be able to do that. If it is done correctly, if you don't step on people. There are some people you cannot communicate with. But they are few ... I think that you often sense it, if you have done something wrong. And you wish to have confirmation [of this], and you think about it. How you could have done otherwise. But of course it is a question of real maturity to be able to do that. And I demand a lot of my colleagues as well ... when I feel that it is important that high ethics are maintained between us as well. I might feel at those times that I would not like to have certain people as colleagues, because I think that they are breaking rules that are fundamental to police work. So, basically, I may have really high standards. But sometimes I think that there are often people who go to extremes on both sides by doing things ... that I may become almost judgmental because of their actions. (Interview with a police officer in Selrot, 2001, p. 31, our trans.)

This quotation also reflects the other side of the relationships between police colleagues – the risk of police officers' mutual trust turning into the tendency to protect each other in unethical situations, for example when officers are accused of using unnecessary force on citizens. Among police officers who uphold law and order, but also among police officers in general, there is a tendency not to report or testify against a colleague (Knutsson & Granér, 2001, p. 96), that is, an 'undesirable team spirit' exists. Metaphorically, one could speak of the occurrence of ethical blinders that hinder the police officers from seeing the ethical fundamentals that they are supposed to live up to. Consideration of others, for example, citizens, is forgotten about, but unreserved trust and loyalty relationships with colleagues have no place in a democratic community governed by law. Such ethical blinders are contraproductive when it comes to upholding citizens' trust in the police force.

Furthermore, insecurity arises if the colleague an officer is supposed to work with is unpredictable. Previous experiences from working with the colleague may, for example, have included sudden provocative or threatening behaviour from the colleague, such as the use of excessive force. We can re-examine a previous quotation: 'He [the colleague] must be predictable and not submit you to any dangers; you must know what he will do' (police officer interviewed in Ekman, 1999, p. 97, our trans.)

This quotation illustrates a consciousness of one's personal vulnerability and the awareness that a colleague's behaviour can have the potential to cause dangerous situations to develop. The need for predictability also applies to the other person's intentions/motives and knowledge. Conversely, dubious motives or a lack of knowledge or both may give rise to insecurity.

Strategies when encountering different citizens

An effect of being subjected to danger and threats is that police officers develop a suspicious nature. This may even be considered part of the job, as one police researcher stresses:

> Police work (just like other control oriented operations, such as criminal care) includes a number of clearly distinguishable trying elements. It is always dangerous. Suspiciousness is a healthy quality in this trade. The police are constantly submitted to the violent, distrustful, hostile, dishonest, brutal and using side of human nature. They are rarely in contact with nobler activities. (Stone 1981, p. 52, as cited in Lundquist, 1988, p. 223, our trans.)

At the same time – like many moral philosophers – one may claim that trust is a moral requirement that ultimately involves showing other people respect. The police, however, are responsible for those who may be affected if this trust is misplaced (cf. Maclagan, 1998, p. 54). Police officers seem to develop different strategies for handling the distrust–trust dilemma regarding citizens.

One method that police officers use to resolve this dilemma when they wish to run a check on a citizen is to refer to it as being a simple routine check, emphasizing that the citizen should not take it personally (Lipsky, 1980, p. 124).

Another approach is to gather *situational* knowledge and specific relations. For example, in his study of police work in slum areas, Bittner (1967) found that the police officers gathered knowledge about locations as well as individuals in the slum areas. These police officers were always prepared for violence, and their focus was targeted more on the dangers in the area than the dangers in society in general. It was a preconceived notion that, in reality, they were there to uphold peace and order in the slum area. They were there to protect the criminals, troublesome individuals, and potential criminals from each other. Other individuals that were not part of the area were quickly identified as outsiders and were left undisturbed by the police. Their attention was instead directed at those who lived or belonged in the area and the occupational groups who provided them with services. By knowing people from both groups they were able to maintain control of the area:

> If I want to be in control of my work and keep the street relatively peaceful, I have to know the people. To know them I must gain their trust, which means that I have to be involved in their lives. *But I can't be soft like a social worker because unlike him I cannot call the cops when things go wrong. I am the cops!* [italics added]. (Interview with a police officer in Bittner, 1967, p. 709)

The words in italics above emphasize the dilemma that police officers must face, namely, sympathy versus neutrality and closeness versus distance. At the same time as they become highly involved in people's lives they must still keep a certain distance. They cannot call for someone else if something goes wrong.

A corresponding problem or dilemma is discussed in Sweden regarding important skills in the recruitment process to the Police Training Programme. In a Department Series report from the Ministry of Justice, the characteristics of a *relation-focused policeman* are outlined:

The applicant should be able to communicate with other people orally as well as in writing, and also have the ability to relate to other people's situations. At the same time, the applicant should be able to look on situations at some distance, sometimes combined with humour. Hence, the identification cannot become too great. (Ds 1996:11, p. 57; as cited in Stensöta, 2004 p. 136, our trans.)

One way to reduce this complex reality and thus handle insecurity and stress is for police officers to categorize citizens into stereotypes such as villains and Swedes/the public (Lipsky, 1980 p. 141; Ekman, 1999, p. 182; cf. Knutsson & Granér, 2001, p. 88):

The origins of bias in street-level bureaucracies may be sought in the structure of work that requires coping responses to job stress ... Stereotyping thus may be thought of as a *form* of simplification. While simplifications are mental shortcuts (of many different kinds) that summarize and come to stand for more complex phenomena, stereotypes are simplifications in whose validity people strongly believe, and yet they are prejudicial and inaccurate as summary characteristics for groups of people with nominally similar attributes. (Lipsky, 1980, pp. 141–142)

Stereotyping could increase the risk of being biased, an idea that is supported by Hydén and Lundberg's (2004) analysis of the police force's domestic control of foreigners. It is a police task that entails a dilemma, in which the core issue is to find a balance between national interests on the one hand, and the respect for individuals' privacy and human rights on the other.

'Police culture is made up of perceptions, values, and practices, in which suspicion and the "we/them" stereotype is a characteristic' (Oskarsson, 2002, p. 111, our trans.). Oskarsson claims that a concrete example is the stereotype used in the Police Authority's evaluation of the EU-meeting in Gothenburg in 2001, namely, activists. 'Furthermore, there is the change in the public linguistic usage that has become more and more frequently used in the last few years, in which the term "activist" also includes groups and individuals who, in words as well as action, profess themselves as being part of the Swedish democratic principles' (ibid.). The *activist* stereotype, which is defined both as any 'person who committed or prepared for a crime' and any person who (from a democratic standpoint) participated in a demonstration, becomes problematic when seen from a democratic point of view.[7]

'Political order and political rights are ultimately a question of negotiation, [it is] difficult and tricky; it is a question of balance. If this balance is disturbed, so is democracy' (Petersson & Oskarsson, 2002, p. 43, our trans.). And the main task of the police force is to protect the values that democracy is based on. It includes handling both order and political rights, that is, creating safety and safeguarding democratic rights in the public sphere. It concerns the citizens' expectations of the police. This can be linked with what may be identified as different types of expectations of the police:

1. Those concerned with normal social life and the maintenance of persistence, stability and order.
2. Those that we have of 'technically competent role performance' such that we trust, for example, the surgeon to perform the operation well, or the official to pay out benefits correctly.
3. Those that we have of others to carry out their fiduciary responsibilities and obligations. (Lawton, 1998, p. 71)

The police have a duty to create safety and order, are expected to have the necessary knowledge and experience to be able to perform their tasks well, and are expected to live up to the responsibilities and obligations that come with their role as guardians of democracy. This involves the trust and expectations of citizens, and the citizens' perception of the police as authority. As we will see, the concept of authority involves both trust and knowledge.

Being perceived as an authority

According to relevant dictionaries, authority includes the overlapping phenomena of knowledge and trust. Dictionary definitions of the term *authority* include words and phrases such as *professional, expert, source of trust, value of trust, trustee, reputation, person with acknowledged ability/knowledge, awe-inspiring behaviour,* and *the right or possibility to use force.*

Perceptions of danger and threat involve looking for safety within relationships with and/or in relation to someone else. The insecurity of violence is handled with authority (Ekman, 1999, p. 187). For example, police officers often speak about the importance of not provoking citizens when interacting with them (cf. Ekman, 1999; Knutsson & Graner, 2001; Shearing & Ericson, 1991). There is an important distinction between being an authority and being authoritarian.

Dictionary entries suggest that the word *authoritarian* signifies someone who has exclusive right to use force, to command, to dictate, to be autocratic Chapter 5, § 1 of the Police Ordinance states:

> In his or her work, a police officer shall behave in a way that promotes trust and esteem. He or she shall act civilly, respectfully and with firmness, as well as with self-restraint and avoid that which may be perceived as unfriendly or petty. (our trans.)

This statement implies that police officers are to act with authority in the sense that the phenomenon has been discussed in this chapter. Police officers are to promote trust and esteem. Authority can be seen here as legitimacy. The wielding of power must be justified. To induce such respect, one is required to use an approach that includes calming, soothing, etc. One way to transmit this knowledge/approach is exemplified in Shearing and Ericson (1991): "'Always act,' said an experienced officer, 'as if you were on vacation'" (p. 492).

The point is for officers to have just the right amount of relaxed attitude so that they do not provoke the people they are dealing with. At the same time, as previously mentioned, officers must be able to mark that they are able to act if the situation so demands. Police officers learn different ways to soothe people and defuse hostile situations. One technique is to divert attention from people who are arguing with each other. Using humour is another example of the types of technique that are mentioned in police stories and anecdotes.

On the other hand, police officers also need to make it clear that they are authorized to use restraint and force, and ready to do so if necessary. The general public must be sure that the officers will always be able to sort out the situation, an idea that is emphasized in a document from the National Police Board:

> The objective of supervision work is to offer security to the general public. The police can provide this security experience in two ways: first by being visible and second by showing up when called for. However, the sense of security of the general public demands more than visibility when it comes to police surveillance. It also requires the surety that the policeman – if called for – will intervene firmly but friendly, make things right and actually report offences against the law. At the same time that this provides the law-abiding citizen a sense of security, it also has the opposite effect on those who are not prepared to abide by the rules of society. (Rikspolischefens grundsyn 85, 1985, Rikspolisstyrelsen; as cited in Åse, 2000, p. 80, our trans.)

Police officers' opportunities to perform their work seem to depend on their being perceived as authorities; this is what gives them legitimacy. They also expect citizens to obey them. When citizens obey, the authority of the police force is confirmed. The notions that exist regarding the approaches police officers need to develop if they are to be perceived as authorities are double-sided. On the one hand, the police should exude a calm, secure, relaxed attitude (in accordance with the vacation analogy); on the other hand their physical actions (body language, uniforms, and weapons) must suggest the potential threat of restraint and force. However, it is important to avoid overt demonstrations of physical power. Instead, police officers' actions should merely hint at the potential for threat and punishment (Lipsky, 1980, p. 63).

Citizens are expected to obey the law. That is the norm, and violations against this give rise to sanctions. There is also, according to Ekman, a dimension of danger linked to this norm. 'The more police officers interpret things as being dangerous, the more important it is to uphold the norm' (Ekman, 1999, p. 163). There is also a preconceived notion among police officers that it is the behaviour of citizens/members of society that determines how to treat them:

> If a citizen is 'correct' the police officers should also act correctly (and of course vice-versa). If a citizen is unpleasant, the policemen should also be unpleasant. If a citizen uses force against the policemen, they should also use force. (Ekman, 1999, p. 164, our trans)

Police officers learn to develop an instinctive cautiousness in accordance with what one policeman called 'well-planned lay-back' and to act 'with a margin of force just beyond what their would-be opponents might use' (Shearing & Ericson, 1991, p. 492).

'Reality rules,' say police officers, and to serve the public is 'real police work'. If citizens feel safe in knowing that the 'bad guys' view the police as authorities, sanctions against the bad guys are especially important. Ekman (1999) also maintains that the sanctions against bad guys are particularly forceful. Bad guys are considered security risks and are thus 'kept on a short leash' in a strict hierarchy determined by the police. We will also look at examples in which police officers interact with 'junkies':

> 'What the hell are you doing! Take it out of your pockets and put it on the ground!' Reluctantly the 'junky' does what the officers order him to and at the same time says: 'I was only checking if my mate

was on the bus, and then I was going to go into the gangway and buy some.' The officers take no notice of this but interpret the man's explanation as an attempt to trick them ... Eriksson takes up the belongings that the 'junky' put on the ground and says: 'Come with us.' The police lead the 'junky' into a guardhouse nearby. Inside they thoroughly search the man. Not even a close examination of the man's socks and feet shows any signs of drugs. What they do find, however, is a screwdriver.

Thulin holds up the screwdriver and asks: 'What are you going to do with this?' 'It's mine and I need it to fix my bike,' says the man emphatically. 'We'll take that; if you protest we'll write a report about a violation against the knife act, or we'll just throw it in the garbage can,' says Thulin. 'No, I want my screwdriver,' responds the man, who after a few minutes' discussion is allowed to leave the scene with his screwdriver. When he leaves, however, he receives a warning: 'The next time we find a screwdriver on you it goes, is that clear?' 'Yes, yes,' says the man and walks out. (Ekman, 1999, pp. 108–109, our trans.)

The hierarchy and obedience norm are upheld because bad guys obey the police (Ekman, 1999, p. 188). Sanctions may act as a form of confirmation that the 'general public' can feel safe. On the other hand, sanctions are deterrent examples for potential criminals. Sanctions are, in other words, a way to uphold authority so that it may be used to reduce insecurity and avoid violence.

To establish and maintain social relationships and to show respect can, as we have seen, be a way to reduce insecurity in uncertain situations. We will now look at two quotations from interviews with a Swedish police officer:

I hope that those you meet are satisfied with what you do, so to speak. Both those who have been affected but also those you take care of, so to speak, like thugs or suspects. You have to try to treat them with some respect, too, because that is always a good thing in the end. You learn this more and more in the profession. In the beginning you were more inconsiderate of those who are our clients or criminals, but I guess you become more open-minded. You should not have prejudices and such, because you profit from treating them with a little bit of respect in any case. You then have a better connection and are more successful in your work. (Interviewed in Selrot, 2001, p. 18, our trans.)

But you are on the underbelly of society in many respects and espe-cially now that there are so few of us, or perhaps we are not fewer policemen now than when I started my career, for example, when you could help an old lady cross the street who had been standing there waiting. Now it is only when bad things happen that we come into the picture – when there has been a break-in, for example, when some-one has been beaten or has disappeared – then you call the police. Before, if someone had taken a fall you could, for example, help them up and take them home and make a pot of coffee and have some cof-fee together with them and make sure that everything settled down. There is no time for that anymore. So the social contact with people has completely disappeared. (ibid., p. 28)

As we can see, the quoted police officer speaks of the importance of everyday social contact, and not only of interacting with people when something troublesome has already happened.

A different way to look at *interactions with citizens* is if the inter-action takes place between identified individuals or between uniden-tified collectives. This may influence the level of frustration, for example, in connection with demonstrations, and may lead to the cre-ation of a mutual spiral of violence:

In the Metropolitan Police the difficulties to control the use of batons are known as 'the red mist'. This refers to a cocktail of mixed socio-psychological extracts that influence a person's self-control in a negative manner, also within the police force. The use of batons forces constables to act aggressively in a situation, in which you also remain anonymous ... you are most likely wearing protective gear with a visor, which makes identification difficult; furthermore it is about moving forward, not as individuals, but as an unsigned collective. 'We', the police, will then portray a striking resemblance to 'the others', the masses. In that way the level of frustration and anger will rise at the same time as the police go to action, and by using a method that min-imizes individual responsibility. (Waddington, 1991, as cited in Peter-son & Oskarsson, 2002, p. 140, our trans.)

In conclusion, we can confirm that there are built-in oppositions in the police role. These oppositions originate in police officers being sub-jected to danger, being perceived as an authority, and having the authority to use restraint/force at need.

As mentioned in the example above, Police officers are supposed to safeguard citizens so that they can exercise their democratic rights in public spheres. They are also responsible for keeping general order. We have also looked at the double-sidedness of having to be soothing and calming while at the same time needing to indicate that you are in the position to use restraint and force.

In order to be perceived as an authority and hence be given legitimacy, the police must be able to balance these contradictory demands and prerequisites. This balancing act must, furthermore, often be upheld even when making quick decisions and when acting under time pressure and stress. The latter aspect is further discussed in the next section.

The demand for quickness and efficiency

So far the discussion has concerned how police officers have to handle exposure to danger and threats and the factors that influence the development of an authoritarian role. An additional demand on police officers is that they act quickly and efficiently. As a short addition to the previous discussion, we would like to point out how quickness and efficiency are linked to questions about threats and authority. Our point is that the different characteristics of police work are presupposed and linked together. The demands for quick decisions are illustrated by this police officer's words:

> As a police officer…I found myself forced to make the most critical choices in a time frame of seconds rather than days: to shoot or not to shoot, to arrest or not to arrest, to give chase or to let go – always with a nagging certainty that others, those with great amounts of time in which to analyze and think, stood ready to judge and condemn me for whatever action I might take or fail to take. (George Kirkham, as cited in Lipsky, 1980, p. 32)

Fear, pressure, anger, and stress may, for example, be reasons for random behaviour. The effects of stress found in experimental research include an increased number of random behaviours, impaired verbal ability, and regression that makes the response more primitive (Holsti, 1971, p. 58). We will now look at an example of a situation in which police officers feel threatened:

> 'What the hell are you doing, you son of a bitch!' he [the police officer] cries out loudly and is all flushed with anger. 'I didn't know that you were police officers [these officers were dressed in civilian

clothes]. You should be made to show ID; all I saw was how my friend fell over,' the man responds in broken Swedish. 'You knew bloody well who we were; you were being threatening; you should bloody well not have done that,' Vandin shouts. 'You shouldn't have done that; you've had it, you son of a bitch!' (The two dark-skinned men had become upset and approached the civilian-clad police officers while they wrestled a third man. The men had done nothing physically, but the policemen had felt threatened.) 'We thought that they were going to attack us,' the policemen said later. (Ekman, 1999, p. 143, our trans.)

It seems as if the police depend on being perceived as authorities in a different way than, for example, physicians. Physicians are seen as authorities by virtue of people's trust or their medical knowledge. Their authority and legitimacy comes from in the general acknowledgement that the medical profession is based on scientific knowledge and well-developed ethics.

The police must *make use of their authority*, and in order to do so they must *be seen as authorities*. For police officers, authority seems to be the tool with which they deal with work tasks and terms. Being perceived as an authority also entails, as we have shown, various demands on the police, some of which are contradictory.

A well-developed norm within police culture is, as we have shown, that their authority needs to be defended often in order to be maintained. If, for example, citizens do not abide by a police officer's instructions, the authority of the police force is threatened. An infraction of the obedience norm becomes a threat to the authority norm.

We have witnessed that 'the specific work of the police force' includes a number of contradictory and complex demands. In order to reconnect with Weick and Robert's concept of the collective mind, we should, when discussing the demand for efficiency regarding police officers, observe that performance may be judged from different perspectives: productive versus unproductive, adequate versus inadequate, or heedful versus heedless (Weick & Roberts, 1993, p. 377). In some situations, acting quickly may be contraproductive with regard to heedfulness. Quantitative measures for tasks may be counterproductive in relation to what is adequate, and so forth.

Regarding dilemmas and complementary attitudes

Under the circumstances of the general dilemmas mentioned by Lundquist (1991) – that is, the dilemmas that may arise when an official has to simultaneously abide by the law, adhere to directions from superiors, and show consideration towards citizens – and the more specific dilemmas mentioned in the literary overview, we may distinguish some examples of dilemmas in police work:

Formal regulations and discipline	Situation-oriented actions
Support of colleagues	Independent (ethical) action
Trust in the general public	Professional caution
Exuding security and calm	Preparedness for threat and danger
Quick actions	Heedfulness

Concrete work is about managing the tension generated by these dilemmas. It is not a question of either-or, but rather of both-at-the-same-time. However, it is not a question of imprecise 'just enough' or wishy-washy compromise, but rather about consciously balancing the oppositions and constantly remaining alert to the inherent risks of extreme attitudes. This may be described as needing to have a *split vision*. (This expression, first used in the field of pedagogy by Fritzell (1996), refers to the ability to see many things at one time; for example, when people drive they focus their attention on the road while simultaneously registering their surroundings.)

From this starting-point, the terms *counterproductive* and *complementary attitudes* are used as tools in the analysis (cf. Jenner, 1995). These terms were introduced in work-ethical contexts by Fagerberg *et al.* (1988), and originate in a theory by the German philosopher Knauer (1967). The reasoning, which originated with Aristotle, starts from the statement that an approach is (morally) correct if it is not counterproductive in the long term, that is, if in a long-term perspective it does not undermine or destroy the values that it is intended to promote. In short, this thesis implies that good values should not turn into something undesirable.

This thought can be illustrated by examining the quality of *courage* (to begin with a classical Greek virtue). Too much courage leads to foolhardiness. In order to avoid courage turning into foolhardiness there is a need for a certain amount of caution. However, too much caution may turn into cowardice. In this example, caution and courage *complement* each other; hence, they are not in opposition. They counterbalance each other, or provide a mutual guarantee that this approach will not turn into something undesirable (thus becoming counterproductive). This issue may be further illustrated as follows (extreme attitudes have been stated, as well as complementary attitudes):

• Cowardice – *caution* – *courage* – foolhardiness
If the dilemmas mentioned above are analysed correspondingly, among other things you find the following:

The first dilemma can – upon close inspection – involve weighing: *loyalty* (towards regulations and superiors) versus *autonomy* (the officer's independent assessments).

The role of the police officer entails being able to assess what type of effort is adequate. To do this, officers need to have a certain amount of autonomy and to be free of detailed control. At the same time, it is important that police officers abide by the rules so that their actions do not become merely arbitrary. On the other hand, too much docility and loyalty may lead to blind obedience, which could also be devastating. The fundamental problem can be illustrated as follows:

• blind obedience – *loyalty* – *autonomy* – arbitrariness

One needs to consider both loyalty and autonomy, so that the need for autonomy does not turn into arbitrariness, or loyalty into blind obedience.

The second fundamental dilemma can be analysed in terms of:
• undesirable team spirit – *support from colleagues* – *independent action* – disloyalty

Independent action is mainly about having personal ethical judgment. This serves as a counterbalance, so that the support of colleagues does not turn into 'undesirable team spirit' (symptoms of which include keeping abuse a secret and having unfavourable attitudes toward the surroundings). However, if a police officer always – even when not required to – acts on his or her own accord, it may jeopardize police work in critical situations. This then becomes a question of disloyal actions that should also be avoided. Police officers need to find a balance between the complementary attitudes.

The third dilemma can be analysed in terms of:

• naïveté – *trust in the public– professional attention* – cynicism

Professional operations cannot turn into cynicism, and trust in the society cannot be signified by naïveté.

Correspondingly, other dilemmas of police work can be analysed. The point is, consequently, that the police officers' task is to strike a balance between the different approaches and – as pointed out above – to do this in full awareness of the risks involved in extreme attitudes. We do not claim that this is an easy task, but it is a task that is part of the role of police officers. The demands on police officers are often contradictory. Some part of their competence in action consists of handling both objective conflicts and value conflicts. Police officers win respect only if these complement each other:

> It is not admirable to be objective unless there is also compassion and commitment, or to have integrity unless there is openness, or having moral courage unless there is loyalty. (SOU 1997:57, p. 150, our trans.)

In a public organization, officials have special responsibilities linked with their duty towards society, and this is no less so when it comes to police work. This includes demands regarding public ethics and legal rights for citizens. Officials must – as requested by Lundquist (1998) – be able to function as guardians of democracy.

How to ensure the (further) development *a reflective practice* in this social climate – a practice in which police officials have both the tools *and* the possibilities to critically examine police work – is an issue that needs to be addressed in Police Training Programmes as well as in the working organization of the police force itself.

Notes

1 This chapter is a revised version of an article that has previously been published in Swedish (Agevall & Jenner, 2006). It is based on an eclectic theoretical approach, in which public organizations' multi-functionality is the starting-point for the analy-

sis of the demands on the police role as described in police research (by e.g. Skolnick, 1994; Ekman, 1999; Granér, 2004). The reasoning is linked to Lipsky's (1980) theory regarding street-level bureaucrats and research about 'competence in action' (e.g., Schön, 1983; Ellström,1998).

2 Contradictory demands on the police may be seen as tension *between* the police and organization, and as tension within the 'police role' – tension *within*.

3 *Knowing how* is understanding linked with that which varies (cf. Aristotle's concept *phronesis*) and deals with attention, perception, and judgment. Know-how understanding can provide a full picture – an understanding of units, patterns, and contexts. It is context-based and transmitted by examples, stories, maxims, analogies, etc. Reflection and dialogue are important for knowledge development. Reflection in this sense means that individuals distance themselves from and try to problematize what they already know. This means speaking quietly within. Rolf, Ekstedt & Barnett (1993, p. 68, our trans.) maintain that reflection 'is a process in which one distances oneself from the knowledge that is expressed by others or oneself. Reflection opens the way to processing: one defines, investigates alternatives, studies cause and effect, weighs pros and cons.' Dialogues as well as reflections are ways to reorganize knowledge.

This may be seen as a contrast to *knowing what*, which is universal context-free knowledge – logical knowledge – which is regulated and based on connections, terms, regulations, and what these entail. Logical knowledge is analysed in a step-by-step process (cf. Aristotle's concept *episteme*). This is knowledge that individuals acquire via literature, lectures, etc.

4 'Competence means the ability to reflect and – via criticism and visions – renew one's traditional work. Competence requires a wide public debate in the work field in order to raise mutual awareness regarding the problem areas of the occupation and how to possibly solve them' (Rolf, Ekstedt & Barnett, 1993, p. 72).

5 At the same time, writes Bittner, the police force expressed that they had not been thinking along these lines. They were not aware of how these standards ruled their work.

The professions define to a great extent the standard or rules that apply to the assessment of their work. However, no profession has a complete 'knowledge monopoly'. Comments are also provided by, for example, citizens and other professions (Rolf, Ekstedt & Barnett, 1993, p. 40).

6 A socially tight-knit couple is something other than technical. Weick and Roberts (1993) maintain that common accidents are more likely to be caused by social processes that one does not comprehend rather than by technical mistakes. 'Inadequate comprehension can be traced to [a] flawed mind rather than flawed equipment... Reliable performance may require a well-developed collective mind in the form of a complex, attentive system tied together by trust' (p. 378).

7 The Police Authority defined the term *activist* as a 'person who committed or prepared crime on the 11th to 16th of June in 2001 in Gothenburg,' but this term is also used in a broader sense, according to Oskarsson (2002, p. 111).

Preamble

The concept 'time-formative' provides us with knowledge of what new demands on the organization of working hours have been created by recent school reforms. It helps us see that new stress fields have developed between profession and organization, leading to an increased fragmentation of teachers' work, among other things, in the form of 'intermittent work'. The chapter is built on material collected in the research project *Teachers' work planning*, funded by the Swedish Research Council.

Carola Aili

Time-formatives
and intermittent work

School and teachers' work in practice

Introduction

Questions about what teachers are supposed to do in their working hours and how much time various types of teachers' work actually take and are allowed to take have long been central in discussions between teachers and the State. In a conference arranged by Swedish municipalities and county councils on this issue, one principal, a propos all that teachers claim they work on, sighed and said, 'We don't need to have names for everything, do we? Surely it's enough to look at all the work as pedagogical work.'

The principal was insisting that keeping the different types of jobs apart was the very thing that was making difficulties. It is an interesting remark. It demonstrates that when the school as an organization is going to manage different forms of teachers' work, it is considered to be more efficient the fewer categories one has to work with. When individual teachers are going to perform the work, however, they have a need to categorise the work effectively, according to what is needed in the form of time, type of time, space and tools. The school as an organization has one rationality and the teachers' professional mandate another. The statement from this principal shows how, within the world of the school, other parties attempt to gain power over the work by preventing teachers from giving their own account of their work. His statement is an attempt to counter the teachers' reports of stress as a consequence of their being constantly interrupted and never having time to finish anything. The principal was suggesting an alternative understanding: If the entire work teachers do were considered to be one and the same activity, pedagogical activity, then they would never be interrupted. Lack of time could in that perspective only arise as a result of an idea about a demarcation between projects related to a specific entity of time. This chapter, however, is an argument for there being actual stress fields, stress fields about which we may have ideas but on which our influence is limited.

If we view the stress fields as actual, we can develop new ways of looking at school development. To a large extent, school development projects and reforms have been a matter of getting teachers to apportion their working hours differently. In Sweden, for example, it has been a matter of getting teachers to put more time into work on basic values and into collaboration with colleagues. How the 'new' time for this work is to be created has seldom been treated in reform documents and contracts. If the stress fields that are pointed out here are conditions that individual teachers are hardly able to change, then reforms may come to nothing because individual teachers are not able to create the kind of time that is needed. Instead, from a professional perspective, school development could be a matter of the organization's striving to make it easier for the teachers to do what they are already trying to do. This type of school development project would involve bringing about an institution in which the organization supports the teachers' duties.

Ideally, an organization provides the individual professional with strength by offering a number of supports and resources (cf. Ahrne, 2000; Svensson, 1990). The profession provides the individual with support in a similar way, through the profession's accumulated knowledge, for instance, or through the identity and the ethics the profession offers. Professions as well as organizations have an interest in time management, in questions of how activities are most appropriately arranged in time or how various activities are prioritised in time for optimal administration. Some researchers maintain that the possibilities for teachers to shape their work themselves have decreased and that the profession's independence has been called into question (Lundahl, 2003), or that their influence has decreased but their work still differs so markedly from contract work that, in comparison with other occupational groups, it is still relevant to regard them as independent (Murphy, 1999). Others maintain that the possibilities for influence have increased and that the teachers have greater prospects for designing their work themselves (Carlgren & Marton, 2000). Rothstein speaks of professional bureaucracies, where power is found to a large extent within a group of the professionals themselves (Rothstein, 1991). The teachers did not and do not have sole control of the overall goals of their work, over its social purposes, over guidelines and policy. Today the mandate of teachers is a negotiated and compromised mandate to which teachers must relate under the conditions of their work at school.

The teaching profession, to use Murphy's words, is not proletarianised but bureaucratised (Murphy, 1990). Even if the teachers to a large extent have a monopoly on teaching in school, they have a bureaucratic apparatus around them and, as Ahrne (1994) maintains, 'What you gain in access to resources and possibilities by organizational affiliations you lose in autonomy and independence' (p. 35). Those professionals, according to Ahrne, must sacrifice portions of their autonomy. The situation in which Swedish teachers find themselves today is a situation in which reforms of the school system are constantly replacing each other and in which new operating systems are constantly taking shape (Aili & Brante, 2007). Often they come in contradictory forms in which processes of decentralising and centralising are going on simultaneously. Management by objectives has increased at the same time that economic tightening and cutbacks have hit the schools; this is accompanied by a rhetoric about teachers' work that is expressed in terms of flexibility, responsibility and professionalism at the same time that it entails their constantly being given new mandates and new areas of responsibility. This is a development that appears to encompass large parts of the western world and has already been under discussion for decades as the intensification of the teaching profession (Sarfatti-Larson, 1980; Apple, 1989; Hargreaves, 1994; Day, 2000; Grundy & Bronser, 2000; Aili & Brante, 2007).

Teachers' work has changed, as much other work has changed. Fragmentation is one such change that manifests itself in a number of different ways for the individual. One does not have time to make oneself familiar with all information, only certain fragments, and one does not have influence and control over an entire process or issue, only over small parts. There is not enough time to finish tasks, and so one must divide them up and do them off and on, inserted amongst other things, since one has control over only small segments of one's working hours. Nor does one have shared breaks with colleagues over an extended period so that one is able to develop relationships and knowledge; people run into each other irregularly, and work colleagues are replaced frequently. The fragmentation of work life demands a flexible person, a person who does not need to build long-lasting relationships, who is not interested in long-term goals and who assumes responsibility for his or her own activity (cf. Sennett's discussion of fragmentation, Sennett, 1998). The professional mandate of the teacher, on the other hand, requires good relations with pupils, which take time to build, meaning that the teacher works for the long term as one part of the pupils' world. A number of other teachers, other professionals, parents and friends also exert an influence on situations at school. The fragmentation of working hours generates a specific stress between the teachers' mandate and the organization, something that the individual teacher must develop strategies to handle.

What do teachers do to handle circumstances where they are often disturbed by interruptions and where they often have difficulty finding time to finish? As far as the location of the work in time and space is concerned, this has repeatedly been a central issue in the negotiations on working hours between the teachers' union and the state trough Swedish Local Authorities and County Councils. The question of what kind of time teachers need in order to do a good job is also central and often discussed when changes are to be implemented. When working-hour reforms are implemented there are often a number of different, simultaneous consequences. In the 1990s, for example, a policy specifying the number of hours of work that must be done on-site at the workplace was inaugurated in Sweden.[1] This decreases the teachers' options to take work home but at the same time increases their presence in school and, with that, their accessibility and opportunity to work with other staff. With less chance to work at home and a greater number of on-site working hours, questions about the opportunity to be able to work undisturbed have been stirred up, and many people report constant interruptions in their work as burdensome.

The school principal who was quoted in the introduction was saying quite simply that everything would have been simpler if there were only a single form of teachers' work, not a number of different ones that were differently weighted, that required different amounts of time, different types of time and different types of rooms. If all work were looked on as a single 'pedagogic job' then a number of discussions and demands on organizing would be hard to legitimate. One can of course understand the irritation of the principal at the teachers' points of view about how the expenditure of time for various tasks should be assessed, but this is unavoidably one of the most important issues, and with the decentralization processes that have been taking place in Swedish schools, more and more time will have to be devoted instead to organizing and job sharing: What is going to be done? By whom? When? Where and how? The organization provides assistance, in a limited sense, in determining what is going to be done and how it is going to be organized, but at the same time the organization limits and shapes what is possible.

What happens when a profession is bureaucratised and, at the same time, the practitioners of the profession are charged with practicing and organizing their work independently? Might it mean that teachers are becoming more occupied by the institutional problems than by the pedagogical workday? Does the teachers' use of time proceed from the pedagogical challenges or from the challenges the local organization of work confronts them with? Do they have to take time from preparing instruction to constantly discuss their work situation with the principal?

On the temporality of teachers' work, on time-formatives and intermittence

Teachers have to arrange their working hours and they have to keep to the time arrangements. Different components of the teacher's work require different forms of time arrangements. These act on the teacher as inherent time-formatives. They are inherent in the sense that they logically must follow in certain sequences, have a certain time scope and, if necessary, happen in a certain place. There are other forms of time-formatives as well. The school as an organization is supposed to coordinate the activities of a number of individuals and in addition has its own projects and goals and consequently has to manage time. The organization's shaping of time acts on the teacher as organizational time-formatives. But projects that the organization is pursuing can also have an effect on the teachers' time, even if unintentionally. This too constitutes one kind of organizational time-formative.

Meaning making is not the main interest of time-geography but it seems impossible to study interruptions in teacher's work without also addressing the issue of the local creation of meaning. The intention, however, is to point out what stresses may arise between organization and the professional mandate, here studied as organizational time-formatives and inherent time-formatives.

Time-geography gives us a number of law-like propositions. These describe the temporal and spatial scope within which everything must be enacted. Of necessity these are determined, for example, by sequential arrangements, by coordination with other people, by coordination in space, thereby creating patterns and life-paths, which are called *trajectories* (see e.g. Hägerstrand, 1974). From the perspective of a 24-hour day, the maximum time-space for a teacher consists of 24 hours multiplied by the space that is accessible to the teacher in the course of those hours. In this time-space the teacher must in fact accomplish the teaching work, and in this time-space teachers will experience interruptions in their projects which they will perceive as disruptive elements in their work. To look at the work of teaching in a time-geographic manner involves looking at the teacher as acting intentionally, as someone who has a number of different specific projects. The focus, however, is not on intention but on the conditions required for it, and on what intentions those requirements make possible.

Project is time-geography's concept for the process in which an individual or group tries to achieve something. When a collective or an organization is working jointly to bring something about, time-geography speaks of the *activity bundle* (Hägerstrand, 1970). The essence of education in itself can be regarded as one such collective project with a number of different activity bundles (Hägerstrand & Lenntorp, 1974). Projects always require a certain time in order to be carried out. Moreover, as a rule all projects compete with other projects. Projects always have an *inherent time*. Given that something is to be done under given conditions, it will take a certain time. Given that an absence report is to be entered in a class-book when the lesson starts and four pupils are absent, it takes barely a minute. Given that an absence report is to be entered in a computer that is in a workroom one flight of stairs below, it takes four minutes including log-in. This is a matter of the same project, but it is enacted in different types of time-space, with different types of artefacts. Interruptions must involve people's projects getting interrupted, given what they regard as a project. Just as in everyday life, interruptions in work may occur frequently, but not necessarily as problematic, at least not as long as we have time to resume what we were doing and get it done to our satisfaction.

For the purpose of examining interruption, the concept 'intermittence' is used here (presented for the first time in Aili & Brante, 2004). *Intermittent work* is all forms of division in the work's operation which mean that the project is not accomplished in one sweep but that other projects are woven in, regardless of whether it is a question of one's involuntarily being interrupted or whether one chooses to divide the work up or whether the nature of the work is such that of necessity it cannot be accomplished in one continuous period.

Time-formatives are forces the teachers have to manage. They can be conceptualised as work conditions. Here a distinction is made between organizational time-formatives, such as the teachers' schedules, centrally established deadlines, fixed meeting times, etc., and inherent time-formatives. Hägerstrand (1974) is of the opinion that projects and processes always have inherent time, that they have an extension in time but also often have an inherent sequentiality. A seed that germinates under optimal conditions has its germination time, but even a seed that finds itself in less optimal conditions has a germination time. The germination always happens in fixed sequences, the shell of the seed splitting before the sprout develops, the sprout developing before the first leaf-pair appears, etc. This is outside our immediate possibility to influence. People's projects also have inherent time. Of necessity, unlocking a door takes time and is performed in a certain order: the key is brought out, pushed into the lock, turned, etc. Of necessity, developing, carrying out and following up a project on gender equality at school require not only a certain time but also a certain sequentiality and particular forms of time, for instance, that groups of teachers have time together, that teachers have time on their own to read texts with concentration, that gender-equality issues are given time in team meetings, and so forth. In this sense the equality project has inherent time, which acts on those involved as a time-formative, that is, as an inherent time-formative.

The concepts 'intermittence' and 'time-formative' help us note specific forms of sequentiality that tend to create problems in working life. They also call our attention to forces that variously affect people's actions in such a way that these often undesired forms of sequentiality arise. The aim of this chapter is to show that the concepts 'organizational time-formatives' and 'inherent time-formatives' make it possible for us to gain knowledge of how work, of greater or lesser necessity, becomes intermittent. This type of knowledge, together with knowledge about the creation of meaning that takes place around time, is important, in part for the purpose of being able to see how individuals' work takes shape in the stress field between profession and organization.

If we inspect the workday of teachers, it is full of intermittence. The teacher, let us say, is introducing the Nordic countries as a topic when some pupil asks if the physical training instructor has recovered or if they are going to have a substitute. After an interruption the teacher returns to the introduction. The teacher is interrupted for the third time while sitting down to test a new computer program. This time it is a colleague who reminds him that she has not received information before the developmental conversation she is going to hold. Activities with different purposes and separate rationalities are woven into one another in this way. There emerges a swarm of activities of which the majority are intermittent, are interrupted and taken up again. Yet in some way we can experience this at the same time as an incessant stream of activities. Thus the fact that different activities are intertwined with one other need not, in itself, be a problem. But something in the daily working life of teachers causes them to be put into a great many problem-generating interruptions. Intermittent work may be one of the manifestations of the new time management that the teachers' new mandate has brought with it and may even be a contributing cause to the fact that in thirty years the teachers of Sweden have gone from being one of the healthiest bodies of professionals to one of the most unwell (Alexanderson, Brommels, Ekenvall, Karlsryd, Löfgren, Sundberg, & Österberg, 2005).

Time-formatives are thus forces outside the individual which that person must relate to in dealing with the time-space. The most interesting time-formatives, from a perspective of organization, are those the organization creates, since, in principle, these are possible to change. Other time-formatives, e.g. inherent time-formatives, are difficult to change, but they are linked to the teachers' mandate. New teachers' mandates, naturally enough, yield new inherent time-formatives. The concept 'inherent time-formative' helps us see what type of time various activities actually need. It is possible to identify other forms of time-formatives, e.g. *biological time-formatives*. Things of this sort, such as visits to the toilet, food intake or sleep, can make it necessary to take breaks and interrupt ongoing activity, particularly if they have a long extension in time. However, biological time-formatives have not been focused on in this chapter.

The interests of the profession and the organization do not support one another automatically. The premise here is that there can be a stress between the organizational time-formatives and the inherent time-formatives, in the way the organization draws people together or apart, for example, and the way different projects require getting hold of people or working in peace and quiet at the same time. In the case study presented here, the point of departure is that a teachers' mandate exists. A teachers' mandate is always under negotiation, where certain responsibilities and certain tasks are self-evident, while disagreement may prevail regarding others. Conversely, the organization can instead, when it is a force that supports the teacher's intentions, cause the teacher's autonomy to be strengthened.

The case study deals with three mandates that the teachers in the study regard, in self-evident fashion, as their responsibility. These deal with 'reporting absence', 'going after absences' and preparing and conducting developmental conversations. Whatever strategy the teacher chooses, it tends sooner or later to lead to ill health. It is fully possible, of course, in the situation that has arisen, to inquire after knowledge about the way teachers best handle the stress fields that new forms of organization and teachers' new mandates are generating, i.e. to individualise the complex of problems. Another interesting question is how, on the whole, we can understand organization and teachers' mandates in terms of time-formatives. This kind of knowledge gives us the possibility to change the organization so that it harmonises to a greater degree with the teachers' mandate, but it also affords the possibility to challenge the reasonableness of various teachers' mandates.

Material and data generation

In order to further investigate the fragmentation of teachers' work, a body of information is used from a longitudinal study of how teachers organize their work and deal with situations of inadequate time. Over a three-year period, sixteen teachers working in school years 1–12 were interviewed in detail about their preceding days of work and about the current period of work in relation to other parts of the year. The interviews were held on one to three occasions per term in order to cover different work episodes in the course of a school year and in the course of a three-year period. Of the sixteen teachers, eight teach in 'grundskola' (nine-year compulsory school), and eight in 'gymnasieskola' (comprehensive upper secondary school), where five are teachers of core subjects and three are teachers of programme-specific subjects.

All sixteen teachers have elements of intermittent work every day during the research. Tasks and activities are divided up to be done at different times, and the teachers are interrupted and must reprioritise. The amount of intermittent work varies. Certain teachers appear to be subject to an extreme number of interruptions that they talk about as being unable to control, and they simultaneously perceive these as having consequences for those projects they consider truly important. In an explorative analysis of small scope, it is an advantage if all the teachers are working in the same kind of instruction. For this reason the three teachers of programme-specific subjects were selected; all three teach subjects in which proficiency training is a central part of the instruction. Unplanned interruptions can occur in everything teachers do. There are examples in the whole body of information of everything from time-consuming work like handling a burglary in a changing room, or even a death, to quickly-resolved interruptions like answering whether a colleague is present today or lending a catalogue to a pupil. As a rule, the interruptions are manifestations of two or more projects that collide in the time-space, and the teacher must prioritise. At the same time, of course, one can debate whether the teacher is supposed to deal with thefts as yet another project and if so, how and in what way. In this chapter, we investigate developmental conversations and work involved in going after absences. Not everything teachers do, however, is as self-evident as the work on developmental conversations.

In the case analysis, teachers Eva, Ann and Tom (fictitious names) are introduced and analysed. Then we discuss the question of how one determines intermittence and time-formatives. The following scenario took place during the first interview with Eva.

Determining intermittence and time-formatives

Eva is a teacher in an arts activity. After one interview with her during the first term in the study, she and the interviewer are going to pick up her work schedule. They walk through the school after leaving the room in which the interview was held. Four times Eva meets people who need to talk with her. First, she encounters the principal and introduces the interviewer. Eva takes the opportunity to exchange a few words with the principal about the technical equipment in the photo lab. She then meets pupils once and colleagues twice. The pupils say they are going to be late for class the next day. Eva talks with the pupils for a moment about what remains to be done in their projects and what they will have time to do before the term ends. The first colleague talks about a meeting they are going to have and the second takes care of some practicalities about a collaboration that the arts teachers have with the history teachers. The transit from one place to the other takes nearly a quarter of an hour. The interviewer experiences this as if they have been interrupted the entire time on the way to the workroom but Eva says nothing to indicate that she experiences herself being interrupted. The interviewer asks how common it is for her to be caught by other people like this and is given the answer that it is typical: 'As soon as you show yourself, there's someone who needs to talk with you,' Eva responds, without calling attention to it as especially problematic.

The concept 'intermittent work' is intended to designate the fragmented work, the chopped-up work, where interruptions or reprioritisations cause one to constantly have to shift focus. The example, however, shows in part the difficulties in determining what, for instance, an interruption is and in part the way different people may behave towards the interruptions. What the interviewer perceives as interruption the informant perceives as the normal flow, and what the interviewer perceives as reprioritisation the informant perceives as interruption. The term 'interruption' places the emphasis on the external force, whereas the term 'reprioritisation' places the power rather on the internal force. In the latter case, one may view the situation as one where the teacher makes a choice: Eva 'chooses' to stop and exchange some words with the principal. If, instead, the external force is emphasised, we would say that the teacher is being interrupted: e.g., Eva is interrupted by the principal's arrival.

Is it relevant to presuppose the teacher as having either an active choice on the teacher's part or being a passive victim of the circumstances? Might it rather be a manifestation of a time strategy the teachers have developed for the purpose of getting their work accomplished despite inadequate time-space? Eva has a number of things she must arrange with the principal. They are on her mental 'to-do list' and are activated when she sees the principal. In order to get them done she must seize the opportunity of the chance encounter. This is what she and others in this study do. The teachers settle joint matters when they run into each other. As time starts growing short they move to actively seeking each other out, and if that does not work either, then the work does not get done. This applies particularly when the teachers' projects have definitive deadlines. From a time-geographic perspective one can note that Eva has several projects going on, and the more projects the greater the risk that they will collide in the time-space. Eva's situation could be said, time-geographically, to be a matter of her and the principal's time-space trajectories crossing one another. The more people there are in motion in a limited area, the greater the likelihood that they will encounter each other and deal with things that concern joint projects, in spite of the fact that this disturbs other projects that are going on.

What, then, are the teachers' projects? Eva's meeting with the principal actualises several projects: (1) her work with the school newspaper on the Web; (2) her participation in a research project that she wants to tell the principal about; (3) her responsibility for the photo lab continuing at the same time as the project she started in connection with the interview which is going on; (4) going to her workroom to get her schedule. If she had not had these projects, she would not have spoken with the principal, nor the principal with her, but now some of their projects are included in the same activity bundles. Nor would the conversation have taken place if she had not encountered the principal there in the corridor. From a time-geographic perspective, it is, if anything, the number of projects and her and the principal's coinciding trajectories that generate the intermittence. An organization, through bringing trajectories together or keeping them apart, can create or prevent intermittence. The more projects are initiated and maintained, and the more simultaneous activity bundles are created in an organization, and the more transits from place to place and opportunities for chance meetings there are, the greater the risk of intermittent work and of collisions in the time-space. This becomes an inherent time-formative that teachers, especially teachers with a lot of projects, must of necessity deal with.

In order to get closer to intermittence and intermittence-generating time-formatives, the study analyses projects that the teachers are carrying on and that all teachers in the body of information regard as obvious parts of the teachers' mandate, such as developmental conversations.

Working with developmental conversations

A common task of Swedish teachers is preparing and holding developmental conversations with pupils and parents.[2] The teacher is often responsible for a number of pupils, alone or together with someone else, in the capacity of 'form teacher' or 'mentor'. To a large extent, form teachers in school years 1–6 have the class alone, but there are often handicraft teachers or physical training instructors, for instance, who are involved and will provide their assessments to the form teacher. Subject teachers in school years 7–12 are responsible for their own developmental conversations but are also involved in those of other teachers, since they must provide information on all the pupils they have. The three cases and their work on developmental conversations are presented below.

Eva

Eva's school has no form-teacher system; every teacher is a mentor for a certain number of pupils, with whom developmental conversations are held. For Eva, the first year involves some twenty pupils. The fifth interview with Eva is held in December, which she considers a 'heavy month', but then she says after a moment's reasoning, 'November is tougher because you've got the developmental conversations at that time and then it's the planning before you can level off in December. So November is worst' (Eva). For Eva, the developmental conversations are bound up with her duties as a mentor. Eva says that, with the pupils, they do not actually refer to the events as developmental conversations: 'We don't do that because the pupils have hated developmental conversations since the senior level of the "grundskola", so we call it something else, "having coffee with you and your parents", or something like that.' Eva talks about how her 'classes' no longer actually exist. Quite simply, one cannot reach everyone in a class because 'they're almost never all together'. This is due to the large number of individual curriculum options but is also connected with the level-grouping they are working with, which means that pupils in the same class may have three different teachers in maths. This also means that it is not simple to reach all of one's pupils' teachers. Each pupil may have a unique set of teachers.

The developmental conversations are preceded by the teachers' having what is called a *mid-term conference*. It appears not to be easy for Eva to get information from all the teachers. Eva starts collecting information from the pupils' various teachers two weeks before the mid-term conference, and after the mid-term conferences the developmental conversations are held. During one interview she says, 'We were actually supposed to have had the mid-term conference this Tuesday, but it's been postponed. And then of course all the teachers are supposed to, and I don't think I've received reports from the English teacher... yes, orally... a little bit from [the] Swedish [and] history [teachers].' Despite the fact that she had put out a request two weeks before the mid-term conferences she has not yet received information from everyone. Eva says that she usually goes through one pupil's information at a time but that this cannot be done during the day between classes. She does not think it works to tuck them in between. It needs too long a time. A great deal of work is done, therefore, after the day's classes or at home in the evenings. Eva must sequence the task of information gathering from the pupils' teachers because not everyone responds to her e-mail in the appointed time and because some want to submit oral reports. She must also sequence the assessments since there is not room to go through everyone in one sweep. Booking the times must also be sequenced if everyone does not respond in time or if parents and pupils cannot come at the offered time.

Preparing developmental conversations is evidently not a task that can be done in one sweep in the course of one day, regardless of whether it concerns a single pupil's conversation or the conversations of a group of pupils. Setting a time requires contact with parents and pupils, a process that may take a week or more. The analysis of assembled information can also take time, and the teacher may need to ponder the assessments, suggestions for measures to take, and perhaps also consider how various issues should be raised and discussed so as to yield best results. Developmental conversations have inherent time-formatives that result in the work having to take place intermittently, spread out over time.

Tom

Tom works in a school with a form-teacher system. He is a form teacher in two classes when the study begins. The classes are small, only seven pupils in school year 11 and seven in school year 12. He has conversations with all fourteen pupils in his classes. In Tom's workplace they have a system with a file folder for each pupil: 'The pupil's entire folder is sitting there, with tests, with problems, in fact everything is there. We put papers in there as we go along, always. So it's collected for when the parents come. Then we can just take it out and show notes I've made on the situation and the development. And it's followed up [...] and then all their theoretical tests are there. Then their programme choices are there' (Tom). Tom says that he puts things in and tends to the files from time to time. He does this more coherently on the Wednesdays when he has on-site working-hours but does not teach, or on days his visits to on-the-job-training sites in the community do not take the entire day, but he also sometimes does it in the evening. He has the developmental conversations outside his teaching, primarily in the evening. Tom says that as a rule the only preparation he needs before a conversation is to look through the folder. He also says that he knows all the pupils well and that he meets their other teachers continually at breaks and lunch. He experiences himself as knowing where he has the pupils. Tom compiles information and makes assessments for developmental conversations in a single ten- to fifteen-minute sweep before the conversation takes place. The systematic set up of pupil documents means that the developmental conversations have only the simple sequence: booking of time – assessment – conversation – decision.

Ann

Ann has developmental conversations with close to thirty pupils, and school-report conversations in courses for adult pupils besides. At Ann's workplace they have no regular telephones. They have one mobile phone that everyone shares and that they 'have to hunt round for'.

This results in her often trying to phone from home in the evenings and parents phoning her at home in the evenings as well. There are extra conversations when times for developmental conversations have to be changed. At the time of one interview Ann had been having developmental conversations on afternoons while she set the pupils to work on their own. She thinks it would be better to have the conversations in the evening, but she does not have time for this. The evenings are filled with planning work and she is going to be starting completely new courses.

During the second interview Ann says: 'And then I have my class and then after the class Jane and I talk a bit about this class, which we have jointly. And then I phone a parent who I'm going to have a developmental conversation with.' When I ask Ann what she spoke with Jane about, whether it had to do with planning, Ann replies: 'Since Jane is a computer teacher, we sort of don't have anything in common to have a discussion about, exactly. But this had to do with the pupils and these developmental conversations that we're working on. Because in fact it's a hassle. Certain parents don't come when we have developmental conversations, and then we're supposed to phone and then book a new time and when will we book the time for, or shall we just have a telephone conversation? So that's probably what it was about that time. There was a pupil whose parents hadn't come. No message, either ... just didn't come.'

The practical routine work has many twists and turns. Ann has to write letters with times she is offering – send the letters with the pupils – get the answers from pupils and parents – possibly offer a new time – communicate to the colleague with whom she shares space that she will be having conversations in their common workroom – ring and book a new time with parents who failed to appear. Moreover, it becomes apparent that the conversations themselves might be interrupted, with all that this involves. During the interview with Ann, the second term of the period of the study, she sighs and says that even the developmental conversations with pupils and parents are impossible to carry out without interruption. The day before, she had had a developmental conversation and had got the pupils underway in their work. She is sitting with a parent and a pupil when she sees through the window that several pupils are standing outdoors smoking. She says that she excuses herself, breaking off the conversation to go outside and bring the pupils back to the classroom. Five minutes later, she is back in her workroom with the waiting parent and pupil to resume the developmental conversation. She expresses despair that she is never able to do a good job.

One part of Ann's work involves doing an analysis of the pupil's development and possible needs, and may have this sequencing: urge current teachers to submit information – urge pupil and parents to come with viewpoint on what to talk about – assemble information and viewpoints received and do assessments – carry out developmental conversations – make decisions, if any. In addition, Ann may be interrupted in any part of the sequences, even during developmental conversations. Since Ann is a form teacher along with a colleague, parts of the assessments are also of necessity sequenced and separated in time, since she must adjust herself to the opportunities that exist to talk over issues with the other form teacher.

Developmental conversations do not happen only on these organized occasions, however. Through the years it becomes apparent that many conversations take place towards the end of term when the pupils start to realise that they have problems:

Excerpt 1

Ann: [...] So that it got terribly stressful here because suddenly I had a number of pupils outside here and I said, I don't have time for so many. Because later they in their turn were going to begin a new class at 10.40. So that between 10.15 and 10.40 I'd intended to take a little coffee break. I had to see that the lecturer got away because I also had to get a little information from her... a fee and a few things like that. I managed that, in fact, after 10.15. But then when I got there, the pupils were standing outside. So then I had to take care of them or talk with them, as many as I had time for. They wanted to look at their projects, didn't they, and I had written evaluations. But in any case it took time, so I said I don't have time for so many.

Interviewer: That means it's a job you have to carry on with?

Ann: Yes, I've got to do it. Now they're coming again next Monday. And later, when they were done, two pupils from form two were standing outside wanting to discuss marks in a basic medical course, which ends at Christmas and where they're a bit shabby. So they wanted to know a little bit what to do to be able to raise their mark, retake a test and so on. So there was a discussion about that. It's always like this towards the end of the term. Suddenly the pupils wake up and realise that, oops, I expect I've got to pull my socks up here if I want to get a certificate. It's that which is, everything comes suddenly then, the bad conscience over them. Now I've got to make an extra effort here to get a good mark.

For Ann, guiding pupils on issues concerning their development in general and in specific subjects is something that takes place in many contexts over and above the developmental conversations.

Intermittence-generating time-formatives and developmental conversations

Seen from a time-geographic perspective, developmental conversations are almost a separate form of activity bundle at school, assembled for a limited period of time every term. This means that a number of trajectories are coordinated during this time for the purpose of bringing about developmental conversations. Further, once the time for the conversations is set, the teacher has a deadline to work against (for a longer discussion of deadlines in teachers' work see Aili & Brante, 2004). Preparations of developmental conversations are a matter of collecting and systematising information from a number of people; in many cases conversations may also be necessary for the purpose of investigating a pupil's situation. The teachers need to analyse their material, make an assessment of what is problematic and consider what measures may be of immediate importance.

Holding developmental conversations is an integral part of the professional mandate of the teacher. Here the teacher is to assess the pupil's learning in relation to course objectives and educational achievement objectives in the teaching plan, and to suggest measures for improving the fulfilment of objectives. Even the pupil's general situation in school and relations with school friends are made into objects for assessment. This requires time in order to be able to study the documentation about the pupil and reflect on possible measures to take, something that may have to happen in dialogue with other school staff. The *inherent time-formatives* of the developmental conversations are further characterised by *fixed sequentialities*. First the conversations must be booked and prepared and then they can be held. There are expectations that pupil information will be submitted in time. If it is, the sequences run without intermittence being noticed. One could almost say that it is erased. Information that fails to appear creates discontinuity. The teacher has to act over and above the routine. The work plan is disrupted. Even though teachers realise that the quality is deficient when they lack information, the rules of the organization require that the developmental conversations be held, that class conferences be held, etc. On the one hand, teachers must deal with the organizational time-formatives, e.g. deadlines, but on the other, they must also produce well-substantiated assessments.

The cases show how the sequencing and its content can vary. It may imply that with the administering of time-booking, teachers gain new impetus to prepare the conversations or that they must make new contacts to confer privately with colleagues and school administrators. The partly unpredictable patterns of sequencing mean of necessity that work on developmental conversations has a number of different sub-elements that must stand separate in time. It is also the case that new issues which come up while the developmental conversations are in progress are not possible to prepare but may instead involve new measures on the teacher's part during workdays that follow, with subsequent feedback to pupils and parents, events that also must happen in a fixed order. The teacher cannot give the feedback about the possibility of extra support in mathematics before the teacher has investigated the possibility.

Thus, for two of the teachers, the project of preparing developmental conversations is of necessity spread out in time, off and on, as small sub-projects. But what is it, then, that leads to these sub-projects, already spread out in time, being further interrupted in themselves, or having to be made intermittent? A number of organizational time-formatives enter in here. Several of them are tied directly to reforms. Organizational time-formatives that can be identified in the narratives of the interviewed teachers are described below. The time-formatives are handled by teachers in such a way that their work on developmental conversations is constantly mixed with other work, both because the teachers themselves in one sense choose to tuck such work into 'gaps', and because they are more or less forced to divide the work up and tuck it into 'gaps' because no other way is possible, since there is no continuous period of time to be had or because colleagues are not accessible and are not possible to control.

Work on developmental conversations can be said to have two components. On the one hand, it is a matter of simple routine work, of booking time and space and assembling information, and on the other, of making assessments and pedagogical deliberations and possibly making decisions about advice or measures to take.

Individualisation and developmental conversations

A great number of *individual options* and different types of *level-groupings* have characterised the school's organization of instruction in recent decades. The individual options have been a way to shape pupils' influence on their education, but they are used also as means of competition among comprehensive upper secondary schools. The particular options offered are politically determined and constitute one of the bases of the schools for creating curricula and distributing resources. Level-groupings are a means of creating more homogeneous instructional groups but also a means of allocating attention through the possibility of determining group sizes so that teaching time per pupil varies. However, these ways of organizing also operate as organizational time-formatives in more contexts than the teaching itself. With regard to developmental conversations, for instance, they involve far more complex demands on collegial coordination. The individual options shape time through the fact that pupils have more or less unique educational programmes, which means that the pupils the teacher is responsible for have extremely different constellations of teachers by whom they are being taught. The teacher must therefore contact more colleagues than previously, often in unique constellations around respective pupils.

Eva deals with this by spreading her information gathering over a two-week period, and during these weeks she must repeatedly occupy herself with it. This involves her sending out mail with her inquiry about time, something over which she has control, and receiving answers spread out over time, something over which she does not have control; however, she can decide when she will deal with them in relation to the spaces that come up. She speaks with teachers she runs into in the corridor or encounters in the staff room. There are certain elements of the preparations that Eva does not manage to 'tuck in between' because those elements require a longer continuous period of time and no organizational time-formatives exist that guarantee her that sort of time. For instance, she needs time to go through which teachers each pupil has so that this is included in the mail, and time to compile the information that comes in. Parents and pupils may have a need to change times. It also happens that the offered times do not work, and the teacher has to look for new times to offer. In a number of concrete ways, the increasing individualisation of the pupils' education, but also increased demands for respect for individual circumstances, become organizational time-formatives.

The teachers' geographical placement and developmental conversations

With those teachers who are close by, even in the same room, one has a continuing dialogue about the pupils. In the same way, Tom, who meets his pupils' other teachers every day, has continual contact with these teachers and knows what is working and what is problematic for his pupils in their various subjects. In certain cases, however, the geographical placement of teachers in the school contributes to the intermittence of their work on developmental conversations. The teachers simply do not get hold of each other, and time and again must fit in attempts to find the teachers they need to catch. For example, physical training instructors, who are to be found in the gymnasium, are hard to get hold of. In that case, the teacher interrupts other work or waits until the next day.

The teachers' schedules and developmental conversations

The teachers' schedules are an organizational formative, but does this contribute to intermittence in their work on developmental conversations? Teachers' schedules can yield an intermittence effect in the same way teachers' geographical placement does. Only in Tom's workplace do the teachers regularly have a break at the same time. Here too, getting hold of the people one needs to talk with is never experienced as a problem. As for the rest, during the period the teachers are working with developmental conversations it is a matter of 'chasing after people' or else being chased and stopped themselves when they are on their way somewhere.

Limited access to computers and developmental conversations

The limited access to computers and placement of computers means that a teacher who is sitting with e-mail from colleagues for the purpose of working on developmental conversations is under pressure at the same time from colleagues who also want to get at the computer. It may also be the computer's placement in a workroom shared with six others that causes the teacher to be interrupted by questions, by telephone calls, or by pupils who come on various matters.

The organization's deadlines and developmental conversations

The mid-term conference that Eva speaks of seems to function as a planning horizon for her, but not as an absolute deadline. It happens that she has not collected all the information before the conference. As times assigned grow close, the teachers seem to increase their intermittent work by inserting as much as will fit into various intervals. Even if one does not have time to finish, one has time for something, and the chance that one will have time to finish before the appointed time increases.

The stress field

The professional mandate to plan and hold developmental conversations makes demands on the possibility to organize the work on developmental conversations into fixed sequences and with fixed time intervals. The organization may insist on when the information is to be compiled, for the class conference/mid-term conference, for instance. Nonetheless, Eva has to go to the conference without having finished her compilation, and thus without a comprehensive picture of the situation of her various pupils. The individual teachers do not have control over their colleagues' work, nor over pupils and parents. This in turn makes demands on their ability to book premises when they have space to do it and getting access to computers when that is needed. The mandate makes demands on the possibility of giving concentrated deliberation to assessment issues and possible measures, along with the need to do this with other concerned staff. But this is not guaranteed, either, and so the teachers must leave work undone or increase its intermittence.

Ann's and Eva's organizational forms offer the teacher opportunities to do the work, but these do not necessarily recur at appropriate time intervals or have appropriate scope. The organization does not guarantee that one will reach colleagues one needs to get hold of, that the person who does room assignments is available when one needs him or that functioning computers are available. Nor does the organization offer guaranteed, undisturbed time for analysis and assessment.

Tom's organization offers a chance to collect information about the pupils continually during the term, a system used by all teachers of his pupils. This means that as a rule Tom does not need to ask teachers for information before the developmental conversation. It is already assembled. As the teacher is continually meeting the teachers his pupils have in their other subjects, he is continually getting an updated picture of his pupils' situation. He is also working continually with the pupil file folders. The organization has earmarked time for this. Still, it does not always suffice. The rooms are such that it is always possible to find undisturbed places to be in, but the organization does not offer guaranteed undisturbed time for analysis and assessment. It is unusual now for Tom to have to have to converse with pupils and parents over and above the developmental conversations: 'It might happen that you sit for half, three-quarters of an hour chatting with parents. It's like that some years, but in the last few years the social work with the pupils has decreased thanks to our having had so many applicants' (Tom).

Intermittence-generating time-formatives and reporting absences

A second analysis was performed on the three cases, this time to address the issue of reporting absences.[3] The professional mandate is to create a correct basis for the assessment and handling of pupils' absences. This requires that teachers have the opportunity to discover absence and report it as quickly as possible, so that those teachers who are accountable can make their assessments. Reporting absences has inherent time-formatives in that it is supposed to be done as soon as possible after an absence is discovered and, where appropriate, is to contain information on the cause of absence. There is also an inherent time-formative in the form of imperative sequencing. The teachers cannot submit the week's absences as early as Monday, nor can they wait until Friday to submit the entire week's absences in one sweep. The three teachers work in schools with computerised reporting of absences. Tom reports absences directly via the computer in the offices of the workshop premises. Ann and Eva share computers with colleagues. Ann says of the reporting, 'I think it's important for you to do it sort of immediately when you've had a class. Otherwise it's easy for you to forget it' (Ann). But Ann is not always able to work according to her intentions. In the course of interviews over the years Ann sometimes says that she had not had time to do absences but had to do them at the end of the day or the day after.

Individualisation

The increased pupil-centredness, with more individual options and a point of departure based more on the pupil's prior knowledge and situation with level-grouping and the like, appears to have had consequences for the teachers' work on reporting absences and act as organizational time-formatives. Eva describes it this way:

Excerpt 2

Eva: The school was smaller. There were more units. I mean, if you took the general studies programme, then you took the general studies programme. And in those days you had a form teacher who handed out the schedule and handed out the class list. And took care of attendance. And in those days the class was together. All the time. And they had a book with them, attendance-book, class-book, and you put absence and attendance in there. And that's how that got taken care of. But now they're almost never all together. Except they're together in a couple of core subjects. Maybe. Because sometimes they do level-groupings [and in that case they are not together in the core subjects, either; author's note]. […] There's no routine for absence, and a mentor has an awful job of trying to get people to report. Because in spite of everything we're supposed to keep track of the pupils.

Deficiencies in the infrastructure

Eva talks about how both she and pupils have to go round to teachers checking on absences and sorting out what's what. She works via the computer with an absence program that has major shortcomings and is sometimes even impossible to get into. One and a half years later Eva is still talking about the problem of getting her work on reporting absences to function. Of the software she says:

Excerpt 3

Eva: You bring up a little place and so the fixed number of pupils is there and then you [...] how many minutes of absence and then you mark an X and click and then you wait until the page loads and after that you bring it up and after that you're supposed to be able to see the pupil's absences, but at best you only get the name and number of hours in the subject, but not when, and mostly it's been wrong. It hasn't worked.

Interviewer: Wow.

Eva: You can't go in and look and you don't find out whether they've been on a medical leave of absence or what's happened with them. So it's a complete disaster.

Interviewer: But can't you print out how much absence the pupil has had?

Eva: Well, sure, how many hours in one subject, but it doesn't say anything about when or why she's been out that time. No free text or anything like that. Then, when we have been able to print out how many hours, it hasn't tallied. Students have come to me. 'It says here that I've been absent, but I haven't been,' and it's true, she hasn't.

Eva tells how they have marked X's in file folders for so long, waiting to be able to enter the absences when the technology has gone wrong. In practice, this has meant keeping double accounts. Eva says that as things are now, just before Christmas, there are 'a whole lot ill' and furthermore, a great deal is happening, so many pupils have excused absences, e.g. for chorus practice. The celebration of Christmas and the preparations leading up to it are in the school's cyclic temporality. These schedule-breaking activities act on the teacher as time-formatives. This increases the number of absences to report, so that more time has to be put into it at the same time that there is too little time and the intermittent work is increasing. Moreover, it is apparent that the sparse supply of computers, poor IT support and inadequate software shape the spreading out in time of their work on absences as the work is impossible to complete, becoming a job that is constantly in progress and that has to be inserted into a number of different situations in order to get done. Here the *organizational time-formatives* generate intermittence in the teachers' work on reporting absences, in opposition to their professional interest.

Increased complexity

The class-book Eva speaks of made reporting absence into part of the lesson. Absence was nothing one needed to commit to memory; when the class monitor put the book out on the teacher's desk, it was filled in. Now the teachers have to remember that absences are supposed to be written in and check reasons for absence with pupils who have not given notification of their absence. If one is interrupted on the way to the computer and a mass of other things show up, it may very well be that one forgets to record the absences, something that was not possible with the class-book system. Reporting absences has become a project that is performed everywhere in the school, no longer only in the classroom. Ideological decisions with new management rationalities and changes in technologies of management make a relatively simple task into not just a complex, constantly unfinished task, but also into an element that is quite evidently capable of generating frustration in individuals.

Once the reporting becomes a job that is performed across the entire school, the likelihood increases that trajectories will coincide in ways that suddenly lead to more absence reports competing for the time-space with a number of other projects. In essential respects reporting absences is a standardised routine, but one that demonstrably does not always allow itself to be carried out easily. Ann organizes her work on reporting absences intermittently, in the sense that she logs on to the computer several times a day to record absences after each class session. For the most part it works, and reporting absences seems to be something that is suited to doing in the intervals that come up during the day between otherwise locked-in activities, as long as the space is not filled by a number of competing projects.

Intermittence-generating time-formatives and the work of 'going after absences'

A third analysis was focused on what the teachers call 'going after absences'. This signifies projects with work on everything from making a single phone call, to years of pupil conversations, meetings with parents, pupil care and treatment conferences, cooperation with school welfare officers. It becomes apparent in this analysis that the time-formatives which were active in the projects 'preparing developmental conversations' and 'reporting absence' return also in projects that deal with 'going after absences'. This is due to the fact that many parts of the nature of teachers' work have similar 'inherent' time-formatives: the fact, for example, that these are not individual but group projects, thus requiring coordination among colleagues, with demands on possibilities of being able to get hold of people one needs to catch, and the fact, for example, that individualisation makes the processes difficult to standardise, predict and plan.

Further, 'going after' unauthorized absences in complicated cases was seen to involve inherent demands for concentration, focus in connection with analysis and processing of information, something that teachers often see themselves having difficulty getting time and space for. One day, all of Ann's work during her breaks dealt with 'going after absences'. As she was about to have some coffee in the late morning the special education teacher came in, wanting to discuss a pupil who had a great deal of work to make up. Ann recounts that she cannot say no and has to consider the fact that the special education teacher is at school only on certain days of the week, and then for a brief time. The next break Ann is supposed to take is the lunch break. At that time her work in connection to pupils with absences continues. The physical training instructor has had a conversation with the class about their high absenteeism:

Excerpt 4

Ann: During lunch, or before I started eating lunch, the physical training instructor came into the classroom wanting to discuss this second-year class. He's had a conversation with the class, and what's come out during this conversation. So he says, 'While you're heating your food in the microwave, can I talk with you a bit?' 'Yes, of course.'

He's in a hurry, too. So then there's a high-speed little discussion there, about important things actually, which I feel were very pressing and I really did want to hear from him how the discussion in the class had been. So that it turned into a bit more time than I'd imagined for that.

Then, when I finally got under way eating, the school welfare officer comes in. And she's going to meet a pupil in this class. It's a class that there are quite a few social problems in. And so she's going to meet a pupil at 1 o'clock and it's 12.45 and she has to get a little information about certain things. So she has to interrupt me while I'm sitting eating. I think I have difficulty saying, No, you can't. One has to do one's bit, somehow. It feels as if... so that it turns into a bit of a broken-up lunch. Then once I've eaten I pull out some overhead pages for this lesson I'm going to have at the end of the day. And then I've got my class and then after the lesson Britt [fictitious name] and I talk for a bit about this class, which we have jointly. And then I phone a parent who I'm going to have a developmental conversation with.

Ann would have liked to talk with the special education teacher, the physical training instructor and the school welfare officer in peace and quiet, but it takes place over food on her own breaks instead. Ann experiences this as stressful and trying, but what is most trying, according to Ann, is not the meal that did not happen in peace and quiet but the fact that she is uncertain about whether she is doing right and is doing enough for her pupils.

This case demonstrates that teachers need access to different kinds of time in order to be able to do their work in ways that they perceive as good. It is not simple to create that sort of time oneself. Instead, they are left to try to do their work with the kind of time the school makes available to them, and this may be when trajectories meet on their own lunch break. It is an organizational challenge to synchronise trajectories of teachers and other staff members at school in such a way that the staff, to the greatest extent possible, get the kind of time they need, alone and with one another. Organizational time-formatives like scheduling, distribution of rooms, etc. no longer suffice as organizational thinking for the new type of mandate teachers face. Collisions in the time-space are thus possible to point to as absolute. They exist as a greater or lesser necessity in the world of the school. But for all that, absence of collisions is something the teachers appreciate.

When Tom describes a good week, he says it is when 'the pupils' education is flowing along and they're taking part and doing their assignments and where nothing is falling apart. You don't need to phone around getting hold of things and details, that we have all the working material in stock if we need to weld or something [...] and that you don't need to sit in any pupil conversations and that you're not having difficulties with your colleagues [...] and that you get home on time.' What Tom is describing is a week without interruptions for unforeseen things that make difficulties in some other aim. Even if Tom does not know when things are happening, he is able, without major consequences for other work, to allow interruption or plan intermittent work. It is not necessarily the case that the interruptions in themselves pose problems for the teachers in the body of information; in fact, it is rather the content of the interruption, its extent in time and what consequences the interruption has for other activities that appear to be crucial for the way it is experienced.

With regard to absences, Tom's work has certain common principles of conduct in relation to time. It is short intervals of time that count. When it is discovered, the teacher is to prioritise the matter. These are tasks that come up chiefly at the beginning of the terms; later they occur more rarely, according to Tom, who says that he telephones pupils immediately when they do not show up in the morning. Student care and treatment tasks that come up unplanned are unusual on the whole in Tom's workday. They did not occur during the period the study was in progress. He says in addition that he holds adamantly to the principle that pupils who are late must check with classmates about what has been said if he has called the group together with information or a run-through and they missed it. Ann, on the other hand, has obligatory elements in her teaching that result in her having to arrange, again and again, new occasions for giving instruction to those who have been absent. Consequently, the content of the instruction may be composed of completely different kinds of inherent time-formatives that vary from subject teacher to subject teacher.

Intermittence-generating time-formatives and individualisation

Many reforms have had the purpose of increasing pupil influence, individualising the instruction and increasing the individual options with regard to school and educational content. It is shown in the foregoing analyses that individualisation creates time-formatives in different contexts. No unanimity prevails on exactly what individualisation in school is supposed to involve. That it can involve giving individual consideration to every pupil in the everyday work many may perhaps agree on, but where the boundaries lie with regard to this consideration is unclear. Individualisation which requires that the teacher acts and reacts immediately in interaction with the pupils and is prepared to be sensitive vis-à-vis the pupils' attitudes and needs, is of course work with inherent time-formatives that generate constant interruptions and, with that, intermittent work. Ann recounts, for example, how they had decided with the pupils that they would go to the cinema together. But going to the cinema with the pupils one evening is not just a question of putting in a few hours of work at night. The decision affects Ann's entire workday in the days before the cinema visit:

Excerpt 5

Ann: [...] we have bought cinema cheques and that's been a lot of hassle back and forth, at first they couldn't but then we are going to go, so can we go this evening, right? and then there are certain pupils who come and say, I can't go then, I won't get home and how are we going to solve that and I'm supposed to go to emergency and I'm supposed to go to the maternal care clinic and, sort of, things like that, so the pupils come into the corridor and catch me there, [...] Ann, I want to talk to you, I want to talk to you [...] Is it important, can it wait? [...] No, I've got to talk to you now [...] and so there I am, maybe on the way to something else and have planned ... something and so I get interrupted ... so I'm experiencing it terribly much now ... that you're getting interrupted by something all the time ... that somehow you never complete things without there being something that gets in between.

Teachers' work is predictable to a relatively low degree, something that Ann illustrates well above. Half of the work over and above instruction is unplanned and comes up spontaneously (Aili & Brante, 2007). This is due not only to the fact that teachers work with people whose conduct is unpredictable (cf. Lipsky, 1980; Hasenfeldt, 1983) but also to the fact that it is the mandate of the teacher to deal with pupils and teaching as if they were unpredictable; that is, the teacher is to regard pupils as heterogeneous, unique and unpredictable, with temporary states of mind, special life circumstances, etc., and one is to be prepared to allow the instruction and other activities to take unforeseen turns. Seeing pupils as unique individuals involves a different use of time than seeing pupils as a group with similar needs.

Intermittent work: as the tension between organization and profession

The reforms in schools are creating new projects that will take up time-space. New technology and new duties not only create demands for new working methods but also constitute new time-formatives in the teachers' workday. Time-formatives can be a useful analysis concept for understanding time management in working life, particularly in relation to change. Here it is used to distinguish between the organization's rationality through organizational time-formatives and the profession's rationality through the work's inherent time-formatives, and the chapter has shown that these rationalities can generate stress fields which the individual teachers are left to deal with. Interruptions are manifestations of collisions in the time-space, a number of different projects going on simultaneously. This means that teachers often have to deal with a tension between the time-space that the organization offers and the projects they have to accomplish. Both the time-space and the projects have changed. The time-space is to a greater degree a space in which the teacher is accessible on the one hand, but on the other hand has his own temporal trajectory, which may differ considerably from those of colleagues or pupils. At the same time, the projects are becoming increasingly numerous, particularly the activity bundles, and this makes demands on coordination and collaboration. The project also becomes increasingly independent of time and space; that is, it can be done whenever one likes and wherever one likes.

The cases also show examples of the fact that organizational time-formatives can harmonise with the professional mandate of the teacher. But it is impossible to exclude the fact that a new type of scarcity has most likely arisen in the teaching profession. This is the scarcity of long continuous sequences of time. For many teachers, getting work finished has become only a dream.

Studies of time-formatives are able to provide us with knowledge about what limitations teachers' professional freedom has and in what sense teachers can be said to plan and organize their work freely for the purpose of accomplishing their professional mandate. This explorative case study shows that the possibilities of accomplishing one's professional mandate vary. However, this is no argument for the growing intermittence being an individual phenomenon, something the teacher personally creates. Both organizational and inherent time-formatives are phenomena outside the individual. The school reforms of recent decades in Sweden are usually spoken of as necessary for 'the teachers' new mandate'. The teachers' new mandate, seen from a time-geographic perspective on organization, can create time-formatives that impair teachers' working conditions and their experience of control over the workday. It is striking, for example, how repeatedly reform consequences like individualisation and collegial coordination turn out to be organizational time-formatives that generate negative intermittence.

The understanding of time is a path to understanding cultures (cf. for example, Castells, 1996; Nowotny, 1994) and by that means also to understanding modern working life. Individualisation has created new ways of looking at time in teachers' work, yet at the same time the organization does not necessarily support the teacher with regard to the new demands on time management. The teachers are working in a potent stress field – potent insofar as generating unhealthy teachers. Within the last thirty years Sweden's teachers have gone from being one of the healthiest occupational groups to one of the sickliest.

The results of this study have shown that there may be contradictions of principle between organization and profession. There may also be conflicts of principle between the professional mandate itself and the school as a work environment.

Notes

1 As a rule, Swedish teachers have a 45-hour work week along with 10 weeks of summer recess (holiday). In the past, teachers could decide where they would put in their working hours, e.g. whether they wanted to do pre- or post-work at school or at home. Instruction (could encompass 16–24 clock hours) and certain meetings were timetabled and to a large degree, place was determined. The on-site working-hours policy means that of their 45 hours, teachers freely allot about 10 hours, so-called trust time. The rest of their time, 25–31 hours, is to be located in the school.

2 These are to be held once per term; their purpose is to give a picture of the pupil's learning in relation to knowledge goals and skill goals, but also to talk about other aspects of the pupil's situation in school and to discuss how the work will be

continuing so as to create good learning and good development. The form teacher/mentor is responsible for and conducts developmental conversations with these pupils and their parents. In the comprehensive upper secondary school, where pupils may be 18 or older, the conversations may be held only with the pupil, if the pupil so wishes.

3 In the comprehensive upper secondary school the reporting of absences is used, among other things, to assess the right to State pupil grants, which can be withdrawn in the event of unauthorized absence. For the teachers' part, pupils' absence sometimes leads to other tasks. It may be a matter of extra support so pupils will be able to make up what they have missed. It may also be that unauthorized absence is a symptom of a larger complex of problems and the pupil health service must be called in.

Preamble

Clinical teachers sowing seeds between theory and everyday practice – a knowledge-transforming process requiring intimate social relations and trust.

Sören Augustinsson & Elvi Richard

Balancing and bridge-building with difficulties ...

Clinical nursing teachers

Introduction

This text mainly focuses on a group of professionals – in our case hospital nurses – who belong to two organizations, on the one hand higher education and on the other healthcare. Their work consists of two main tasks. The first task is to make sure that students' clinical training is based on a scientific approach. The second task, which is further discussed in this article, is to support medical staff and nursing development, primarily with a scientific focus.

The relation between science and practice has proven to be one of the dilemmas that clinical teachers need to deal with. Their staff does not always deem it valuable to implement and utilise new knowledge, since it is considered to be too scientific. The interviews that were conducted with a majority of the clinical teachers in a county council illustrate that this is often the case. In total, twenty-one out of thirty-four clinical teachers and an additional eleven people in managerial positions in this county council were interviewed, the interviews were recorded and then typed out in their entirety. Analyses have been conducted via close-reading and categorisation of the content. Furthermore, a conference regarding the study's result was conducted with some eighty participants from the county council in question and material from this conference was also analysed (Augustinsson & Richard, 2006).

The aim of this article is to contribute to an understanding of how working conditions affect the clinical teachers' experiences of and views on the relation and dilemmas between science and practice.

Dilemmas are more or less part of our participants' – in our case the clinical teachers' – everyday life when it comes to dealing with ambiguous or equivocal situations. One example of what is to be considered a dilemma is when a clinical teacher organizes a seminar about new research regarding the treatment of wounds, but the staff is feeling sceptical or dissociated since the belief is that the current treatment is working just fine. Thus, there are two oppositional forces at work. Clinical teachers need to deal with these and similar situations in their work.

This does not imply that all dilemmas are considered to be of a negative nature. If dilemmas were to be completely eliminated, there is a risk that human dynamics would also disappear and that learning and development would fail to occur (Bird, 2003; Kauffman, 1993; Stacey 2001). Consequently, dilemmas are to be looked at as things that exist in practice and are prerequisites for development (cf. Czarniawska, 2005; Stacey, 2003; Streatfield, 2001).

To understand why dilemmas occur and how to deal with them, the social rule systems theory (Burns & Flam, 1987, Machado, 1996, Richard, 1997) can be employed. According to Burns & Flam, the basis of the social rule systems theory is that all human actions are organized and controlled by socially predetermined rules and regulations. One might say that human participants – individuals, groups, organizations, and societies – become producers and carriers of different social rule systems.

More to the point, what are rule and rule systems? Burns and Flam (1987) ascribe these concepts a wider meaning than the term norm. Different types of rules and rule systems can be identified, for example in terms of their cognitive, behavioural, and institutional status. Norms and laws, moral principles, behaviour codes, the rules of the game, administrative regulations and procedures, technical rules, conventions, habits and traditions are other examples. Consequently, norms are only an isolated form of rules. Burns and Flam (1987, p. 8) say:

> The rule systems governing transactions among agents in a defined sphere specify to a greater or lesser extent who participates (and who is excluded) who does what, when, where and how, and in relation to whom... The theory deals with the properties of social rule systems, their role in patterning social life and the social and political processes whereby such systems are produced, maintained,

and transformed as well as implemented in social action and interaction.

The theory about social rule systems is referred to complex rule structures. It is assumed that different social participants will often adjust to opposing rule systems that they use to structure and regulate their social lives. Furthermore, they need legitimacy, in a sense, from these opposing systems. There may, for example, be some uncertainty regarding how to interpret mutual values. In our case, the clinical teachers are linked with two different organizations – higher education and healthcare – with goals and rules that are partially dissimilar, which produce dilemmas in the work situation for clinical teachers. Simply put, one might say that they are exposed to different types of dilemmas that arise when scientific knowledge systems meet practice.

These social rule systems, however, must not be generally perceived as social obstacles or limits for action (Burns & Flam, 1987). The rule systems reduce social insecurity. On the other hand, they also make it possible for social participants to incorporate news and look for alternatives, which for clinical teachers may include implementing scientific knowledge in practice (Wenger, 1998).

This article is constructed in the following manner. First, the reader is provided with a short description of the roles of the clinical teachers and their tasks, which are partly based on the scientific view on the professional role of hospital nurses that exists today. Second, some characteristics are given that distinguish the difference between, at least some, science and practice, as well as the difference between knowledge and knowing. After this, there is an attempt to try to emphasise some areas in which clinical teachers support the development of operations and the dilemmas that appear in the meeting between science and practice. The article is concluded with a discussion regarding how dilemmas may be understood based on the social rule systems theory.

Clinical teachers

In the year 2000, thirty such positions were introduced in a healthcare sector based on the number of hospital nurses active in the region's healthcare system.[1] The content of the positions varies depending on specific prerequisites and requests from universities/colleges and operations. The actual work is not specified further than what is determined in central documents. These are established between colleges and county councils. Consequently, the actual content of the positions varies to a great extent, basically meaning that it is the individual clinical teacher's responsibility to organize his or her work according to the demands of the organization.

In accordance with political decisions, those employed as clinical teachers, within the framework of the teaching function, will teach students, participate in their examination and planning, as well as conduct courses and seminars. An additional task for the clinical teachers is to strengthen the development work within clinics/equivalent. This entails taking an active part in the development work at clinics, coaching medical staff in the development work, and also conducting seminars and development work for the medical staff. An additional task is to stimulate hospital nurses in their roles when it comes to supervising the clinical training of nursing students.

These are situations in which clinical teachers are intended to support the development of operations. One of the clinical teachers who were interviewed claims that the initial idea was that new clinical teachers were to be positioned on the field in order to 'ensure that the clinical part of training was also scientific since there were no demands for academic training for nurses'.

In order to guarantee high quality training of hospital nurses clearly linked with clinical operations, as of 2001 there is a principle agreement in Sweden between the Ministry of Education, Research and Culture, and the Federation of Swedish County Councils. The aim of this agreement is to provide trainee posts at the disposal of colleges. This agreement is a general agreement for healthcare. One of the reasons for the introduction of clinical teachers is that the new Swedish hospital nurse training as of 1993 required a scientific basis (Janson, 2005; Lindberg-Sand, 1996). The clinical and practical part of training should also have a scientific basis (Chekol, 2003). In other words, similar to the rest of the training, this part should also be based on science and evidence (Abrahamsson, 2004).[2]

The clinical teacher positions that previously existed were disposed of and new positions demanding some level of academic education were introduced, junior lecturers with Master's degrees and senior lecturers with PhDs.

One of the clinical teachers who were interviewed claims that the initial idea was that new clinical teachers were to be positioned on the field in order to 'ensure that the clinical part of training was also scientific since there were no demands for academic training for nurses'. In the article it is illustrated how the demand for academic skills in nursing constructs a dilemma; between science and practice or as a clinical teacher puts it: 'We need to be bridges between colleges and hospitals in order to introduce knowledge into operations'.

Clinical teachers often use the metaphor of 'being a bridge' in order to describe their roles. A typical answer is: 'I very much feel like a bridge-builder, which was originally intended.' To a great extent, this bridge seems to involve implementing scientific knowledge systems in practice '... going from theory, project, research, to implementing this in nursing.'

The following section will in short deal with some of the characteristic aspects on science and practice.

Some aspects on science and practice

In this section science is emphasised, at least within some fields of knowledge, and practice seem to have dissimilar content. One dilemma that, in our opinion, illustrates this is the difference between 'knowledge' and 'knowing' (it is also possible to use the word 'doing'). The difference between knowledge and knowing is that they seem to have entirely different content, which results in dilemmas when they meet in practice. To illustrate the difference between knowledge and knowing, Gustavsson (2004), Toulmin (1996) and Uhlin (2001) use Aristotle's classical division into 'episteme', which means knowing something, and 'techne' as art, for example cooking, which means that something is happening (Aristotle 'On "Techné and Ephistéme"' in Scarff & Dusek, 2003).

The concept 'knowing' implies action, doing something and a practice (Orlikowski, 2002, p. 250). Thus, knowing is bound to a context. There are similarities between this and what Molander (1996) calls *knowledge in action*. If similar to Gustavsson (2004) the concept of knowing is ascribed roughly the same meaning as 'episteme' (knowing something) and statement knowledge, Tsoukas (1998, p. 45) says that 'propositional knowledge on its own is of limited utility', since 'propositional statements are predicted on the assumption that the phenomenon they refer to is patterned, composed of objectively available elements which can be represented via an abbreviated formula'. Similar arguments are also found in Cunliffe and Shotter (2006, p. 234) in their distinction between 'knowledge versus knowing'. The first mentioned is described by them as: 'bounded in disciplines and categories, and only ever expressed explicitly' whereas 'knowing' represents: 'unbounded, fluid, bodily sensed, and often tacit i.e., implicit in one's practices and expressions'.

A reason for the problems between 'knowing' and 'knowledge', say Christensen and Kreiner (1997), is that practice is often dynamical and includes a certain measure of uncertainty that needs to be dealt with. Toulmin (1996, 2001) also takes a similar stand. He compares what he calls 'high science' to that which he claims characterises practice. In his opinion, science is: abstract, general, non-determined by space, logical, and characterised by linear causality – explanation and possible to explain. In contrast there is practice and its active knowledge that is concrete, bound to time and space, and dynamical. The authors of this text also concur with Schön (1983, p. 234) who writes about 'knowing in practice' that includes: 'a self-reinforcing system in which role frame, strategic of action, relevant facts, and interpersonal theories of action are bound up together'. He also stresses the complexity of practice.

If these prerequisites and the complexity of practice are not taken into account, say Alvesson and Deetz (2002, p. 211), practice will be lost. Consequently, existing practice cannot be viewed as being: 'natural, rational and neutral'. The situations in which knowledge results in action are complex and depend on a number of phenomena that science does not always take into account (Wenger, 1998).

The current attempts to make healthcare more scientific often originate in 'knowledge' based on scientific knowledge systems, in which knowledge is central and should be implemented in a complex and real practice. Janson (2005, p. 17) stress that 'the transmittal of knowledge and how to implement central evidence-based guidelines on a local level is given comparatively little notice in the discussion regarding evidence-based medicine and treatment'.[3] What these authors also seem to suggest is that it is unusual that science in practice is considered a problem when the problem has been reduced to a question of implementation of scientific knowledge in practice. This point-of-view is a reoccurring general theme in many of the clinical teachers' stories. Although some consider themselves as being bridge-builders in both directions, it is more common that they perceive themselves as being representatives of research, science and evidence and the legitimacy of these in society in general (Benner, 2001).

Almost without exceptions the terminology order is theory – practice. In their roles as clinical teachers, they claim that they are there to 'stimulate treatment research and organize seminars and internal training for the staff' and 'seek more evidence-based references and literature and discuss this with the staff'. However, as previously mentioned, they also state that they often meet a practice that is not always open-minded when it comes to science. In the next section, there will be examples of how clinical teachers speak of the meeting between science and practice, more specifically when knowledge is used in practice.

Stories about the meeting between science and practice

One of the most apparent images of how science has become important in nursing is when the clinical teachers time and time again tell us about the various activities that originate in scientific or evidence-based knowledge (or what is called 'episteme') in order to promote development in operations. This suggests that, in various contexts, they contribute to or give support to hospital nurses to enable them to seek evidence-based knowledge primarily in scientific articles. They tell of meetings in networks or private clinics in which medical staff has gathered and are aided by librarians in the search for articles. That there are some problems is evident from the following quotation:

> We tried to conduct a really ambitious article search in the beginning, but we could not find the time. We had decided that we would look up a certain thing in order to establish a standard treatment plan... But there just was not enough time.

Activities to encourage nurses to search for research-based knowledge are, hence, part of the clinical teachers' assignment. At the same time, they see in practice that there is resistance, or at least a lack of commitment, that is not only due to lack of time. A clinical teacher says the following:

> Something I would like to do is work more with research and make it more tangible; however, since there is resistance toward all of this science and research... I hosted a nursing forum that met once a month and discussed nursing issues and this was going all right as long as this was the only issue. But as soon as science was mentioned no one showed up...

The stories of several clinical teachers regard their attempts to involve the staff when it comes to acquiring general evidence-based knowledge. No one, however, seems to be completely satisfied with their achievement. Rather they express a will or opinion that things could have been better. Several clinical teachers say that more staff members should participate in courses or theme days organized by the college. However, a clinical teacher tells us that 'when you first visit a ward, you do not start off by saying that you are working on a research project. Definitely not'. One reason for this is that 'we are in a culture in which research and science is something foreign and anti many things'. 'We cannot become involved in that here, where we deal with patients.' The staff's somewhat negative attitude to science and evidence also seems to apply to more research-oriented hospitals.

Clinical teachers also tell us about what clinical hospital nurses consider to be 'a real nurse'. She (this term is generally used) is 'on the floor' and meets patients. The climate is such that she is supposed to work with patients, many of them claim. One clinical teacher describes this when he relates to students who are hired within the organization:

> I have given this a lot of thought, on the one hand I believe that the socialisation process from being a student to becoming a co-worker is very difficult and there is a rather small loop hole one needs to pass through in order to fit in.

Although nursing science is important, something happens when one is employed as a hospital nurse, which entails that one abandons science and goes into practice described as a 'loop hole' above. Consequently, one does not become a hospital nurse until one has done some hard labour. Somewhat ambiguously, a number of clinical teachers state in their accounts that new hospital nurses bring their academic Bachelor's degrees with them, and hence a scientific background that they themselves lack. This provides the new hospital nurses with a different basis than the rest, which may lead to higher demands for career moves and development. Others say, as stated above, that new hospital nurses are quick to incorporate the terms of practice that are different from their academic way of thinking. There is a tension between new hospital nurses with academic schooling and old hospital nurses who have 'always done their rounds and in the same way and aided the doctor and put out prescription notes and all of that'. The first-mentioned demands much of operations as well as of personal development. Here there is a certain distinction between old hospital nurses who are well-equipped with silent knowledge and new hospital nurses who have evidence-based skills based on knowledge.

To a large extent, most clinical teachers seem to perceive themselves as being bridge-builders between on the one hand science, colleges, research, and evidence-based knowledge, and on the other hand clinical operations in which there are patients. In this role, they are alone and can rather smoothly 'claim' this territory.

Above some of the activities that clinical teachers devote their time to were illustrated and some of the dilemmas that both theoretically and practically emerge between science and practice were emphasised. A second task that clinical teachers often talk about in great detail in our interviews is their effort to develop the documentation in healthcare as regards what and how to document. This is the focus of the next section.

Documentation

In the roles of future researchers, the authors of this text were quickly struck by the extensive work that seems to be performed in order to develop routines and live up to the rules. Agevall and Jonnergård, in this anthology, discuss how regulating via documents may result in de-professionalism. Documentation is a difficult area to address. In all kinds of healthcare in 1985, hospital nurses and others were obligated to keep a journal (SFS 1985:562). Ever since, the keeping of journals has obviously become more and more equal to documentation as a means to control healthcare and not solely as a support for the hospital nurses' diagnoses of patients. If possible, what was discuss in this section may be stated in the words of Friberg (2002, p. 4), with reference to Sarvimäki: 'an element of military discipline has been part of nursing tradition from the 19th century up to our days', with inflexible hospital routines as a consequence. This military discipline is also found, for example, in Grimby (2001) who says that documentation should be executed in a general manner, follow a logical structure, demand objectivity, be explanatory, and give possibilities for various healthcare professions to utilise and interpret the content (cf. Jonazon, 2002). According to Grimby, documentation should thus be abstractly written and in general terms.

It is in the light of this that several clinical teachers say that they try to implement documentation and the keeping of journals. Based on the interviews, documentation and the keeping of journals seem to take up a lot of time. It is extensive work and: 'We could spend all day talking about it... it is a huge problem and has to do with attitudes and power...', says one clinical teacher. One of the interviewees shows a handbook and adds that it is written in: 'a very high-flown language' that the staff has difficulties to interpret. A fairly common description by clinical teachers regarding their work with documentation is the following:

> We meet in networks once a month. We also have a documentation group that also meets and we convene several times a month and produce a journal that we discuss and if I have time... as soon as I can and have the possibility I join in and we discuss the journal with documentation and try to develop it. We do not criticise but try to develop. It is an awful lot to do regarding this. You could work full-time just doing that.

Documentation and keeping journals seem to take a lot of time from the rest of the work, not only for clinical teachers. This fact is confirmed by the National Board of Health and Welfare (NBHW, 2000), which claims that hospital nurses at hospitals spend an average of 7.2 hours per week documenting. Doctors as well spend the equivalent number of hours documenting. In addition to this, all of the activities that are focused on implementation of documentation should be discussed, which the clinical teachers also mention. Although documentation and the keeping of journals have been in effect for a long time, as one clinical teacher says, there is still a 'lack of documentation and accurate documentation'. Consequently there are possibly in all parts of the county council the types of documentation groups that the clinical teachers talked about.

Several clinical teachers tell us about the problem with new hospital nurses who have been taught to do scientific and evidence-based documentation but do not always use this in practice. On the contrary, nurses are socialised into how the staff documents, which is different from the scientific approach. In practice, nurses document what they do, i.e. real actions. The problem is making them 'document thoughts, our problem analysis,' as a clinical teacher puts it. Hence, he says that they have: 'An important task when it comes to translating the scientific language into everyday language and make it more common'.

One clinical teacher says that problems arise when colleges teach a different type of documentation than the medical. What one learns is called nursing documentation, 'but that is not used in real life. Here you are socialised into a system in which you sometimes write medically about your nursing.' Instead, the hospital nurse should in her documentation refer to:

> the list of pharmaceuticals or write down if a patient desires apple mash when taking his pills. Then you write the list of pharmaceuticals. But in this you write which medicine and how much has been given. Sometimes the hospital nurse also writes the prescription.

The problems with documentation are often described in terms of the student's approach when it comes to documenting and the staff's. A clinical teacher says: 'I could not tell the students to do it a certain way and then do it differently in reality'. This clinical teacher is trying to balance that which is taught in college and his or her work in the documentation group that clinical hospital nurses in the organization also participate in. Consequently, this work is important since 'the documentation that the students observe in reality is not always what we teach them'. Several clinical teachers tell us that the documentation that the students are taught is required to be general, logically structured and objective.

Above it was demonstrated that there are a number of dilemmas between on the one hand the general and objective (science and evidence), and on the other hand situated practice that is specific and subjective (Lave & Wenger, 1993; Orr, 1996; Suchman, 1987, p. 49). The documentation should be based on actual meetings with specific patients. Documentation also includes dilemmas other than that between general and specific. Other dilemmas occur between what the doctors document and what the hospital nurses document. It should be noted in this context that there is a problem between different professions that manifests itself as a dilemma.

Essays

The task of the clinical teachers is to promote development in clinical operations. One example of this is when clinical teachers say that it is beneficiary when hospital nurses to greater extent continue with their education and receive Bachelor's[4] and Master's degrees in nursing science. Clinical teachers say that they try to make hospital nurses pursue this to a greater extent. It is also part of their training on these levels to write a thesis, which, among other things, teaches the hospital nurses 'the scientific work method and the systematic way of working'. Theses written by hospital nurses, however, are not frequent. One clinical teacher responds to the question of how often she supervises such theses: 'this term there has been none, last term there were two. Before that there were two each term so it is not a lot…'. The reason for the relatively small number of hospital nurses in higher education is that they claim that it is difficult to leave their patients and experience that there is not enough time to do this.

Higher education often results in desires to use one's newly acquired knowledge and do other things. A clinical teacher speaks of how one could make use of those who have Master's degrees:

> How are we to use them? We discuss that perhaps we will need to institute project positions so that they are relieved of their other duties for a while and can do other things, and later return to working on the floor again.

A dilemma mentioned by Spencer (2005) and our clinical teachers is that in order to make a career move, one needs a Master's degree, which implies that one has to leave the operations that work closely with patients.

The problem, or dilemma, seems to consist of knowing that a Master's degree does not contribute when it comes to strengthening, or supporting, the hospital nurse in her meeting with patients. Most clinical teachers are aware of the tension in one way or the other that exists between knowledge and knowing, but how to define this conflict and how to resolve it is difficult to put into words (Pfeffer *et al.*, 2001).

In view of this, Gerrish *et al.* (2000) and Hardwick and Jordan (2002) may be mentioned who claim that the academic training of hospital nurses is said to lessen their ability to make decisions in practice. However, this is not clearly found in our material, but should be noted as a tendency. In the concluding section, examples of how to deal with some of the dilemmas in connection with the social rule systems theory are illustrated.

Dealing with dilemmas and social rule systems

Participation of clinical teachers in practice is sanctioned based on decisions and agreements between the regional healthcare and colleges/universities. Their assignment is also evident in these documents. Actual meetings and discussions, however, create the relations that transpire and are maintained. Since they are at colleges and in healthcare at the same time, they need to adjust to two different social rule systems better known as knowledge and practice. It is not predetermined whether they are members of the college world or the healthcare world.

The dilemma is that they are at the same time part of and not part of both organizations whose social rule systems differ. Social rule systems are constructed from the content of the organization, how work is governed and controlled, and of course from its history (Augustinsson, 2006). Science and scientific knowledge systems differ from clinical healthcare, and the meeting between these manifests itself in dilemmas that are actualised in the work of clinical teachers. When they act on the terms of the organization they are so to speak accepted. If, on the other hand, they represent the other organization (the college) they are not automatically accepted into the staff group and its time. Consequently, formal rule systems, decisions, and agreements between both organizations (college/university and healthcare sector) do not offer clinical teachers automatic access to respective organization. Hosting seminars, for example, about science in practice is obviously not a simple task; to represent the bridge between science and practice. It has been described how they try to be the bridge by teaching hospital nurses to look for scientific articles, educate themselves further, and write Master's projects, document nursing efforts etc. In this work, however, they face a certain resistance that creates dilemmas in their work. They try to solve these dilemmas via strategies such as 'planting seeds', acting 'as a mole', via casual conversation, showing perseverance etc. i.e. via formal and informal conversations with hospital nurses and thereby establish a relation between the two organizations. A clinical teacher speaks of how she has dealt with the staff relation:

> For me, it includes actual visits to the ward, sitting down with the employees and reason with them, perhaps regarding a case or something… I strongly believe in working actively with those who are here, i.e. speaking to people, making people realise things… to increase awareness. If you understand why you are doing something you are able to continue doing it. If you do not understand it, you cannot continue doing it and will consequently stop doing it.

They continuously describe the small, everyday close human relations. In order to function, one needs to have someone to 'invite someone to dance, there must be a partner'. One clinical teacher describes it as follows:

> We only show up and we show up a lot and speak to the assistant nurses, we speak to the hospital nurses and we speak to the managers. But it is not like I will show up on Thursday at 3 pm, and have a talk with you. It is just casual conversation. You are in the organization and chat.

How they deal with dilemmas is often manifested in negotiations with hospital nurses and others in practice. This is what is called action strategies. It seems that the more dilemmas there are, the more negotiations occur. When, on the other hand, they show up and introduce themselves as being representatives of scientific knowledge systems and experts, they are met with incredulity. There is often talk about informal meetings with hospital nurses, so as to overcome their incredulity against science.

Perseverance and closeness are two other key words that emerge in the stories about how they work as clinical teachers. One clinical teacher speaks of an initiative regarding the implementation of new administrative routines at a clinic. Rather than having different patients' journals in one file, as before, the staff now has one file for each patient. The reason for this change was that when several patients were hospitalised at the same time, the use of the files was limited. However, it took three years before she managed to change the routines. The staff, at first, could not see the benefits of the new system that she suggested but only the drawbacks, she tells us. As part of the process, she describes a ward that over the weekend went back and put all the patients' journals in a mutual file once again. This was done out of pure protest and anger; however, they had to surrender and take up the new system. Today they would not wish to return to the previous system.

One effect of the mole work and being a negotiator, say many of the interviewees, is that the supervising status of the hospital nurse has increased significantly. One clinical teacher tells us:

> We are in a culture in which research and science is foreign and anti, very much so. We cannot do that here, here we deal with patients. In this you need to be a mole, working as a mole, and I have done a lot of that. Got many things started. What I have done, is that I have worked with the supervisors 'mole-style' in order to get them motivated to take a tutor's course and continue in nursing science in order to gain a tutor's competence.[5]

Several reports regarding increased demands and wishes from hospital nurses to take tutor training exist. This is said to prove that more and more see the importance of education based on science: 'This is something that I'm promoting. More and more turn to us and ask what training you need in order to move forward.' The reason for this could be previous contacts. Someone speaks of contacts that were established more than ten years ago and that are now revived when she has become a clinical teacher:

> in part it is because we had a mutual project many years ago, sometime in the 90s when I was out and giving undergraduate studies in vips and treatment documentation in all municipalities. At that time we had a mutual project between hospitals, rehab and municipalities that was supervised by our counsellor and that was where it all started...

Others speak of how they use their relations with former classmates to establish networks. The relations that were created via tutors are always described as being important for the clinical teachers' opportunities when it comes to fulfilling their work in organization development. They say that they, when visiting their tutors or meeting them in other contexts, use these meetings on purpose in order to discuss problems and needs that exist in reality. This is what some referred to as 'mole-work' in the relation between science and practice. This could be approached differently, but aim at the same thing. Some use a number of previous relations in order to be included in organizations. If one wants to say hello to someone one knows one cleverly does this in time for break. Consequently, one has unofficially attempted to make oneself known in the organization. The clinical teachers also take the opportunity to join the organizations' 'nurse meetings', so as to make an appearance among the staff. As clinical teachers, they are responsible for 'paving the way' as someone comments.

Another approach when it comes to establishing networks is to maintain contact with previous students so as to have a natural link to the organization. It might be suggested that the clinical teachers have an underlying desire to establish a trust that lasts a long time.

Recommendations to new teachers often include: 'Establish a network'. Those who originally lack a network must, consequently, establish one. If one does not have a network:

> you must find and know the ways of how to make things happen. All clinical teachers need some form of network that has been established for a long time ... Yes, it takes a long time to establish one, especially if you are straight out of school 'cause then you are a bit of a threat. It is perhaps simpler if you are a hospital nurse. But contacts are very very important and that you take it slow, that you realise that these things take time...

Based on the idea of social rule systems, the clinical teachers' situation can be described as the frames of interpretation that enable them to meaningfully interpret contradictory circumstances and deal with these. Social rule systems are mainly dynamic, since rules are constantly created and recreated in the interaction between participants.

The strategies they use to deal with dilemmas, such as documentation and academic essays compared with practical knowing, may be viewed as an attempt to gain room for manoeuvre. For clinical teachers it seems to be an issue regarding how to navigate and balance the different rule systems in their attempts to participate in the development of operations. In this context, it is maintained that the resources previously open to clinical teachers have been important in order to give autonomy. In short, it deals with what one is equipped with in order to face the dilemmas in practice. Having resources is necessary in order for clinical teachers to be able to develop clear strategies for handling various problems and thus gain control of the situation. Richard (1997) describes this similar to a work leader's position, which is constructed by different social rule systems. Ambiguity, consisting of a number of different dilemmas, arises and that results in the development of action strategies. In her study there are the social rule systems within an organization. In this study there is the one between two overlapping social rule systems (higher education and healthcare) as well as the one between two knowledge systems (knowledge and knowing).

Conclusion

In this article it was demonstrated how working conditions affect the clinical teachers' experiences of and views on the relation and dilemmas between science and practice. Their assignment to contribute to a more scientifically oriented health care is one of the factors that manifest itself as a dilemma: that of being a bridge between science and practice, or as a clinical teacher describes it: 'we need to be a bridge between colleges and hospitals in order to implement knowledge in the organization.' It is common that clinical teachers perceive themselves as being representatives of science and research; almost without exceptions the terminology order is theory – practice. However, when they continue to describe what they actually do and how they handle the actual contents of the bridge, a different picture emerges. In order to deal with these complex dilemmas and other obstacles, they use various networks for daily talks and dialogues primarily with hospital nurses in practice. One emerging principle seems to be that one deals with dilemmas via close relations and communication with the target group. To be successful, one needs to be skilful when it comes to utilising different action strategies depending on the local terms.

Since clinical teachers simply put belong to different social rule systems in the form of higher education and healthcare, there is also room for them to decide which strategies and networks that are of importance in order to be successful as a clinical teacher and in the tasks that they consider important. This article attempted to illustrate that it is only then that the bridge between science and practice can result in increased knowledge for the staff that meets patients. Attempts to reduce dilemmas between knowledge and knowing as a linear relation, in which the problem is more often seen as an implementation of science in practice, often seem to result in failed action strategies. This also shows that dealing with dilemmas should result in development, as in this case, when the complexity of practice forms the basis for action.

Notes

1 There has also been some movement in that some people have quit their jobs and new positions have been filled. For some their work tasks have changed. A number of clinical teachers aim for, or have gained, a Master's in nursing science while being employed.

2 Evidence-based knowledge roughly means that something seems to imply that a certain connection applies (cf. Latin *evidentia* that means clarity). Evidence is the result of scientifically qualitative observations and is consequently seen as being confirmed via the best evidence available. Possibly there are links to standard analysis. In order to say something one must believe it. Secondly, what one believes must be true, and finally, thirdly, one needs good reasons for believing it (Haglund, 1998). According to Plato, if these three conditions are fulfilled, knowledge could be determined as being epistémé, which is distinguished from doxa, which is thought and opinions (Augustinsson, 2006). Consequently, in this article evidence and science will be used synonymously.

3 Other common concepts are statement knowledge, theoretical knowledge, expressed knowledge, and knowing what. All of these indicate some form of limitation.

4 Other common concepts are skills, practical knowledge, knowing how, familiarity knowledge, orientation knowledge, and silent knowledge. All of these imply some form of a holistic view.

5 In 'The Nicomachean Ethics', Aristotle calls episteme scientific knowledge and techne craft-knowledge (Scharff & Dusek, 2003). However, there is some uncertainty whether the latter in fact lacks judicious action. Nonetheless, this will not be discussed further.

6 They seem to use the word evidence in connection with scientifically acquired knowledge.

7 The new nurse training programme awards students with a Bachelor's degree.

8 These 'tutors' are nurses who supervise students in their clinical training. The tutors take a course for this purpose that is offered either via clinical teachers or via col-

leges. This is one way for clinical teachers to establish relations with hospital nurses. The clinical teachers look at the work with tutors, indirectly, as a means to develop clinical operations in an evidence-based and scientific spirit.

Preamble

Collaboration is a fashionable word in the current welfare state. But why? What is it? And how does it work? This chapter explores collaboration between different organizations from the perspective of practitioners. Some of their experiences are mirrored in a wider context that could contribute to the understanding of tensions in daily practice.

Agneta Abrahamsson

Uncovering tensions in an intersectoral organization

A mutual exploration among frontline workers

Introduction

An increasing number of family centres have been implemented during the last few decades all over Sweden and also in others countries in Europe and the USA. Although they look different in different countries, they are all focused on welfare and health among families with younger children (Cannan, 1992). In Sweden, family centres are run in cooperation between health services such as child and maternity care and kindergarten and social services. Because of the long tradition of child and maternity care in Sweden, this co-location means that almost all families in an area are reached by social services. Family centres provide comprehensive and voluntary service to families in the neighbourhood, with an overall aim of creating social networks among parents. Other common specific goals include: better physical health of children, enhanced child development, better parenting skills and facilitation of parents' independence (Bak & Gunnarsson, 2000; Bons, Lundström Mattsson, Nyberg, & Pettersson, 2003; Gärdsmo Pettersson, 2000; Niklasson, 2001; Perdal, 1998; Svensson, 2001; Söderström-Claeson & Granberg-Wennberg, 2003).

This study focuses on a family centre that was launched two years ago, called Family House. It is situated in an area with higher unemployment, higher social welfare expenses and higher levels of immigrants than the municipality as a whole (Kristianstadskommun, 2000). In total eight staff members work regularly at the family centre: three district nurses, two midwives, one assistant nurse, one preschool teacher and one social adviser, who is also coordinator of the team that can be labelled frontline workers (Lipsky, 1980). The entrance to the premises is situated in the middle. Receptions rooms and waiting room for maternity and child health care are situated to the left and a big room with kitchen, two smaller rooms, and an office for social advice and kindergarten are situated to the right.

The common area for everyone in the family house is the kindergarten, in which the preschool teacher spends most of her time, whereas other frontline staff work in this area more (social adviser) or less (other staff) temporarily. Midwives and district nurses spend most of their time in reception rooms where they carry out individual consultancy with families. The social adviser/coordinator does individual consultancy and administrative work approximately half-time. In the preschool area the preschool teacher is the central person who has a combined role of being supporter, host and facilitator for families. In the ongoing development of service and activities, families are encouraged to participate since this is expected to improve service by starting from the perspectives and needs of families.

Professionals work on a daily basis in a joint location, although they are employed in and managed by their parent organizations which control the resources on which they rely. They are expected to create a synergy of competences and activities that will meet the needs of families in a better way than in the traditional parent organizations in local authorities and county councils (Kristianstadskommun, 2000), which according to Hill and Lynn (2003) is a common precondition for interagency collaboration. The focus of this paper is on the tensions that occur in organizing interagency collaboration. Tensions that might be significant for the development of collaboration during the first two years after the opening of the family house have been uncovered together by frontline workers and the researcher.

Background

The increasing numbers of family centres in different countries could be seen as a part of the development of human service organizations, since endeavours at new organizations emerge in an empty space in the social landscape (Ahrne, 1994). Historically, an empty space originated with the development of human service organizations from fragmentation to coordination between agencies. The traditional bureaucratic model has increasingly been found to be insufficient to meet complex needs in social and health care and eventually an empty space for a new model of organization, built on collaboration, was born (Brechin, Brown & Eby, 2000). New models for organizing work have thus been tried out to improve both the quality and the efficiency of service (Ahrne, 1994).

An important drive in the development of health and social service has been to make the service more person-centred, in contrast to the traditional way in which service users went from one specialist to the other to have their needs met (Nylén, 2005). Coordination and integration of resources and competence from different service organizations, through co-location in a family house as in this study, requires collaboration between different agencies. This collaboration, however, means that boundaries have to overlap on different levels (Hornby & Atkins, 2000). It involves a complex social change with both competitive and cooperative elements, since the interaction between organizations is both instrumental and strategic in character (Ahrne, 1994). Both material and symbolic elements of differing origin have to be reviewed. Formal rules and regulations originate on a macro-level. The structures within and management of the agencies involved have to support professionals when collaborating. Barriers in planning and budget procedures together with funding bases need to be sorted out in a way that facilitates everyday work. Informal values, norms, interests, and taken-for-granted beliefs originate on a micro-level. The ideology, values and self-interest of individual professionals as well as the concern for threats to autonomy and domain have to be handled in a way that makes service integration possible (Brechin, Brown & Eby, 2000). In the development of service these material and symbolic elements may imply tensions and shape actions, although both can be seen as opportunities and constraints for the development of service.

According to a review by Carlström *et al.* (2004), the frequent use of teamwork in organizations originates from an assumption that it contributes to the creation of synergy of competences and activities around the end user. The underlying idea is a rationality that is seldom questioned. Some common and taken-for-granted assumptions are that teams are effective, increase motivation and satisfaction with work, they are harmonious and create consensus among the members, and there is a common interest shared by the organization and individuals. Old-fashioned knowledge is replaced by new knowledge if teams are decisively constructed and implemented. Stereotypes about what teamwork will result in are taken for granted and have resulted in a common use of teamwork. This is a way to demonstrate good order and to legitimize an organization (Carlström & Berlin, 2004). This part of the development of organizations with teamwork as a way to increase effectiveness can be traced to the rationale of New Public Management (NPM) (Montin, 2002). In the following definition this is overt: 'interdisciplinary collaboration is an effective interpersonal process that facilitates the achievement of goals that cannot be reached when individual professionals act on their own' (Bronstein 2003, p. 299). Great demands are thus made of frontline workers to meet the expectations of their organizations.

The family house is one of many examples of interagency collaboration in health and social care in which the beneficence of teamwork has been taken for granted. The pitfalls in the development of teamwork need further research, for example about how consensus and conflicts are handled in the implementation phase of teams (Carlström & Berlin, 2004). In the second year after the launch of the family house, the researcher and the frontline workers together explored this development. A pre-understanding was that since the team consists of individuals from different professions and parent organizations, conflicts and negotiations in the common overlapping area are natural. The focus is on tensions as preconditions for development in an organization, potentially leading to new solutions to old problems in order to improve activities to meet families' needs better.

Action research approach and methods to generate data

An action research approach was used to generate empirical data for this study (Greenwood and Levin 1998; Waterson 2000). The acknowledgement of everyday experience among frontline workers was seen as crucial in the development of a reflective practice. The objective was to improve frontline workers' skills to reflect and to see everyday work from different perspectives.

Different sources of data have been used. Observations with informal interviews formed the main part of data. These were brought up in discussions when the frontline workers as a group communicated their experiences of the development. Documents were used as complementary data on how decisions had been made. Feedback from analysis and preliminary interpretation of this data to staff in sessions with further analysis and interpretation was used as a mode of action. In-depth understanding of how individuals talk about issues in common with others was constructed in open-ended individual interviews.

The 'us and them' wall
– the defensive posture against insecurity

During the first year, the frontline workers had constructed a symbolic wall in the middle of the house that was named 'us and them'. On one side of this wall were midwives and nurses and on the other side the preschool teacher and social adviser. The disappointment about the lack of success in cooperation was often described as: 'It was not as easy as we thought it would be.'

The individual frontline worker may be seen as carriers of various tensions in an organization, which may result in feelings of insecurity that disturb collaboration. Tensions felt by individuals had resulted in the creation of building blocks for the 'us and them' wall. In the following section these tensions are presented in different areas. Data on these areas were compiled from issues that occurred in the researcher's observation, in discussions between the researcher and individual frontline workers and with all the members of the team together. These issues have been investigated further in special reflection sessions. The researcher and frontline workers tried together to reach a deeper understanding of frontline workers' experiences. In the reflection sessions, the current situation was analysed by posing the general questions: 'What is going on here?' and 'Why?' Different sources were used to mirror the ongoing situations, such as other research findings and reflections on frontline workers' previous experiences of working in other organizations. It was expected in this way to uncover the meaning of the situations for each frontline worker, together with the implications that situations for the team as a whole could contribute to the improvement of collaboration.

Structures in the organizations as a source of tensions

Availability of time for collaboration was one building block in the construction of the 'us and them' wall. The frontline workers commonly said, 'Collaboration takes time, and more time has to be allowed by our managers to make it possible for us to develop collaboration.' However, data from observations of how staff used their time in common (two hours a week) demonstrated how this time was employed to sort out practical, administrative and economic issues, but discussions of how to develop activities were unusual. These data were used as a source for reflection. It occurred to the staff that in other organizations clerical professionals did these tasks. These observations and insights were discussed in a special session when the steering group (managers from each parent organization and coordinator) attended a reflection session together with the team of frontline workers. The outcome of this session was that frontline workers were asked to present a list of issues that were later solved at a higher level in each parent organization.

This obstacle could be seen as a tension for each frontline worker originating at a higher level in each parent organization. From an agency perspective, endeavours at collaboration could, according to Hill (2002), be seen on a management level as benefits in the form of politically correct action, whereas costs tend to be overlooked. Managing in agencies necessarily has to consider both costs and benefits to improve conditions for frontline workers' cooperation. Although the parent organizations are expected to fulfil some obligations, rules and regulations, they need to design mechanisms for handling routines in a way that fits frontline workers' everyday collaborative work (Hill & Lynn, 2003). This lack of administrative routines was also a lack of collaboration on a management level that caused insecurity and contributed to the construction of the symbolic wall in the family house. As soon as this lack of collaboration became obvious to all involved, it could be solved on the level in the organization where it belonged.

Another building block for the 'us and them' wall was the '*have tos*'. Health care personnel felt that the daily routines were more specified and obligatory than the social adviser and the preschool teacher. Health care personnel saw this as a reason why it was so difficult to spend time and to work on the whole idea of family house. A clear and realistic profile in each agency is viewed by Hornby and Atkins (2000) as facilitating collaboration. Good communication, well-defined working roles and support were ways to prevent role insecurity. Otherwise defence will risk disturbing collaborative practice among frontline workers because of personal and role insecurity (Hornby & Atkins, 2000). The reliance on the 'have tos' could be a defensive posture to prevent feelings of insecurity in the new organization. In order to test the strength of the 'have tos', all personnel further investigated steering documents in the different agencies. At a workshop it was concluded that programmes on surveillance in the health care organization were more precise, whereas social and preschool organizations were more about principle. However, in steering documents for all staff, collaboration was as important as other obligatory activities.

Professional development as a source of tensions

On the individual level, however, each frontline worker ascribed a different meaning to the 'have tos'. They could be regarded as superior, more like objectives that had to be fulfilled, whereas other frontline workers saw them as inferior, more like tools for achieving objectives from the families' perspective. Aili (2002) shows how midwives saw autonomy as crucial for how they handled the working situation and related to steering documents. Either autonomy was about solving everyday problems together with women, which could imply that steering documents were an obstacle they had to deal with in an acceptable way. Autonomy could also be about fulfilling tasks originating in steering documents (Aili, 2002). One of the frontline workers described how she had changed her way of seeing and handling steering documents. She had modified her way of working since

> I'm now more open to needs of the family, if I haven't done what I 'have to' by the time I intended, it will be done some other time. This time other things were more important to focus on. I don't bother anymore because I feel secure in that, and I hope this will make families feel that they could become more open to me when I'm more open to their needs.

Prioritizing needs among families was one area in which the 'us and them' wall was seen. The overall aim of the family house is to meet family needs, but families' needs vary considerably depending on their social circumstances and other factors. The health care personnel primarily saw needs among more 'ordinary' families from a public health point of view, in which service would be available for families in special temporary situations. The social worker and the preschool teacher were more focused on social prevention and on more continual needs among socially vulnerable families and on immigrants' needs.

This difference was presented as an obstacle to collaboration when all frontline workers met, and it became most obvious when the content of the preschool activities was discussed. However, the researcher found the differences in beliefs ambiguous. While it was set up as an obstacle, the frontline workers individually presented a shared interest in meeting the needs of socially vulnerable families in the preschool activities. Before the opening of family house, health care personnel had to work on their own with these families without having the expert social knowledge required. An advantage now was that they had been relieved of some work and responsibility. They also had some positive experiences of successful 'treatment' of these families in the preschool since they had observed changes in parents' and children's behaviour in families. This common interest among individuals on their own had been ignored. Instead the different views on the priority of needs were emphasized when they met as a group. Why?

One way to understand the ambiguity in individuals' opinions, inside or outside the team, is in the light of professional identity and development. In early stages of professional development on a collective and individual level, it is important to set up limits *vis-à-vis* other professions or professionals. This may lead to a resistance towards approaching each other and recognizing interdependence. As soon as the individual feels safe in his or her professional role, it becomes easier to open up limits. One of the frontline workers said:

> Now I feel secure in my role as ..., before I was so focused on my role, what I had to do, and didn't open up to find new ways to see problems and work. Now I'm beginning to find my feet and feel secure enough to let others help me.

According to Abbott (1988), a profession is a system that consists of an essence and an outer zone. The essence is the limitation of work to a particular profession, which implies a mandate to complete tasks serving a special category of user. This limitation is based on special training, skills, knowledge and a theoretical base and code of ethics. The outer zone is not limited to a particular profession since it consists of tasks and a knowledge base shared between different professions. Continuous negotiations about who is going to do what take place in the latter area between the professions involved (Abbott, 1988). The positive thing about a strong professional identity for the individual is the strength to carry out difficult tasks on one's own, whereas the negative aspect could be the reluctance to use the resources of the whole team and to collaborate (Hornby & Atkins, 2000). This will occur if the individual frontline worker feels insecure and tries to expand his or her own limits towards others in order to feel more secure in handling tasks. In a team consisting of different professions who are focused on drawing borders between professional groups, there is a tendency to focus more on differences and to make similarities between the professional groups invisible (Aili, 2002). This situation was reflected on in a group session and a decision was made to continue work by setting objectives for the family house in each professional group and in the next group session to investigate the differences.

The parent organization's culture and knowledge base a source of tension

In line with Bronstein (2003), each professional's cultural background in the parent organization could have implications for beliefs, norms and use of language. This could be seen in the way they talked about families' needs. The health care personnel proceeded from the perspective of public health, whereas the social worker and preschool teacher considered things from the perspective of social prevention. Language and cultural understanding rather than objectives could thus be the origin of tensions among the frontline workers.

The system of shared norms and values about what is important for how the organization members carry out their work may create tensions for the individual (Hill & Lynn, 2003). Health care personnel valued the order and a clear planning process as important cultural characteristics in their parent organization. This may be seen in the light of the belief system in health care, based on rationality and cause-effect relations originating in natural science. Additionally, the traditional hierarchical decision-making processes in health care entail a clear and systematic order. This is in contrast to the social adviser and preschool teacher, who attached greater value to facilitating social relations and problem solving in everyday life as cultural characteristics with roots in social science.

The frontline workers all ascribed value to proceeding from the family's needs. They talked about the importance of creating insights for learning in relationships with parents, while acquiring knowledge and experiences from the knowledge base in each profession was simultaneously important. In the context of health care, Mischler, Clark *et al.* (1989) have discussed differences in what is meant by being an expert as the 'voice of life-world' and the 'voice of medicine'. These voices may result in ambivalence for the individual since she sees herself as representing one knowledge system (medicine), whereas she primarily wants to proceed from the perspective of the life-world of the parent. These voices could be transferable to the context of the family house as a whole. The knowledge base for the preschool teacher was based on playing and doing practical things, whereas for health care personnel it was about giving information based on medical evidence.

Reflection and learning together

In line with Hill and Lynn (2003), the notion of these voices, the 'voice of life-world' and 'the voice of medicine/preschool' may be seen as beliefs based on cultural differences that are often unconscious to the individual. Reflections on inherent traditions and knowledge use in the organization may thus improve learning, as in the quotation above. The preschool teacher described it this way:

> At the beginning I focused exclusively on building relationships and avoided doing craft work, which is usually what they do in open preschools. But now I see it differently, it could be useful to do both, if you know why you are doing it.

Reflection on implications from the parent organization about how different tasks are valued (Abrahamsson, 2004) may raise awareness of why you do what you do. You may become able to combine and use the notion of being an expert differently in different situations. In one situation it might be a matter of achieving something and in another situation it could be acting as a facilitator to build relations, and to create an environment for learning and change. The frontline workers as a group may together learn by reflection on the origin of tensions to transcend inbuilt structures they carry within themselves. Recognizing likeness between professionals may contribute to development, while disparities may cause hindrances unless they are acknowledged as natural and even seen as an asset for the improvement of the service (Reed & Harvey, 1992).

In line with Manz and Neck (1997), the individual professional has to shift focus from being a professional in an independent agency to the team as a whole that can meet the family's needs. There is, however, a pitfall in the danger of group thinking. Especially in the initial phase, this can easily happen because group members endeavour to agree with one another in order to create a positive and secure climate in the group. Internal pressure towards conformity may result in less consideration of alternative suggestions, which in turn may lead to less creative and functional decisions. This danger of group thinking may be counteracted by encouraging an open debate based on individuals' divergent roles. In this 'team thinking' the aim is to facilitate synergic thinking as a means to more creative decision-making (Manz & Neck, 1997).

So far, feedback sessions had shown how anxiety and excitement about the creation of something new had led to tensions within the team of frontline workers. Ambiguity and tensions are essential prerequisites for achieving emancipatory learning (Cranton, 1994). However, to make learning possible requires 'dynamic in the communicative interaction that is fluid enough, when there is diversity, tension and conflict in the thematic patterning of communicative interaction, analogous to the edge of chaos' (Stacey, 2001, p. 189). If this dynamic is hampered, at worst the opposite may happen and at best the development of the group may stagnate.

Dynamic in tensions in an organization as fuel for development and learning

This chapter demonstrates some aspects of complexity in tensions among a group of co-located frontline workers that is originated on different levels in each parent organization. The individual frontline worker carries them more or less unconsciously, although reflections on the implications for collaboration are crucial in team building. One of the frontline workers described the team as follows:

> How can you get something out of us? We are a confused group of women who talk a lot forward and backwards. We are here and there and everywhere when we are trying to find out what we are doing and what direction we are aiming for.

The quotation illustrates the insecurity that may be generated in complex patterns of tension related to and displayed in identity and roles, relations between individuals and organizational levels and communication (Stacey, 2001). This study suggests that conflicts and ambivalence cause tensions that are not so obvious to the individuals that they can discuss them. According to Esquivel and Kleiner (1997), a common misunderstanding is that conflicts are an obstacle to a team's efficiency in solving problems. If conflicts are focused on a special individual this may be the case, but if the focus is on a special task, conflicts may generate more alternatives and better solutions. The difficulty from a management perspective is to distinguish and to balance between the two. It is suggested here that a way to deal with conflicts at an early stage in team building is to view them as originating in the organization and not in personality.

The tensions that are created in a co-located facility with four professional groups could be seen as fuel for knowledge building. They may facilitate or hinder the improvement of service to families and the development of new ways of working if the team does not reflect on their implications in this particular context. A model for interdisciplinary collaboration between social workers and other disciplines presents components that have been identified in management literature as achieving optimum collaboration. Recognized interdependence between disciplines, newly created professional activities, flexibility, collective ownership of goals and reflection on the process will make collaboration more likely (Bronstein, 2003).

The origins of the tensions that have been explored are complex. They all derive from administrative and managerial procedures, economic incentives for collaboration, professional education and development, organizational culture and personal preferences. In Reed & Harvey (1992) (see also Bhaskar, 1998) a transformational model of social action posits three levels of social reality that could be seen as important for how change is achieved in the improvement of social welfare. The first is the structural level, 'society', the second is the individual level, which consists of a significant power of agency, and third is the intermediary level in which the interaction between society and individual takes place. This last level is a position-practice system of rules, roles and relations that condition how a group of individuals make decisions based on their interpretations and intentions. The complex role of the intermediary level is important when improving social welfare.

The frontline worker is viewed in this study as a carrier and a creator of complex patterns of tensions at the intermediary level.

Organizing collaborative work like the family house is what all the stakeholders believe in. On a rhetorical level in the social welfare system, collaboration has been taken for granted as a doctrine for achieving efficiency. New public management is still a way of steering welfare systems with incentives for short-term economic cutbacks, production of service, denial of political interests, free choice of the end user, and control of measurable goals (Montin, 2002). Among the frontline workers, however, the current doctrine on collaboration is to meet families' needs and involve them in the development of activities in which values of democracy, social networking and also economic savings in the long run are discussed. Since successful organizing is usually built on strength in doctrines rather than research, the question is which doctrine of collaboration will win.

Tensions in the organization of collaboration have been explored in this chapter, but this does not mean that all existing tensions have been explored. According to Stacey (2001), knowledge is meaning that is constructed in a communicative interactive process between people. In this process the researcher has worked as a facilitator to encourage communication about experiences in organizing work. The objective has been to improve frontline workers' ability to see the everyday practice from different perspectives. The causes to tensions in the new organization have been explored. In these meetings, focus was set on structures in organizations, professional development and organizational culture. A metaphor that could be used is that the researcher has observed and pointed out stones on the road ahead. Also, she has suggested that the staff lift the stones and have a look at what could be beneath them. In an ever-changing context there will always be new stones that need to be lifted. Therefore, it would be ambitious enough to claim that this study can only say something about the process of knowledge creation in this context. Hopefully, this way of working can contribute inspiration and 'reflection tools' that could be useful to other frontline workers in other contexts.

Preamble

This chapter illustrates how teachers position themselves and are positioned in terms of rights, duties and obligations as users of information and communication technology. This is done against the backdrop of the emergence of a system-level bureaucracy concerned with the design of a new organizational backbone in a local school district. An overarching concern is whether there is a shift from system-level to street-level bureaucracy discretion and the possible implications of such a shift. Data for this chapter have been drawn from material collected by the research project *ICT and Learning in Teacher Training*, funded by the Knowledge Foundation through its research programme LearnIt.

Lars-Erik Nilsson

'Shutting down the network'

System level discretion and teacher discretion in talk about technology

Introduction

This study discusses how teachers position themselves and are in turn positioned in terms of their rights, duties, and obligations as users of information and communication technology (ICT), and whether this positioning constitutes a bureaucratic shift. Browsing information about education at different municipal websites uncovered the following text that can serve as a starting point:

> An operation governed by goals and results requires continuous follow-up and assessment. Some of these [i.e., follow-up and assessment measures] have been determined by government, [measures] such as quality accounts, cost accounts, national tests, and grades. Others have been initiated and devised by the municipality of Nacka by itself or in collaboration with other municipalities, for example, municipal tests, observations, customer surveys, and analysis of different parts of the operation. (Nacka: Title utvärdering active 2007-08-27)

The above text summarizes some of the concerns involved in quality management carried out by the municipality of Nacka, Sweden, and how these are framed. What is particularly interesting in the case of Nacka is that much of what it does is done using ICT. Data for reports to national administrative bodies are gathered through forms on the Internet. Requests for data are disseminated to professionals who feed these data into the system; results are disseminated to professionals and concerned citizens. An up-to-date plan for follow-up and assessment is linked to the information. That way the citizens of Nacka can, at least in theory, stay informed using the web. Management by documents, as it is aptly called in another chapter (Agevall & Jonnergård, chapter 2, this volume), seems to have become an important part of the bureaucracy. At first glance, this networked model closely resembles a traditional hierarchical bureaucracy with professionals at 'street level' doing discretionary work, the difference being that there is more information to manage.

Professional tools and professional discretion and autonomy

This study presents ICT implementation as a rhetorical dilemma. Teacher use of ICT extends beyond simply answering demands for data registration. Technology is used in a range of educational practices, including those that support direct classroom activities, such as classroom activity planning. Teachers need to communicate with students and peers; they need to search for and publish information, set up courses and lessons, use training programmes, prepare online lectures, and tutor students on their projects – to cite just a few examples. Will managerial control of ICT mark the end of discretion and autonomy, or will teachers be able to use technology to strengthen their position as professionals? In short, what kind of space is being constituted for teachers and for pedagogy?

Professional work is generally regarded as characterized by discretion. While decisions are supposed to be based on a shared professional knowledge base, every case needs to be treated as unique. Professionals therefore must have a high degree of autonomy. It can be argued that discretion extends to the use of available tools – at least to how tools should be used in individual cases – to arrive at the best possible results. Applications such as documentation systems with standardized forms, limitations on the sources of information professionals may tap, and design solutions that dictate particular professional actions all would seem to go against such an understanding.

A point of departure of this chapter is the understanding that there is a field of tension between organizations and professions concerning the use of ICT. This tension refers to more than simply management by documents, instead extending from the implementation of particular forms of infrastructure to the choice of tools professionals can use and how these may be used. Professionals will be differently positioned when it comes to influencing decisions in these matters:

some positions will increase their autonomy while others will leave them little power to influence how they do their work. Indeed, as new technology is put in place, new groups may claim the expertise to make decisions (Postman, 1993). Tensions between professions and organizations concerning the rights and duties to use professional tools thus imply consequences for the individual teacher and the kinds of positions made available to them.

Street- and system-level bureaucracy and the discretionary use of tools

From a historical perspective, discourse on tensions between organizations and occupations/professions on the issue of tools has a long history. These tensions were of central importance to Marx and formed part of his class struggle concept (1974). In contemporary discourse on technology, tensions between organizations and occupations/professions about technology cover a wide spectrum of matters: design, implementation, and diffusion, technology assessment, and professional use – to mention but a few. Bovens and Zouridis (2002) pick up on the idea that workers (in their study, professionals) may become 'objects of the machine', and they ask what legal consequences such a development would have for the bureaucracy in the constitutional state. They assert, much as was suggested in the introduction to this chapter, that technology is rapidly changing the workings of traditional bureaucracy. Their study found that system analysts and software designers have intervened in bureaucracy and, in some realms, through particular system designs, replaced traditional bureaucrats. According to Bovens and Zouridis,

> Window clerks are being replaced by Web sites and advanced information and expert systems are taking over the roles of case managers and adjudicating officers. Instead of noisy disorganized decision-making factories populated by fickle officials, many of these executive agencies are fast becoming quiet information refineries, in which nearly all decisions are pre-programmed by algorithms and digital decision trees. (p. 175)

Bovens and Zouridis suggest that street-level bureaucracy is being replaced first by 'screen-level' then by system-level bureaucracy. They identify some differences between the workings of organizations, professionals, and technology in the different bureaucracies. In street-level bureaucracy, technology is designed to support and ICT is primarily used to register and store data. Case managers still make up the organizational backbone and manage individual cases using their professional discretion. In system-level bureaucracy, technology now effectively has been given a decisive role, executing controls and communicating externally. Categories are predefined and for each category there is a fixed solution. In the organizational backbone case managers are replaced by system designers who implement the rules for handling cases. Communication between databases causes the boundaries of organizations to dissolve. A legal system incorporating detailed control and allowing for little discretion has replaced the traditional open system with its ample discretion.

Such discourses are also present in this volume. Agevall and Jonnergård (this volume) argue that documentary systems can be used as control mechanisms, for steering purposes, and to standardize professional work, shifting control from the individual professional to the organization. Hansen (this volume) describes how control of national health registers, set up by the medical profession to serve as professional knowledge bases, is being threatened by health authorities and those who construct such information systems and want to use them for managerial purposes. In contrast, Ljung-Djärf (this volume) argues that pre-school teachers are trying to resolve organizational/professional tensions by invoking different rationales as to what it means to be a teacher working in a pre-school. Thus, introducing ICT has various influences on the discretionary nature of work and professional autonomy.

A problem with Bovens and Zouridis' study is that it draws on data from agencies dealing solely with traffic violations and student grants. According to their description, these have already been transformed into screen-level bureaucracies in which the process of handling cases has been routinized. These agencies have now become system-level bureaucracies in which the role of ICT is no longer simply one of data registration and storage. ICT has taken on a decisive role and, as a result, street-level bureaucracy is disappearing. The question posed by Bovens and Zouridis is whether introducing ICT will 'eventually transform all street-level bureaucracies into system-level bureaucracies' (p. 180). As early as Lipsky's (1980) work on street-level bureaucracy, it was argued that some professional work, for example, that of 'patrolmen assigned to traffic duty or gun permit applications' (p. 15) had 'relatively little bureaucratic discretion' (ibid.). Should we assume that Bovens and Zouridis' observations about the use of ICT are restricted to the particular line of work under study, or that messages such as those on the Nacka website prefigure what will also happen to street-level bureaucracies that are non-routine and non-legal, such as teaching?

Drawing on Bovens and Zouridis (2002), Agevall and Jonnergård (this volume), and Hansen (this volume), one would expect that teacher discretionary work would, if not be replaced, at least eventually be circumscribed by managerial routines that will interfere with professional autonomy. A pressing issue is whether this type of governance will also extend to pedagogy. Ljung-Djärf (this volume) indicates that while teachers do not openly resist implementing technology, they allow their professional judgement to influence how technology is used. Rather than being technological drones, teachers turn technology itself into an object of knowledge and use their professional knowledge to make sense of it.

Data and analysis

The kind of analysis employed here to examine the possible effects of ICT on discretionary work and teacher professional autonomy draws on positioning theory. The particular interest when analysing this data in this way is the dynamics of identity mediated by tension between stable roles in the moral order and new work tools introduced in the organization. The suggestion is that roles such as teacher, head teacher, ICT pedagogue, or support technician are too stable and all inclusive to guide analysis of the effects of technology on professional identity.

In studying how identity is defined and formed, data have been analysed using positioning theory. This theoretical perspective asserts that 'assessment talk' is ubiquitous in any encounter between groups of people and technology (van Langenhove & Bertolink, 1999, p. 123). In such talk, storylines are produced about technology in which rights and duties feature as resources that make positions available and in which contextually sensitive clusters of rights and duties are deployed to sustain different positions. People position themselves or are positioned as controlled or autonomous, interested or disinterested, included or excluded – to cite just a few examples. An almost limitless number of categories can logically be applied (Harré & Moghaddam, 2003, pp. 3–4), some of which may harmonize well with the idea of the autonomous professional carrying out discretionary work in street-level bureaucracies. Others are in line with the idea of professionals who have been forced to relinquish discretion and become dominated by technology in what may resemble a system-level bureaucracy.

What is essential here is that studying such assessment talk allows researchers to address how cultural tools are used to produce positions. From this perspective, cultural tools may be said to be positioning devices. Rather than assuming that technology determines action, that professional work is discretionary, or that street-level bureaucracies are becoming system-level bureaucracies, such descriptions are treated here as discursive resources that feature in storylines that outline professionals' relationships to technology. Stories can also be told about their rights or duties to fill in forms, install software, use particular software, access other people's accounts, or report students who interfere with the configuration of a system.

Drawing on positioning theory, I argue that it matters what positions professionals are afforded when we talk about professional tools. These positions are consequential for the rights and duties of both the profession and the individual professional. A teacher may claim to have excellent knowledge of how to use technology to support writing and, from that position, expect to influence how the technology is to be used. A teacher who claims not to know how to use technology is less likely to be asked for opinions on the design and use of technology. Whether teachers are empowered or disempowered by technology, both individually and as a profession, can arguably be analysed through considering the acts/actions that are made available to them.

The owners, the intermediaries, and the disowned

The data used in this study were collected in ethnographically inspired research carried out in a local school district from 2000 to 2005. Meetings of ICT support teams and reference groups, and 'local talk' between administrators, technicians, teachers, and students were video taped, audio taped, or recorded in field notes. The data used here are from audio recordings and field notes; they are used to illustrate how the rights and duties to influence the design, implementation, and use of technology have become topics of conversation at work.

We will consider four stories or texts: the first is a transcribed excerpt from a reference group meeting in an ICT support organization, the second is a transcribed excerpt from a meeting of technicians in a local school district and the third a recreation from field notes describing a conversation during a coffee break in a reference group meeting. The fourth is a story retold from field notes describing a conversation between personnel at a newly opened school equipped to give teachers and students access to state-of-the-art modern technology. What these texts share is that they all deal with different ways of positioning teachers as ICT users. The transcriptions are verbatim, and our aim has been to preserve the language of the participants – even when ungrammatical or incomplete. To note pauses in speech, parenthetical indications such as '(.)' for a short pause and '(2.4)' for a 2.4-second-long pause have been used following the conventions of Jeffersonian transcription.

We now turn to data gathered at the local level in a reference group tied to a local IT centre. The group comprises those sometimes referred to as the 'ICT responsible' (*IT-ansvariga*) and other times as 'ICT pedagogues' (*IT-pedagoger*). It is rather unclear to the group what their function and their mandate is. At times they position themselves as 'just a group that discusses ICT in schools', while at other times as 'responsible for implementation'. The interlocutors, Ivar, Rut, Reidar, Roger, and Rune, have all been given pseudonyms.

The excerpt involves talk about access to the educational network. The conversation starts with a complaint about access to the public network used by local schools. This network is very slow and the question is what can be done about it. Access to the public network is turned into an object of knowledge that makes different positions available for those employed in the school system.

Text 1: Excerpt 1

1	*Ivar*	How they want this, it is something we can bring up – hey now
2		it's lagging [inaudible] the public network.
3	*Rut*	Lagging very much.
4	*Ivar*	Lagging very much.
5	*Reidar*	When they are shutting down the public network and then go
6		to the administration and tell them that now the public net-
7		work isn't working.
8	*Ivar*	Yeah, yeah.

9	*Roger*	It's just a lot of laughs [laughter].
10	*Rune*	Didn't get that.
11	*Reidar*	So there is a red flag. Then you have to rush down and (.) shove
12		the school secretary aside so you can see (0.8) if you have access
13		to it, administratively, somewhere else (1.5) when people are
14		breathing down your neck
15	*Ivar*	Hmm (1.9). And it's a lot, there's like now no view of the whole
16		um (1.3). No coherence in the work done. Neither on the edu
17		cational network nor this about lag and who you're supposed
18		to contact and who runs what (.) And now it takes about four
19		weeks more – well like you know, we have been harping on the
20		same theme with the central city authorities about the special
21		schools since I don't know when eh (0.8). Going on a two-year
22		anniversary. I think it is unbelievable.

The issue raised here can be described as one of ownership. Ivar presents the problem of the lagging 'public network' and suggests that the group should act on it. This indicates that at least they own the problem in the sense that they *can* act on it. Their action has the rhetorical construction of a complaint. The 'public network' is the one used by teachers and students to do school work. It is a primary work tool for thousands of people. Lagging is a nuisance, especially when teachers need to deal with a group of irritated students who cannot access the applications and information they need. The complaints are unanimous and all members of the reference group agree that the network is too slow.

The next storyline begins at line 5, where we learn that some unidentifiable 'they' have the power to shut down the network when it is lagging. The reference group may own the right to complain but they do not own the right to decide on network operations.

Reidar jokes about this and makes a connection between shutting down 'the network' and the right to be informed. The unidentified group that has the power to cut the power 'then go to the administration and tell them that now the public net isn't working' (lines 5–7). The use of 'then' implies a sequential ordering that connects the incidents. First we have a lagging network, then a decision to shut it down, and then finally the administration is informed – but no information is given to the thousands of students and teachers left without a network connection. The way people are informed – or not informed – is presented as premeditated. Those responsible knew beforehand and had the opportunity to inform students and teachers by disseminating a message, about an upcoming shut down through 'the public net'. They are positioned as though they do not need to inform teachers and students of their actions, but must or at least can chose to inform administration afterwards. Not only do they own the right to make decisions concerning the running of the local network, but they also own the right to determine where the information should go. Roger's remark 'it's just a lot of laughs' is the type of underplayed sarcasm that signals agreement about that something is wrong.

Ivar seconds this, sharing Reidar's perception, and experience, of how rights and duties are distributed in the organization: teachers and students are effectively disowned, stripped of any right to know why their tools do not work. It may be hard to reconcile this appraisal with certain notions, for example, that this technology is the backbone of a new educational infrastructure and that the applications that run on it are new tools of learning. Such a point, however, is not raised. In this storyline, teachers are not the owners of their tools; they are just professional users who have been stripped of their rights. The power to determine when they can use their tools resides elsewhere. How the members of the reference group position teachers and systems people is consistent with Bovens and Zouridis' (2000) suggestion that ICT gives system analysts and designers discretionary power, and that system-level discretion appears to impede street-level discretion, in this case restricting teachers' actions as pedagogues.

So what rights do teachers and students have? They cannot use some of their work tools and they are not informed, but they can still act to get information. Reidar states that when there is a 'red flag' and 'people are breathing down your neck' (line 11 through 14) he has to get to a computer that can access the administrative network quickly, so he can find vital information. The rhetorical construction '*when* there is' suggests that what is described is not an isolated event. Reidar can and repeatedly does act as an intermediary between the owners and the disowned to make sure teachers are informed. His story line positions teachers (and students) as people who need to know – and indeed, should have the right to know – why their work tools are not working and himself as resourceful enough to get to that information. All it takes is to act as though you have the right to find out and to 'shove the school secretary aside' (lines 11–12).

Neither teachers nor ICT pedagogues, however, have the right to decide when they should have access to the public network; that right rests elsewhere in the organization. Teachers have found out to whom they should direct their complaints, but ICT pedagogues have not. It is not clear 'who you're supposed to contact and who runs what' (lines 17–18). Decisions about running the technology have become hidden at a system level and subject to discretionary judgements at that level. Faceless figures control teachers' use of technology and limit the efforts of ICT pedagogues to intervene as intermediaries on teachers' behalf.

The supportive, the competent, and the less competent

The data used in the second example were collected at the IT centre, a support organization in a local school district, at what we understand from the TV series *Hill Street Blues* would be called a 'roll call', but in the context of this organization is called a '*teknikerbönemöte*' – literally, 'technicians' prayer meeting'. Ingemar is the pseudonym of the head of the department, and Tomislav, Tommy, and Tryggve for the technicians present. What transpires can best be described as institutional assessment talk involving an 'appreciation' of operations. Technicians are asked to account for how they support computers issued by the government – ITiS project (ICT in Schools for a description see chapter 3, this volume) and their users.

Text 2: Excerpt 1

1	*Ingemar*	How much of a burden do you feel ITiS computers are to you (1.1)?
2	*Tomislav*	It has begun to become become too much (0.6). It has be (.) I
3		feel this bur-, this pressure, really, and the main reason is the
4		connection to Internet from home (1.9). That and a lot of stuff
5		that they cannot manage by themselves and you know it's sen-
6		sitive particularly on portable computers (0.3).
7	*Ingemar*	Hmm.
8	*Tomislav*	So repeatedly (1.1). At least eh once or twice a week I have a
9		client who comes with a computer and says I can't connect it
10		to the Internet (0.4). So we should perform a test for errors. I
11		haven't said 'no' to them but this is.
12	*Ingemar*	No.
13	*Tomislav*	Then also come with applications, to update anti-virus programs.
14		Why can't I do this or that – I mean, from stupid to sophisti-
15		cated questions (2.4).

Ingemar starts by asking about how much of a burden a particular aspect of support is for the technicians. Tomislav's answer reveals that it is not ITiS computers *per se* that are the problem; rather, it is the competence of the teaching staff. Working with ITiS computers has become 'too much' because of the teachers' lack of competence. He refers to problems with Internet connections from home that 'they cannot manage by themselves' (line 5). This can be seen as an act of demarcating two different occupations. Tomislav positions teachers, as a group, as incompetent and technicians, as a group, as competent when it comes to solving problems with Internet connections. In the context of relationships between technicians and their clients, such a description may be consequential. Setting up computers so as to allow teachers to access Internet from their homes becomes a technical problem that currently must be solved by the technicians. A demand is placed on technicians to be supportive, but in turn, they are given the right to monopolize such work.

At first glance, it appears as though Tomislav allocates rights and duties only to technicians, and that teachers' rights are limited to asking for help. In lines 13–15 Tomislav extends this to actions such as using and updating applications and the duty of technicians to support anything from 'stupid to sophisticated questions'. It becomes apparent that teachers' rights and duties, like those of technicians, may have something to do with positions that draw on competence. As we recall, Tomislav says that it has 'become too much', a comment that speaks against any notion that he is trying to monopolize the right to provide such support. This becomes even clearer when Tommy, another technician, states that it was only a temporary problem when teachers needed help 'with mounting' the network cards (lines 17–20, excerpt 2). He indicates that some teachers do have problems of a more technical nature, but that his support cases are few.

Text 2: Excerpt 2

16 *Ingemar* Tommy what do you feel ITiS computers?
17 *Tommy* Eh yes, for some time there were many that came, but it was
18   because of that mounting of eh
19 *Ingemar* No.
20 *Tommy* Network cards
21 *Ingemar* Yes.

24 *Tommy*   That they were going to use like (1.9). But it's not something
25   special. It's mostly that way [inaudible] ITiS. But the others don't
26   need to [inaudible].
27 *Ingemar* What you can say is that (0.6). The interesting if we compare
28   your two areas then 'M' school (0.9). Those who have entered
29   the ITiS project. They have relatively high (1.5) personal ICT
30   competence. Most of them (1.8) really, they are high up (.) on
31   the scale. So we have been spared dealing with these problems
32   there. But your schools (0.6), on the contrary, G school espe-
33   cially.
34 *Tomislav* And 'L' school too.
35 *Ingemar* And 'L' school too there are n-
36 *Tomislav* there are not so many
37 *Ingemar* There are, there are not such high competence levels.

Tommy's response prompts one in turn from Ingemar (lines 27–33), who suggests that teachers may not be incompetent as a group. Indeed, there are schools where teachers have sufficient competence to deal with technical issues and are not prevented from doing so. Teachers' discretionary use of technology seems, at this point, to depend on their competence.

'ITiS computers' seem to be indexical to those speaking at this meeting. Why do teachers insist on using ITiS computers when there are other computers at their schools? Why are ITiS computers not treated the same as other computers? Why is support of ITiS computers a particular problem? ITiS computers are not really the concern of this support team. They have been given by the state to those participating in the ITiS project, and there is a special support organization responsible for them; this was a government decision. In this case, however, the local school organization installed network card in ITiS computers, so teachers could use them in the local school network. This was a decision made at a managerial level to enable teachers to use their ITiS computers at school. The installation of these cards caused problems that have become a support problem for local technicians, simply because the cards' installation in the computers was a local management decision.

Tommy does not, however, turn technical issues *per se* into work tasks that should be carried out only by technicians, or by the external support organization for that matter. Ingemar claims that they 'have been spared dealing with these problems' because of the 'relatively high personal ICT competence' of personnel at the 'M' school. The network card thus functions as a boundary object (Bowker & Star, 1999, pp. 296–298) in the storyline, shedding light on teachers' rights to obtain support and on the competent users' right to self support. Teachers positioned as competent appear to have the right to solve particular technical problems without asking for help.

There is an obvious similarity between how teachers are positioned in this text and in the previous one about the lagging net. In both texts, teachers are *objects* of decisions made by other groups. Instructions are built into the system, the network is shut down, and network cards are added to the computers – these actions are 'done to' teachers but mediated by technology. In all environments, however, teachers have the right to exert some control, depending on the position they can assume. The first text described how they were disowned, stripped of access; 'faceless others' could pull the plug and leave them without access. Even as disowned parties, however, they could still ask for information about the lagging network and base their actions on the answer. The second text affords two teacher positions mediated by the network card. The way to make sense of Ingemar's response seems to be that teachers' rights and technicians' duties must be seen in relation to teachers' technical competence rather than in relation to their professional status. If they cannot mount network cards they are entitled to support, but if they can they are free to mount them without help. Teachers are thus positioned as both competent and incompetent and are empowered to make decisions based on their competence. They cannot, however, influence how their computers are configured or when they should have access to the network; that right is not based on competence.

The surveyed and the surveyors

That rights are not distributed according to a strictly hierarchical model becomes obvious in the next text. Text 3, excerpt 1 comes from field notes describing a conversation during a coffee break in a meeting of the same reference group that also figured in the first excerpt. Present at the table are Ivar, Ingemar, Ralf, Helena, and the author. During the meeting, the competence of school management has been an issue, and members of the group have contributed stories that have caused group members to laugh. During the coffee break an old anecdote is retold, one that had previously been told to the author at a universi-

ty in another city. According to the field notes, the conversation went
something like this:

Text 3: Excerpt 1

1	*Ivar*	You remember I told you about mail.
2	*Helena*	You mean about privileges?
3	*Ivar*	Yes, they had forgotten to set privileges so the head teachers were
4		set as super users.
5	*Ralf*	And they managed to delete all mail for all teachers believing
6		they had only deleted their own.
7	*Ivar*	Lots of fun. Not much competence there. We had to revoke
8		their privileges.
9	*Ingemar*	I remember when one of them turned up at a staff meeting and
10		started by saying that one issue on the agenda could not be dis-
11		cussed, because some staff had not read their mail and had not
12		prepared.
13	*Ralf*	Yeah, people were really pissed off and wanted to know who
14		and what he based this information on.
15	*Helena*	And then he said he had looked at the message history.
16	*Ingemar*	And two people told him their work group had printed out the
17		information and discussed it, and another one said he had his
18		mail forwarded to Outlook and never opened it in the local mail
19		system.
20	*Ralf*	Good story.
21	*Author*	Yes, I remember when I first heard it at a school several years ago.
22		They said it happened there.

There are several things to say about this passage, one being that the
present author has used both these anecdotes many times in lectures
to illustrate how power may be exerted and how we leave traces in
the systems we use. Once, however, it was a real-life story told by the
group of teachers who had actually attending the particular staff meeting. In this coffee-break conversation, head teachers are positioned as
another group with dangerously little competence. We learn that they
had super-user privileges in the local mail system, probably assigned
to them because of their role in the moral order, and thus could erase
all mail – unfortunately, also mail that belonged to others. This
would seem to indicate that those placed at a high level in the school
system are also placed high in the communication system.

Ivar, who is responsible for running the mail system in the local school district, makes the point that this should not necessarily be the case – at least not when one considers the damage that could result. What is interesting is how privileges seem to be distributed. A head teacher's privileges seem to be established at the discretion of some unspecified administrative body, yet can be revoked by Ivar, a lower-ranking official. Being responsible for the mail system, albeit at a local level, seems to carry with it discretionary power that extends to setting privileges for those more highly placed.

The second part of the anecdote concerns management by documents, what traces we leave, and how these can be used. Documents are disseminated to teachers to be read and commented on; teachers have a right to be informed and a duty to send back their responses to the documents. The text illustrates one feature of this form of surveillance. Not only is it transparent to those involved what information is sent out and how it is being responded to; the head teacher brings into the discussion the fact that it is also transparent what has been read. Somewhere at a system level it has been accepted that the communication system used for mail in the organization should be equipped with a feature called 'history' that lets users see whether a message has been opened. The head teacher positions himself as a surveyor with the right to use this feature to survey the actions of his teachers. Do they read his messages promptly? This feature works in both directions, also letting teachers see whether their head teacher has read their mail. As far as surveillance goes, what has actually been done to a particular message is not as transparent as the head teacher would have it, and there are suggestions that the accuracy of the surveillance should be checked more carefully before blame is assigned. Among the rights of the surveilled in this case is the right to respond to accusations. There is no claim, however, that such surveillance encroaches on the integrity of the teachers, merely that the information obtained must be checked for accuracy before it is used. Thus integrity is not treated as an issue in their discussion of surveillance.

The excluded and the resourceful

The final story is retold from field notes on a conversation between the author and a teacher at a newly built lower secondary school, a school designed to support science and technology work. It is equipped with laptops, wireless access, video projectors, IP addresses for media broadcast, and a range of devices such as scanners, USB microscopes, and music equipment. Elena has just finished a lesson and we are standing beside the trolleys that carry the laptops the students can use. The story goes something like this:

Elena complains that 'the distribution of computers takes a lot of time', but also claims that teachers constantly find ways to solve problems, such as 'connecting the laptops to power directly at the trolley'. In the initial storyline, teachers are positioned as resourceful: as professionals they find ways to solve problems even if circumstances are less than optimal. She also positions teachers as incompetent ICT users. She claims that their lack of competence has led them to let their students use computers without knowing why they should use them:

> ... today I haven't had time to help anyone with their work, well, or hardly anyone. It seems like those who plan ICT believe that all students know everything about computers.

Elena has been forced to spend all her time on problems concerning students' use of computers; no time was left to help students with the actual *contents* of their projects.

The field notes indicate that teachers have not really been involved in designing this particular environment; Elena claims that there

> ... were some people in administration and some head teachers who wanted a school like this with lots of technology. We should have been hired early to take part in the design but it didn't happen.

The initiative has emanated from the system level. Teachers were supposed to participate in discussions affecting the learning environment, but were never invited. Elena positions teachers as excluded from design but included in implementation. Being excluded suggests being absolved from responsibility for decisions made in the design process. Decisions were made without taking account of important factors, such as teacher skills, student skills, and professional demands on learning environments. This omission is presented as consequential. Poor student skills present a problem. 'Hardly anyone can use a graphics program', and 'if you tell a student that they must send something to another student, you must help them'.

Unfortunately it has become a case of the blind leading the blind, as teachers only know enough 'to keep from going under'. Her conclusion is that

> in a school like this where we are supposed to use computers a lot, you really need a teacher who is a computer specialist.

Another kind of urgency is built into Elena's storylines, despite the fact that they do depict teachers as resourceful. Teachers need to solve problems in an environment that has been designed by others; they may not have been involved in design, but they are constantly involved in assessment and re-design. While observing that laptop docking is too slow, that student and teacher competence is lacking, and that some technical devices cannot be used, she nevertheless tries to think of how to improve operations. She voices ideas about computer labs, recruiting people who know the software, and setting up basic computer training for students, so that teaching time is freed up and students can do the type of work they need to do.

Elena alternates in her narrative between 'I' and 'we', using 'I' in her tired description of what has just transpired and 'we' when talking about the situation in general. Teachers as a group should have been included, but in practice are excluded from the 'big' decisions about setting up learning environments. She mentions others who have the right to make such decisions: head teachers and local technical administrators, but also systems people.

Elena does not suggest they should not use computers in school. Resourceful teachers have a right to deal with problems locally using their professional discretion. It is clear that she makes professional judgements about what does and does not work. Teachers are positioned as resourceful in her storylines. They find it within their rights to assess technology and to make suggestions, even changes. These rights and duties are, however, restricted. They are restricted in terms of what can be influenced and also by teacher competence. Despite being resourceful herself, she feels a need for *teachers* who are specialists; technicians they already have. She is willing to invite in other occupational groups with higher competence in certain areas, to help deal with the immediate needs in this particular learning environment.

Rights, duties, and positions

This study was introduced as a discussion of how teachers position themselves and are in turn positioned in terms of their rights, duties, and obligations as ICT users. A Swedish municipal website was cited as an example of how new managerialism has introduced forms of 'management by documents' that force professionals to perform certain work in a certain way. A study by Boven and Zouridis (2002) was cited to illustrate that, for some professions, introducing ICT has already meant doing away with street-level bureaucracy, replacing it with system-level bureaucracy. Bovens and Zouridis left readers with the question of whether this could happen to all professions, teachers being one example. This study in a sense both narrows the question down to whether this could happen to the teaching profession in particular, while broadening the scope of the question to encompass the overall control of professional tools in general. Who is in control and for what can technology be used?

According to Bovens and Zouridis (2002), system-level discretion impinges on the moves street-level bureaucrats could make, binding them to certain approaches, circumscribing their professional decision-making, and ultimately threatening to replace them with technology. The data cited in the present study suggest an impact from system-level bureaucracy that is no less dramatic. Here it is teachers' *access* to technology that is subject to system-level discretion, rather than their professional application of technology to perform their work. The shutting down of the network without prior notice could be likened to removing all surgical tools from a ward because they were needed elsewhere, without notifying the staff about to perform surgery. Teachers are effectively being stripped of their professional tools and the only professional response they have is to ask for information. Teachers' total reliance on technicians for simple questions bind them together as a group possessing little knowledge of what kind of technology support they need to be able to carry out their work. They know how to access the library but many of them do not know how to access the network. At the same time, they are loaded with expectations; they are supposed to read their mail, and they fear whether or not they have done so can be checked. How does this fit with Bovens and Zouridis' question as to whether teaching work can be turned into system bureaucracy work? A preliminary answer would seem to be that teaching work is still discretionary and that teachers have professional autonomy – at least if they can manage to position themselves as competent and resourceful professionals who own the question of how to use ICT in education.

What is evident in the data presented here, however, is that teachers do want to use the new technology: they try to get access to the network, they try to get support. It is not management by documents that is their problem. It is access to tools that can support pedagogical work and the competence to use these tools skilfully. Teachers, however, are seldom portrayed as a group in this data; rather, they are individuals working under particular local conditions. There are a number of positions they can take up or become forced into as individuals. Those who are positioned or manage to position themselves as owners or as competent and resourceful play by one set of rules. They can influence technology, at least when it comes to local decisions. They can influence access to technology and even have a say about the workings of their own computers; in the extreme, they can even add hardware to their computers. In many cases, they can install particular software they need and access the websites they want to access; there are few local restrictions. Furthermore, judging from the Elena's example, finding their own local solutions is what teachers do, even when they have been excluded from all other stages of design.

Another way to answer the question posed by Bovens and Zouridis is to say that teachers are not quite there yet. Prior research suggests that teachers as a group have acted as gatekeepers, keeping ICT out when they have not been convinced that it can add something to how they solve problems (Cuban, 1986, 2002; Jedeskog, 2000; Robertson, 2000). Furthermore, there has been strong political resistance to the idea that teachers should be controlled or replaced by technology. This may be changing. 'Shutting down the net' illustrates an important aspect of networked technology. Decisions about access and surveillance in networked systems indicate that at least some *individual* professional decisions are becoming impossible. Teachers cannot leave their mail unopened or not report absences; it will be noted. There is also the further question of management by documents. Such systems were not yet in place by the end of this study, but application launchers, surveying software, and the like had already been tested.

However, Bovens and Zouridis' (2002) question still lingers, and should be linked to questions about the danger that discretionary power 'could cause an open society to be smothered in the bud' (174).

Boven and Zouridis pose their question in relation to Hayek's assertion that discretionary power threatens democracy, and Durkheim's assertion that a society without regulation faces anomie. Boven and Zouridis consider the opposite to be the case. Can system-level discretion replace street-level bureaucracy, even in such professions as the teaching profession, and if so, what will the consequences be? In answer to the first question, the data analysed in this chapter instead suggest a dynamic relationship more along the lines of an irreducible tension between professional agents and bureaucracy at system levels. Decisions made at system levels are treated as ubiquitous challenges to professional discretion, in this case, to teachers' agency. These decisions are presented as dilemmas rather than threats, and are assessed for their consequences. Here they appear as issues concerning the running of networks, design of local learning environments, surveillance tendencies, and decisions concerning technical support in a local school district. The seriousness of such decisions does not, however, go unnoticed. Teachers both are described and describe themselves as a group lacking control of their tools, possibly even being controlled by their tools. Most teachers share experiences of being unable to perform work because of restrictions put in place by hidden system-level agents.

One question is left hanging. Is there a shift in progress from street-level to system-level bureaucracy, or vice versa, and could such a shift threaten to smother an open society? In answering, it is pertinent to reflect on what has come to pass since the data here were collected at this particular local school district. This is a question that greatly concerns the space allowed for pedagogy. Since the study, access to sites and resources on the net has been limited through the use of a variety of filters, Novell Application Launcher objects have been used to set standards for anything from the right to save data to the right to install software, and rights to privacy are being discussed. On a last visit to a school in the same municipality, but in another school-district, the teachers had all the hardware – video projectors, DV cameras, tape recorders, 'smart boards', and computers – but could not insert memory sticks and save work. After taking photos with her students, one teacher was informed that she did not have access rights allowing her to import them to her computer and display them on the smart board. Head teachers were instrumental in acquiring the artefacts but have been unable to influence the rules for their use.

Professionals' rights to discretion do not go unchallenged – this is true in both everyday life and science – and do not automatically pose a threat. Boven and Zouridis, assert that history has proved constitutional and welfare states to be reconcilable. Initially, this has happened through constructing a *cordon sanitaire* around welfare state organizations, a project that now needs to be repeated when it comes to system-level bureaucrats. Ultimately, their belief rests on faith in a strong constitutional state that can implement checks and balances, but not on professionals' unconditioned right to their tools. It does, however, point us towards a need for further exploration of the effects of the democratic system on teachers' access to the tools of their profession.

Preamble

This article concerns the ways in which pre-school teachers respond to expectations that the computer, as a new and challenging form of technology, is to be incorporated into the institutional practice of the educational system. Pre-school staff faces a dilemma in terms of what these expectations mean for pre-school activities. The article addresses an area of tension where pre-school staff and their traditional discursive approaches to pre-school activities are challenged by organizational expectations and demands for computer implementation – the tension between a central 'ICT vision' and the pre-school teachers' professional knowledge base.

Agneta Ljung-Djärf

ICT and pre-school

Teachers' professional knowledge

The Swedish pre-school as an arena of change

Swedish pre-school implies full-day activities involving children from 1 to 5 years of age (Skolverket [National Agency for Education], 1998). Pre-school as a locale for care, nurturing, and teaching has a long and strong tradition in Sweden. The 1990s, though, brought a number of radical changes in pre-school activities. In addition to comprehensive financial cutbacks resulting in a lower staff-to-pupil ratio and a higher number of children per section (Lidholt, 1999), a number of other pervasive changes were introduced.

First, pre-schools came under the oversight of a different authority, moving in 1996 from the Socialstyrelsen [National Board of Health and Welfare] to the Utbildningsdepartementet [Ministry of Education and Science]. Second, the first official pre-school curriculum, Lpfö 98, was introduced by the Ministry in 1998. The curriculum was intended in part to foster equivalence among pre-schools at a high level of quality. The new governing regulations, which replaced what had previously been general guidelines for pre-school activities (Socialstyrelsen, 1987:3), spelled out the goals of such activities in various areas of childhood learning and development. Although the curriculum gives pre-schools a more clearly defined educational mission, it also stipulates that pre-schools must offer activities in which care, nurturing, and learning form a cohesive whole (Utbildningsdepartementet, 1998). Third, the institutions were to be referred to as pre-schools rather than day-care centres (Skolverket, 1998). Fourth, universal preschool was introduced, the need for care being no longer a prerequisite for participation, at least not in the case of children above the age of four (Regeringens Proposition [Government Bill] 1999/2000:129). The elimination of the need for care as a requirement for a place in pre-school not only gave pre-schools a more clearly defined educational rationale, but also indicated the importance of pre-school in a unified school system, and in the lifelong learning of the individual (Skolverket, 2004). These sweeping changes in pre-school activities have increased the focus on the content of the instruction and how it is to be provided, thereby confronting pre-schools with a major challenge in terms of maintaining and developing their unique character in the face of an intensified educational mission.

ICT in pre-school

Since the end of the 1990s, at the same time as Swedish pre-schools were being charged with this intensified educational mission, information and communication technology (ICT) and computers have become increasingly prevalent features of everyday pre-school activities. Educators themselves have only to a small extent driven this initiative. The trend toward computer use has instead been driven by political decisions and municipal investments. The computer was discussed and promoted in political rhetoric at the central government level as the tool of the future, and especially of education (Regeringsskrivelse [Government Communication], 1997/98:176). Ambitious visions were associated with its use in various educational contexts. When the decision was made, as of 2001, to incorporate knowledge of ICT and its areas of application at all levels of the educational system (Regeringsskrivelse, 1998/99:2), Swedish pre-schools figured prominently among those confronted with a major challenge. There were many aspects to this challenge, but I will limit discussion here to only the four main ones.

First, there was major uncertainty as to how pre-schools were actually factored into the key documents behind the investments in ICT within the educational system. It was unclear whether these investments were made at the time pre-schools were transferred from the oversight of one government authority to another because this timing coincided with political decisions about ICT. *How then were pre-school staff to relate to central directives formulated for school activities without risking 'schoolification'[1]?*

Second, there was also uncertainty as to why ICT should be incorporated in pre-school activities. The political rhetoric noted that there was a risk that digital advancements in the form of ICT use might create a gap between those with and those without knowledge of and access to such technology (Regeringens Proposition 1995/96:125; Regeringens Proposition 1996/97:112). There was also a lack of documentation describing just what would be achieved by using ICT in pre-schools specifically. *How were pre-school staff to relate to the use of ICT when the answer to the question of 'why' was not concretely related to activities in the pre-school?*

Third, the documentation that was presented provided few or no concrete proposals as to how the technology could or should be used, or at least none with which pre-schools could readily identify. The situation was rather that what was understood and defined within the pre-school profession as the mission and core of pre-school practice was challenged by ICT and the potential ways of using it that the educators could identify. *How were pre-school staff to relate to the use of ICT when there were no concrete examples of how the technology could contribute to fulfilling the pre-school's mission and developing its content?*

Fourth and finally, the lack of ICT knowledge and experience by pre-school teachers was perceived in many cases as restrictive, not least by the educators themselves (Ljung-Djärf, 2004). These limitations in terms of experience and insight in the area entailed that many of those who worked in pre-schools had no real opportunity to question or discuss educational visions and issues associated with the technology, or various experts' opinions on the possibilities of the technology and its educational applications. *How were pre-school staff to relate to ICT use when they lacked competence in terms of both the practical use of the technology and insight into the possibilities it would actually offer?*

Regardless of the answers to these questions, the official discussion produced signals and expectations that ICT was naturally an area and a mission that pre-school personnel could handle. It thus became the task of educators to transform political visions and plans into practical activities, and a large number of issues on computer implementation were thus placed in educators' hands. Most importantly, despite municipal investments in both technical equipment and training, a major challenge was now posed to educators (Ljung-Djärf, 2004). The purpose of this article, therefore, is to elucidate the tension that arose as a consequence of organizational requirements to implement ICT and the ways in which pre-school educators handled ICT in relation to the pre-school mission. In other words, to better understand the tension between the centrally generated 'ICT vision' and the pre-school teachers' professional knowledge base.

Theoretical framework

A sociocultural perspective on *ways of acting*, as described by Säljö (2005), is used as the point of departure for the study. Situated aspects of ways of acting and ongoing development of knowledge, are central in meetings between individuals as well as between individuals and artefacts. The sociocultural theoretical framework implies that understanding of the context in which the individual acts is taken as a point of departure for understanding that individual's actions. Institutional practices are thus to a great extent regulated by overriding goals and functions as well as by historical and cultural traditions.

Whereas pre-school is embedded within a well-established institutional practice with its equally well-established discursive patterns, ICT is of relatively recent date. When the use of computers was imposed upon pre-schools, it may be assumed that the question as to how the new artefact would be regarded was related to the existing pre-school discourse. In institutional practices such as pre-school, collectively held beliefs and ways of acting and thinking are developed about the activity and what takes place there. Conventions and expectations are constituted about what appears to be appropriate and reasonable within the practice. These systems of meaning-making exclude and include various ways of relating to different tasks. Modes of acting thus grounded in the institution constitute and reconstitute discursive patterns (Dahlberg & Lenz Taguchi, 1994; Säljö, 2005). When pre-school teachers act in their daily work, they act in accordance with the discursive patterns of the institution. Or, in other words, they act within a *discursive practice* (Mäkitalo, 2002; Säljö, 2005). Thus, different ways of acting are expressions of different ways of meaning-making within a particular discourse.

Ways of acting are situated in the practice and constitute a collective, ongoing, meaning-making process (Harré & van Langenhove, 1999b). The individuals' ways of acting imply different ways of *positioning* themselves, each other or the artefacts within the discursive practice. Positioning is understood in this study as constituting the ongoing play around and in relation to the computer within the pre-school practice.

Methdology of the study

Data were collected in three different municipal pre-school units with children from three to six years of age. The study involved about 60 children and 9 adults representing these pre-school units. Three of the pre-school personnel[2] were trained child minders (one in each unit) and six were pre-school teachers. All of the pre-school personnel were female. At the time of the study (1999–2000) the pre-school units had access to one computer each. The data collected from each unit consist of observations and interviews. Video recordings were made in addition to field notes of what took place around the computer. The activity in each unit was followed for 10 to 12 days over a period of three to four weeks. Approximately 13 hours of video documentation were collected and transcribed into written text.

Audio- and video-recorded interviews were also carried out with nine pre-school teachers (three from each unit). An interview guide with open-ended questions was used. Recordings were transcribed verbatim. The transcripts were scrutinised in a number of readings as well as in frequent re-readings to verify the texts against the original video or audio recordings. During this process of analysis, the researchers searched for differences and similarities in the ways of relating to computer use with respect to the particular discursive practice of pre-school.

Settings and subjects

Three pre-school units were selected for the study:

Bridge Street pre-school had enrolled children from an area with private houses and another area. The unit in the study had 20 children from 3:1 (3 years, 1 month) to 6:3 years of age. All but one had a computer at home. Of the four teachers at this unit, three agreed to an interview.

City pre-school had enrolled 21 children between 3:2 and 6:3 years of age. A majority of the children lived in a multi-racial area in public apartment housing, whereas a minority came from an area with private houses in the neighbourhood. Eight children had a computer at home. Four teachers worked at this unit, and three of them were interviewed.

Dale Street pre-school is situated in a socially well-established area with private houses. The unit taking part in the study had 21 children aged 3:2 to 6:0 years. All children had a computer at home. All three teachers working at the unit were interviewed.

Findings

The analysis showed how the teachers were striving in some way to realise the centrally formulated wishes or 'vision' for ICT implementation in pre-school activities. The teachers' ways of acting are found to be more or less in line with political visions, at least on a rhetorical level. They all, for example, describe the computer as a tool with possibilities. The possibilities, though, are typically described in terms of the future, for example use in school or in a future job. The importance of coming into contact with a computer is talked about in terms of equality and giving all the children the same opportunities to be introduced to and to use a computer. Nonetheless, the teachers' ways of describing computer use do not imply that the computer is seen as one of the main activities of pre-school, and it is seldom talked about as particularly useful in its own right. Computer use is, rather, an activity allowed between other pre-school activities regarded by the teachers as 'real' or 'important.' The computer is positioned as something to play with during time for free play, a sort of relaxing and entertaining break-time activity.

Beyond this common ground, the teachers' ways of acting are also found to be varied and constituted what, from the teachers' perspective, appears to be appropriate within the institutional practice. Three ways to manage computer use were identified at the three pre-school units participating in the study: *(A) as a threat to other activities, (B) as an available option*, and *(C) as an essential activity*[3]. Teachers tended to adopt one of these styles of classroom management.

A. Computer use as a threat to other activities

These teachers expressed the opinion that the computer use was important but should not be given a high priority, as the children need other things more. They are very eager to help and support the children in developing their verbal skills, but do not ascribe to the computer any role with respect to these efforts. Instead, the computer is described as a threat against other more important activities, as for example play and communication. When Catarina, one of the teachers, talks about the computer use, the children's needs are referred to as *special* needs.

Excerpt 1

Interviewer (I): Do you think that the way that you use the computer is the way you'd want? [...] does it turn out the way you'd want it to work?

Catarina: For these children I think there are other things that are more important. It's a little different, if I think about the other group of kids I had there, then maybe I could think about developing that a bit more.

I: Do you mean when you were at X pre-school?

Catarina: Yes

I: That was another reception area for pupils?

Catarina: Yes, because here they need to, they need to play and they choose to do that most of the time.

I: Mmmm

Catarina: Because we aim somewhat to do what the kids want, I don't think we should force things on them.

The choice to use the computer is left to the children, and the personnel do not take any responsibility to make the children use the computer. Instead, the teacher seems to see a risk of the children spending too much time at the computer. For this reason it seems to be important not to encourage an increased interest among the children.

The teachers are continuously supporting the children with different materials, supervising, playing games, and suggesting activities. But when a child has chosen to use the computer, they only intervene when absolutely necessary – for instance, if there is a risk of harm or damage. Obviously the teachers give priority to other tasks, judged as more important and valuable. Time appears to be an important feature in the teachers' ways of explaining this approach. As (teacher) Catarina, for example, who says that 'there's so much else, so much that it's hard to find enough time. It is not just the time used when working with the children; it is also a question of time to learn how to use the computer and different software.' Catarina continues, 'It's time-consuming to learn all that yourself as well.' But also, she says, if there is a computer problem to be solved, it takes time from more important activities like playing with the children, supervising them, or controlling their activities and behaviour.

Teachers hope the children will learn not only by themselves but also without causing any damage or problems on the computer. The teachers are not confident in their own abilities to handle problems that might occur with the computer, so the less it is used the lower this risk.

In this pre-school unit computer use is a low priority activity, for teachers as well as children. When the computer was new, the children were crowding around it, many conflicts occurred, and yet, as the teachers express it, at the same time there was passivity among the children. The activity now is described as more relaxed and as not causing many problems. The teachers stated they were relieved by the children's reduced level of interest.

B. Computer use as an available option

These teachers express the opinion that the computer use is a collective project, comprising those who want to participate. The computer is treated as a valuable option, but it is left to the children to decide whether to use it or not. The teachers say that some of the children never use the computer and the explanation given is that they prefer, as Boel says, 'to play other games'. If a child does not want to use the computer, it does not demand an intervention. Instead, the teacher waits for the interest to 'wake up' as teacher Bibbi puts it, 'It'll come when it comes; when they're mature enough to use it then they'll do it.'

The teachers are conscious of whether each child is using the computer often, seldom, or not at all. And even if the teachers assume that it is the children who use computers at home who also use the computer in pre-school, this is not treated as a problem. Also the position the child chooses at the computer (e.g., owner, participant, or spectator see Ljung-Djärf, in press/2008) is conditioned by earlier experiences.

Excerpt 2

I: But the kids that sit here a lot, do you think they are the kids that have a computer at home, or the ones that don't?

Bibbi: I think it's the kids that have a computer at home that sit here.

I: Mmmm

Bibbi: I think that the ones that don't have one at home, they don't know how to use it.

I: No?

Bibbi: Those kids usually sit a bit away or behind.

When children gather around the computer and participate in the play with comments or suggestions, it is talked about as a valuable activity. Participation in the common play affords (a) individuals with limited ICT experience an opportunity to watch and learn, as well as (b) the more experienced children an opportunity to express and share experiences within the group.

The teachers often make comments to the children at the computer and appear to be interested in what is happening on and around the computer. The teachers also try to provide help when it is needed, either by trying to help themselves or by asking a skilled child to help. For example, Bibbi suggests that the children help each other: 'Benny, can you show him how to exit, or maybe Björn can?' Help, support, and previous experiences are used in a practically continuous ongoing process among the participating individuals, peers as well as adults.

C. Computer use as an essential activity

These teachers are of the opinion that the computer is important and that all children should be included in the ICT activities. The same opportunities, they say, should be available for everyone, as a matter of equality and justice. Doris, one of the teachers, describes it as follows:

Excerpt 3

I: What are the advantages for kids in pre-school when they work with computers?

Doris: [...] That all children, regardless of whether they have a computer at home or not, can use them and aren't afraid of them, and can turn them on and know a little about how they work. That, I think, is important, so that everybody stands at the same level. Then, of course, there are some that are way ahead that use computers a lot more.

The teachers say that it is important that every child use the computer and they actually initiate computer use if the children do not initiate it themselves. Their way to deal with low interest on the part of the child is using easy software during a calm and quiet time of the day and with teacher guidance.

The teachers stress the importance of children learning 'this computer stuff,' as Doris puts it, and this aim becomes discernible as a strategy including a high level of control. For example, teachers record children's computer use. This, states Doris, helps the teachers to see to it that 'all the children sat some time at the computer, and we didn't miss anyone... everybody learned the basics ... everyone got an introduction.'

Even if playing computer games implies learning, this is not enough for this group of teachers. They also want the children to do other things with the computer, and for this reason some days are organized as writing or drawing days at the computer, and during these days playing computer games is not allowed. In this way, the teachers want to make the children understand that playing is not 'the whole thing,' and that thus there are other possibilities. As teacher Disa expresses it, 'I'd like to teach the children all the different things they can use a computer for, because, I mean, I hear the kids talking about what mom and dad do at work – they play computer games – that's all they think a computer is for, and that's not they way it should be.'

Except when the teachers have other plans, for example a circle time, there is continuous activity around the computer in these rooms. Most of the time it is crowded around the computer and it is seldom that a child is playing alone. This is mentioned as a problem concerning both the playing child (who is not allowed to take independent decisions) and the other children (who become passive). For this reason some rules are formulated to regulate the children's behaviour. It appears as important that use of the computer is equitably distributed among the children. The focus on justice in the formulated rules is to afford all children the same opportunities and equal time to use the computer.

Teachers described it as important that the children manage to do as much as possible without the teachers' help, for example being able to change programs. The role of the teachers is described as follows:

Excerpt 4

I: What do you see as your role in the kids' work with computers?

Doris: I want to be a kind of instructor. I want the kids to be doing things, but with me there in the background, so I can help out when things get difficult or when they don't know how to do what they want to do. But I also want them to learn how to explore and figure things out themselves.

I: That they try themselves?

Doris: Yes

But, all the same, it is held important that it is the adults who are in charge:

Excerpt 5

I: Who decides when and what the kids do at the computer, the kids themselves or you adults?

Doris: It's the adults that decide because the kids have to ask if they can sit at the computer and we can say 'No, we'll do something else' or 'Yes, that's fine'; so we're the ones that decide.

The teachers' decisions concern not only whether one is allowed to play or not, but also which program should be used. The teachers try to guide the use of different programs, making each child use software at a 'proper level.' By first using easy programs and then more complex ones, the children are supposed not only to learn from the content of the software, but also to learn how to manage the computer hardware.

Many visions and plans related to ICT use are expressed by the teachers. For example, when Disa is asked what she wants the children to learn when using the computer she says:

Excerpt 6

Disa: You'd like to teach them, first, how to turn off and on the computer, how to open their folder, every child has their own folder, how to open it and how to save, like that [...] Yeah, I think it feels like there's so very much that you'd like to do. I'd want, like, some simple computer certificate for kids you could have for kids when they begin school.

Time, though, is never sufficient and for this reason it is seldom possible to live up to the teachers' visions and plans.

Discussion

This study has focused on various aspects of the tension which exists between organizational requirements for computer implementation and the ways in which pre-school educators deal with them. Beyond the fact that the computer has been characterised in common parlance as a 'teaching tool', the responsibility for finding ways of applying the technology in the pre-school has been left to educators. The answers to the questions of if, when, and how computers can be used and incorporated in pre-school activities, and at the expense of what, have been assessed in relation to the teachers' professional knowledge base.

The study has shown that the computer is in use in Swedish pre-schools in a variety of ways, but also that the pre-school teachers have to solve a number of dilemmas when ICT is handled in local practice. Three dilemmas are identified and discussed in this section of the article: (A) a dilemma between the computer use and play in pre-school practice; (B) a dilemma between a central 'ICT vision' and dominant rationalities, and (C) a dilemma between a central ICT vision and teachers' actual competence in ICT.

A. Dilemma between computer use and play in pre-school practice

The study has shown that the computer is positioned as something to play with during time for free play in the three pre-school practices. It is also shows that there is some doubt as to how ICT can be developed and incorporated into ongoing pre-school activities. Such doubts can be viewed as a reflection of pre-school teachers' professional knowledge base and their ways of making sense of computer use. Pre-school teachers' professional knowledge base comprises preconceptions about what pre-school activities constitute and contain, and what things can be considered correct and expected in such a context. Goals, methods, and ways of understanding and describing pre-school activities have developed over time. These specific ways of understanding and defining the practice and its mission and core have developed and become self-evident, even as the identity of the pre-school continues to evolve.

The pervasive changes which have occurred in relation to the Swedish pre-school system over the last ten years have resulted in pre-school activities being given a clearer educational mission, while play has at the same time been emphasised as an important path to childhood learning. Today, play and learning, but also play *as* learning, is emphasized in the curriculum (Utbildningsdepartementet, 1998) as well as in studies of early education (see e.g., Lindqvist, 1995; Pramling Samuelsson & Asplund Carlsson, 2003). Play is part of the mission of education, and *variety* and *activity* are held as some of the ideals of play, which implies that educators steer the children's play away from those activities that are perceived to be stereotypical and passive (Tullgren, 2004). As a result, a conflict has arisen in the minds of many educators, as the computer and its use have been perceived as in fact being stereotypical and passive in many cases (Ljung-Djärf, 2002).

Such doubts can also be seen as an expression of pre-school teachers' ways of defining and assessing the computer in relation to children's play. It may be that the tension that arises between the assessment of the computer as a play artefact set off against a perceived 'schoolification' and the computer as a teaching artefact is another possible explanation of why computer use sometimes looms as a challenge in the pre-school environment. Earlier studies of toys in pre-schools indicate that there is a tendency to distinguish between good and bad toys, and also between those toys that fit or do not fit into pre-school activities (Selander, 2003). Almqvist's study (1994), which involved 340 pre-schools,[4] shows that so-called 'educational toys' designed to promote childhood learning in various areas dominate the field, while commercial toys such as Barbie™, My Little Pony® or Mc-Mice, are clearly not accorded the same space in pre-school activities (Fredricson, 2003). The educational tradition requires that such toys be viewed as non-educational and excluded from pre-school activities. The intrinsic opposition that is expressed in educators' statements regarding the computer and its use thus does not mean that the computer is being treated separately and distinguished from other play devices.

When it comes to computer use, educators have not, however, been faced with the choice as to *whether* computers are to be incorporated into their activities, but rather *how*. This study has shown that computers are being used in pre-schools, albeit not always with the conviction that they are actually good for either the pre-school per se or the children who are participating. Some of the findings that have emerged can thus be viewed as an expression of the ways in which professionals work within a framework to which they actually, or at least to some degree, take exception. This is manifested in that, for instance, some educators let the children sit at the computer if they take the initiative to do so, while at the same time trying to limit and tone down any interest that may be present. The tension between the introduction of the computer as the 'tool of the future, and of education' and a sometimes clearly dubious attitude toward its ultimate necessity and value in the pre-school is managed through efforts to make the computer less visible and promote other alternatives in its place.

B. Dilemma between a central 'ICT vision' and dominant rationalities

The study has revealed variations in terms of the purposes and tasks for which computers are used and how computer use is organized during the day. One such variation discussed here is constituted in the tension between a central 'ICT vision' and ways of defining the professional practice – to be more specific, in the meeting between the pre-school teachers' assumptions about the computer and the dominant rationalities within the three pre-school settings. It is argued that the computer is treated differently according to whether a caring, nurturing, or teaching rationality dominates in the practice. The rationalities constitute three different meaning-shaping practices with the computer. These practices, discussed below and summarized in Table 1, are categorised as *protective, supporting,* and *guiding.*

The computer within a caring rationality

Within a caring rationality the computer is used as a leisure activity of low priority. The main aims for the children are having something to do and taking turns. It is obvious that the teachers give priority to other tasks, judged as more important and valuable. The computer is held as important, *but* should not be prioritised, as the children need other things more. For example, the teachers express themselves as very eager to help and support the children to develop their verbal skills, but they do not seem to ascribe to the computer any part in these efforts. Instead, computer use is described as a threat to other and more important activities, as for example play and communication.

A playing child is supposed to be active, and teachers are conditioned towards activities connected to variation and activity to fulfil such presumptions. In this practice the teachers use a protective way of relating to computer use, which implies that they give the children the opportunity to use the computer but also try not to improve or expand their interest and time spent around the computer. This may be explained by the image of children's free-time use of the computer, in which a host of threatening elements, such as violence, sedentary inactivity, and undesirable experiences are identified, not least in the media, as constantly present. Of course, the sort of games played in pre-school are not comparable with the violent games referred to in the media, but encouraging free-time computer use could, in the long-term, lead to undesirable effects and experiences. The teachers also seem to see a risk of abuse, in the sense that the children spend too much time at the computer. The risk of 'getting stuck' and forget to play ordinary games, paint, and participate in other traditional pre-school activities implies that the teachers should not encourage an increased interest among the children.

The computer use is organized to fulfil an aim of equal access for all who want to play. But this is not a large problem as the children do not seem to be very interested in using the computer. The teachers strive against limitations, and peer interaction is restricted. It is only the situation of the child playing at the computer for the moment that is described as something possibly valuable. Against that is weighed the risk of passivity or the risk of the other children interrupting, disturbing or even taking over control of the computer. This is not a risk if the playing child is sitting alone at the computer, and for this purpose the children are not allowed to gather around it. The children's opportunities to interact, support each other, or share experiences appear to be nearly non-existent. The teachers themselves even seldom intervene with the child using the computer. The playing child is left alone and is supposed to play and learn how to manage the computer and the software on their own, preferably without causing too much trouble. If something should happen to the computer, the teachers do not see themselves as capable of handling the incident. The less it is used, the less this risk.

The computer within a nurturing rationality

The computer as an available choice can be associated with a nurturing rationality where social interactions around the computer are primary in terms of the opportunities they provide for responsibility, initiative, and cooperation. When children are given extensive freedom and encouraged to gather around the computer in groups, demands are at the same time placed on their ability to get along, and to help and support each other. The computer is an available option, but the choice of whether to use it or to do other things is left to the children.

The children use the computer now and then, but not all of them. The explanation given by the teachers is that some children prefer to do other things. If a child does not want to use the computer it is not a problem, and not anything demanding an intervention. Instead the teachers wait, as they say, for the interest to wake up. Peer interaction is encouraged, and when children assemble by the computer and participate with comments or suggestions, focusing on what are happen on the screen, it is talked about as a valuable activity. They describe the participation in the learning situation as valuable not only to individuals with limited experiences within the field, as they get a good opportunity to watch and learn, but also to more skilled children who get opportunities to express and share experiences in the group. In this practice the teachers use a supporting way of relating to the computer use, which implies that they stand by and support when needed and that peer interaction is encouraged. Teachers as well as children are treated as sources of knowledge. It is important to note that both children and teacher can choose whether or not to be involved in the computer use.

The computer within a teaching rationality

The main characteristic of the teaching rationality is that the computer is a tool for learning and teaching. The computer is an essential activity and using the computer implies learning, but playing computer games is not enough. The teachers with this rationality also want the children to do other things with the computer. For this reason, some days are organized as writing or drawing days at the computer and during these days playing computer games is not allowed. In this way, the teachers want to make the children understand that playing is not, as they say 'the whole thing', and that there are other possibilities. The teachers are eager for the children to manage to do as much as possible without help, for example, moving from one program to another. But when it comes to ultimate decisions about the use of the computer, it is held important that the adults are in charge. The teachers' decisions concern not only whether one is allowed to play or not, but also which program should be used. Moreover, the teachers try to guide the use of different programs, having each child use software 'at the proper level.' When children play, at first using easy programs and then more complex ones, they are supposed to learn not only from the content of the software, but also to manage the computer. The computer is treated as something important and the teachers are very concerned that everyone is using it.

The aims of learning are related to fulfilling political visions and goals related to equality of opportunity. The focus for everyone is what each individual needs. It is the teachers' responsibility to initiate the computer use if children do not initiate it themselves. Using easy software during a calm and quiet time of the day and teacher guidance is a way to deal with low interest. In this practice the teachers uses a guiding approach relating to computer use, which implies that they not only stand by and provide support when needed but also intervene in a more active way. Using the computer is a project involving all children and all teachers and the social practice around the computer affords opportunities for the children to learn together and from each other.

C. Dilemma between a central ICT vision and teachers' actual competence in ICT

The various ways of managing computer use can ultimately be understood as a question of the educators' ICT knowledge base, as earlier studies have also concluded. It is, of course, unreasonable to expect a concurrent development of ICT knowledge among pre-school staff to have taken place within the relatively short time that computers have been widely available in pre-schools. However, it is possible to discuss what the various ways of handling this dilemma may entail in terms of practical activities. The educators' ICT knowledge base appears in many cases to be so limited that it is scarcely possible for them to deal with computer use in a more advanced and reasoned manner. Clearly, it is essential that the level of knowledge be raised

Rationality	Content and aim	Organisation	Learning environment
Caring	The computer as leisure activity. Main aims are having something to do and taking turns.	Equal access for all who want to play. Peer interaction is restricted.	Protective: the computer is a threat to other activities
Nurturing	The computer as nurturer. Many aims are to stimulate responsibility, initiative, co-operation, and ensure the children help and support each other.	All who want to may play, and agree about the rules. Peer inter- is encouraged.	Supporting: the computer is an available option.
Teaching	The computer as a tool for learning and teaching. Main aims are related to fulfilling political visions and goals with regard to equal opportunity.	What each individual needs. Peer interaction is allowed.	Guiding: the computer is an essential activity.

Table 1. Computer use within a caring, nurturing, or teaching rationality.

and become more consistent, so that pre-school personnel as a group can develop a common knowledge base which involves ICT in their educational mission. A higher and more consistent level of knowledge could also enable educators to take responsibility for ICT and discuss its use and forms of use critically both among themselves and with outside experts. A broader knowledge base will also enable educators to view the ways in which the computer can be used from a broader perspective than simply being something perceived as standing in opposition to the elements involved in the pre-school ideal, i.e., imagination, creativity, variety, and activity. Instead, they should be enabled to develop ways of using the computer as one of many tools serving to facilitate childhood play and learning in the pre-school environment.

Conclusions

Teachers' ways of acting have been discussed as a positioning in relation to the use of the computer use as situated in the discursive practice of the pre-school. The tension between a central vision for ICT and the pre-school teachers' professional knowledge base has been examined in terms of the three dilemmas: between computer use and play in pre-school practice, between a central ICT vision and dominating rationalities, and between the central vision of computer use and the teachers' current ICT competence.

The results indicate that the way in which the computer is to be assessed is not self-evident when pre-school teachers' professional knowledge base and the ICT vision confront one another. The assessment of the computer as a tool for learning or play poses a key dilemma. When the computer is assessed as a play artefact, as opposed to a teaching artefact, with perceived schoolification as the result, it is possible to view the technology as a threat to the pre-school's basic values. The computer can fall short of both perspectives, unless it is defined as a choice for children who want to use it, as is the case in the nurturing rationality.

Notes

1 By schoolification, I imply when a traditional 'school discourse' is dominating the pre-school teachers' ways of making sense of pre-school education.

2 The term 'pre-school personnel' is used synonymously with the term 'teacher'.

3 These results are also reported in Ljung-Djärf, A., Åberg-Bengtsson, L., & Ottosson, T. (2005). Ways of relating to computer use in pre-school activity. *International Journal of Early Years Education, 13*(1), 31–43.

4 At this time the term 'pre-school' encompassed both full-time and part-time pre-school.

Preamble

The demands on the police are so heavy and often contradictory that it seems impossible to answer to all of them. What happens to police officers' occupational identity when they find out that they cannot live up to expectations. How do they deal with the dilemma of efficacy and legitimacy? In this article I argue that one solution to the dilemma to 'Do what's most effective as long it won't get public', is to develop a partly independant policy with managable internal standards in terms of an occupational culture. This form of discretion, however implies conflicts with ethical guidelines set up by the state and the police organization.

Rolf Granér

Police work between legitimacy and efficiency

Handling the expectations on the role of the police

Introduction

The contradictory demands put on the role of the police have been discussed by Jenner and Agevall (chapter 12). Here my point of departure is police officers who primarily in patrol duty and during emergencies fulfil their task of enforcing law and order and being of service to the public. The aim is to show that the expectations and demands put on the individual police officer are so wide-ranging and contradictory that they only to a limited extent can serve as a basis for a clear professional identity. Instead the professional identity is informed by a professional ethics and/or culture which quite often goes against the officially sanctioned social mandate of the police.

This professional ethics/culture which can be seen as way of handling contradictory demands is often in opposition to the sanctioned organizational and administrative ethical ideal. Individual police officers will thus be confronted with the dilemma of either subordinating themselves to the legal power that has invested them with their authority or to the norms of the professional group even if this means resorting to illegal methods. I will describe this administrative ethical ideal in terms of a legalistic perspective and the professional ethics as an autonomous perspective.

This clash between the legalistic and autonomous perspective puts different emphasis on legitimacy and efficiency. The legalistic perspec-

303

tive represents 'doing things the right way' while the autonomous tends towards an attitude of ends justifying the means. Legitimacy does although presuppose a certain degree of efficiency. From an organizational point of view you can detect a hidden agenda where efficiency in police work is appreciated and even expected even though it might entail breaking the rules of the legalistic perspective, but only as long as the legitimacy relating to the organizational power structures is not threatened.

With a free interpretation of Lundqvist (1991) you can distinguish between a private, individual ethics, based in the professional collective and an administrative ethics sanctioned by the authorities.

Professional identity is here defined as those elements in the self that consist of the mental images of the profession formed by individual officials. A fundamental assumption is that if these images are to create a positive self-image they must correspond to the individuals' idea of their own needs and resources. You can also, in accordance with Lundquist, distinguish between a private ethics, a professional ethics and an administrative ethics sanctioned by the authorities (cf. Agewall & Jenner) A professional ethics is a vital part of the culture in certain professional areas. A professional culture is here defined as the collectively founded mental processes of a profession such as notions, values and assumptions that determine the professionals' view of themselves, their situation and tasks. These general assumptions and values are the basis both of the accepted ways of performing a task and the shared norms for what is right and wrong (Manning, 1979).

Andersson (2001) describes police culture as a male hegemony expressed and demonstrated by both women and men. In line with this I will refer to the individual police officer as 'he'.

This description is founded on an ethnologically inspired study of the professional culture of policemen on patrol duty. The empirical base of the study consists of a number of field studies among patrolling police comprising 18 shifts and 25 interviews of 3 to 4 hours each. I have also had the opportunity to test my analyses in discussions with several hundred active police officers taking part in further training. The theoretical framework is interdisciplinary. From social psychology I make use of symbolic interactionist role theory (Mead, 1976; Goffman, 1998) and from organizational sociology have used critical organization theory especially neoinstitutional theory (Meyer &

Rowan, 1991; Johansson, 2002) and taken into account the emphasis put on the deep structures of organization cultures as presented in symbolic cultural theory (Alvesson, 2001).

Expectations on the role of the police

Police work in general and the professional role of the patrolling officer is subject to a range of different types of expectations. It is reasonable to assume that there is an overall consensus that the primary object of the police is to fight crime and supervise traffic. Views might differ though when it comes to which crimes are relevant and the methods of fighting them. Traffic supervision and crime prevention are fairly well defined as to rights and duties. Upholding public order is also seen as part of the basic duties of the police. The instructions concerning this are, however, fairly general. At the same time it is hard to reach consensus about when the limits for public order have been transgressed and what methods should be employed by the police. In addition to this there are a number of other expectations about what are the duties of the police. This includes various service functions, assistance at accidents and seconding other authorities.

In the standard work on Swedish legislation regulating police work, Berggren and Munck (2005) it is noted that in a number of studies right from the preparatory work on the police law of 1925 onwards there is nowhere a detailed description of the role of the police. The tasks of the police have been seen as so dependent on the development of society that a legislation defining them would risk becoming quickly obsolete. Here you can detect a tendency for other institutions to have well-defined operative areas whereas the police are expected to cover a number of different areas that for different reasons are not covered by others. This interpretation is confirmed by the study on police work which maintains that the police have been landed with a number of tasks that have little or no relation to the core functions. It is even claimed that these tasks 'have become so wide-ranging, vague and far from core functions that the police in certain respects cannot adequately uphold its main task' (SOU 2001:87, p. 8). A result of this is that the area of police work is considerably wider than the economic resources allow. This also leaves more room for varying interpretations of the role of the police.

The police can be described as the ultimate guarantor that the legislation is observed. Patrolling police are expected to react and intervene in a number of areas which require a wide competence. To control the adherence to legislation presupposes police resources that, to a large extent, are beyond what the organization can achieve. As Berggren and Munck (ibid.) note, the tasks of the police are so wideranging that in practice there is a great need to prioritize.

The organizational regulation of police work is attained both directly and indirectly, both inside and outside the police organization. The direct regulation is done by parliamentary legislation which is then defined by the judiciary system in the form of sentencing, pronouncements by the judicial ombudsman and the interpretations of prosecutors. The government defines, in its annual regulations, what should be the priorities of the police. Here the emphasis has been put on crime prevention and intensified contact with the public rather than repressive policies. On the other hand there have been demands for tougher repression when it comes to certain crimes highlighted in public discussions such as street violence, racial crimes and violence against women. Similarly objectives descriptions on different organizational levels define the priorities such as traffic and drug violations. Periods for selected targeting are defined. Recurrent police criticism has been directed at the fact that low priority tasks are never properly defined. Instead these priorities are expected to be combined with regular emergency and supervisory duties as if all this was actually backed up by the resources. You could however claim that if the government or the police organization officially declared which parts of the legislation were low priority this would result in a total disregard for these legislative areas.

The objectives of the police organization should instead be seen as largely symbolic. It's about creating the impression of a police force that can guarantee law observance and the safety and security of the public. As Ekman (1999) notes, the citizens' mental image of the police upholding public safety is more important for the experienced sense of security than any amount of actual practical police work.

In addition to this there is the classical conflict between legality and efficiency typical of all states governed by law. Policing is subject to a number of fundamental judicial principles. The police need to have a well-founded suspicion to invade anyone's personal integrity. Efficiency in police work can never override legal rights. All citizens are to be treated equally and the individual police officer is required to perform his duties with fairness and impartiality. In this way the authority of the police officer is restricted when it comes to controlling people, traffic and private property. At the same time this restricts his capacity to make use of the 'quiet' knowledge based in experience described by Jenner and Agevall.

The overall objectives of the police imply that a police officer is required to combine a number of different social roles. He is expected to react instantly to incidents even if his perspective on the situation is limited. He is supposed to be able to offer support and assistance and at the same time keep an eye on possible crimes and whether he himself or members of the public are at risk. He should be able to judge what level of intervention is most adequate in a situation and be aware of relevant laws. Klette (Cedermark & Klette, 1979), for example, claims that the two roles of crime prevention and community service are in opposition to each other since they require different skills and capabilities. You can't in an instant jump from one role to another. Punch (1979) refers to Bittner, who stresses that 'peace-keeping' entails handling a very wide spectrum of frequently complex and serious human problems. In general the police receive no instructions, guidance or above all, attention for doing this kind of work.

A number of different types of expectations come from society at large. There is the popular picture of police work as a dangerous and thrilling tracking down of villains which children learn early. The same view is represented in media coverage of police work. Policing also seems to be the profession that attracts most media attention. In the news, and even more in fictional representations, the stereotype of the police as more or less successful crime fighters in an action-packed job is prevalent.

Critical scrutiny is also a constant in media coverage of police work. The police often focus on this and claim that they are frequently misrepresented and unfairly criticised in news reports describing the police as either too complaisant or too arbitrary.

The direct relations to the general public are also seen as problematic. The police frequently see themselves as unfairly treated by the public they are required to protect (see Smångs, 2001; Statistiska centralbyrån, 1998). The public is considered ignorant of the rights and obligations of the police and also to have a primitive view of how police work should be done. Police officers often talk about being criticised for showing too much leniency in dealing with criminals and hooligans. Gunnar Ekman quotes an informant who claimed that: 'They [the public] expect you to be wearing animal skins, going around whacking hooligans' (Ekman, 1998, p. 184, cf. Finstad, 2000).

Encounters with the police are also described as calling forth an irrational behaviour in the public where the police role seems to act as a catalyst for regressive reactions where the police are seen as either omnipotent protectors or unjustly punishing parental figures (cf. Bonifacio, 1991). On the one hand you come across unrealistic ideas of the capacity of the police to control a situation. On the other hand police interventions can be met with great indignation when you feel that attention to your own minor offence takes valuable time away from the tracking down of real criminals. Even outside work, police officers often see themselves as under constant scrutiny and moral censure. Their gardens and cars are expected to be in perfect order and their children immaculate. Alcohol comsumption and drinking habits are observed and commented on.

Consequences for the professional identity

As can be seen from the examples above, the role expectations directed at the police officer constitute an insufficient basis for a professional identity. The patrolling officer who tries to meet all these expectations risks feeling inadequate at his job. He will also discover that by meeting some of the expectations he will disregard others. From this you would expect a certain distancing from these role expectations. At the same time the sheer mass of expectations could give a certain leeway, at least on patrol duty.

In conformity with a number of other researchers I have observed a considerable freedom of action in the priorities and methods used by individual police officers as well as what they 'take note of' during patrol duty (cf. e.g. Ekman, 1998; Holmberg, 2003; Finstad, 2000; Holgersson, 2005). There are then great variations in the views on how police work should be done. These variations depend not only on individual choices and the style developed by the team but also on gender, geography and the type of job being done. Like the researchers above and supported by a large number of international studies on the police (for an outline see Reiner, 2000) you can observe that the professional ethics not infrequently come into conflict with the officially sanctioned administrative ethics.

The legalistic versus the autonomous perspective

I hold that the professional culture of patrolling police can be described as a continuum between two dominating perspectives, the legalistic and the autonomous ones. The former – that of the loyal civil servant – is characterized by loyalty to the officially sanctioned societal mandate, loyalty to the directives and the policy documents of the police organization – altogether forming a broad view of police work.[1] The latter celebrates ideals of the police as an independent force and puts the emphasis on repressive crime fighting in way that brings back memories of the old-style sheriffs and samurais we have met on the screen.

In both perspectives it is the public at large that constitute the client. From the legalistic viewpoint the public comprises everybody. But from the autonomous point of view it is only by leading a law-abiding life that you qualify as a member of the public. Here it is the police and the public jointly that represent all that is good and respectable.

In the legalistic perspective it is the elected representatives of various political bodies that lay down the framework for what the police should do and how, then the judiciary including the police with its hierarchic structure execute this policy. In the autonomous system then it is assumed that the police are acting on a direct mission from the public. The police and the public are seen as organically linked to each other. Officers are recruited from and identifies themselves with the pool of law-abiding citizens. The public then are assumed to share in this autonomous view of how policing is to be done (see Carlström, 1999; Ekman, 1999).

In contrast to the broad view of police work that the legalists maintain, the autonomous view stresses the primary aim of protecting the public. The protection can consist of handling emergencies where people are at risk, e.g. in accidents. Foremost is, however, to protect the public by making sure that ordinary people can feel safe and live in 'peace and quiet'. This entails not only fighting clearly criminal activity but also guaranteeing moral guidelines such as basic principles about justice and showing consideration for others.

The threat to the security of the public partly consists in what the police refer to as habitual criminals and disturbers of the peace. The hard core of habitual criminals are then surrounded by a number of hangers-on. This group will be perceived as a distinct social group in the community held together in an informal network of pals and relations. Typical for them is that they more or less exclusively support their existence by committing crime. Whereas the legalistic perspective is based on the fundamental legal principle that there has to be an actual, concrete crime to make a criminal, the autonomuos view is that you can take it for granted that a villain is bound to commit crime. It becomes a matter of being able to pin the crime on the criminal so that he can be punished in a proper legal process (cf. Carlström, 1999). The autonomous view is that the chances a criminal has of changing lifestyle are very slim indeed. The fundamental attitude is: once a thief – always a thief. The best way of fighting crime then is to go for the known criminals. In addition to going for convictions you make sure that you disrupt their activities as much as possible. In conjunction with these methods they can also count on (as noted also by Jenner & Agevall) a much harsher treatment and stricter law enforcement than members of the general public.

Those who disturb the peace come in a variety of categories united in their capacity to threaten the public's sense of security. Here you find the social misfits: alcoholics, the mentally ill but also gangs of youth and activists on either of the political extremes. They might all commit crime but they mainly constitute a threat to the public's sense of security by deviating from the conventional norms of decency. Reiner (2000) refers to this category as 'police property' since the police, though not formally but in practice, have a mandate to use their powers in a totally different way from what they can in relation to other more well-established groups in the community. Alcoholics can be ordered to leave their bench in the park just on the grounds of their position in the community.

Real – 'hands on' policing

Jenner and Agevall in their article address the tacit knowledge, the know-how that is evolved in a professional group and, for example, include rules about what the collective consider good work. In my study as well as in Scandinavian and international police research, you frequently come across a similar divide between on the one hand the legalistic broad perspective on policing in terms of real, practical work and on the other what is considered as totally meaningless ('crap jobs') (cf. van Mannen, 1978; Reiner, 1992; Carlström, 1999; Ekman, 1999;

Holmberg, 2003; Finstad, 2000; Smångs, 2001). This involves fundamental considerations of the priorities and methods deemed relevant
for policing. Three types of criteria for real policing are easily distin-
guishable: there should be a clearly identifiable crime where the
demarcation line between right and wrong is unmistakable. In this
way, robbery, theft, assault and battery for example constitute clear-
cut cases for police intervention. Drunken brawls on the other hand
are at the opposite end from real policing and so considered a 'crap'
job. In these cases it is hard to tell perpetrator from victim and drink-
induced fights are not considered proper crimes anyway.

Added to this there is the efficiency aspect. The crime must be of
a reasonably severe nature, the perpetrator must be identifiable, be of
some importance and finally, you must be able to get a conviction.
'Crap' jobs on the other hand are all those cases that don't result in
arrests or where the arrest doesn't lead to conviction or substantial punishment. To pick up a shoplifter who is then unable to pay the subsequent fines is not considered proper police work. Domestic violence
is another area that has been considered out of bounds of real policing (cf. Lundberg, 2001).

The most important criterion for what constitutes real police work
is, however, the method used, the way it is done. Real police work
involves drama. The hunt supplies the metaphoric framework: it is a
matter of tracking down, catching and bringing home the quarry. This
is when the police can make use of all the professionel skills, the practice and training, fitness and authority. One of the interviewed police
officers described car chases and burglars caught redhanded as a real
feast for everyone on the force irrespective of speciality. The prospect
of a car chase could tempt all patrols to compete for a bit of the action
even though they really had no business there. Desk jobs, such as documentation or assisting other authorities, on the other hand, are considered very low status.

The term 'practical policing' was coined in opposition to all kinds
of theoretical desk work which is perceived as designed by 'desk-jock-
eys', i.e. the bureaucrats on the National Police Board who are quite
out of touch with reality. Practical policing requires being constantly on the alert for the emergencies of real police work and so being
able to put aside less the important desk duties (crap jobs again.) The
fundamental assumption, if you take the autonomous perspective, is
that anything could happen and you should be prepared for all even-

tualities. Because of this, work is only partly organized on the basis of what happens in an ordinary day's work.

Practical policing also means upholding the respect for the police as well as maintaining the freedom of action of the force. This can, as maintained by Jenner and Agevall, be seen as a way of emphasising the position of power vis a vis the public. It is the police that dictate the terms and character of the interaction with the public. An often voiced fundamental assumption among my interviewees was that it was the people the police had to deal with that determined the level of intervention. The police did what the situation demanded and it was the other party that was responsible if the reaction was harsh. The person who didn't do what the police asked him had to expect what was coming to him. Acting on this assumption could although come into conflict with the directives on police conduct. The law on taking into custody of drunks could, for example, be used against people taunting or in other ways provoking the police.

In relation to legislation

A fundamental difference between the legalistic and the autonomous point of view can be found in their respective attitudes to legislation and the statutes governing policing. In the legalistic view it is taken for granted that every aspect of policing, and especially the use of force, is based on the legislation. From the autonomous viewpoint it is a matter of upholding a certain moral stance concerning right and wrong, acting on behalf of the public and securing results according to the principles of 'real' policing. It is not deemed possible to do efficient police work and follow the regulations (cf. Skolnick, 1994; Ekman, 1999; Reiner, 2000). In police training you are taught how to do your job according to rules and regulations but it is in practical work you learn how to stretch and sometimes break the rules. At the same time practical work requires that you avoid acting in a way that results in disciplinary repercussions. A prerequisite in practical policing is to be able to justify your actions so that it appears as if you didn't make a mistake. In police jargon there are special expressions describing how you write yourself into and out of trouble. In practical work you need to know the legislation well enough to be aware of when you stretch a law and when you break it so that you can, in retrospect, justify your intervention (cf. Holmberg, 2003; Ekman, 1999).

In the same way that you can describe the legalistic perspective as founded on a number of constitutionally based legal principles, you can describe the autonomous perspective from a number of moral guidelines. Thus the legalistic principles above could be amplified with the 'moral rights principle' of the autonomous view. The police take the liberty of morally determining the righteousness of the legislation. When it comes to more serious crime this is no problem, but when handling minor offences you can come into conflict with the legislation. In these cases you often start from determining the character of the perpetrator and his or her motives. You are reluctant to take part in punishing a member of the public for making a mistake or having done something that isn't a crime according to the general sense of justice. You also have to take into consideration what consequences this offence has for others. To distil spirits in your own home could be considered a private matter, especially if it was done discreetly. Selling alcohol to under age youths, on the other hand, would be seen as a serious offence. You also have to take the status of the victim into consideration (Christie, 1987). If the victim of, for example an assault, is a defenceless and innocent member of the public it is treated much more seriously than if the victim was a drunk in rude health.

The equality, objectivity, legal rights and applicability principles of the legalistic perspective can be contrasted to the norms about efficient crime-fighting and the selective uses of penal law. The applicability principle, i.e. the rule that a law should only be used for the cases it was designed for, is more or less disregarded from an autonomous point of view. Here traffic regulations could be utilized for flagging down cars to check up on suspects or the laws on drunkenness could be used for taking presumtive lawbreakers into custody. The laws about interrogating minors in the presence of their parents could be circumvented by redefining 'questioning' as an 'interview' and making sure no report was written.

Fundamental legal principles are only granted to a law-abiding general public who also, according the autonomous view, should be interfered with as little as possible. On the other hand, it is seen as essential for practical police work to have a thorough knowledge of potential offenders, their characteristics and foibles. To be able to do this a typology is created that goes against principles such as equality in general and more relevant, equality before the law. When the police identified potentially 'interesting' presumptive offenders it was low-income groups such as immigrants of low status, the down-and-outs and the deviants that were focused on. The more intensified monitoring of these groups also emphasised their criminality in opposition to groups with more Nordic looks who could make a well-ordered, steady impression (cf. Finstad, 2000). This can be seen as prejudiced. The police justify it in terms of efficiency. You fish where you are most likely to catch something. Random supervision of the public would not only be a waste of time it would also disregard the professional know-how of experienced police officers.

Another aspect is the public's access to power. The police show more care dealing with groups that can assert their rights, but can take greater liberties with groups that lack such powers. It ought to be easier to take a tough repressive line with drunk youths than with a group of tipsy middle-aged men on their way home from an office party. With the familiar clientele it is no problem to gain access to a flat on the pretext of 'having a chat' but when it comes to better placed people you make sure you have a warrant.

The code of silence

From the legalistic viewpoint you are required to report on a colleague you suspect of crime whereas the autonomous view requires you to do the opposite – not report on or testify against a colleague. The code of silence was previously even stricter and more absolute: you just didn't report a colleague almost irrespective of the seriousness of the crime. Even if this still goes for colleagues that you have a close personal relation to, the code is most frequently referred to in crimes that could be described as 'within duty', i.e. they have been committed in the line of duty, for no personal gain and in line with the norms of the professional group. The code of silence of the police has often, as in Jenner and Agevall, been seen as connected to the use of excessive brutality and other violations of justice. I hold that the code of silence in a more general way can be seen as a prerequisite for the relative freedom of the police in relation to the legislation as described above. When it comes to use of violence the norm states that it was not condoned if the perpetrator was already incapacitated. There might, however, be mitigating circumstances concerning the use of violence in a state of affect. In the condoned uses of violence there could also be an element of informal punishment. If the feeling is 'he got what was coming to him' the offence was more or less excused. The norm also held for what is considered minor offences and didn't apply to professionally related crimes such as fraud, theft, receiving and sex crimes. It is maintained that there has been a change in attitudes over the last 10 to 20 years. The verdicts of colleagues have been hard. The offender has been seen as a 'bad egg', the result of a bungled recruiting process.

The hidden agenda of the police organization

So far I have been treating the administrative, legalistic ethics, and the professional ethics as opposite poles. The individual officer has to find a balance between the two ends of the spectrum. But there are also reasons to claim that the limitations of the role of the police, and the emphasis put on efficiency that characterizes the autonomous perspective, can be found in the police organization as a whole.

In neo-institutional theory a distinction is being made between technical and institutional operations. Typical of technically characterized operations is for example that they have a well-defined core, i.e. aims and means of production are fairly unambiguous. Institutionally characterized operations – which mostly deal with people – are typical for their lack of a clear definition of what is to be produced and how to go about it. The technical core thus becomes vague. Instead they rely on the world around it to see it as legitimate, i.e. the organization itself has to create its own legitimacy that make others put trust in their performance. This is done via a number of expectations put on the institutions (Meyer & Rowan, 1991). Scott (1995) defines the idea of institutions as 'cognitive, normative and regulatory structures and activities that provide stability and meaning to social behaviour'. The cognitive aspect implies that the institutional notions have become 'social facts' that have come to be taken for granted, the normative aspect that the institution is expressed via collectively rooted values and subsequent norms for what is considered morally right and desirable. Finally, the regulative aspect deals with how the institution is expressed via an official set of rules such as legislation. The expectations directed at the institution can come from public opinion as expressed in mass media, from important partners or from knowledge legitimized in the education system or via governmental regulations.

The kind of expectations directed at the police that I have described above can be seen as institutional expectations. The technical centre can be described as upholding law and order and fighting crime even though opinions differ as to how this is to be done. At the same time the police depend on being able to show a good record on 'law and order' and the number of cases solved. A solution to the problem of establishing legitimacy and at the same time show a good record could be reached through the notion of 'loose linking'. This means on the one hand that there are structures within the organization that pay attention to institutional expectations and thereby can create an impression that the organization as a whole acts accordingly. At the same time there have to be other structures that put more emphasis on safeguarding direct production and the technical essence of the organization (Scott, 1998).

On paper the police organization is a regulated bureaucracy with sanctions directed at those who deviate from the body of regulations. At the same time, only a very limited number of police officers are convicted for breaking the law or not following regulations. This can be construed as evidence of how law-abiding the police are. On the other hand a recurrent notion among my informants is that most experienced patroling police officers at least once have been guilty of conduct that if it had reported and documented would have led to serious consequences. Deviating from the officially sanctioned policy for police work such as redisigning priorities of tasks and methods produce no such repercussions (Ekman, 1999). The existence of an autonomous perspective is well-documented in police organizations all over the western world. In spite of this there have been no radical measures taken to fight it (Skolnick & Fyfe, 1994). Even leading representatives of police organizations admit that there is a large grey area between legitimate and illegitimate police practices and that this is the area that the individual police officer has to negotiate with great care. Several informants describe how after an arrest or after seizing stolen goods no questions are asked about how this was achieved. When it comes to keeping informed about the legislation you are required to uphold, further education is neglected and legislation doesn't keep up with practice (cf. Holgersson, 2000). An officer has to pass a shooting test every year to be allowed to carry firearms. No such tests regarding jurisprudence are carried out once he has left the police academy.

How is this to be interpreted? Have the authorities and police organizations realized the impossiblity of keeping a check on the activities of the police in the streets or could it be that the legalistic and the autonomous perspectives complement each other. Starting from the latter viewpoint you could maintain that within the police organizations of the western world the autonomous view is not attacked because it is frequently seen as a more efficient method of policing than it is possible to officially sanction. To allow a repressive police practice based on categorising citizens according to superficial characteristics or prior convictions could for example prove an efficient method for patrolling police even though innocent citizens risk being caught in such a wide-meshed net.

To combine the legalistic and the autonomous perspective can be seen as a practical solution to the problem of combining, on the one hand, technically motivated demands for an efficient enforcement of law and order and, on the other hand, institutional demands of subordination under fundamental rules of law. What could look like a profession taking too many liberties could in effect be an instrument for dealing with institutional demands about equality before the law. 'Ordinary decent people' deserve their legal rights as citizens. But the rules that apply for them could be set aside and the police be given free reign to choose methods when dealing with socially disadvantaged and criminally implicated groups. Institutional notions of equality before the law prohibit legislation targeting specific segments of the population. Instead you can leave it to the individual police officer to make more practical dispositions. It will, however, become problematic when this practice is made public or the 'victim' actually is in a position to protest and take action. Thus, even though it is not admitted openly, this point of view that corresponds to what in the autonomous perspective is described as 'real and practical policing' is also the view of the police organization when it comes to what is expected of the police officer.

Consequences for the professional identity of patrolling police

In developing his professional identity as a patrolling police officer both the legalistic and the autonomous perspective have to be taken into consideration. Both sides can, as it were, back up their claims on him.

Of the various institutional demands that are directed at the role of the police the autonomous perspective can claim an affinity with popular notions of policing. Compared to all the other demands it has the attraction of limiting the field to what is unique for policing. By adopting the professional ethics represented by the autonomous perspective you become part of a professional community in the form of the police force (Van Mannen & Barley, 1984).

The autonomous perspective can also be seen as a strategy for dealing with work-induced anxiety and ambivalence. By focussing on clearly defined situations you avoid the ambivalence a wider perspective might induce. The in-group, out-group dichotomy emphasised in social identity theory (Brown, 2000) is in itself identity boosting. It is also a way to negotiate the problem of the police to further a good cause by repressive means (Muir, 1977). By idealizing your own group you gain a moral right to give priority to your own judgements and exercise authority over others. Dividing people into good and bad could also justify subjecting the latter to suffering.

The legalistic perspective can back up its power with the police organization's authority to use both legal and administrative sanctions. On the legal side, breaking the laws and regulations for police work could result in penal or disciplinary consequences. Although I have maintained that these sanctions are seldom used, nevertheless my informants frequently claim that they adhere to the rules to avoid the risk of being punished (cf. Lundberg, 2001). Examples of administrative sanctions are, for example, not being promoted or being assigned to less popular duties. To work in reception is often looked upon as a form of sanction. This type of sanction can also be used in maintaining those parts of the autonomous perspective that are informally supported by the police organization and can be found somewhere on the axis between legality and efficiency. If you adhere strictly to laws and regulations you will never fall foul of the legal system but you can be labelled inefficient, averse to work or untrustworthy.

Legal back-up is, however, a prerequisite for a case to be brought forward in the judicial process. The freedom of action for the individual police officer increases in proportion to the distance from the station. On patrol duty the officer can choose to see or not see and so make his or her own priorities. More or less against the law a patrol can decide to file a report or solve the problem on the spot. They can take liberties when apprehending someone or securing evidence, they can influence the prosecutor by their choice of words in the report (cf. Lundberg, 1998). Once back at the station this independence is limited by the regulations of the legalistic perspective.

On a routine basis or depending on the case at hand, an officer can choose the professional rather than the administrative code. On an overall level it is the legalistic perspective that lends legitimacy to the police role. The autonomous attitude can be used as a motivating ideology when it comes to making priorities and deciding on methods of conduct. But to keep your professional identity it would be very hard not to accept the rules that officially constitutes it. It would mean not being loyal to the democratic state governed by law that you are a part of.

The sliding scale between the two perspectives is reflected in the field studies. When an officer talks about policing with an unitiated outsider he takes care to stick to a legalistic perspective. When he talks more generally about policing, in my interviews or field studies the autonomous perspective often dominates with its notions about a direct link betwen the public and the police, the duty to disrupt criminal activity as much as possible and the idea that efficient policing is impossible without breaking regulations. When the discussion touches on how to handle actual situations the legalistic perspective becomes more prominent in referring to a number of laws applicable in different situations. A similar double-sided picture characterizes the actual interventions I have observed. My main impression is that the police more or less adopt a legalistic perspective in terms of following police regulations. Deviations from this are, however, fairly regular.

Two types of factors are essential for when an autonomous perspective is allowed to dominate in practice. One is founded on the degree of commitment in a case the other on whether the officers involved risk censure for their actions.

The degree of commitment can be described with the help of the division between real police work and 'crap' jobs. Crimes that are sufficiently serious, where there is a good chance of actually apprehending the criminal, are a boost to the level of commitment. Rules about house searches and that a law only can be applied for what it was intended for are of little consequence in this situation. Especially if there is a real chance of something dramatic happening, like a car chase.

The autonomous perspective is however most prominent in a situation where motivation is lacking. Crap jobs such as petty crimes and minor offences with little likelihood of a conviction are often avoided or disregarded. In these cases the obligation to report a crime is overlooked.

The level of commitment is also determined by who you are dealing with. Those who are considered representatives of a law-abiding general public are often treated with greater leniency and consideration than what the police actually are allowed to. Those who are labelled troublemakers receive much tougher treatment than the crime would warrant. There is also the tendency to get emotionally involved in victims of crimes or accidents who are considered morally irreproachable, defenceless and innocent.

Another determining factor for the degree of commitment is the level of perceived provocation. When the police have their authority questioned this could result in minor offences being reported.

The attitude that the police meet plays a role also in cases of excessive brutality as for example when someone tries to escape or is violent.

The second reason why the autonomous perspective is given such scope is the need to keep out of trouble. Here the principle is that if you are able in retrospect to motivate your action you secure quite a lot of freedom of action irrespective of motive. You also have to know who you are dealing with. You had better keep within the law if there is a risk that those you are dealing with or potential witnesses are in a position to file a credible complaint. If this is not the case the limits are decided by internal norms.

Summary and comments

From the perspective of an administrative ethics the individual police officer has to be loyal to the social mandate of the police, subordinate himself under the legislation and other regulations for police work and be loyal to the police organization. But is it possible to form a coherent professional identity when the social mandate is perceived as too wide to be implemented in practice, when legislation and regulations are seen as obstacles to the efficiency of upholding law and order and fighting crime, and when the directives of the police organization answer to institutional demands rather than being concrete guidelines for practical work. A result of this is that the personal ethics of individual police officers are given wide scope. If you are not supplied with the means to do all that is expected of you, you are left to make your own choices. Within the police (and other institutions) a professional culture has evolved – an autonomous perspective – which also comprises a professional ethics for rights and wrongs in policing. With its base in popular conceptions of the police as guardians of justice fighting crime, it presents an identity boosting ideology where the administrative ideal is perceived as insufficient.

While the official professional ethics has to consider institutional demands about the legal rights of the individual and personal integrity for everybody, the autonomous perspective gives notions of efficiency priority over general considerations regarding legal rights. Thus you find within the autonomous perspective strategies for disregarding, stretching and in certain cases breaking against the official administrative ideal. The situation is further complicated by the fact that the police organization has a need to show results in order to achieve legitimacy. As a result the methods of the autonomous perspective are accepted as long as they are not made public and threaten the legitimacy of the organization. For the individual police officer this means that he is expected to do what he is not allowed to, according to the official administrative ethics. But if caught, he personally is left to suffer the consequences.

Note

1 The basic administrative ethics for the Swedish police as well of other civil servants is regulated in the *initial articles of the Constitutional Law (Regeringsformen)*. The police service is regulated more precisely in the *Police Act and the Police Statute* and the *Code of Judicial Procedure*, judgements from courts and opinions from the *Parliamentary Ombudsman* (Justitieombudsmannen – JO). There is also the *National Police Board* (Rikspolisstyrelsen) which presents recommendations and directions from the abovementioned sources of Law. Another central governmental policy document isthe letter of regulation

Katrin Hjort

Epilogue: What's new, Doc?

Old tensions between or new knowledge about tensions between professions and organizations?

Tension between professions and organizations is nothing new. Despite the fact that professionals have always attempted to fight for their independence and autonomy, professional autonomy has historically remained more of an ideal than an actual condition. The clergy and church were not independent of kings and feudal lords. Lawyers and solicitors have never been independent of the state; on the contrary, legislation has been a prerequisite for their very existence. Doctors have never been independent of the pharmaceutical industry or the healthcare system.

So what new insight can emerge from a preoccupation with tensions between organizations and professions, a preoccupation typical of the papers in this anthology? Do they not simply rehash old, well-researched issues brought to light through professional ideals that exclusively convey the self-image of professional groups, or their wishes for the ideal world? A world where professionals, by virtue of their education, have exclusive knowledgebases, earning them the right to monopolize certain occupational areas, the right to set their own quality standards, and the right to decide, unilaterally, what is in the client's best interest?

This issue becomes even more acute with reference to professions that have developed in close association with the welfare state, such as nurses, teachers, and social workers. These groups of 'relational workers' – people who work with people – can scarcely be understood without first making sense of the type of welfare arrangement of which they are part. Their work is done in public institutions, and the def-

initions of the aim of their work and consequently of their professional ethoses are inseparable from the basic social and democratic values
of Scandinavian welfare models. In this respect, the professionals are
already placed in a field of tension in which political struggle or negotiations regarding the distribution of affluence and social goods are
at stake. Professions in public service are not, and have never been,
autonomous, enjoying the luxury of exclusive preoccupation with their
own internal interests. Instead, they are, and have always been, pressured by several stakeholders pulling in different directions.

So, what's new?

The research contributions in this volume confirm that change is ubiquitous and that the decisive changes currently being carried out affect
the working conditions of welfare state professionals. Such changes
multiply and intensify the tensions of which the professionals are part,
thus contributing greatly to producing dilemmas the individual professional must take into account and address day to day.

Professionals caught in the crossfire

The decisive changes in professional conditions can, as the papers in
this anthology demonstrate, be localized at several levels. We can focus
on 'real reforms', understood as national political decisions, passed at
a central political or administrative state level, involving all institutions or organizations and representing both professionals and clients
in the area in question. Changes of that kind can be exemplified by
the new type of documentation and quality-assurance systems that
Karin Jonnergård and Lena Agevall examine, the implementing of
workplace-located time (implying that teachers must stay at school
for most of their preparation-time) that Carola Aili describes, and the
implementing of new infrastructures based on information and communication technology (ICT) that Lars-Erik Nilsson highlights in his
study of the working conditions of teachers and technicians. Reforms,
however, can equally well be in the form of changes decentrally determined at a local level, in collaboration between municipal authorities, groups of citizens, and groups of committed professionals, for
example, the creation of a community centre for families, which Agneta Abrahamson has been following, or the local political decision to

give all preschool children access to computers, as analysed by Agneta Ljung-Djärf.

Regardless of circumstances, these changes involve a shift of focus for the professionals in question. Karin Jonnergaard and Lena Agevall examine how new forms of 'management by documents' affect established professional knowledge and institutional norms and values. Lars H. Hansens describes what happens when individual-based data concerning healthcare diagnoses, treatments, and outcomes not only come to serve quality-development purposes, instead becoming quality-control tools informing patients about hospital rankings in order to let patients choose the best healthcare service provider. In this situation, doctors responsible for reporting quality-development data are likely to shift their focus to data that indicate good practices and results. The focus is shifting: new concerns will need to be attended to and new assignments defined. This does not necessarily imply that old tasks have become superfluous, but it does increase tensions for the employees. Increased attention to customer service, for example, implies increased attention to satisfying the individual citizen. Irrespective of this, traditional professional standards cannot be ignored; professionals cannot refrain from using their professional knowledge to assess what serves their clients best in the long term. Similarly, increasing demands on public institutions for operational and economic efficiency have contributed to a shift in focus to the productivity of public institutions, i.e., the number of clients, students, patients leaving an institution and with what results. However, these demands do not imply that professionals can ignore either the particular characteristics of the specific human life processes – learning, developing, etc. – that are at the core of their work, or their clients' various physical, psychological, social, and cultural resources. Nor do increasing demands for self-governance and governance in professional and cross-professional teams alter the fact that public institutions in the end are required to fulfil politically defined aims and do so subject to given economic constraints. All these matters entail different dilemmas, as seen in the case of the police work discussed by Lena Agevall and Håkan Jenner. Like most activities carried out by street-level bureaucrats, this work is characterized by many dilemmas and a constant lack of absolute answers as to how to act in various situations.

Viewed thus, one can claim that decentralization, management by objectives, and exposure to market forces place public servants in a field of tension where they are subject, in a new way, to pressure exerted by conflicting rationales and interests. Those employed in health-care, education, and social services carry out their daily work in a field subject to tension between state and market, between communal welfare state ideals and the aim of serving individual customers, between professional quality standards and the personal wishes of professionals to secure the survival of their institutions and to further their own careers. Many often-conflicting matters must be taken into consideration, forcing public professionals to deal with various dilemmas – not least the need to take the interests of their own professions into account. These interests include furthering their own professional knowledgebase and ethos, which in the long run secures their work, social legitimacy, and, in the final analysis, their pay and working conditions as well. These are interests that are just as legitimate in relation to public professionals as in relation to any other labour market groups. Lars-Erik Nilsson covers these questions in two articles in which contemporary threats to teachers' professional legitimacy and right to control their professional tools are highlighted and the possible consequences discussed.

Differences and shared traits

Taking a closer look at issues of contemporary processes of change, the papers present two tendencies pointing in different directions. Both strands of research represented in the articles clearly indicates a trend towards differentiation. Tensions between professions and organizations manifest themselves in different ways; they are dealt with in different ways by different professions, and also by different professionals. Conceptualized in this way, one can claim that the era of mass production in relational work has ended. Different organizations and different (groups of) professionals must confront different conditions and challenges in different ways. One can observe shared traits in the descriptions of the problems professionals confront and in their approaches to dealing with them; these approaches are as follows:

1. Increased individualization: A common feature described in the papers is an increased individualization or a still stronger focus on individual differences. For better or worse, the focus on the individual has become more pronounced. Interest in human differences has grown and interest in seeing oneself as a unique individual has accordingly enlarged. Looking after individual interests and engaging in individual competition for benefits has become more legitimate. Client demands for personalized assessment and treatment (for example, students' individual choice of courses and subjects) have become stronger, in many respects challenging the professionals' ways of coping with their work. This is illustrated in the chapter by Carola Aili. She describes how individualized options, have been introduced, so as to let students shape their own educations. A consequence is that teachers have trouble gathering the information they need for academic supervision and guidance. They simply do not meet their students often enough, and the numbers of teachers involved in the students' education has increased dramatically. In practice, individualization implies new forms of social selection or, put differently, new forms of social inclusion and exclusion. With regard to clients, it becomes decisive whether individuals have the needed resources and ability to take advantage of the 'free choice' of public services. With regard to professionals, it becomes important to be resourceful enough to position oneself favourably as a (successful) member of a (successful) institution in the process of quality development. In the course of these changes, professionals must develop their own personal styles and competence profiles. This entails professional possibilities as well as threats. In her chapter, Agneta Abrahamsson demonstrates how pre-school teachers, district nurses, midwives, and social workers in a new community centre for families became more secure in their professional roles when they moved in the direction of multi-professional co-operation, simply because other professional groups could then relieve them of tasks they lacked the competence to perform. Sandra Jönsson, in contrast, describes conflicts among staff at a drug abuse treatment centre and how the employees experienced role conflicts arising from the contradictory expectations of individual clients, relatives, management, different municipal agencies, and colleagues.

2. *Increased complexity:* Professional tasks and the organization of professional groups have increased in complexity. The abundance of information, growth of professional knowledgebases, and the trend towards specialization mean differentiation of functions in various areas. Efforts geared to co-ordinating and integrating the many special

functions in cross-professional and multi-professional collaborative relationships are on the increase. These efforts themselves may lead to the emergence of new specialists and special functions for co-ordinating differentiated specialists, that is, to a higher degree of complexity. Söran Augustinsson and Elvi Richard describe how nurses who become clinical teachers responsible for education and development, also need to assume the difficult task of building bridges between two distinct forms of practice, scientific and clinical. Increasing institutional complexity implies the ongoing development of new and specialized forms of professional management and leadership – centralized and decentralized, political and economic – and a desire to link these different forms of governance practices together in what has been conceptualized as 'advanced liberal management' (Rose, 1999; Dean, 1999). Carl Rosengren and Michael Ottosson describe, for example, nurses' and ward managers' experience of organizational change. By the late twentieth century, the professional role of ward managers had shifted from an emphasis on clinical to administrative work, without an automatic reassessment of systemic norms and expectations regarding their nursing role. In the same period, still more interest groups became involved in defining the agenda of welfare institutions, groups such as user organizations, professional groups (with their own private practices and interests), and groups of systems specialists and producers behind ICT implementation in the public workplace. As described in Lars-Erik Nilsson's chapter dealing with system bureaucrats, these groups not only claim particular work as their own purview, but also have considerable influence on how professionals carry out their work.

3. Increased relativism: Individualization and complexity challenge in new ways the knowledgebases on which professionals have traditionally relied. The individual client has become an 'expert on his/her own life', and internal and external stakeholders compete for the right to define the kind of knowledge on what (public) work must be based. On one hand, the professionals face a situation in which there is fundamental uncertainty about their knowledgebase as well as about their professional status and legitimacy. On the other hand, demand for professional knowledge is increasing, because it is assumed that a future knowledge society or knowledge economy will rest on such knowledge. In her analysis of ICT in Swedish preschools, Agneta Ljung-Djärf describes how the divergence between a central 'ICT vision' and the preschool teachers' actual professional knowledgebase creates tensions leading to very different ways of handling ICT in different preschools. This situation is not simplified by demands for cross-professional collaboration. Cross-professional collaboration not only entails different professions collaborating to solve a shared task; often, it also involves competition between different scientific paradigms and knowledge definitions., i.e., power struggles for hegemony over the great issues of truth and knowledge. However, the people directly involved are not necessarily completely aware of what is going on. Instead they may interpret these disputes as related to more personal or inter-personal questions.

4. Increased pace of work: More numerous, more complex, and more contradictory assignments, needing to be completed in less time, are being combined with demands for decentralized administration and collaboration. Employees in public institutions experience, for better or worse, the innovations of flexible and autonomously organized cross-professional work. Agneta Abrahamsson demonstrates how the interest of leaders and street-level bureaucrats in collaboration in family centres for families builds on different motives. Leaders who carry out their work guided by new public management theories harbour expectations regarding financial restraint and efficiency. The rank-and-file personnel, in contrast, hope to provide for the families that are their clients and to assert more influence at work. Personnel argue that if they can provide better for their client families and have more influence at work, this will lead to sustainable restraint, while the underlying 'mother organizations' of the multi-professional centre expect both immediate improvement and better economic performance. Consequently, the professionals have to 'do it all' – handle all tasks at the same time. The same general picture is presented in the analysis carried out by Marie-Louise Österlind, Pamela Denicolo, and Curt R. Johansson, which finds that head teachers in Sweden are caught in the middle, being forced to deal with conflicting demands from the local school administration and the teaching profession. Head teachers' responsibilities have increased while their authority has diminished, and financial restraint combined with organizational restructuring has led to more turbulent everyday activities being added to their already heavy workload.

5. Increased fragmentation of work: This implies both increased vertical and horizontal division of labour (i.e., dividing and standardizing work assignments) and efforts to create more hierarchical structures for co-ordination and control (i.e., creating leadership teams to co-ordinate leadership). In this process, there is a tendency to divide performance teams from planning and assessment teams – a division between premier and second league, as it were. In this regard, it must be questioned whether what is going on in the public sector is actually a process of *deprofessionalization*, rather than one of professionalization. In her article on Swedish municipal adult education, Ingrid Henning Loeb describes how conflicting incentives arising from decentralization, coincide and create tensions both in the organization and between professionals. While flexible adult education entails political demands from the state regarding professionalization, teachers' work is becoming increasingly defined by local expert groups that deliver precise models of how education is to be carried out. Relevant to this debate is Joakim Caspersen's chapter about professionalism in teaching and nursing, where he emphasizes the difficulty of saying whether new forms of control are today undermining professionalism. There is great variation between public-sector professions and threats may come from many directions – even from the professions themselves. A more definitive response to the matter of trends of professionalization versus deprofessionalization must build on empirical studies of concrete cases.

Future research

This volume makes a solid contribution to establishing new, theoretically and empirically based knowledge of the tensions in the professional/organizational field arising from contemporary changes in the Scandinavian welfare states. It is broad in scope and renders a nuanced picture of the many ways in which tensions between professions and organizations are manifested in public-sector work.

We still lack knowledge, however. A central concern remains with respect to concrete changes in professional relational work. What kind of knowledge is developed and used professionally? What types of reorganization and restructuring are taking place? What practices are being developed? What new demands are being placed on the professions? How is work being anchored and given legitimate status? How are the most important objectives of professional work to be defined, seen from an ethical or a social perspective? These are questions that concurrently relate to more general questions about the mission, organization, and financing of the welfare state, questions that are notoriously hard to answer. Or rather, they are questions that never can be fully answered in a democratic society but must be subject to ongoing public debate. Precisely for that reason, it is important to establish and discuss knowledge of these issues, not least with reference to the education of the professionals who are going to take care of our common welfare in the future.

References

Abbott, A. (1988). *The system of professions: An essay on the division of expert labor.* Chicago: The University of Chicago Press.

Abernethy, M. A., & Stoelwinder, J. U. (1995). The role of professional control in the management of complex organizations. *Accounting, Organization and Society, 20*(1), 1–17.

Abrahamsson, A. (2004). *Addressing smoking during pregnancy: The challenge to start from the woman's view* (Department of Community Medicine, 148). Lund: Lund University.

Acker, G. M. (1999). The impact of clients' mental illness on social workers' job satisfaction and burnout. *Health and Social Work, 24*(2), 112–119.

Agevall, L. (1994). *Beslutsfattandets rutinisering* [The routinization of decision-making] (Lund Political Studies, 84). Lund: Lund University.

Agevall, L. (2002). Kvalitetssystemens paradoxer. In L. Agevall & L. Zanderin (eds), *Organisering, ledning, miljö* [Organizing, leadership and environment] (328–385). Växjö: Växjö University.

Agevall, L. (2005). *Välfärdens organisering och demokratin: En analys av New Public Management* [Democracy and the organization of social welfare: An analysis of new public management]. Växjö: Växjö University Press.

Agevall, L., & Jenner, H. (2006). Polisarbetet som en uppgift att hantera dilemmas. In L. Agevall, L. & H. Jenner (eds), *Bilder av polisarbete: Samhällsuppdrag, dilemman & kunskapskrav* [Pictures of police work: Public mandate, the dilemmas & required skills] (13–33) Växjö: Växjö University Press.

Ahrne, G. (1990). *Agency and organization: Towards an organizational theory of society.* London: Sage.

Ahrne, G. (1994). *Social organizations: Interaction inside, outside and between organizations.* London: Sage.

Ahrne, G., Roman, C., & Franzén, M. (1996). *Det sociala landskapet: En sociologisk beskrivning av Sverige från 50-tal till 90-tal* [The social landscape: A sociological description of Sweden from the 1950s to the 1990s]. Göteborg: Korpen.

Aili, C. (2002). *Autonomi styrning och jurisdiktion: Barnmorskors tal om arbetet i mödrahälsovården* [Autonomy, governance and jurisdiction: Midwives' talk about their work in maternity health care welfare]. Stockholm: Stockholm University.

Aili, C., & Brante, G. (2004). *Developing categories to study teachers daily work in a perspective of organising.* Paper presented at Nordic Educational Research Associations Congress in Reykjavik, Iceland, 11–13 mars 2004.

Aili, C., & Brante, G. (2007). Qualifying teacher work: Everyday work as basis for the teacher professions' autonomy. *Teachers and Teaching, Theory and Practice, 13*(3), 287–306. London: Routledge.

Alexanderson, K., Brommels, M., Ekenvall, L., Karlsryd, E., Löfgren, A., Sundberg, L., & Österberg, M. (2005). *Problem inom hälso- och sjukvården kring handläggning av patienters sjukskrivning* [Problem in health services about dealing with patients sick leave] (Report, January 2005). Stockholm: LIME Karolinska institutet, Sektionen för personskadeprevention, Institutionen för klinisk neurovetenskap och Medical management centrum.

Allen, J., & Mellor, D. (2002). Work context, personal control, and burnout among nurses. *Western Journal of Nursing Research, 24,* 905–917.

Almqvist, B. (1994). *Approaching the culture of toys in Swedish child care: A literature survey and a toy inventory.* Uppsala: Uppsala University.

Alvesson, M. (2001). *Organisationskultur och ledning* [Corporate culture and leadership]. Stockholm: Liber.

Alvesson, M., & Due Billing, Y. (1999). *Kön och organisation* [Understanding gender and organizations]. Lund: Studentlitteratur.

Andersson, S. (2003). *Ordnande praktiker: En studie av status, homosocialitet och maskuliniteter utifrån två närpolisorganisationer* [Ordering practices: A study of status, homosociality and masculinities based on two community police organisations]. Stockholm: Stockholm University, School of Education.

Andreen Sachs, M., & Theodorsson, E. (2002). Övergripande kvalitetsindikatorer framtagna för hälso- och sjukvården [Comprehensive quality indicators, developed for health services]. *Läkartidningen, 99,* 797–803.

Apple, M. (1989). *Teachers and texts.* New York, Routledge & Kegan Paul.

Aristoteles (1988). *Den nicomachiska etiken* [The Nicomachean ethics] Translation Mårten Ringbom. Göteborg: Daidalos.

Åse, C. (2000). *Makten att se: Om kropp och kvinnlighet i lagens namn* [The power to see: On the body and femininity in the name of the law]. Malmö: Liber.

Augustinsson, S. (2006). *About organised complexity: Suggestions for integration of organisation, learning, and knowing.* Luleå: Business Administration Department, Luleå University.

Augustinsson, S., & Richard, E. (2006). *Balancing and bridge-building with difficulties* (Utredning kliniska lärare). Kristianstad: Region Skåne.

Babbage, C. (1835/1971). *On the economy of machinery and manufactures* (repr. ed.). New York: Kelley.

Bak, M. & Gunnarsson, L. (2000). *Familjecentralen: Framtidens stöd till föräldrar och barn?* [Family centres: The support of the future for parents and children?] (Folkhälsoinstitutet utvärderar, 14). Stockholm: Folkhälsoinstitutet [Swedish National Institute of Public Health].

Barnard, C. J. (1938). *The function of the executive.* Cambridge, MA: Harvard University Press.

Barth, F. (1994). *Ethnic groups and boundaries.* Oslo: Pensumtjeneste.

Bauman, Z. (1991). *Modernity and ambivalence.* London: Polity.

Beach, D. (2004). The public costs of the restructuring of adult education: A case in point from Sweden. *Journal for Critical Education Policy Studies, 2*(1), Retreived October 19, 2007, from http://www.jceps.com/?pageID=article&articleID=25.

Beck, U. (1992). *Risk society: Towards a new modernity.* London: Sage.

Becker, H. (1962). *The nature of a profession. Sixty first yearbook of the National Society for the Study of Education, Part II* (24–46). Chicago: National Society for the Study of Education.

Becker, H., & Riel, M. (2000). *The beliefs, practices, and computer use of teacher leaders.* Paper presented at the American Educational Research Association, New Orleans, 24–28 April.

Beckman, S. (1989). Professionerna och kampen om auktoritet. In S. Selander (ed.), *Kampen om yrkesutövning, status och kunskap: Professionaliseringens sociala grund* [The struggle for practice, status and knowledge: The social basis of professionalization] (57–88). Lund: Studentlitteratur.

Bejerot, E., & Hasselbladh, H. (2001). *Kvalitetsstyrning och professionell autonomi.* Projektansökan.

Benner, M. (2001). *Controversy and consensus.* Stockholm: Swedish Institute for Studies in Education and Research (SISTER).

Benner, P., Tanner, C., & Chesla, C. (1999). *Expertise in nursing practice: Caring, clinical judgment and ethics.* Lund: Studentlitteratur.

Bennet, L., Ross, M. W., & Sunderland, R. (1996). The relationship between recognition, rewards and burnout in AIDS caring. *Aids Care, 8*(2), 145–153.

Berg, G. (2003). *Att förstå skolan: En teori om skolan som institution och skolor som organisationer* [To comprehend schools: A theory about the school as an institution and schools as organizations]. Lund: Studentlitteratur.

Berger, P. L., & Luckmann, T. (1966). *The social construction of reality.* London: Penguin.

Berggren, N.-O., & Munck, J. (2005). *Polislagen: En kommentar* [The police statute: A commentary]. Stockholm: Norstedts.

Bergman, B., & Klefsjö, B. (1995). *Kvalitet från behov till användning* [Quality, from demand to use]. Lund: Studentlitteratur.

Bertilsson, M. (1990). The welfare state, the professions and citizens. In R. Torstendahl & M. Burrage (eds), *The formation of professions: Knowledge, state and strategy* (114–133). London: Sage.

Biesta, G. (2004). Against learning: Reclaiming a language for education in an age of learning. *Nordisk Pedagogik, 24*(1), 71–82.

Bijker, W. E. (1995). *Of bicycles, bakelites, and bulbs: Toward a theory of sociotechnical change.* Cambridge, MA: MIT Press.

Bijker, W. E., Hughes, T. P., & Pinch, T. J. (eds). (1987). *The social construction of technological systems: New directions in the sociology and history of technology.* Cambridge, MA: MIT Press.

Billquist, L. (1999). *Rummet, mötet och ritualerna: En studie om socialbyrån, klientarbetet och klientskapet* [The room, the encounter and the rituals: A study on the social services agency, client related work and clientship] (unpublished doctoral thesis). Göteborg: Göteborg University.

Bird, R. J. (2003). *Chaos and life complexity and order in evolution and thought.* New York: Columbia University Press.

Bittner, E. (1967). The police on skid-row: A study of peace keeping. *American Sociological Review, 32*(5), 699–715.

Bjørk, I. T., Hansen, B. S., Samdal, G. B., Tørstad, S., & Hamilton, G. A. (2007). Evaluation of clinical ladder participation in Norway. *Journal of Nursing Scholarship, 39*(1), 88–94.

Björklöf, A, (2006). Kall eller profession hänger på könet [Calling or profession, a question of gender]. *Genus, 2,* 21–22.

Blomberg, S. (2004). *Specialiserad biståndshandläggning inom kommunala äldreomsorgen. Genomförandet av en organisationsreform och dess praktik* [Specialized aid administration within municipal elders' care. Implementation of an organizational reform and its practice]. Lund: Lund University.

Blomgren, M. (1999). *Pengarna eller livet? Sjukvårdande professioner och yrkesgrupper i mötet med en ny ekonomistyrning* [Your money or your life? Healthcare professions and occupational groups in the encounter with new financial management]. Uppsala: Uppsala University, Department of Business Studies.

Blossing, U. (2002). *Skolförbättring i praktiken* [School improvement in practise]. Lund: Studentlitteratur.

Bonifacio, P. (1991). *The psychological effects of police-work: A psychodynamic approach.* New York and London: Plenum Press.

Bons, T., Lundström Mattsson, Å., Nyberg, E., & Pettersson, S. (2003). *Familjehuset: Ett resurscenter för barnfamiljer: En studie av ett storstadssatsningsprojekt i initialskedet, 30/03* [The Family Center: A resource center for families with children. A study of a metropolitan initiative project in the initial phase, 30/03]. FoU-Södertörn.

Bottery, M. (1996). The challenge to professionals from the new public management: Implications for the teaching profession. *Oxford Review of Education, 22*(2), 179–197.

Bovens, M., & Zouridis, S. (2002). From street-level to system-level bureaucracies: How information and communication technology is transforming administrative discretion and constitutional control. *Public Administration Review, 62*(2), 174–184.

Bowker, G. C., & Star, S. L. (1999). *Sorting things out: Classification and its consequences.* London: The MIT Press.

Brante, T. (1988). Sociological approaches to the profession. *Acta Sociologica, 31*(2), 119–142.

Brante, T. (1990). Professionals types as a strategy of analysis. In M. Burrage & R. Torstendahl, R. (eds), *Rethinking the study of professions* (75–93). London: Sage.

Brante, T. (1999). Professional waves and state objectives: A macro-sociological model of the origin and development of continental professions, illustrated by the case of Sweden. In I. Hellberg, M. Saks & C. Benoit (eds), *Professional identities in transition* (61–81). Stockholm: Almqvist & Wiksell.

Braudel, F. (1972). *The Mediterranean and the Mediterranean world in the age of Philip* II (2. ed.). London: William Collins & Sons.

Braverman, H. (1977). *Arbete och monopolkapital: Arbetets degradering i det tjugonde århundradet* [Labor and monopoly capital: The degradation of work in the twentieth century]. Stockholm: Rabén & Sjögren.

Brechin, A., Brown, H., & Eby, M. A. (2000). *Critical practice in health and social care.* Thousand Oaks, CA: Sage.

Brint, S. (1994). *In an age of experts: The changing role of professionals in politics and public life.* Princeton, NJ: Princeton University Press.

Brown, R. (2000). Social identity theory, past achievements, current problems and future challenge. *European Journal of Social Psychology, 30,* 745–778.

Brytting, T. (2001). *Att vara som Gud? Moralisk kompetens i arbetslivet* [To be like God? Moral competence at work]. Malmö: Liber.

Burke, R. J. (2002). Work experiences and psychological wellbeing of former hospital-based nurses now employed elsewhere. *Psychological Reports, 91,* 1059–1064.

Burns, T. R., & Flam, H. (1987). *The shaping of social organization: Social rule system theory with applications.* London: Sage.

Calltorp, J. (1999). Kvalitetsutveckling i vården – dags för strategiska val! Öppen redovisning utmanande men ofrånkomlig [Improving the quality of healthcare – time for strategic choices! Open accounting a challenge but inevitable]. *Läkartidningen, 96,* 2566–2568.

Cannan, C. (1992). *Changing families, changing welfare: Family centres and the welfare state.* London: Harvester.

Carlgren, I. (2000). The implicit teacher. In K. Klette, I. Carlgren, J. Rasmussen & H. Simola (eds), *Restructuring Nordic teachers: An analysis of policy texts from Finland, Denmark, Sweden and* Norway (325–390). Oslo: University of Oslo, Institute for Educational Research.

Carlgren, I., & Marton, F. (2002). *Lärare av i morgon* [Teacher of tomorrow] (new extended edition.). Stockholm: Lärarförbundet.

Carlström, A. K. (1999). *På spaning i Stockholm: En etnologisk studie av polisarbete* [Reconnaissance in Stockholm: An etnographic study of police work]. Stockholm: Stockholm University.

Carlström, E., & Berlin, J. (2004). *Boken om team: En kunskapsöversikt om team och teamarbete inom hälso- och sjukvården* [The Team Book: A research overview on teams and teamwork in healthcare]. Stockholm: Landstingsförbundet.

Caspersen, J. (2006). *Kallet eller dannet? Motivasjon og yrkessosialisering hos sykepleiere og lærere* [Motivation and work-place socialisation among Norwegian nurses and teachers]. Oslo: Høgskolen i Oslo, Senter for profesjonsstudier.

Cassel, C., & Walsh, S. (2004). Repertory grids. In C. Cassel & G. Symon (eds), *Essential guide to qualitative methods in organizational research* (61–72). London: Sage.

Castells, M. (1996). *Rise of the Network Society: The Information Age: Economy, Society and Culture.* Cambridge: Blackwell Publishers.

Castro, F. (1999). After the wave: The welfare state professionals in Sweden. In I. Hellberg, M. Saks, & C. Benoit (eds), *Professional identities in transition* (43–59). Stockholm: Almqvist & Wiksell.

Cedermark, G., & Klette, H. (1973). *Polis, myndighet – människa* [Police, authority – man]. Lund: Studentlitteratur.

Checkland, P. (1981). *Systems thinking, systems practice.* Chichester: Wiley.

Chekol, I-M. (2003). *Supervision as an educational activity in practical training in the nursing programme: A description of variation in understanding* (Department of Education, 368). Lund: Lund University.

Christensen, S., & Kreiner, K. (1997). *Project management under uncertainty.* Copenhagen: Academia Adacta.

Christensen, T., & Laegreid, P. (1999). New public management: Design, resistance, or transformation? A study of how modern reforms are received in a civil service system. *Public Productivity & Management Review, 23*(2), 169- 193.

Christensen, T., Lægreid, P., Roness, P.G., & Røvik, K. A. (2005). *Organisationsteori för offentlig sektor* [Organization theory for public sector]. Malmö: Liber.

Christie, N. (1987). The ideal victim. In E. Fattah (ed.), *From crime policy to victim policy: Reorienting the justice system* (17–30). London: Macmillan Press.

Collin, S-O. (1990). *Aktiebolagets kontroll: En transaktionskostnadsteoretisk inlägg i debatten om ägande och kontroll av aktiebolag och storföretag* [The control of the corporation: A transaction cost approach to ownership and control of large joint stock companies] (Lund Studies in Economics and Management, 9). Lund: Lund University Press.

Cooper, T. L. (1990). *The responsible administrator.* San Francisco: Jossey-Bass Publishers.

Cranton, P. (1994). *Understanding and promoting transformative learning: A guide for educators of adults.* San Francisco: John Wiley & Sons, Inc.

Cuban, L. (1986). *Teachers and machines: The classroom use of technology since 1920.* New York: Teachers College Press.

Cuban, L. (1993). Computers meet classroom – classroom wins. *Teachers College Record, 95*(2), 185–210.

Cuban, L. (2002). *Oversold and underused: Computers in the classroom.* Cambridge, MA: Harvard University Press.

Cuban, L. (2001). Why are teachers infrequent and restrained users of computers in their classrooms. In J. Woodward & L. Cuban (eds), *Technology, curriculum and professional development: Adapting schools to meet the needs of students with disabilities* (121–137). Thousand Oaks, CA: Corwin Press, Inc.

Cunliffe, A.L. & Shotter, J. (2006). Wittgenstein, Bakhtin, Management and Dialogical. In D.M. Hosking & S. McNamee (eds), *The Social Construction of Organization.* Malmö: Liber.

Czarniawska, B., & Joerges, B. (1996). Travels of ideas. In B. Czarniawska & G. Sevón (eds), *Translating organizational change* (13–48). Berlin: de Gruyter.

Czarniawska, B. (2005). On Gorgon Sisters: Organizational Action in the Face of Paradox. In *Niklas Luhmann and Organization Studies,* (eds), D. Seidl, K.H. Becker. Copenhagen: Liber.

Dæhlen, M. (2005). Change in job values during education. *Journal of Education and Work, 18*(4), 385–400.

Dahlberg, G. & Lenz Taguchi, H. (1994). *Förskola och skola: Om två skilda traditioner och om visionen om en mötesplats* [Preschool and school: On two discrete traditions and a vision of confluence]. Stockholm: HLS.

Dahle, R., & Thorsen, K. (2004). *Velferdstjenester i endring: Når politikk blir praksis* [Changing welfare-state services: when politics become practice]. Bergen: Fagbokforl.

Day, C. (2000). Stories of change and professional development: The costs of commitment. In C. Day, A. Fernandez, T. Hauge & J. Møller (eds), *The life and work of teachers: International perspectives in changing times.* London: Falmer Press.

Day, C. (2003). The UK policy environment for school leadership: Uneasy transition. *Leadership and Policy in Schools, 2*(1), 5–25.

Dean, M. (1999). *Governmentality: Power and rule in modern society.* London: Sage Publications.

Denicolo, P. M., & Pope, M. (2001). *Transformative professional practice: Personal construct approaches to education and research.* London: Whurr.

Derber, C., & Schwartz, W. A. (1991). New mandarins or new proletariat? Professional power at work. *Research in the Sociology of Organization, 8,* 71–96.

DiMaggio, P. J., & Powell, W. (1983/1991). The iron cage revisited: Institutional isomorphism and collective rationality. In W. Powell & P. J. DiMaggio (eds), *The new institutionalism in organisational analysis* (147–160). Chicago: University of Chicago Press.

Dreyfus, H. L., & Dreyfus, E. S. (1986). *Mind over machine: The power of human intuition and expertise in the era of computer.* New York: The Free Press.

Dreyfus, L. H., & Dreyfus, E. S. (2005). Expertise in real world contexts. *Organization Studies 26*(5), 779–792.

Dufwa, S. (2004). *Kön lön och karriär: Sjuksköterskeyrkets omvandling under 1900-talet* [Gender, salary and careers: The transformation of nursing profession during the twentieth century] (Acta Wexionesia, 40/2004). Växjö: Växjö University.

Ehn, P. (1993). Scandinavian design: On participation and skill. In D. Schuler & A. Namioka (eds), *Participatory design: Principles and practices* (41–77). Hillsdale, NJ: L. Erlbaum Associates.

Ekholm, M. (1992). Evaluating the impact of comprehensive school leadership development in Sweden. *Education & Urban Society, 24*(3), 365–385.

Ekholm, M., Blossing, U., Kåräng, G., Lindvall, K., & Scherp, H-Å. (2000). *Forskning om rektor: En forskningsöversikt* [Research on Head Teachers – A research review]. Stockholm: Skolverket [National Agency of Education]/ Liber.

Ekman, G. (1999). *Från text till batong: Om poliser, busar och svennar* [From text to baton: On police officials, and ruffians] (Dissertation, 510/1999). Stockholm: School of Economics, the Economic Research Institute.

Ekstrand, P. (2005). *"Tarzan och Jane": Hur män som sjuksköterskor formar sin identitet* ["Tarzan and Jane": How men in nursing practice form their identity] (Uppsala Studies in Education, 109). Uppsala: Uppsala University.

Ellström, P.-E. (1997). The many meanings of occupational competence and qualification. *Journal of European Industrial Training, 2* (6–7), 266–273.

Eraut, M. (1994). *Developing professional knowledge and competence.* London: Falmer Press.

Eriksen, E. O. (1998). *Kommunikativt ledarskap: Om styrning av offentliga institutioner* [Communicative leadership: On managing public institutions]. Göteborg: Daidalos.

Eriksson, B., & Karlsson, P.-Å. (1990). *Utvärderingens roll i socialt arbete* [The role of assessment in social work]. Göteborg: Göteborg University.

Erlingsdóttir, G., & Jonnergård, K. (2006). *Att trolla med kvalitet: Om kvalitetssäkringens framfart inom hälso- och sjukvården och inom revisionsbranschen* [Conjuring up quality: On the advance of quality assurance in healthcare and accounting]. Lund: Studentlitteratur.

Erlingsdóttir, G., & Lindberg, K. (2005). Isomorphism, isopraxism, and isonymism: Complementary or competing processes? In B. Czarniawska & G. Sevón (eds), *Global ideas, how ideas, objects and practices travel in the global economy* (47–70). Malmö: Liber & Copenhagen Business School Press.

Erlingsdóttir, G. (1999). *Förförande idéer: Kvalitetssäkring i hälso- och sjukvården* [Seductive ideas: Quality assurance in health services]. Lund: KFS AB.

Evans, R. (1999). *The pedagogic principal.* Edmonton: Qual Institute Press.

Evetts, J. (2002). New directions in state and international professional occupations: discretionary decision-making and acquired regulation. *Work Employment and Society, 16*(2), 341–353.

Evetts, J. (2003). The sociological analysis of professionalism: Occupational change in the modern world. *International Sociology, 18*(2), 395–415.

Evetts, J. (2006). Trust and professionalism: Challenges and occupational changes. *Current Sociology, 54*(4), 515–531.

Fagerberg, H. (ed.). (1988). *Medicinsk etik och människosyn* [Ethics and outlook on mankind in medicine]. Stockholm: Liber.

Fenlason, K. J., & Beehr, T. A. (1994). Social support and occupational stress: Effects of talking to others. *Journal of Organizational Behavoiur, 15*, 157–175.

Finstad, L. (2000). *Politiblikket* [Police vision]. Oslo: Pax Forlag.

Flyvbjerg, B. (2001). *Making social science matter: Why social inquiry fails and how it can succeed again.* Cambridge: Cambridge University Press.

Fournier, V. (1999). The appeal to 'professionalism' as a disciplinary mechanism. *Sociological Review, 47*(2), 280–308.

Fransson, A., & Larsson, S. (1989). *Who takes the second chance? Implementing educational equality in adult basic education in a Swedish context.* Göteborg: Göteborg University, Department of Education and Eduacational Research.

Fredricson, A. (2003). The preschool's meeting with Barbie, Mc-Mice and computers. In A. Nelson, L. E. Berg & K. Svensson (eds), *Toys as communication: Toy research in the late twentieth century, part 2* (131–148). Selection of papers presented at The International Toy Research Conferens, Halmstad University, Sweden, June 1999. Stockholm: KTH, Sitrec.

Freeman, C., & Perez, C. (1988). Structural crisis of adjustment: Business cycles and investment behaviour. In G. Dosi, C. Freeman, R. Nelson, G. Silverberg & L. Soete (eds), *Technical Change and Economic Theory* (36–66) London: Pinter.

Freidson, E. (1971). Editorial foreword. *American Behavioral Scientist, 14,* 467–474.

Freidson, E. (1986). *Professional powers: A study of the institutionalization of formal knowledge.* Chicago: University of Chicago Press.

Freidson, E. (1988). *Profession of medicine: A study of the sociology of applied knowledge.* Chicago: University of Chicago Press.

Freidson, E. (1994). *Professionalism reborn: Theory, prophecy, and policy.* Chicago: University of Chicago Press.

Freidson, E. (2001). *Professionalism: The third logic.* Cambridge: Polity Press.

Friberg, F. (2002). *Pedagogical encounters between patients and nurses in a medical ward* (Göteborg Studies in Educational Sciences, 258). Göteborg: Acta Universitatis Gothoburgensis.

Fritzell, C. (1996). Pedagogical split vision. *Educational Theory, 46*(2), 213–216.

Fritzén, L. (1998). *Den pedagogiska praktikens janusansikte: Om det kommunikativa handlandets didaktiska villkor och konsekvenser* [Pedagogical practice – the face of Janus: The didactic conditions and consequences of communicative action] (Lund Studies in Education, 8). Lund: Lund University.

Fritzén, L., & Gerrevall, P. (2001). Bedömning av yrkeskunnande inom gymnasieskolan: Några principiella utgångspunkter. In G. Svingby & S. Svingby (eds), *Bedömning av kunskap och kompetens* [Assessing knowledge and competence] (Rapport från PRIM-gruppen, 18). Stockholm: Stockholm University, Institute of Education.

Gaines, B. R., & Shaw, M. L. G. (1990). *RepGrid II.* Computer programme for the analysis of repertory grids.

Gärdsmo Pettersson, E. (2000). *Att verka tillsammans: En bok om familjecentraler* [Working together: A book about family resource centers]. Stockholm: Svenska folkhälsoinstitutet [Swedish National Institute of Public Health].

Gergen, K. J. (1999). *An invitation to social construction.* London: Sage.

Gerrish, K. Macmahon. (2000). Research and development in nursing. In K.Gerrish & A. Lacey (eds), *The research process in nursing.* Oxford: Blackwell pub.

Gilbert, S. (1996). Making the most of a slow revolution. *Change, March/April,* 245–258.

Gilligan, C. (1982). *In a different voice.* Cambridge, MA and London: Harvard University Press.

Goodson, I. F., & Hargreaves, A. (eds). (1992). *Studying teachers' lives.* New York: Teachers College Press.

Granér, R. (2004). *Patrullerande polisers yrkeskultur* [The professional culture of patrolling police officers] (Lund Dissertation in Social Work, 18). Lund: Lund University, School of Social Works.

Granér, R., & Knutsson, M. (2000). *Etik i polisarbete* [Ethics in police work]. Lund: Studentlitteratur.

Greiff, M. (2006). Kall eller profession? Yrkeskultur och skapandet av manligt och kvinnligt mellan klient och arbetsköpare [A calling or a profession? Occupational culture and the construction of male and female between client and customer]. In H. Peterson, V. Leppännen, S. Jönsson & J. Tranquis (eds), *Villkor i arbete med människor: En antologi om human service arbete* [Conditions of working with people: An anthology on human service work] (111–137). Stockholm: Arbetslivsinstitutet [National Institute for Working Life].

Grimby, U. (2001). Dokumentation av *Documentation of quality system in health care*. Ellös: Kaprifolen Utveckling AB.

Grundy, S., & Bronser, S. (2000). The New Work Order and Australian Schools. In C. Day, A. Fernandez, T. Hauge & J. Møller (eds), *The life and work of teachers: International perspectives in changing times*. London: Falmer Press.

Gustavsson, A., (ed.). (1996). *Silent knowledge: What is it really?* Stockholm: Stockholm University, Department of Education.

Gustavsson, B. (ed.). (2004). *Knowledge in Practice*. Lund: Studentlitteratur.

Hägerstrand, T. (1974). Tidsgeografisk beskrivning – syfte och postulat. *Svensk Geografisk Årsbok*, 50, 86–94.

Hägerstrand, T. (1970). What about people in regional science? *Papers of the Regional Science Association*, 24, 1–12.

Hägerstrand, T. (1991). What about people in regional science? In G. Carlestam & B. Solbe (eds), *Om tidens vidd och tingens ordning: Texter av Torsten Hägerstrand* [On the vastness of time and the order of things: Texts by Torsten Hägerstrand] (143–154). Stockholm: Byggforskningsrådet. (Original manuscript 1970.)

Hägerstrand, T. (1982). Diorama, path and project. *Tijdschrift voor Economische en Sociale Geografie*, 73(6), 323–339.

Hägerstrand, T., & Lenntorp, B. (1974). *Samhällsorganisation i tidsgeografiskt perspektiv. SOU 1974:2*, 221–232.

Häggroth, S. (1991). *Offentlig sektor mot nya mål* [Public sector towards new objectives]. Stockholm: Publica.

Haglund, B. (1998). What is knowledge? In M. Eivergard (ed.), *Philosophical questions. adventures in the world of ideas*. Stockholm: UR [Swedish Educational Broadcasting Company].

Hallsten, L. (1983). *Utbränd i jobbet: En litteraturgenomgång av burnoutfenomenet* [Burn-out at work: A review of the burn-out phenomenon]. Stockholm: Länsarbetsnämnden.

Halmos, P. (1970). *The personal service society*. New York: Shocken Books.

Hansen, L. H., & Adam, K. (2004). *Från forskningsprojekt till kvalitetsverktyg:*

En professions- och organisationsstudie av de nationella kvalitetsregistren [From research project to quality instrument: A professional and organizational study of Swedish national quality registers] (Arbetslivsrapport, 2004:22). Stockholm: Arbetslivsinstitutet [National Institute for Working Life].

Hansen, L. H. (2001). *The division of labour in post-industrial societies.* Göteborg: Göteborg University, Department of Sociology.

Hargreaves, A., & Goodson, I. F. (1996). Teachers' professional lives: Aspirations and actualities. In I. F. Goodson & A. Hargreaves (eds), *Teachers' professional lives* (1–27). London: Falmer Press.

Harré, R., & van Langenhove, L. (1999a). The dynamics of social episodes. In R. Harré & L. van Langenhove (eds), *Positioning theory: Moral contexts of intentional action* (1–13). Malden, MA: Blackwell.

Harré, R., & van Langenhove, L. (eds). (1999b). *Positioning theory: Moral contexts of intentional action.* Malden, MA: Blackwell.

Harré, R., & Moghaddam, F. M. (2003). Introduction: The self and others in traditional psychology and in positioning theory. In R. Harré & F. M. Moghaddam (eds), *The self and others: Positioning individuals and groups in personal, political, and cultural contexts* (1–11). Westport, CT: Praeger.

Harré, R., & Moghaddam, F. M. (eds). (2003). *The self and others: Positioning individuals and groups in personal, political, and cultural contexts.* Westport, Conn.: Praeger.

Hasenfeld, Y. (1983). *Human service organizations.* Englewood Cliffs, NJ: Prentice Hall.

Haug, M. (1973). Deprofessionalization: An alternative hypothesis for the future. In P. Halmos (ed.), *Professionalism and social change* (195–211). Keele, UK: University of Keele.

Haug, M. (1988). A re-examination of the hypothesis of physician deprofessionalization. *The Milbank Quarterly, 66*(2), 48–56.

Heggen, K. (2005). Fagkunnskapens plass i den profesjonelle identiteten [The role of formal knowledge in professional identity]. *Norsk Pedagogisk Tidsskrift, 89*(6), 446–460.

Helgøy, I. (2003). Fra skole til tjenesteleverandør? Endringsprosesser i norsk grunnskole [From school to provider of services? Processes of change in Norwegian primary school]. *Norsk Statsvetenskaplig Tidsskrift, 1*, 55–79.

Henning Loeb, I. (2006). *Utveckling och förändring i kommunal vuxenutbildning: En yrkeslivshistorisk ingång med berättelser om lärarbanor* [Development and change in municipal adult education: Life history studies and narrative analysis of teacher trajectories] (Göteborg Studies in Educational Sciences, 237). Göteborg: Acta Universitatis Gothoburgensis.

Henning Loeb, I. (2007). Development and change in Swedish municipal adult education: Occupational life history studies and four genealogies of context. *Policy Futures in Education, 5*(4), 468–477.

Henriksen, E. (2002). *Understanding healthcare organizations*. Uppsala: Uppsala University.

Henriksen, J-O., & Vetlesen, A. J. (1998). *Etik i arbete med människor* [Ethics when working with people]. Lund: Studentlitteratur.

Hill, J. C., & Lynn, J. L. E. (2003). Producing human services: Why do agencies collaborate? *Public Management Review, 5*(1), 63–81.

Hjort, K. (2001). *Moderniseringen i den offentlige sector* [Modernization of the public sector]. Roskilde: Roskilde Universitetsforlag.

Hjort, K. (ed.). (2004). *De Professionelle – forskning i professioner og professionsuddannelser* [The professionals – research into professions and education of professionals]. Roskilde: Roskilde Universitetsforlag.

Hjort, K. (2005). *Professionaliseringen i den offentlige sektor* [Professionalization in the public sector]. Roskilde: Roskilde Universitetsforlag.

Holgersson, S. (2001). *IT-system och filtrering av verksamhetskunskap: Kvalitetsproblem vid analyser och beslutsfattande som bygger på uppgifter hämtade från polisens IT-system* [IT systems and filtering of organizational knowledge: Problems with analysis and decisions based on information taken from the Swedish Police IT system] (FiF-avhandling, 49). Linköping: Linköping University.

Holgersson, S. (2005). *Yrke POLIS: Yrkeskunskap, motivation, IT-system och andra förutsättningar för polisarbete* [Profession POLICE: Occupational knowledge, motivation, IT system and other requirements for police work]. Linköping: Linköping University.

Holmberg, L. (1999). *Inden for lovens rammer: Politiets arbejdsmetoder og konkrete skøn* [Policing Stereotypes: A qualitative study of police work in Denmark]. Copenhagen: Gyldendal.

Holsti, O. R. (1971). Crisis, stress and decision-making. *International Social Science Journal XXIII*(1), 53–67.

Hood, C. (1991). A public management for all seasons? *Public Administrations, 69*, 3–19.

Hood, C. (1995). The 'new public management' in the 1980s: Variations on a theme. *Accounting, Organizations and Society, 20*(2/3), 93–109.

Hornby, S., & Atkins, J. (2000). *Collaborative care: Interprofessional, interagency and interpersonal*. Oxford: Blackwell Science.

Hovdenakk, S. S. (2004). Et kritisk blikk på Reform 97 og dens grunnlagstenkning [A critical view of "Reform 97" and its foundation]. *Norsk Pedagogisk Tidsskrift, 4*, 316–330.

Hultman, G. (2001). *Intelligenta improvisationer: Om lärares arbete och kunskapsbildning i vardagen* [Intelligent improvisations: On teachers' work and every day knowledge formation]. Lund: Studentlitteratur.

Hyden, H. (2002). *Normvetenskap* [Norm science] (Lund Studies in Sociology of Law, 8). Lund: Lund University.

Hydén, S., & Lundberg, A. (2004). *Inre utlänningskontroll i polisarbete: Mel-*

lan rättsstatsideal och effektivitet i Schengens Sverige [Inner aliens' control in police work: Between the ideals of the rule of law and efficiency in Sweden as a Schengen state] (Linköping Studies in Arts and Science, 291 / Malmö Studies in International Migration and Ethnic Relation, 1). Linköping: Linköping University, Philosophical Faculty.

Hyland, T. (1996). Professionalism, ethics and work-based learning. *British Journal of Educational Studies, 44*(2), 68–180.

Imsen, G. (2003). *Skolemiljø, læring og elevutbytte: En empirisk studie av grunnskolens 4., 7. og 10. trinn* [School environment, learning environment and students' outcome: An empirical analysis of 4th, 7th, and 10th grade]. Trondheim: Tapir Akademisk Forlag.

ITiS98/Government Communication (1997/98:176). *Tools for learning. A national programme for ICT in schools.* Retrieved February 27, 2003, from http://www.itis.gov.se/publikationer/eng/IT_iskolan.pdf

Ivarsson Westerberg, A. (2004). *Papperspolisen: Den ökande administrationen i modernarganisationer* [Paper Police: The growing administrative burden in modern organizations] (Dissertation, 660). Stockholm: EFI.

Jacobsson, B. (2000). Standardization and expert knowledge. In N. Brunsson & B. Jacobsson (eds), *A world of standards* (40–49). Oxford: Oxford University Press.

Janson, P. (2005). *Competence for evidence.* Stockholm: Swedish Institute for Studies in Education and Research (SISTER).

Jedeskog, G. (1996). *Lärare vid datorn: Sju högstadielärares undervisning med datorer 1984–1994* [Teachers at computers: Seven upper intermediate teachers' use of computers in teaching]. Linköping: Linköping University.

Jedeskog, G. (2000). *Teachers and computers: Teachers' computer usage and the relationship between computers and the role of the teacher, as described in international research.* Uppsala: Uppsala University, Department of Education.

Jenner, H. (1995). *Nytta och etik i det sociala arbetet* [Utility and ethics in the social work]. Lund: Studentlitteratur.

Jensen, K., & Lahn, L. (2005). The binding role of knowledge: An analysis of nursing students' knowledge ties. *Journal of Education and Work, 18*(3), 305–320.

Jensen, K., & Tveit, B. (2005). Youth culture: A source of energy and renewal for the field of nursing in Norway. In H. M. Dahl & R. Eriksen (eds), *Dilemmas of care in the Nordic welfare state: Continuity and change* (161–175). England: Ahgate.

Johansson, R. (2002). *Nyinstitutionalismen inom organisationsanalysen: En skolbildnings uppkomst, spridning och utveckling* [The new institutionalism in organization analysis: The origin, dissemination and development of a new school]. Lund: Studentlitteratur.

Kahn, R., Wolfe, D. M., Quinn, R. P., & Snoek, J. D. (1964). *Organizational stress: Studies in role conflicts and ambiguity.* New York: Wiley.

Kalliath, T., & Morris, R. (2002). Job satisfaction among nurses: A predictor of burnout levels. *Journal of Nursing Administration, 32,* 648–654.

Karlsen, G. (2002). *Utdanning, styring og marked: Norsk utdanningspolitikk i et internasjonalt perspektiv* [Education, politics and governing. Norwegian educational policy in a comparative perspective]. Oslo: Universitetsforlaget.

Karlsen, G., & Kvalbein, I. A. (2003). *Norsk lærerutdanning: Søkelys på allmennlærerutdanningen i et reformperspektiv* [Norwegian teacher education: spotlight on the education of the generalist teacher in a reform perspective]. Oslo: Universitetsforlaget.

Karlsson, M. (2004). *An ITiS teacher team as a community of practice* (Göteborg Studies in Educational Sciences, 216). Göteborg: Acta Universitatis Gothoburgensis.

Karseth, B., & Nerland, M. (2007). Building professionalism in a knowledge society: Examining discourses of knowledge in four professional associations. *Journal of Education and Work, 20*(4), 335–355.

Karsten, S., Koning, I. & Schooten J. F. (2007). Individual and School-related Aspects of Stress and Job Satisfaction. In J. Löwstedt, P. Larsson, S. Karsten & R. Van Dick (eds), *From intensified work to professional development.* Brussels: P.I.E. Lang.

Kauffman, S. A. (1993). *The origins of order: Self-organization and selection in evolution.* New York: Oxford University Press.

Kaufmann, G., & Kaufmann, A. (1998). *Psykologi i organisation och ledning* [Psychology in organisation and management]. Lund: Studentlitteratur.

Kelly, G. (1955). *The psychology of personal constructs, volume one: Theory and personality.* London: Routledge.

Kjekshus, L. E. (2003). Når sykehus blir butikk: Effekter på styring, profesjoner og brukere [When hospitals become shops: Effects on management, professions and users]. *Norsk Statsvitenskaplig Tidsskrift, 3,* 444–459.

Knauer P. 1967). The hermeneutic function of the principle of double effect. *Natural Law Forum, l2,* 132–162.

Knorr Cetina, K. (2001). Objectual practice. In T. R. Schatzki, K. Knorr Cetina, & E. von Savigny (eds), *The practice turn in contemporary theory* (175–188). London: Routledge.

Knutsson, M., & Granér, R. (2001). *Perspektiv på polisetik* [Perspectives on police ethics]. Lund: Studentlitteratur.

Koehn, D. (1994). *The ground of professional ethics.* London and New York: Routledge.

Kollerbauer, A., Jansson, C.-G., Köhler, H., & Yngström, L. (1983). *Datorstöd i undervisningen: En presentation av PRINCESS-projektet* [Computer support in teaching: A presentation of the PRINCESS project] (Slutrapport 1983). Stockholm: Clea.

Kristianstads kommun. (2000). *Familjehus på Näsby* [Family centre at Näsby].

Kullberg, C. (1994). *Socialt arbete som kommunikativ praktik: Samtal med och om klienter* [Social work as a communicative practise: Talk with and about clients] (unpublished doctoral thesis). Linköping: Linköping University.

Larsson, P., & Löwstedt, J. (2007). Refining the expedition: Individual and organisational development. In J. Löwstedt, P. Larsson, S. Karsten & R. van Dick (eds), *From intensified work to professional development*. Brussels: P.I.E. Lang.

Lave, J. & Wenger, E. (1993). *Situated learning. Legitimate peripheral participation*. Cambridge: Cambridge university press.

Lawton, A. (1998). *Ethical management for the public services*. Buckinham: Open University Press.

Le Blanc, P., de Jonge, J., & Schaufeli, W. (2000). Job stress and health. In N. Chmie (ed.), *Introduction to work and organizational psychology: A European perspective* (148–177). Oxford: Blackwell.

Leppänen, V., Jönsson, S., Petersson, H., & Tranquist, J. (2006). Villkor i arbete med människor: En inledning. In H. Petersson, V. Leppänen, S. Jönsson & J. Tranquist (eds), *Villkor i arbete med människor: En antologi om human service arbete* [Conditions of working with people: An anthology on human service work] (1–18). Stockholm: Arbetslivsinstitutet [National Institute for Working Life].

Lidholt, B. (1999). *Anpassning, kamp och flykt: Hur förskolepersonal handskas med effekter av besparingar och andra förändringar i förskolan* [Adjustment, fight and escape: How preschool staff cope with effects of financial cutbacks and other changes] (Uppsala Studies in Education, 83). Uppsala: Acta Universitatis Upsaliensis.

Light, P-C. (2002). The content of their character: The state of the non profit workforce. *The Nonprofit Quarterly, Fall 9–16*.

Linander, C. (2002). *En för alla, alla för en: Sjuksköterskors och ingenjörers syn på ledarskap. En enkät och repertory grid studie sista terminen i utbildning och efter ett till ett och ett halvt år i utbildning* [One for all, all for one: Nurses' and engineers' views about leadership. A questionnaire and repertory grid study during the last term of study and at work, one and a half-years later]. Lund: Lund University, Department of Psychology.

Lindberg-Sand, A. (1996). *The spider in the glue: The impact of clinical training on the development of professional nursing competence* (Scripta Academica Lundensia, 339). Lund: Lund University, School of Education.

Lindén, J. (1996). Theoretical and methodological questions concerning a contextual approach to psychological issues in working life. Development of a diary-in-group method. *Science Communication, 18*(1), 59–79.

Lindén, J., & Torkelsson, E. (1991). *Yrke: Skådespelare – kritiska moment i arbetslivet* [Occupation: Actor – critical moments at work]. Lund: Lund University, Department of Psychology.

Lindgren, G. (1992). *Doktorer, systrar och flickor: Om informell makt* [Doctors, sisters, girls: On informal power]. Stockholm: Carlsson.

Lindh, J. (1997). *Datorstödd undervisning i skolan: Möjligheter och problem* [Computer supported teaching at school: Possibilities and problems] (2 expanded ed.). Lund: Studentlitteratur.

Lindqvist, G. (1995). *Lekens estetik: En didaktisk studie om lek och kultur i förskolan* [The esthetics of play: A didactic study of play and culture in preschools] (Research report 95:12). Karlstad: Karlstad University.

Lipsky, M. (1980). *Street-level bureaucracy: Dilemmas of the individual in public services.* New York: Russell Sage Foundation.

Ljung-Djärf, A. (2002). Fröken får jag spela data? Datorn i förskolans lärandemiljö. In R. Säljö & J. Linderoth (eds), *Utm@ningar och e-frestelser: IT och skolans lärkultur* [Ch@llenges and e-temptations: IT and the learning culture of schooling] (280–301). Stockholm: Prisma.

Ljung-Djärf, A. (2004). *Spelet runt datorn: Datoranvändande som meningsskapande praktik i förskolan* [Play around the computer: Computer use as meaning-shaping practice in pre-school] (Malmö Studies in Educational Sciences, 12). Malmö: Malmö University, School of Education.

Ljung-Djärf, A. (in press/2008). The owner, the participant and the spectator: Positions and positioning in peer activity around the computer. *Early Years, 21*(1).

Ljung-Djärf, A., Åberg-Bengtsson, L., & Ottossson, T. (2005). Ways of relating to computer use in pre-school activity. *International Journal of Early Years Education, 13*(1), 31–43.

Lloyd, C., King, R., & Chenoweth, L. (2002). Social work, stress and burnout. *Journal of Mental Health, 11*(3), 255–265.

Lortie, D. (1975). *School teacher: A sociological study.* Chicago: University of Chicago Press.

Lumsden Wass, K. (2004). *Vuxenutbildning i omvandling: Kunskapslyftet som ett sätt att organisera förnyelse* [Restructuring adult education: The adult education initiative as a way of organizing change] (Göteborg Studies in Educational Sciences, 219). Göteborg: Acta Universitatis Gothoburgensis.

Lundahl, L. (1997). *Efter svensk modell: LO, SAF och utbildningspolitiken 1944–1990* [According to the Swedish model: LO, SAF and the education policy 1944–1990]. Umeå: Boréa.

Lundahl, L. (2003). Sweden: Decentralization, deregulation, quasi-markets – and then what? *Journal of Education Policy, 18*(1), 87–97.

Lundberg, M. (1998). *Kvinnomisshandel som polisärende: Att definiera och utde-*

finiera [Woman-battering as a police matter: Definitions and redefinitions] (Network for Research in Criminology and Deviant Behaviour, 1). Lund: Lund University.

Lundberg, M. (2001). *Vilja med förhinder: Polisers samtal om kvinnomisshandel* [Intention with impediment: Police conversations about woman-battering]. Eslöv: Brutus Östlings Bokförlag Symposion.

Lundquist, L. (1988). *Byråkratisk etik* [Ethics in bureaucracy]. Lund: Studentlitteratur.

Lundquist, L. (1991). *Etik i offentlig verksamhet* [Ethics in public work]. Lund: Studentlitteratur.

Lundquist, L. (1992). *Förvaltning, stat och samhälle* [Public administration, state and society]. Lund: Studentlitteratur.

Lundquist, L. (1998). *Demokratins väktare* [Guardians of democracy]. Lund: Studentlitteratur.

Lysgaard, S. (2001). *Arbeiderkollektivet: En studie i de underordnedes sociologi* [The worker collective: A study in the sociology of submission]. Oslo: Universitetsforlaget.

Macdonald, K. (1995). *The sociology of professions*. London: Sage.

Machado, N. (1996). *Using the bodies of the dead: Studies in law, organization and social processes concerning organ transplantation*. Uppsala: Uppsala University, Department of Sociology.

Maclagan, P. (1998). *Management & morality*. London: Sage.

Mäkitalo, Å. (2002). *Categorizing work: Knowing, arguing, and social dilemmas in vocational guidance* (Göteborg Studies in Educational Sciences, 177). Göteborg: Acta Universitatis Gothoburgensis.

Malmquist, E. (1961). Undervisningsmaskiner och deras användning [Educational technology and its use]. *Skola och Samhälle, årg. 42, 6*, 175–187.

Manning, P. K. (1989). Occupational culture. In W. G. Bailey (ed.), *The encyclopaedia of police science*. New York & London: Garland, 472–475.

Manson, S., McCartney, S., & Sjerer, M. (2000). Audit automation as control within audit firms. *Accounting, Auditing and Accountability Journal, 14*(1), 109–130.

Manz, C. C., & Neck, C. P. (1997). Teamthink: Beyond the groupthink syndrome in self-managing work teams. *Team Performance Management, 3*(1), 18–31.

Marx, K. (1974). *Kapitalet: Kritik av den politiska ekonomin, Bok 1. Kapitalets produktionsprocess* [Capital: A critique of political economy: Book 1] (3rd ed.). Lund: A-Z. (Original work published 1864).

Meyer, J. W., & Rowan, B. (1991). Institutionalized organizations, formal structure as myth and ceremony. In W. Powell & P. DiMaggio (eds), *The new institutionalism in organizational analysis* (41–62). Chicago: University of Chicago Press.

Miller, C. R. (1994). Opportunity, opportunism, and progress: Kairos in the rhetoric of technology. *Argumentation, 8*(1), 81–96.

Mintzberg, H. (1983). *Structure in fives: Designing effective organizations.* Englewood Cliffs, NJ: Prentice-Hall.

Moghaddam, F. M, Slocum, N. R., Finkel, N., Mor, T. & Harré, R. (2000). Towards a cultural theory of duties: The apparent dominance of rights over duties. *Contemporary Culture Culture & Psychology 6*(3), 275–302.

Molander, B. (1992). Att handla med goda skäl. In M. Bertilsson & A. Molander (eds), *Handling, norm och rationalitet: Om förhållandet mellan samhällsvetenskap och praktisk filosofi* [Action, norm and rationality: About the relationship between social science and practical philosophy]. Bergen: Ariadne Forlag, Daidalos.

Molander, B. (1996). *Kunskap i handling* [Knowledge in action]. Göteborg: Daidalos.

Montin, S. (2002). *Moderna kommuner* [Modern local municipalities]. Malmö: Liber.

Morgan, P., & Potter, C. (1995). Professional cultures and paradigms of quality in health care. In I. Kirkpatrick& L. M. Martinez (eds), *The politics of quality in the public sector* (166–189). London: Routledge.

Mowery, D. C., & Rosenberg, N. (1998). *Paths of innovation: Technological change in 20th-century America.* Cambridge: Cambridge University Press.

Muir, W. K. (1977). *Police, streetcorner politicians.* Chicago: University of Chicago Press.

Murphy, R. (1990). Proletarianization or bureacratization: the fall of the professional? In R. Torstendahl & M. Burrage (eds), *The formation of professions. Knowledge, state and strategy* (71–96). London: Sage.

National Board of Education. (1986). *Utbildning inför datasamhället: Information om fortbildning inom dataområdet för skolpersonal* [Education in preparation for a digital society: Information about competence development on computers for school personell]. Stockholm: Skolöverstyrelsen.

NBHW (2000). *Nationella kvalitetsregister inom hälso- och sjukvården 1999* [National Quality Registries in the public health services 1999]. Stockholm: Socialstyrelsen [The National Board of Health and Welfare].

NBHW (2001). *Framtida finansiering av de nationella kvalitetsregistren inom hälso- och sjukvården: Förslag från Beslutsgruppen för nationella kvalitetsregister* [Future financing of the National Quality Registries in the public health services: Propose from the group of decisions for National Quality Registries]. Stockholm: Socialstyrelsen [The National Board of Health and Welfare].

NBHW (2002). *Användningen och nyttan med nationella kvalitetsregister: En undersökning bland deltagande enheter samt sjukvårdshuvudmän* [The use of and the benefits with national quality registries: A study of participated unities and responsibility authority in health services]. Stockholm: Socialstyrelsen [The National Board of Health and Welfare].

Niklasson, L. (2001). Familjecentralen Jorden: Ett andra hem. Samverkan i Haninge kommun. In B. Rasmusson (ed.), *Utan oss ingen framtid: Rapportering från integrations- och demokratiarbete i utsatta bostadsområden* [Without us there is not any future: A report on integration- and democracy-work in exposed housing areas] (53–77). Stockholm: Kommentus.

Nilsson, K. (2005). *Att vara chef och ledare för omvårdnadsarbete* [Being a manager and leader in care services]. Lund: Studentlitteratur.

Nilsson, L.-E. (2005a). *The enemy within: Positioning students as enemy or prey in the design and implementation of digitally mediated learning environments.* Paper presented at the 33rd congress of the Nordic Educational Research Association (NERA) in Oslo, Norway, 10–12 March, 2005.

Nilsson, L.-E. (2005b). *"I've just been shanghaied": Coming out as important in discourse.* Paper presented at the 33rd congress of the Nordic Educational Research Association (NERA) in Oslo, Norway, 10–12 March, 2005.

Nordström, L. (1938). *Lort Sverige* [Dirty Sweden]. Retrieved October 19, 2007, from http://runeberg.org/lortsvrg/kap2p1.html, kap. 2 / §1. prosten och stataren.

Nowotny, H. (1994). *Time: The modern and postmodern experience.* Cambridge: Polity Press.

Nylén, U. (2005). *Coping with trinity human service professionals in interorganisational team work.* Paper presented at the 18th Scandinavian Academy of Management Meeting, Aarhus.

Nyström, P. (2004). Svårt mäta resultat och kvalitet i kirurgi men vårdtiden är en viktig variabel [Difficult to measure the outcomes and quality of surgery, but length of stay is a key variable]. *Läkartidningen, 101,* 184–189.

Nytell, U. (1991). *The school principal in Sweden: A boss or a leader? Implications for the competence of school principals.* Paper presented at the Annual Meeting of the American Educational Research Association. Chicago, IL.

OECD. (1996). *Lifelong learning for all.* Paris: OECD Publications.

OECD. (2005). *Teachers matter: Attracting, developing and retaining effective teachers.* Paris: OECD.

Öhman, P. (2004). *Revisorers perspektiv på revision: En fråga om att följa upptrampade stigar* [Auditors' perspectives on audits: A matter of following well-worn paths]. Luleå: Peter Öhman förlag.

O'Neil, H. F., & Baker, E. L. (1994). *Technology assessment in software applications.* Hillsdale, NJ: L. Erlbaum Associates.

Orlikowski, W. J. (1991). Integrated information environment or matrix of control? The contradictory implication of information technology. *Accounting, Management and Information Technology, 1,* 9–42.

Örn, P. (2004). Starkt stöd för öppen kvalitetsredovisning [Greater support for open quality accounting]. *Läkartidningen, 101,* 1588–1589.

Orlikowski, W. J. (2002). Knowing in practice: Enacting a collective capability in distributed organizing. *Organization Science, 13,* 249–273.

Orr, J.E. (1996). *Talking about machines : an ethnography of a Modern Job.* Cornell: Cornell university press.

Oskarsson, M. (2002). Dialog med förbehåll: Polisens kontaktgrupp, demonstrationsnätverken och det tragiska dilemmat i Göteborg 2001. In M. Björk, & A. Peterson (eds), *Vid politikens yttersta gräns: Perspektiv på EU-toppmötet i Göteborg 2001* [At the frontier of politics: Perspectives on the EU-summit in Gothenburg 2001] (81–113). Stockholm/Stehag: Brutus Östlings Bokförlag Symposion.

Österlind, M.-L. (2002a). Head teachers: Street level bureaucrats or pedagogues? In G. Chiari & M. L. Nuzzo (eds), *Psychological constructivism and the social world* (213–219). Milano: Franco Angeli

Österlind, M.-L. (2002b). Father, friend, visionary leader or business executive? Swedish top head administrative directors' constructions of leadership. In G. Chiari & M. L. Nuzzo (eds), *Psychological constructivism and the social world* (220–229). Milano: Franco Angeli.

Österlind, M.-L. & Denicolo, P. (2006). Extending the catalytic and transformative potential of grids using a congruent technique: An exemplar study of management development. *Personal Construct Theory & Practice, 3,* 38–51.

Ottosson, M. (1999). *Sohlberg och surdegen: Sociala relationer på Kosta glasbruk 1820–1880.* [Sohlberg and the power of tradition: Social relations at Kosta glasswork 1820–1880]. Lund: Bettan och Ottos grafiska.

Ouchi, W. G. (1979). A conceptual framework for the design of organizational control mechanisms. *Management Science, 25*(9), 833–848.

Ouchi, W. G. (1980). Markets, bureaucracies, and clans. *Administrative Science Quarterly, 25*(1), 129–141.

Parkin, P. A. C. (1995). Nursing the future – a reexamination of the professionalization thesis in the light of some recent developments. *Journal of Advanced Nursing, 21*(3), 561–567.

Perdal, A.-L. (1998). *Utvärdering av familjecenter i Vännäs: En stödjande och förebyggande arbetsmodell riktad till barn i förskoleåldern och deras familjer 960101–981231* [Evaluation of the Vännäs Family Center: A supportive and preventive model aimed at preschool children and their families 960101–981231]. Vännäs: Vännäs kommun.

Peterson, A., & Oskarsson, M. (2002). Öppenhet och övervakning: Om sammandrabbningar mellan polis och demonstrationer under EU-toppmötet I Göteborg 2001. In M. Björk, & A. Peterson (eds), *Vid politikens yttersta gräns: Perspektiv på EU-toppmötet i Göteborg 2001* [At the outer limits of

REFERENCES

policy: Perspectives on the EU Summit in Göteborg 2001] (114–143). Stockholm/Stehag: Brutus Östlings Bokförlag Symposion.

Petersson, H. (1993). *Avdelningsföreståndaren, chef eller ledare* [Ward manager, head or leader]. Lund: Lund University.

Petersson-Royce, A. (1982). *Ethnic identity*. Indiana: Bloomington.

Pfeffer, J., & Sutton, R. I. (2001). *The knowing-doing gap: How smart companies turn knowledge into action.* Stockholm: Swedish Publishing.

Polanyi, M. (1973). *Personal knowledge: Towards a post-critical philosophy.* London: Routledge & Kegan Paul.

Polkinghorne, D. (1995). Narrative configuration in qualitative analysis. *International Journal of Qualitative Studies in Education, 8*(1), 8–25.

Postman, N. (1993). *Technopoly: The surrender of culture to technology* (1. pbk. ed.). New York: Vintage Books.

Postman, N. (1996). *The end of education: Redefining the value of school.* New York: Vintage.

Pousette, A. (2001). *Feedback and stress in human service organizations* (unpublished doctoral thesis). Göteborg: Göteborg University.

Pramling Samuelsson, I., & Asplund Carlsson, M. (2003). *Det lekande lärande barnet: I en utvecklingspedagogisk teori* [The playing, learning child: In an educational theory]. Stockholm: Liber.

Prottas, J. M. (1979). *People-processing.* Harvard: University Lexington Books.

Punch, M. (1979). The secret social service. In S. Holdaway (ed.), *The British police* (102–117). London: Edward Arnold.

Reed, M. (1995). Managing quality and organizational politics: TQM as a governmental technology. In I. Kirkpatrick & L. M. Martinez (eds), *The politics of quality in the public sector* (44–64). London: Routledge.

Reed, M., & Harvey, D. L. (1992). The new science and the old: Complexity and realism in the social sciences. *Journal for the Theory of Social Behavior, 22*(4), 353–380.

Regeringens proposition [Government Bill] 1995/95:125. *Åtgärder för att bredda och utveckla användningen av informationsteknik* [Measures to widen and develop the use of information technology].

Regeringens proposition [Government Bill] 1996/97:112. *Utvecklingsplan för förskola, skola och vuxenutbildning – kvalitet och likvärdighet* [Development plan for pre-schools, schools and adult education – quality and equivalency].

Regeringens proposition [Government Bill] 1999/2000:129. *Maxtaxa och allmän förskola m.m.* [The maximum fee and public preschools, etc].

Regeringens proposition [Government Bill] 1999/2000:86. *Informationssamhälle åt alla.* [Information society for all].

Regeringens proposition [Government Bill] 2004/05:175. *Från IT-politik för samhället till politik för IT-samhället* (kapitel 1–29) [From an IT policy for society to a policy for the information society].

352

Regeringsskrivelse [Government Communication] 1997/98:176. *Lärandets verktyg – nationellt program för IT i skolan* [Tools for learning: A national programme for ICT in schools].

Regeringsskrivelse [Government Communication] 1998/99:2. *Informationssamhället inför 2000-talet* [Information society on the eve of the second millennium].

Reiner, R. (1992). Police research in the United Kingdom. In M. Tonry & N. Morris (eds), *Modern policing* (435–508). Chicago: University of Chicago Press.

Reiner, R. (2000). *The politics of the police.* Oxford: Oxford University Press.

Richard, E. (1997). *First in line* (Dissertation in Sociology, 19). Lund: Lund University.

Riis, U. (2000). *The introduction of computers and ICT in the Swedish primary and secondary school: A case of technological push.* Paper presented at the Chinese – Swedish conference "New Technologies – Old Dreams".

Riis, U. (1991). *Skolan och datorn: Satsningen "Datorn som pedagogiskt hjälpmedel" 1988–1991* [School and computers: The effort 'Computers as educational aids' 1988–1991] (Tema T: Tema teknik och social förändring, 24). Linköping: Linköping University.

Robertson, J. (2002). The ambiguous embrace: Twenty years of IT (ICT) in UK primary schools. *British Journal of Educational Technology, 33*(4), 403–409.

Robertsson, O., Lewold, S., Knutson, K., & Lidgren, L. (2000). The Swedish knee arthroplasty project. *Acta Orthop Scand, 71*, 7–18.

Rolf, B. (1991). *Profession, tradition och tyst kunskap* [Profession, tradition and tacit knowledge]. Lund: Novapress.

Rolf, B., Ekstedt, E., & Barnett, R. (1993). *Kvalitet och kunskapsprocess i högre utbildning* [Quality and knowledge processes in higher education]. Nora: Bokförlaget Nya Doxa.

Rombach, B. (1991). *Det går inte att styra med mål* [Management by objectives can not be done]. Lund: Studentlitteratur.

Rose, N. (1999a). *Governing the soul: The shaping of the private self.* London/New York: Free Association Books.

Rose, N. (1999b). *Powers of freedom: Reframing political thought.* Cambridge, UK: Cambridge University Press.

Rothstein, B. (1991). Demokrati, förvaltning och legitimitet [Democracy, public administration and legitimacy]. In B. Rothstein (ed.), *Politik som organisation: Förvaltningspolitikens grundproblem* [Politics as organization: The fundamental problem of the public administration]. Stockholm: Studieförbundet.

Røvik, K. A. (2000). *Moderna organisationer: Trender inom organisationstänkandet vid millennieskiftet* [Modern organisations: Trends in organisational thinking at the millennium shift]. Malmö: Liber.

Sahlin-Andersson, K. (2000). *Transnationell reglering och statens omvandling. Granskningssamhällets framväxt* [Transnational control and the transformation of state: The rise of the audit society] (SCORE report 2000:14). Stockholm: SCORE.

SALAR (2005). *National healthcare quality registries in Sweden 2005.* Stockholm: The Swedish Association of Local Authorities and Regions.

Säljö, R. (2002). Lärande i det 21:a århundradet. In R. Säljö & J. Linderoth (eds), *Utm@ningar och e-frestelser: IT och skolans lärkultur* [Ch@llenges and e-temptations: IT and the learning culture of schooling] (13–29). Stockholm: Prisma.

Säljö, R. (2005). *Lärande och kulturella redskap: Om lärprocesser och det kollektiva minnet* [Learning and cultural tools: On learning processes and collective memory]. Stockholm: Norstedts.

Säljö, R., & Jernström, E. (2004). *Lärande i arbetsliv och vardag* [Learning at work and in everyday life]. Jönköping: Brain Books.

Salvage, J., & Heijnen, S. (1997). *Nursing in Europe: Resource for better health.* Copenhagen: World Health Organization.

Sarfatti-Larsson, M. (1979). *The rise of professionalism: A sociological analysis.* Berkeley: University of California Press.

Sarfatti-Larsson, M. (1980). Proletarization and educated labour. *Theory and Society 9*(1), 131–175.

Samma yrkesetik för alla. *Chef & Ledarskap, 2/2007.*

Savage, J., & Scott, C. (2004). The modern matron: A hybrid management role with implications for continuous quality improvement. *Journal of Nursing Management, 12,* 419–426.

Scarff, R. C., & Dusek, V. (ed.). (2003). *Philosophy of technology: The technological condition.* Malden, MA: Blackwell.

Scheytt, T., Soin, K., & Metz, T. (2003). Exploring notions of control across cultures: A narrative approach. *European Accounting Review, 12*(3), 515–547.

Schön, D. A. (1983). *The reflective practitioner: How professionals think in action.* New York: Basic Books.

Scott, W. R. (1995). *Institutions and organizations.* Thousands Oaks, CA: Sage.

Scott, W. R. (1998). *Organizations: Rational, natural and open systems.* Englewood Cliffs, NJ: Prentice Hall.

Scott, W. R., & Meyer, J. (eds). (1994). *Institutional environments and organizations.* Thousand Oaks, CA: Sage.

Selander, M. (2001). *Mångfaldens problematik: Om mötet mellan Ädelreformen och sjukhemmets verksamhet* [Problems of diversity: On the meeting between the Swedish elder care reform and nursing home operation]. Göteborg: BAS.

Selander, S. (2003). Toys as text. In A. Nelson, L. E. Berg, & K. Svensson (eds),

Toys as communication: Toy research in the late twentieth century, part 2 (39–46). Selection of papers presented at The International Toy Research Conference, Halmstad University, Sweden, June 1999. Stockholm: KTH, Sitrec.

Selrot, J. (2001). *Polisetik: En kvalitativ studie om polisers tankar kring etik samt etiska konflikter och dilemman i yrkesutövandet* [Police ethics: A qualitative study of reflections of police on ethics, ethical conflicts and the dilemma in practice] (Essay in Politology 41–60 points). Växjö: Växjö University, School of Social Sciences.

Sennet, R. (1998). *Chorrosion of character: The personal consequences of work in the new capitalism.* New York: Norton.

SFS 1985:562. *Destruction of journals or parts of journals: Swedish IRS declaration of principle for errands in accordance with 13 § Patient Journal Act.* Stockholm: Regeringskansliet [The Government Office].

SFS 1993:100. *Högskoleförordningen* [The Higher Education Ordinance]. Stockholm: Regeringskansliet [The Government Office].

Shearing, C. D., & Ericson, R. V. (1991). Culture as a figurative action. *The British Journal of Sociology, 42,* 481–506.

Silvén, E. (2004). *Bekänna färg* [Embrace color]. Stockholm: Nordiska museets förlag.

Simon, H. A. (1985). *The sciences of the artificial* (2nd ed.). Cambridge, MA: The MIT Press.

SKAR (2006). *Annual report 2005: The Swedish knee arthroplasty register.* Lund: Lund University Hospital.

Skolnick, J. H., & Fyfe, J. J. (1994). *Above the law: Police and the excessive use of force.* New York: Free Press.

Skolnick, J. H. (1994). *Justice without trial: Law enforcement in democratic society* (3. ed.). New York: Macmillan.

Skolöverstyrelsen [National Board of Education]. (1963). *Undervisningsmaskiner och programmerat studiematerial* [Educational technology and programmed study material] (Utredningar i skolfrågor, 11). Stockholm: Skolöverstyrelsen.

Skolverket [National Agency for Education] (1998). *Nyhetsbrev nr. 16/1998* [Newsletter no. 16/1998]. Stockholm: Skolverket.

Skolverket [National Agency for Education] (2004). *Förskola i brytningstid: Nationell utvärdering av förskolan* [Pre-school in a time of change: A national evaluation of pre-school] (report no. 239). Stockholm: Skolverket.

Skolverket [National Agency of Education] (1998). *Slutrapport från projektet: Hur styr kommunerna skolan?* [Concluding report from the project: How do municipalities govern schools?]. Stockholm: Skolverket.

Skolverket [National Agency of Education] (1999). *Nationella kvalitetsgranskningar 1998* [National quality audits 1998] (report no. 160). Stockholm: Skolverket.

Skolverket [National Agency of Education] (2001). *Rektor: Demokratisk, utmanande ledare* [Head teacher: Democratic, challanging leader]. Retrieved October 25, 2007, from http://www.skolverket.se/publikationer?id=920

Skolverket [National Agency of Education] (2004). *Utbildningsinspektionen 2003 ur ett nationellt perspektiv: En analys av inspektionsresultaten. Sammanfattande del samt skolformsvisa och tematiska redovisningar* [School inspections 2003 from a national perspective: An analysis of audit results. Summary part with form specific and thematic presentations]. Retrieved October 25, 2007, from http://www.skolverket.se/publikationer?id=1405

Smångs, B. (2001). *Polisyrket: Polisers och allmänhetens bilder* [Police work: The images of police officers and public]. Lund: Lund University, Department of Sociology.

Smith, J. (1995). Repertory grids: An interactive, case-study perspective. In J. Smith, R. Harré, & L. van Langenhove (eds), *Rethinking methods in psychology* (162–177). London: Sage.

SNHAR. (2003). *Annual report 2002: The Swedish national hip arthroplasty register.* Göteborg: Sahlgrenska University Hospital.

SNHAR. (2005). *Annual report 2004: The Swedish national hip arthroplasty register.* Göteborg: Sahlgrenska University Hospital.

Socialstyrelsen [The National Board of Health and Welfare]. (2005). *Personlig assistans: Kartläggning av kommunala riktlinjer* [Personal assistance: Surveying municipal guide lines]. Stockholm: Allmänna förlaget.

Socialstyrelsen [The National Board of Health and Welfare]. (1987:3). *Pedagogiskt program för förskolan* [Pre-school policy on education]. Stockholm: Allmänna förlaget.

Söderberg Forslund, M. (2000). *Kvinnor och skolledarskap: En kunskapsöversikt* [Woman and school leadership: A knowlege review]. Stockholm: Skolverket [National Agency for Education]: Liber.

Söderfeldt, B., & Söderfeldt, M. (1997). *Psykosocial arbetsmiljö i människovårdande arbete* [Psychosocial work environment in human service work] (Meddelanden från Socialhögskolan, 3). Lund: Lund University.

Söderfeldt, B., Söderfeldt, M., Muntaner, C., Ocampo, P., Warg, L. E., & Ohlson, C. G. (1996). Psychosocial work environment in human service organizations: A conceptual analysis and development of the demand-control model. *Social Science and Medicine, 42*(9), 1217–1226.

Söderlund, A. (2000). *Det långa mötet: IT och skolan – om spridning och anammande av IT i den svenska skolan* [A long encounter: ICT and school – about diffusion and acceptance of ICT in the Swedish school system]. Luleå: Luleå University of Technology.

Söderström-Claeson, C., & Granberg-Wennberg, C. (2003). *Utvärdering av projekt Familjecenter: Ett samverkansprojekt mellan kommun och landsting i Umeå* [Evaluation of the Family Center Project: A joint municipal/county council project in Umeå]. Stiftelsen Trygghetsfonden för kommuner och landsting.

Sommerfeld, P. (2005). Evidence-based practice: The end of professional social work or architect of a new professionalism. In P. Sommerfeld (ed.), *Evidence-based social work? Towards a new professionalism?* (7–31). Bern: Peter Lang AG.

SOU 1997:57, *I medborgarnas tjänst: En samlad förvaltningspolitik för staten* [In service of the public: A comprehensive administrative policy for the state]. Report from the Administrative Procedure Commission.

SOU 2001:87, *Mot ökad koncentration – Förändring av polisens verksamhet* [Towards greater concentration – Changing police operations] (Polisverksamhetsutredningen 2001). Stockholm: Fritzes.

Spencer, R. L. (2005). Nurses', midwives' and health visitors' perceptions of the impact of higher education on professional practice. *Nurse Education Today, 26,* 45–53.

Stacey, R. D. (2003). *Strategic management and organizational dynamics: The challenge of complexity.* Harlow: Prentice Hall.

Stacey, R. D. (2001). *Complex responsive processes in organizations: Learning and knowledge creation.* London: Routledge.

Starr, P. (1992). Social categories and claims in the liberal state. In M. Douglas & D. Hull (eds), *How classification works. Nelson Goodman among the social sciences* (154–179). Edinburgh: Edinburgh University Press.

Statistiska centralbyrån. (1998). *Så har vi det på jobbet: En rapport om polisens arbetsmiljö.* Stockholm: Svenska polisförbundet.

Stensöta, H. (2004). *Den empatiska staten: Jämställdhetens inverkan på daghem och polis 1950–2000* [The empathetic state: The impact of gender equality on daycare centers and police 1950–2000] (Gothenburg Studies in Politics, 85). Göteborg: Göteborg University, School of Political Sciences.

Stjernö, S. (1983). Stress og utbrenthet: Belastninger i arbeid med mennesker [Stress and burn-out: Strains in work with people]. Oslo: Universitetsforlaget.

Streatfield, P. J. (2001). *The paradox of control in organizations.* London: Routledge.

Stronach, I., Corbin, B., McNamara, O., Stark, S., & Warne, T. (2002). Towards an uncertain politics of professionalism: Teacher and nurse identities. *Journal of Education Policy, 17*(1), 109–138.

Suchman, L.A. (1987). *Plans and situated actions. The problem of human machine communication.* New York: Cambridge university press.

Sundkvist, M. (2000). Analyses of steering documents for compulsory school in Sweden during the 1990s: What is a teacher supposed to know and do? In K. Klette, I. Carlgren, J. Rasmussen & H. Simola (eds), *Restructuring Nordic teachers: An analysis of policy texts from Finland, Denmark, Sweden and Norway* (187–262). University of Oslo: Institute for Educational Research.

Svedberg Nilsson, K., Henning, R., & Fernler, K. (eds). (2005). *En illusion av frihet?: Företag och organisationer i regelsamhället* [An illusion of freedom: Businesses and organisations in the rule society]. Lund: Studentlitteratur.

Svedberg, L. (2000). *Rektorsrollen: Om skolledarskapets gestaltning* [The principal's role: A study of the formation of educational leadership] (Studies in Educational Sciences, 26). Stockholm: HSL.

Svedberg, L. (2003). Att skapa mening i korselden mellan konkurrerade synsätt. In I. Holmberg & R. Henning (eds), *Offentligt ledarskap: Om förändring, förnyelse och nya ledarideal* [Public leadership: About change, renewal and new leadership ideals] (89–109). Lund: Studentlitteratur.

Svensson, E. (2001). *Utvärdering av Sesam familjecentral i Malmö* [Evaluation of Sesam familycenter in Malmö]. Malmö: Persona Eskil Svensson.

Svensson, L. G. (1990). Knowledge as a professional resource: Case studies of architects and psychologists at work. In R. Torstendahl & M. Burrage (eds), *The formation of professions. Knowledge, state and strategy.* London: Sage.

Svensson, L. G. (1998). *Professionalism och politisk decentralisering: En sociologisk studie av skolan och socialtjänsten i en kommundelsreform* [Professionalism and political decentralization: A sociological study of schools and social services in a municipal district reform] (Research report no. 122). Göteborg: Göteborg University, Department of Sociology.

Svensson, L.G. (in press). Profesjon og organisasjon. In A. Molander & L.-I. Terum (eds), *Profesjonsstudier* [Studies of professions]. Oslo: Universitetsforlaget.

Sveriges skolledarförbund [The Swedish Association of School Principals and Directors of Education]. (2007). *Många rektorer lämnar sina tjänster i förtid!* Pressmeddelande [Press release]. Retrieved March 19, 2007, from http://www.skolledarna.se/

Symon, G. (1998). Qualitative research diaries. In C. Cassel & G. Symon (eds), *Qualitative methods and analysis in organizational research: A practical guide* (94–117). London: Sage.

Symon, G. (2004). Qualitative research diaries. In C. Cassel & G. Symon (eds), *Essential guide to qualitative methods in organizational research* (98–113). London: Sage.

Taylor, F. W. (1911). *The principles of scientific management.* Retreived August 26, 2007, from http://www.marxists.org/reference/subject/economics/taylor/principles/index.htm

Thomson, P. (2004). Severed heads and compliant bodies?: A speculation about principal identities. *Discourse: Studies in the Pultural politics of Education, 25*(1), 44–59.

Thylefors, I. (1991). *Ledarskap i vård, omsorg och utbildning* [Leadership in health services and education]. Stockholm: Natur och Kultur.

Toulmin, S. (1996). Beyond theory: Changing organizations through participation. *Dialogues on Work and Innovation, 1,* 203–225.

Toulmin, S. (2001). *Return to reason.* Cambridge: Harvard University Press.

Tsoukas, H. (1998). Introduction: Chaos and complexity. *Organization, 5,* 291–313.

Tullgren, C. (2004). *Den välreglerade friheten: Att konstruera det lekande barnet* [The well-regulated freedom: Constructing the playing child] (Malmö Studies in Educational Sciences, 10). Malmö: Malmö University, School of Education.

Turner, B. (1993). Talcott Parsons, universalism and the educational revolution: Democracy versus professionalism. *British Journal of Sociology, 44*(1), 1–24.

Uhlin, A. (2001). About regional innovation systems, learning, complexity and trust. *Work Life in Transition, 4,* 37–75.

Ure, A. (1835). *The philosophy of manufactures: Or, an exposition of the scientific, moral and commercial economy of the factory system of Great Britain.* Retrieved August 26, 2007, from http://books.google.se/books/pdf/The_philosophy_of_manufactures.pdf?id=_XsBAAAAQAAJ&output=pdf&sig=LXdZZ9tIvPMjO1TC1Jtz9ALFAAg.

Utbildningsdepartementet [Ministry of Education and Research]. (1992). *Skola för bildning: Huvudbetänkande av Läroplanskommittén* [Schools for schooling and culture: Main report of the National Curriculum Committee] (Statens Offentliga Utredningar, SOU 1992:94). Stockholm: Allmänna förlaget.

Utbildningsdepartementet [Ministry of Education and Research]. (1994). *Läroplan för det obligatoriska skolväsendet och de frivilliga skolformerna, Lpo 94, Lpf 94* [Curriculum for the compulsory school system, the pre-school class and the leisure-time centre, Lpo 94, Lpf 94]. Stockholm: Fritzes.

Utbildningsdepartementet [Ministry of Education and Research]. (2004). *Skolans ledningsstruktur: Om styrning och ledning i skolan* [The structure of school leadership: About governance and leadership in school] (Statens Offentliga Utredningar, SOU 2004:116). Stockholm: Fritzes.

Utbildningsdepartementet [Ministry of Education and Science]. (1998). *Läroplan för förskolan, Lpfö 98* [Curriculum for the Pre-School, Lpfö 98]. Stockholm: Fritzes.

Van Gustern, H. R. (1976). *The quest for control: A critique of the rational-central-rule approach in public affairs.* London: Johan Wiley & Sons.

Van Langenhove, L., & Bertolink, R. (1999). Positioning and assessment of technology. In R. Harré & L. van Langenhove (eds), *Positioning theory: Moral contexts of intentional action* (116–126). Malden, MA: Blackwell.

Van Maanen, J., & Barley, S. R. (1984). Occupational communities, culture and control in organizations. In M. M. Staw & L. L. Cummings (eds), *Research in organizational behaviour, Vol. 6* (287–365). Greenwich: JAI Press.

Van Maanen, J. (1978). The asshole. In P. K. Manning & J. Van Maanen (eds), *Policing, a view from the street* (309–349). Santa Monica: Goodyear Publishing Company.

Vermulen, M. (1997). *De school als arbeidsorganisatie* [The school as workplace]. Amsterdam: Proefschrift van de Universiteit van Amsterdam.

Wallenberg, J. (1997). *Kommunalt arbetsliv i omvandling: Styrning och självständighet i postindustriell tjänsteproduktion* [Municipal working life in transition: Management and independence in post-industrial service production]. Stockholm: SNS Förlag.

Warren, W. (2004). Construing constructionism: Some reflections on the tension between PCP and social constructionism. *Personal Construct Theory & Practice, 1*(1), 30–43.

Warschauer, M. (2000). Technology and school reform: A view from both sides of the tracks. *Education Policy Analysis Archives, 8*(4). Retrieved August 26, 2007, from http://epaa.asu.edu/epaa/v8n4.html

Weick, K. (1976). Educational organizations as loosely coupled systems. *Administrative Science Quarterly, 21*(1), 1–19.

Weick, K. E., & Roberts, K. H. (1993). Collective mind in organizations: Heedful interrelation on flight decks. *Administrative Science Quarterly, 38*, 357–381.

Wenger, E. (1998). *Communities of practice: Learning, meaning and identity.* Cambridge: Cambridge University Press.

Whitty, G. (1997). Marketization, the state, and the re-formation of the teaching profession. In A. H. Halsey (ed.), *Education, culture, economy and society* (299–310). Oxford: Oxford University Press.

Whitty, G., Power, S., & Halpin, D. (1998). *Devolution and choice in education: The school, the state and the market.* Buckingham: Open University Press.

Wikander, U. (2006). *Kvinnoarbete i Europa 1789–1950: Genus, makt och arbetsdelning.* [Women labour in Europe 1789–1950: Gender, power and division of labour]. Stockholm: Atlas.

Wildavsky, A. B. (1979). *The politics of the budgetary process.* Boston: Little Brown.

Wilensky, H. (1964). The professionalization of everyone? *American Journal of Sociology, 70*(2), 137–158.

Wilson, J. Q. (1989). *Bureaucracy.* New York: Basic Books.

Wise, A. E. (2005). Establishing teaching as a profession: The essential role of professional accreditation. *Journal of Teacher Education, 56*(4), 318–331.

Wittgenstein, L. (1992). *Filosofiska undersökningar* [Philosophical investigations]. Stockholm: Bokförlaget Thales.

Woodward, J. (1965). *Industrial organisation: Theory and practice.* London: Oxford University Press.

Ziehe, T. (2000). School and youth: A different relation. *YOUNG – Nordic Journal of youth, 8*(1), 54–63.

Ziehe, T., Fornäs, J., & Retzlaff, J. (1993). *Kulturanalyser: Ungdom, utbildning, modernitet* [Cultural analyses: youth, education, modernity] (3rd ed.). Stockholm/Stehag: Brutus Östlings Bokförlag Symposion.

Ziehe, T., Nielsen, E., & Fornäs, J. (1989). *Ambivalenser og mangfoldighed: En artikelsamling om ungdom, skole, æstetik og kultur* [Ambivalence and multiplicity: essays on youth, school, aesthetics and culture]. Copenhagen: Politisk revy.

Zuiderent, T. (2000). *The construction of technology assessment: Stories on the Danish Board of Technology.* Paper presented at the POSTI conference in London, December 1st–3rd, 2000.

About the authors

Agneta Abrahamsson is senior lecturer in Public Health and evaluation methodology at Kristianstad University, Sweden. She is a researcher at the platform of Nearby Care. Her current research projects are in developing programme theory in family centres, and in a development program of Bridge Builders between Swedish society and refugee communities. E-mail: agneta.abrahamsson@hkr.se

Lena Agevall is associate professor of Political Science at Växjö University, Sweden. Her research interests include public administration, public ethics and the governing of professions. She is a member of the management team of Forum for Reseach on Profession, Växjö University. She is currently involved in research projects regarding different forms for governing profession and the consequences of NPM for professional ethics. E-mail: lena.agevall@vpu.vxu.se

Carola Aili is senior lecturer in Educational Science at Kristianstad University, Sweden and director of research for the research team Work at School. She works with projects about time and lack of time situations in teacher work, teacher professionalisation, work division and the use of different forms of knowledge in work divisions processes. Her chapter is built on material collected in the research projects *Teachers' work planning* funded by the Swedish Research Council. E-mail: carola.aili@hkr.se

Sören Augustinsson is senior lecturer in Sociology and Human Work Science at Kristianstad University, Sweden. Ph.D. in Human Work Science and has his interests in complexity science and organizing. E-mail: soren.augustinsson@hkr.se

Joakim Caspersen is Master of Sociology and a research fellow (Ph.D.) at the Centre for the Study of Professions, Oslo University College,

Norway. The working title of his Ph.D. thesis is 'Teachers' Epistemic Trajectories from Education to Work', and he is also affiliated with the project 'Novice Teachers and How They Cope', founded by the Norwegian Research Council. E-mail: joakim.caspersen@hio.no

Pamela Denicolo is professor of Postgraduate and Professional Education at the University of Reading, UK and the Director of the Research Centre for PCP in Education. E-mail: p.m.denicolo@rdg.ac.uk

Rolf Granér is senior lecturer in Police Science at the Police Education and Training Programme at Växjö University, Sweden. His research interests include the relation between formal and informal organizational processes, occupational cultures and ethics in policing. E-mail: rolf.graner@vxu.se

Lars H. Hansen is Ph.D. in Sociology and deputy head of the Department of IT, Göteborg University, Sweden. His main interest is in sociology of work. E-mail: lars.hansen@sociology.gu.se

Ingrid Henning Loeb is senior lecturer at the Department of Education at Göteborg University, Sweden. She teaches in teacher education and works with course development on adult education in teacher education. Her field of research is in adult education, the politics of lifelong learning, working life studies, and on the organization of local adult educational projects. E-mail: ingrid.henning-loeb@ped.gu.se

Katrin Hjort is associate professor of Professionalisation at The Danish University of Education in Copenhagen and guest professor of Pedagogy at Kristianstad University. Her area of research is the transformation of the welfare state and new demands to the professionals within education, health and social work. She has been head of the Danish Network for Research in Professions and Education of Professionals, and she is a member of the Danish State Council for Research into Culture Communication. E:mail: KAHJ@dpu.dk

Håkan Jenner is professor at the School of Education, Växjö University in Sweden with a special interest in professional training. His research has focused on professional attitudes, and the prerequisites for developing a 'reflective practice'. He is a member of the management team of the Forum for Research on Professions, Växjö University. E-mail: hakan.jenner@vxu.se

Curt R. Johansson is professor of the Work and Organizational Psychology Division at the Department of Psychology, and of the UNIVA University Institute, Lund University, Sweden. E-mail: curt.r.johansson@psychology.lu.se

Karin Jonnergård is professor of Business Administration at Växjö University in Sweden. Her research interests include corporate governance and especially the governance of the professions within the corporate governance system (e.g. auditors, financial analysts). She is a member of the management team of the Forum for Reseach on Profession, Växjö University. She is currently involved in research projects regarding different forms for governing profession and organizational entrance strategies for young professionals. E-mail: karin.jonnergard@ehv.vxu.se

Sandra Jönsson is senior lecturer in Leadership and Organisation at Malmö University, Sweden. Her current research involves a project focusing on long-distance commuting, sense of coherence and health. E-mail: sandra.jonsson@mah.se

Agneta Ljung-Djärf is senior lecturer in Educational Science at Kristianstad University, Sweden, and a member of the research team Work at School. Her research interests are focused on the use of information and communication technology in educational settings. She is also working with projects about teacher professionalisation, work division and the use of different forms of knowledge in work division-processes. E-mail: agneta.ljung-djarf@hkr.se

Lars-Erik Nilsson is lecturer in Educational Science at Kristianstad University and Ph.D. student at Göteborg University in Sweden. His research interests include implementation of technology and socio-cultural aspects of information and communication technology. He is in the final stages of completing his Ph.D. thesis on cheating in education, plagiarism and technology. Data for his chapters have been drawn from material collected by the research projects *ICT and Learning in*

Teacher Training funded by the Knowledge Foundation through its research programme LearnIt. E-mail: lars-erik.nilsson@hkr.se

Marie-Louise Österlind is lecturer at the Department of Behavioural Sciences at Kristianstad University, Sweden and doctoral student at the Department of Psychology, Lund University, Sweden. Her field of interest is participative approaches to leadership development in public sector organizations. E-mail: marie-louise.osterlind@hkr.se

Mikael Ottosson is senior lecturer in Working Life Science at the School of IMER, Malmö University in Sweden. His main research field is contemporary social and labour history. His research includes different fields such as the consolidation of Sweden during the nineteenth century; the media picture of the labour movement and different aspects of working time. His current research focuses upon the history of lazybones and the conceptual history of human work. E-mail: mikael.ottosson@mah.se

Elvi Richard is senior lecturer, Ph.D., in Sociology at Växjö University in Sweden. Her research interest is first-line supervision and middle management within the public sector, learning and professionalisation. E-mail: elvi.richard@vxu.se

Calle Rosengren is Ph.D. student in Working Life Science at Kristianstad University, Sweden. His area of research is temporal aspects of work and organization, how changes within social systems correspond to changes in norms and values. E-mail: calle.rosengren@hkr.se

Lennart G. Svensson is professor of Sociology at Göteborg University, Sweden. During his referee work with this book he was guest professor at the Centre for the Study of Professions, Oslo University College, Norway. His main interest is in sociology of work, organization, education and profession. His present research relates to professional organization and practice, and to professional status and trust. E-mail: lennart.svensson@sociology.gu.se

Index